To Dorothy Smith Irwin (1904–1991)
Attending sixty-seven nearly consecutive Detroit Tigers' home
openers must be some kind of record. You couldn't go in
April 1941, because you gave birth to my younger brother.
I'm glad I was born in January.

and

To Betty Huff Lund (1922–1998)
You happily devoted your own life to your man's life in baseball.
He loved the game itself, but not nearly as much as he loved you.

Contents

Foreword

by Bill Freehan

I went to the University of Michigan because of Don Lund. Don was an outstanding athlete there and a nine-letter winner in three sports. I played baseball and football at a small Catholic high school in St. Petersburg, Florida. I thought I might like to play these two sports in college, but I was being recruited by large universities to play baseball. Some of them made it quite clear that they wouldn't let me play football. Don listened to me and said I could play both at Michigan.

Since freshmen weren't eligible to compete in the NCAA at the time, I joined Don's 1961 baseball team as a sophomore catcher and had a successful season, helping them win the Big Ten title. That was when Don became my mentor. That was also when several major league teams came around with offers to sign a professional contract. Don and my dad encouraged me to sign with the Detroit Tigers, and I never regretted that decision. What I did regret, though, was leaving my Michigan teammates, some of whom I had played summer ball with on the Detroit sandlots since the age of fifteen. It wasn't easy to move on.

Nevertheless, the next year, Don led that team to the 1962 College World Series Championship. Over the years, we've all remained friends, and they still tell the same running joke ... that they finally got the monkey off their back and won!

Don was extremely vital to me throughout my career. I could call and talk to him if I was in a slump, and he'd always remind me of something I might be doing wrong.

Don and his wife, Betty, became very close friends with my parents, as well as my wife, Pat, and me. We all followed each other to Michigan, then to the Tigers, and then again back to Michigan. After my father, Don Lund is the most important man in my life.

Michigan's 1962 champion baseball team, with me as an honorary member, has remained a very close group over the years, thanks to our shortstop and reunion organizer Dick Honig. All of these men, without exception, graduated from Michigan and went on to very successful careers. Don was the one who taught us how to win, both on and off the field.

Enjoy this book about an amazing man in his world of sports from high school, through college, and into the major leagues. Have fun with the stories. See for yourself how Don Lund could be a role model for anyone ... especially me!

Bill Freehan

Introduction

Who Is Don Lund?

"Why would you want to write a book about me?"

That was the first thing he said to me when I asked him if he would let me write his biography. I took him by surprise; his question was honest, modest, and straightforward. A measure of the man.

Don Lund is past the midpoint of his eighties as this book is published. He is bright, sharp-eyed, filled with humor, and loaded with friendships that extend beyond America's shores. His memory from childhood is vivid and colorful. Best of all, it's verifiable through documented materials, plus corroboration from family, friends, and associates throughout his career.

So who is this man?

Call him an athlete first. As a three-sport player at Detroit's Southeastern High, the local newspapers bragged about him as the best prep athlete in the entire metropolitan area. At the University of Michigan, he again played football, basketball, and baseball, winning nine letters and three freshman numerals. Not many have done that.

Beyond college, he played professional baseball for nearly ten years. He then went back to his alma mater and coached the baseball team to two titles in four years, one of them the national championship. Then he went back to major league baseball as Farm Director for the Detroit Tigers. Following that, he finished his career as Associate Athletic Director at the University of Michigan.

He never sought or applied for any of those jobs.

Along the way, he focused on making friendships. He schooled himself on techniques for getting people to talk about themselves; to open up lines of mutual trust and cordial bonds. He got to know his fellow teammates, from Jackie Robinson at the start of his playing career to Al Kaline at the end of it.

He made good friends, and he kept them all through his career and beyond. Many of these friends became national legends because they were simply great at what they accomplished. All of them, however, became lasting fixtures within his memory, easily recalled with great pleasure.

But there's more about Don Lund that makes him unique and rather special. Consider that he remains

- The only NCAA college graduate to turn down a National Football League first-round draft pick (Chicago Bears) in favor of playing professional baseball.
- The only person in major league baseball history to serve the same big league franchise as a player, a scout, a coach, and a high-ranking front-office manager.
- Probably the only Detroit High School student to spend the senior year as captain of the football team, the basketball team, and the baseball team, while also serving as class president and winning a major university scholarship.
- The only NCAA Division 1 nine-letter graduate to play major league baseball.
- The only Division 1 nine-letter graduate to retire as a big league player and then go back to his alma mater and coach its baseball team to a national championship.
- The only NCAA rookie baseball coach to lose a shutout game by more than 20 runs (1959: Notre Dame 21, University of Michigan 0).
- The only major league baseball player to work for many years as a live-radio broadcast personality for NCAA football games.

There's something else about Don Lund that takes a biographer to the extreme, when it comes to a typical tendency to support the subject person. It's hard to find anything negative about him. He's not a smoker or a drinker. He doesn't use foul language. He won't exaggerate or lie to you. He lives his life in moderation at all levels. He's generous, devoted to his family, and respectful of others. And, according to the hundreds of people interviewed for this story of his life, he's always been that way. So as you read this, you might think I'm prone to only write the good stuff and overlook the bad. Think again. It took five years to research this book, with objectivity sought constantly. Finally, Don Lund came out as wholesome as anyone could possibly be. That's why I wanted to write his story. You'll see what I mean as you read it.

J.R.I.

1

Rendezvous

Driving through Ann Arbor, Michigan, feels good this morning. A soft breeze carries the midsummer scent of freshly mowed grass. The rising sun drives away any remaining shadows, revealing different shades of green trees, shrubs, and bushes of several types. Flower gardens, swarming with blooms of countless colors, border the houses and stretch out to command Ann Arbor's general landscape.

As I look up through the windshield, I see a Rorschach test in white. Large fluffy clouds, floating lazily, grab my eyes. As I focus on them, I see a laughing dog, a dragon's head, and even a leaping cat. All were sculpted by an invisible wind aloft, just for my amusement. Rorschach can have his inkblots; I'll take clouds anytime.

It's Saturday morning. Traffic is light as I steer through downtown. On the sidewalks, a few people aimlessly saunter, calmly checking out window displays, open storefronts, or each other. Some exchange smiles as they share the serenity of a summer morning. I also notice others in the scene: standouts who contrast sharply from the casual walkers. They're the fitness faithful, the runners and joggers who have their own mission. They weave around and pass their fellow citizens with abandon, like halfbacks streaking for the goal line. Helmeted bicyclists are here, too. But they don't use the sidewalks. They pedal along the edge of the road with impunity, intent on claiming their rightful portion of the pavement. And that's just fine. I'm happy for all of them today. I'm also delighted with myself because, finally, after many weeks of preparation, this is the day I've anticipated. The day I've planned for. If things work out, today could be the best Saturday I've ever spent.

This morning, I'm going to begin a series of interviews with a sports legend. He agreed to meet me after hearing my carefully rehearsed phone presentation a few weeks ago. He was reluctant at first, but when I explained what I had in mind, that his story needed to be told, he consented to see me today. And if I'm successful, he will continue to see me for several more days and weeks to come. My purpose is to learn as much as I can about his life thus far, to find out what drove him to excel in sports, and then to devote his life to helping others excel. Because of the impact he's had on others as an athlete, a teacher, a coach, and a mentor for hundreds of young athletes, his story needs to be told. And I'm going to tell it to you.

This man is special to many folks in Ann Arbor, Michigan. He's also special to legions of sports-loving people in the Detroit area, who have honored him throughout the years. And today, as I drive toward his home, his numerous accomplishments challenge my mind. When I sit down with him, I'm going to break our usual practice of casual conversation. I'm going to ask him lots of questions about his life and the people who shared it with him. He has more than a half-century of stored-up personal memories. He mega-starred in three major sports. He played major league baseball at a time when baseball legends were made following World War II. He became a championship college baseball coach. He's taught hundreds of high school kids the fundamentals of football, basketball, and baseball. Then he officiated at their games as a certified referee. He's made enormous contributions to men and women's sports at the University of Michigan as Associate Athletic Director. And all this merely scrapes the surface of his career. His story serves as an example of excellence in athletics at all levels of competition.

Today, I'm going to get him to start talking about himself, which he doesn't care to do. But I'm also going to get him to reminisce about sports, particularly exploring his memories of pro baseball as he lived it in the forties and fifties. We'll explore the scenes, the places, the personalities, and the attitudes of people he played with and played for. That'll be easy; he talks about those things all the time.

So here I am on this beautiful midsummer morning, driving through Ann Arbor, Michigan. The man calls Ann Arbor his home. He's lived here for decades.

Ann Arbor is a midsize town in southeastern Michigan. Its growth since being founded in 1824 has intentionally merged with that of a world-class institution, the University of Michigan, which moved there in 1837. The two have coexisted agreeably since then. Civic pride, combined with academic renown, creates an especially cohesive "town and gown" environment. Ann Arbor business leaders have also served as university officers or were elected as university regents throughout the years. University executives have been elected to Ann Arbor's City Council or to the mayor's office since the middle of nineteenth century. To underscore the relationship between Ann Arbor and the university, one need only point out that university students are allowed to register and vote in city elections. This fact alone makes town and gown inseparable.

Other things bring the two together, such as the rousing celebrations associated with Michigan sports, particularly those related to football. On Saturdays from September through November, Ann Arbor welcomes thousands of people from beyond its borders. They invade the town and campus to join in familiar rituals associated with Michigan home games. They tailgate with longtime friends. They attend parties. They bask in school spirit and relive memories of famous gridiron wins. Arriving by throngs on game day, they settle into their favorite tailgate spots. Most are dressed in Michigan's colors of maize and blue. Some wear the colors of Michigan's opponent for the game. Eventually, they all march to Michigan Stadium like pilgrims to the holy place, ready to cheer their team to victory. None of this is new, of course; all this has been going on for more than a hundred years. And there's no reason it won't still be going on a hundred years from now.

Ann Arbor and its environs are a near utopia to those who live here, and it's no surprise. People who do demographic surveys rate Ann Arbor among the most desirable residential places in America. The choice is well considered: The town has adapted to generations of cultural modification over the years; the university has supported these, and the result is a cosmopolitan place to hang your hat. Violent crime is relatively low. Schools are among the best in the state. City services are superb. Also, voluntarism is the life blood for highly successful nonprofit organizations, serving Ann Arbor citizens from infancy right through old age.

Ann Arbor also enjoys a reputation for being friendly among its own and hospitable to its visitors. It offers the ambiance of a large, cosmopolitan community. For those who thrive on intellectual stimulation, there's enough for an overdose. For others who seek fine restaurants and popular entertainment places, Ann Arbor has more of these than many cities twice its size. For those who seek a town with profound historical identity, with fine arts, music of all kinds, and a sense of community pride, this small university town in southeastern Michigan has it all.

Beyond the town's boundaries are rolling hills, groves of woods, small farms, high-tech businesses, and expensive homes. Farther out, smaller communities fill the countryside in every direction. Each of them was founded in the nineteenth century to support local agriculture. Detroit is thirty-five miles to the northeast. Lansing, the state capital, is northwest about sixty miles.

The man I'm meeting this morning lives about five miles beyond Ann Arbor's northeast boundary, in a complex of upscale condominiums. My drive meanders through settled country landscape, portioned with a couple of subdivisions, some office buildings, woods with roaming deer, lots of small critters, and the university's botanical gardens. The condos I seek stand just past these landmarks. He lives in one of them. As I turn into the main entrance, I start to feel like an amateur artist about to try his first painting: I know what I'm supposed to do, but what'll it be like when I finish?

The condominiums are a study in black and brown. All paving surfaces are black, right up to the porches. Each of the 103 buildings, containing two or three condos, displays a brown roof, brown brick, brown cedar siding, and brown-trimmed windows, all pretty much the same shade of medium mud-brown. An awfully bleak scene if that's all you saw. But the buildings flow tastefully around thirty acres of lush, green lawn. Trees are planted almost randomly, filling your view with various shades of green. A pond sparkles in light blue; water from its floating fountain splashes in noisy cascades. But the vivid colors, the eye catchers, are thousands of flowers planted throughout the community, tended lovingly by the residents. This is a place where people obviously care about where they live, how they live, and how others live around them. The entire area presents a wholesome impression of domestic serenity.

Most of the residents here are senior citizens—retirees. I sense it's a close community. There are people walking around and greeting each other warmly. I drive slowly. No way am I going to disturb anybody in this peaceful place.

When I pull up to his condo, I note that it's one-half of a two-unit building. Carefully tended flowers and shrubs surround the walls and circle his walkways. One thing I notice right away is the condo's appropriate location: right next to the tennis courts and across from the swimming pool. An athlete's spot, close to the action.

He's expecting me; the door opens before I get a chance to ring the bell. The old man who stands in front of me beams a relaxing welcome. His broad grin shows straight, even teeth and a square jaw. Handsome Nordic features include a straight nose and a high-cheeked full face with few lines. His eyes are a combined brown and green in color, what some people might term "hazel." But those who know him, as well as those who faced him in competition, have seen his eyes darken quickly as his level of intensity increases. From the mound, a pitcher facing him would probably see his eyes as dark brown cannon bores. His once-blond hair now covers his head in a neatly trimmed statement of white. This is a man who does not look in his eighties.

As he welcomes me, his handshake is firm but not crushing. He wouldn't think of trying to create an impression of dominance through a hand squeeze. He's never done that; he doesn't have to.

At six feet and 180 pounds, he's not considered an exceptionally big man. But his shoulders are wide and powerful, his arms are long, and his chest is naturally broad. Looking at him now, no one could deny that his frame once supported 210 pounds of highly toned, highly developed power. His body defined coordination. Balanced perfectly, it was trained to respond instantly to virtually anything he asked of it, time and time again. He was an athlete. A major leaguer. A player in every sense of the word.

Now, as with most who live beyond eight decades, his body doesn't respond as it once did. Age has naturally slowed him. Recurring back pain keeps him awake some nights, and it sometimes bothers him during the day. It hurts him to walk much of the time. But he never complains about the pain. Not to me, not to anyone. Not ever. His knees don't seem to bother him, despite the pounding they took throughout the years. It was his knees that stopped him from realizing his dream of military service in World War II. He thought his knees worked just fine. The U.S. military said no. He still thinks they work okay, but at his advanced age they don't move him around as fast as they used to.

He leads me into his living room. It's an attractive space: square, large, and immaculately clean. Light gray carpeting overlays the floor. The natural fireplace, fronted in grayish-brown marble, dominates the room and captures immediate attention. Hanging around on beige walls are framed prints of common outdoor scenes. One of the more compelling prints shows hummingbirds seeking nectar from the branch of a flowering shrub. The rest of the room is tastefully decorated, but not flamboyant. Sofas face the fireplace at its front and left side; twin chairs, upholstered in a light print, face the sofas. A couple of end tables support decorative porcelain lamps. Standing against the wall across from the fireplace is a colonial desk, topped by a glass-fronted bookcase. Family pictures are carefully arranged on the desk, and a few accent vases and bowls are tactfully placed around. Like the man himself, there is nothing pretentious about this room. His countless awards, trophies, plaques, and memorabilia, which could be here, are not. They're stashed away in drawers somewhere, not forgotten, but not flaunted for the eyes of others.

He settles in his favorite chair by the fireplace, a high-backed light blue, comfortable colonial wingback. I sit facing him on one of the sofas.

On this warm Saturday morning he's dressed for suburban comfort in a light yellow golf shirt, dark blue walking shorts, white socks, and Sperry Top-Siders. He presents the solid image of a typical relaxed, prosperous, carefree retiree. Those who know him well, however, see his true self. He's a man of action, more comfortable outdoors than sitting in his living room on a beautiful Saturday morning. But today his low-intensity hazel eyes and his broad smile show lots of interest. He's glad I'm here. I'm glad for his attention.

Before I have a chance to speak, he asks me about myself, recalling something I told him in the past. He has a knack for putting others at ease by getting them first to talk about themselves. It's a social trait not often found, and it works extremely well. I feel welcome. I'm comfortable.

This is the man I've motored through Ann Arbor to see today. This is the Michigan legend who'll spend the next few days and weeks telling me his life story, and also his stories about others. He'll give me anecdotes about the sports he played. He'll talk about those he played with, played against, played for, and coached. His name is well known by thousands of University of Michigan alumni scattered throughout the world and by hundreds more in amateur and professional sports. He's cherished as a role model by those who proudly call Ann Arbor, Michigan, their home. His name is Don Lund.

I call him Don sometimes, but mostly I call him "Coach," out of respect. I never played for him, but I've been his friend for many years. I knew his wife, Betty, who passed away in 1998. I'm friends with his daughter, Susan, and her loving family. I also knew his sister, Virginia. They all adore him. He adores them back.

"OK, Coach," I say, "Let's start. What's been told to you about the time from when you were born until your first memory as a child?"

"You want to start at the very beginning?" he asks. "Naturally, I can only tell you what's been passed on by my parents and grandparents."

"No problem," I answer. "Just let it flow."

The Coach settles back in his chair. He crosses his legs. His hands relax in his lap. His calm eyes stare at the wall across the room. His memory takes over and he starts talking: "I was born on ..."

2
Hello, World!

The pain was almost unbearable. Much harder than her first childbirth. Marguerite could sense the eagerness of the two others in her bedroom—the doctor at her feet and the nurse standing next to the bed, gently wiping her forehead with a cool towel. The upstairs room felt warm, almost steamy. Window shades pulled completely down isolated the trio from the early morning outside. Three lamps on two bedside tables and a corner dresser provided enough light for all.

"Push, Marguerite, push harder now." The doctor's voice was insistent but gentle. Marguerite could barely see the gray-haired top of his head as she forced herself off the pillow and bore down. "It's the shoulders," the doctor said. "Just a little more now. You can do it."

She knew he held the baby's head in his hands. She pushed. She pushed again, as hard as she could despite the pain. Suddenly she felt the rush of release as the baby seemed to launch from her insides. She gave out a soft cry as her head fell back on the pillow. She lay there collapsed and exhausted. Silence reigned for a moment.

The nurse whispered, "It's a boy!"

Then Marguerite heard a soft slap, followed immediately by a strong infant wail. Happy tears poured down each side of Marguerite's face as Donald Andrew Lund announced his entrance to the world.

It was early morning on May 18, 1923. The baby's cry created immediate excitement throughout the home on Detroit's East Side. Hardly anyone living in the large six-bedroom home had slept, preferring instead to keep a quiet vigil overnight in anticipation of the birth.

The baby's father, Andrew, had waited patiently in the living room through the night, until the nurse came down to tell him the birth would be soon. Andrew then moved to the upstairs hallway and paced deliberately in front of the closed bedroom door. At 5-feet-11 and 180 solid pounds, he would normally produce a heavy sound on the hardwood floor. But his shoes were off, and stocking feet allowed him to move back and forth without making a sound. Fighting the urge to burst into the room, he moved patiently, until the nurse opened the door, smiled broadly, and ushered him in to greet his new son.

Downstairs the grandparents passed the time in soft conversation. Their vigil was finally broken when the doctor, wearing a grin that reassured everyone, came downstairs carrying his black bag. He announced the baby boy's arrival, shook hands all around, and departed. Everyone was excited, but they all suppressed the urge to make a noisy celebration, respecting the moment upstairs. Someone suggested waking the baby's two-year-old sister, Virginia, but the idea was quickly suppressed. It was too early in the morning. Virginia would have her own special time with her brother, introduced properly by her mother and father.

In due time, a proud and smiling Andrew Lund ambled carefully down the stairs, holding the bundle of baby gently in his arms. Grinning like he had just won the Irish Sweepstakes, he presented his son to the rest of the family.

Baby Donald weighed exactly ten pounds at birth. His hands and feet were large, and his overall body was evenly proportioned. But his dominant feature, even as an infant, was his large, exceptionally wide shoulders. People would notice these shoulders throughout his life. They surmounted a solid torso, providing him with a natural, fluid motion in his upper body. These shoulders would later shove aside would-be tacklers on the gridiron, knock away basketball opponents going after the ball, and whip around fast enough to launch a baseball into the left field stands. His shoulders gave him power. They gave him coordination. They would be the positive measure of difference for him in athletic competition.

Donald's early years were spent living at his birthplace at 2183 Lycaste in Detroit, Michigan. The house was owned and occupied by his maternal grandparents, John and Christina Matheson. The Lunds—Andrew, Marguerite, Virginia, and Donald—lived with the Mathesons as tenants, renting the rooms they lived in. But the relationship between Donald's family and the Mathesons extended way beyond that of tenant/landlord. They were all one large, happy family.

John and Christina Matheson were much more than merely hospitable people when it came to family, neighbors, and friends. Their home was always open as a warm and friendly place. No one who visited was allowed to leave without sharing a meal or at least a home-baked roll and a cup of coffee. This was the environment Donald enjoyed as a child. His grandparents and parents were affectionate, attentive, and caring. His sister accepted her little brother more like an equal playmate than as a rival for parental goodwill. His childhood memories recall many hours of wholesome activity around the house. He was constantly exposed to people who loved him, and this exposure could well be seen as a prime source for his own congenial personality. Donald's wholesome beliefs, attitudes, and values, learned as a child at home, would serve him well in later life by giving him a solid social foundation.

Donald's immediate family was his primary childhood example for responsible behavior. His mother Marguerite was a slim, dark-haired beauty with a bright disposition and a ready smile. She was born in Calumet, Michigan, a small town in the state's Upper Peninsula. Her father, John Matheson, had emigrated from Canada near the turn of the century, intending to take advantage of the copper mining boom in the UP. He settled in Calumet, then bought a rooming house in nearby Freda and rented out rooms to itinerant miners.

Marguerite's childhood exposures to the myriad types of adult men, all of whom treated her with courtesy and respect, provided her with prime exposure to worldly human behavior. The miners would tell her stories about their lives, their work in the mines, their goals, and their dreams. She came away from all this with a well-rounded understanding of the working man's frailties; of behavior traits that can lead to both successes and failures. She would carry this insight throughout her life, and she would transfer it to her children.

When Marguerite was still a little girl in 1913, her father sold the rooming house in Freda and moved his family to Detroit. The city had become the automobile manufacturing capital of the world, on its way to earning the nickname "Motor City." John Matheson, eager to share in this exploding economy, bought a large house on Lycaste, took in a few boarders, and got a job in one of the East Side auto factories. The family adapted easily to the move, even though they went from a small town to the big city in only a few days. The move was filled with promise. Detroit was growing so fast that job openings simply waited until people came along to fill them. Workers had cash to spare; saloons sprang up overnight. It was several years before Prohibition would slow things down; everyone was eager to embrace the good times. And Marguerite was eager to grow up.

As a young girl, Marguerite showed a talent for music. She liked to sing, and with encouragement from her parents she studied and learned to play the piano. Others noticed her musical talent, and soon she was playing piano at church and social gatherings around the neighborhood. It was this love of music and her enjoyment of playing the piano that captured the strongest memories Donald would have of her.

He recalls his mother playing the piano and singing in the parlor at home. It's his earliest memory of anything in his childhood. Marguerite would play and sing "Show Me the Way to Go Home" or "Ramona," and Donald would stand next to the piano, a wide-eyed little boy completely captivated by his mom's performance.

Above all things, Marguerite was a powerful source of love and support for Donald, especially in his childhood. Her gentleness, her motherly patience, and her encouragement became a lifeline for her son. She was extremely adept at focusing toward the content of one's character as being most important above all things. She carefully and deliberately transferred this focus onto both of her children. Hers was a lifelong effort to create and perpetuate a wholesome frame of mind. In doing so, Marguerite lovingly touched the hearts of everyone around her. She was the solid core of Donald Lund's boyhood home. And the head of this home was his father, Andrew.

Andrew Lund was also a product of Michigan's Upper Peninsula. Born and raised in Ishpeming, he was the son of Norwegian immigrants who settled in Ishpeming along with several other families from Norway. His father established a bar in town, and it was there that young Andrew learned the rough give-and-take of men in a social setting. As a young man he also found a natural skill in working with his hands. He could fashion small toys out of wood and fix things around the house with ease. It wasn't long before he realized that using his hands would be his livelihood. He learned the art of welding and became skilled at repairing machinery.

When his father contracted tuberculosis and died, Andrew helped his mother sell the bar, then left home and moved to Detroit, where he took a skilled welding job at Detroit Edison. He settled in a rented suite of rooms on Detroit's East Side. Although he needed the work, Andrew's move to Detroit from Ishpeming was bittersweet for him. He loved the Upper Peninsula and the quiet, steady lifestyle it offered. To the end of his life he praised the UP. But in fact Andrew Lund never regretted leaving Ishpeming. After all, his life really began when he arrived in Detroit and subsequently found the girl of his dreams in another UP transplant, Marguerite Matheson. Nevertheless, Andrew always professed that Michigan's Upper Peninsula was "God's Country." His young son Donald couldn't wait to go there someday.

By all accounts, Andrew was a loving husband and a devoted father. He was also a no-nonsense disciplinarian to his children, but he balanced that by being attentive to their needs. There were four things, according to his son's memory, that he wanted to instill in Donald above all others: that America is the land of opportunity; that hard work and knowing the value of a dollar will lead to success; that Babe Ruth was the greatest baseball player in the world; and that if you really put your mind to doing something, you could do it. Andrew was determined to support his son's honest efforts in whatever the lad chose to do. And he had no reservations about doing the same for Donald's older sister, Virginia.

Virginia Lund was born on November 16, 1920, exactly two years, six months, and two days before her brother. She was a precocious child, especially when it came to language communication. She spoke in sentences at a much earlier age than most children. Virginia could recognize letters of the alphabet when other toddlers were focusing merely on pictures. And as she grew through her early years, Virginia learned to conceptualize the written word. She would soon become one of the youngest members of the Young Writers Club at school, and literature would eventually become the focus of her adult life.

It probably was Virginia who started the family calling the baby "Don" instead of "Donald." Whether as a two-year-old she had trouble pronouncing the complete name "Donald" (highly doubtful, since she was adept at speaking even at an early age) or whether she just elected to call him "Don," no one quite remembers. Nevertheless, he was "Don" to her, and the family followed suit.

And so it was, on May 18, 1923, that Don Lund joined a tightly connected, success-driven, and doting family. He became part of a household of role models, which included not only his parents and his sister, but also his grandparents. And beyond that nuclear family extended the regular visitors at 2183 Lycaste. They included aunts, uncles, household borders, and drop-in friends who stopped by in a constant stream. Don first drew breath in that house, and it didn't take long before he became integrated into the frenzy of the household. He also learned early on that he was part of a remarkable lineage of hardworking, decent, and honest people. He quickly assimilated their way of life. He readily accepted their values as his own, embracing them as they became imbedded in his conscious mind.

Don looks back on his childhood with fondness, chiefly because his family talked to him repeatedly about important events in those early years, before his age of memory kicked in. One of the most frequently told stories, a favorite one rendered over the years by nearly every member of his family, was certainly a treasured moment. It's the tale of how Don Lund received his first ball.

3
Uncle Alec's "Baw"

"Mom! Here comes Uncle Alec!" Five-year-old Virginia Lund bounded into the house as the front screen door banged shut behind her. Virginia was the delight of the entire household. At just under four feet, she was taller than many of the neighborhood kids her age. She was also stronger and smarter than most of them. By the age of four, she was a self-taught reader, and few of her friends could match her command of words. She easily became a childhood leader and mostly played with kids one or two years older. Her dad called her a tomboy, but he said it with pride. She'd giggle when he called her that, stomp her foot playfully, and flash her large, brown eyes. As far as Virginia was concerned, Daddy could call her anything. And so, on a typical mid-August early evening in 1925, Virginia pounced into the kitchen.

"Uncle Alec is coming, Mom!" The announcement was made for everyone in the house, not just Virginia's mother. Standing at the doorway with arms folded, feet apart, her short brown hair typically askew, the five-year-old commanded attention with a bright smile. She wore a dark blue calico daytime dress, with short sleeves trimmed in white. White knee-length socks stretched upward from scuffed, black, everyday play shoes.

"All right, Virginia," said Marguerite, "Uncle Alec will be coming by for dinner. We'll set an extra plate for him."

That was fine with Virginia. Without another word, she charged back out to the front porch to wait for Uncle Alec. Grandpa John Matheson, dressed casually in black slacks and a white, open-collar shirt with rolled-up sleeves, joined her. John looked to the left, down Lycaste. Sure enough, shuffling toward them from half a block away came Alec Mackenzie.

Alec wasn't really a sibling-related "uncle." He was a distant cousin to Marguerite Lund, but nobody ever tried to figure out just how distant. They didn't care. Alec was a likable guy who fit in socially wherever he went. And he went to the Matheson home on Lycaste frequently. He loved Christina Matheson's cooking. And her daughter-in-law, Marguerite, was just as good around a stove as Christina. So Alec wasn't timid about showing up several days a week, right around dinnertime. Alec loved to eat. And the Matheson place on Lycaste was the best eatery in town, as far as he was concerned.

Nobody in the neighborhood really knew what Alec Mackenzie did for a living. They did believe, however, that whatever he did was honest work. He seemed to live modestly; he never flashed a wad of cash or hung around with less-than-desirable characters. In fact, Alec Mackenzie was indeed an honest laborer. He didn't hold down a steady job at the nearby auto plant like most of the men in his East Side neighborhood. He preferred, instead, to work random jobs, like sweeping up floors in tool shops or auto parts stores. He stocked shelves. He delivered groceries to people's homes. He "did this and that," as he liked to tell his friends. But in sum, Alec Mackenzie was a down-to-earth plain old good guy. And he loved to grab a free meal at the Matheson's place on Lycaste.

This evening Uncle Alec was moving along the sidewalk toward the Matheson house. He walked slowly, with an uneven gait caused by a slight deformity in his right hip. He was born with the hip that way and wasn't self-conscious about it, despite having to walk with an awkward shuffle. Virginia ran out to meet him. Uncle Alec was thirty-eight years old and rather stout. He stood about 5-feet-9 and weighed about 190 pounds. Today he wore a light brown work shirt with sleeves rolled up, dark brown pants, white socks and black work shoes. His dark brown fedora, stained with sweat, covered a full head of thick, dark brown hair. He carried a small paper sack in his left hand. The sack held a gift he intended to give to Virginia.

As Alec walked up the front porch steps, he was greeted warmly by John Matheson, who held open the screen door and motioned him inside.

"Hey, Uncle Alec," said Virginia as she noticed the sack he was carrying. "What's in the bag?"

Alec smiled at her. "I'll show ya in a minute," he said.

As he walked into the house, Alec placed his hat on the rack by the door and proceeded to the kitchen. The family would be there, he knew. It was close to dinnertime, and the kitchen was the hub of their home.

Alec came into the room with the paper sack held high in his left fist. He shook it. "Here, Virginia," he said. "This is for you." With a ceremony that could rival a performing magician, he reached in and slowly began to pull out his mysterious gift. The sets of eyes following Alec's performance were a mixture of adult curiosity and five-year-old wonder. With deliberate flourish, Uncle Alec plucked forth his treasure.

It was a yellow rubber ball—soft, hollow, about five inches in diameter. It only weighed about six ounces, and it hardly bounced when thrown. But Alec acted as if it was one of the rare artifacts of the world.

"I traded it from this guy for a beer," said Alec. "Down at the tavern on Kercheval." He flipped the ball up and down in his right hand. "And I think it's perfect for Virginia." Alec moved into the dining room, and motioned for Virginia to follow him. "Wanna play catch?" he asked her.

Marguerite, the ever-watchful mother, saw what was about to happen and said, "Wait a minute, Alec. Better wash your hands first. And let me have the ball. I'll wash that, too."

Alec left for the bathroom to wash his hands. Marguerite, wearing a simple pink-and-white housedress under a full white apron, took the ball and carried it to the sink. She wore her dark brown hair softly around her shoulders. Her hands were delicate but strong as she washed the ball thoroughly with soap and water. She dried it on her apron and then handed it to Alec as he walked back into the dining room.

"Now please be careful how you throw it to her," said Marguerite. "She's just a child, you know."

Alec took the ball and winked at Virginia. He knew that this was one little girl who was anything but fragile. He flipped it to her from about six feet. Virginia caught it easily in both hands and returned it right back with a two-handed flip. Easy. So Alec and Virginia started playing catch.

Virginia's two-year-old brother, Donald, was taking all this in from his favorite spot under the kitchen table. Having learned to walk just after his first birthday, Donald showed off his "terrible twos" by grabbing small items from around the kitchen. He would openly pilfer spoons, dish towels, and salt shakers, "hiding" them under the table. Marguerite and Andrew recognized this as normal behavior, and they put up with it without complaint.

Donald was considered big for his age at two, standing about thirty-eight inches and weighing nearly forty pounds. His mother fashioned his straight blond hair in a pageboy style, with bangs in the front going all around, falling over his ears, and cascading down to the bottom of his neck. The hair style was typical for little boys of his age. Like Virginia, Donald was a blur of energy around the entire house. He could walk up and down the stairs, but he chose to crawl because it was faster for him. On the floor he much preferred running to walking. He climbed on every piece of furniture he could. He bounced up and down in his crib every morning until Marguerite or her husband would arrive and lift him out. He practically refused to wear shoes and socks. Almost immediately after someone would put socks on him and leave him alone, he'd take them off. But everyone doted on him, and he was a source for constant home entertainment. Donald laughed. He giggled. He found everything exciting and funny. Andrew would roll with his son on the floor, toss him in the air, hold him upside down for a few seconds, and occasionally bounce him on his knees. The rough play didn't matter to the boy. He loved it and always asked for more.

Now Donald was watching intently as Alec and Virginia played catch with the yellow rubber ball. It wasn't until Virginia tossed the ball high in the air to nearly hit the ceiling that Donald decided to become part of the action.

"Baw!" he said, as he bounded out from under the table, "Baw!" He ran up to Alec and said it again. The hazel-eyed boy wore a light blue play suit with short pants and a round-collared short-sleeved shirt.

"He wants the ball," said Virginia. "Throw it to him, Uncle Alec."

"But it's your ball, Virginia," said Alec. "I brought it for you."

"That's OK, Uncle Alec," she said. "Throw it to Don."

Alec Mackenzie was hesitant. He had played catch with two-year-olds before. Usually they just looked at you as you threw the ball to them, and they wouldn't take their eyes off you as you threw it. They just stood there and let the ball bounce off their bodies. Sometimes you could really hurt them. Alec wasn't

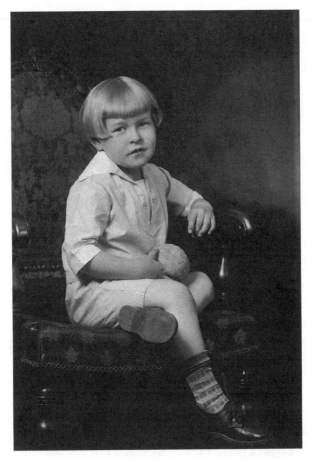

Pageboy Donald Lund, four, in the living room of his grandparents'
house on Lycaste Avenue in Detroit. The house would later be
owned by his parents. Yes, that's a ball in his right hand.
(Lund Family Collection)

about to try that with Donald, no matter how much the kid
yelled "Baw!"

At that moment, Andy Lund walked down the stairs and into
the room. He had cleaned up and changed clothes after coming
home from his job at the factory. He wore his favorite around-
the-house apparel: light brown denim shirt that had been washed
and pressed hundreds of times, dark brown wool pants, brown
socks, and his favorite everyday brown shoes.

Andy looked at the scene and immediately realized what was going on. His son wanted the yellow ball, and Alec Mackenzie wouldn't throw it to him.

"Here, Alec, let me try it," said Andy. Alec tossed Andy the ball, and little Donald turned around to face his father, yelling "Baw!"

"All right, son," Andrew said. He showed Donald how to put his hands together to grasp the ball, placing it repeatedly in and out of the little boy's hands. Finally, Andy stepped about four feet away. His son stood looking at the yellow ball in his father's hands, his own small hands clasped together at his chest.

Andy flipped the ball right at his son's midsection. Donald caught it and held on. "Marguerite, did you see that?" His astonished father exclaimed, "He caught it!" Andy reached over to take it back, so he could toss it again to Donald. But the boy held on tightly. "Baw!" shouted Donald, and it was only after his father assured him he would throw it back again that Donald released the ball. Andy threw the ball again. Donald caught it. Then he caught it again, this time from about six feet. Then again from eight feet.

Every time, Donald caught it. After about five throws from his dad, Donald threw it back, mimicking his father's toss. He wasn't strong enough to throw it the entire eight feet in the air, but the two or three bounces the ball took were right on line.

"Look at his eyes," said Andrew. "They follow the ball, not my hand. "Watch this." He threw the ball about two feet to the boy's right. The ball sailed past him, but Donald's eyes never left it. For the next twenty minutes, father and son played catch. Most of the time Donald caught the ball, his eyes never leaving it, even if it was thrown too low or off-center.

His natural ability, obvious to everyone in the family, astounded his parents. Even Virginia, who lovingly tolerated her little brother, saw how much he cherished that yellow rubber ball. So she gave it to him. And no matter how many toys he had to play with over the next three or four years, Virginia's little brother "Don" always came back to that yellow ball. Thanks to Uncle Alec. Thanks to the patience of his mom and dad. Thanks to Virginia's generosity to her brother. Donald and his "Baw!" were inseparable.

4

Dialogue

"That yellow ball must have been pretty special, I guess. I don't remember much about it. I heard I was never without it as a little kid."

Don Lund's early childhood memories are vicarious, placed in his mind by his parents and other relatives. He doesn't remember who first told him about Uncle Alec and the yellow rubber ball. But it's a good tale and fun to tell.

As he finished the story, he slowly sat up in his chair and stretched. I watched his shoulders as they challenged his chair's "wingbacks." He raised his arms straight up, while at the same time clenching his hands into relaxed fists. Even at his advanced age, the muscles in his forearms rippled with stored energy. I imagined him slapping a hard shot to deep center field.

"Coach," I asked, "how would you compare yourself to Al Kaline?"

He straightened right up. "You've gotta be kidding," he says. "Don't compare me to Kaline. He was great. Better than great. Why, I've seen Al charge a low line drive, make a diving catch off the top of the grass, then double the runner off first base from his knees. Now, how many guys could do that? I'd rather you didn't try to compare me and Al. Except that we both played right field for the Tigers."

"All right, Coach," I said, "I hear you. So let's compare your playing skills to the Tigers' current right fielder, Magglio Ordoñez? Granted, Ordoñez is a superstar at the plate and I wouldn't ask you to compare yourself to him in that regard."

He grinned. "Thanks a lot!"

"But, between the two of you," I asked, "who's the better fielder?"

"Well," he stated without hesitation, "I'd have to give Ordoñez the edge."

"Really?" I asked, assuming he was just being typically modest. "How do you figure that?"

"Simple," he chuckled. "I'm in my eighties!"

We both laughed hard—I had the certain feeling he couldn't wait to get in that old joke. It was funny. And it served as a subtle warning against asking him again to compare himself to anyone else.

"Let's move on to childhood things you personally remember," I offered. "What are your earliest memories?"

The old coach thought for a moment, smiled, frowned slightly, and settled back in his chair. "I suppose the earliest things I remember were around the time we moved to the west side of Detroit ..."

5
West Side Story

"Run, Donnie, run!" The cry came from one of the dozen or so kids lining the railroad tracks on this hot summer morning. They were excited. They were watching one of their favorite games, a contest where two kids competed in running the rails. All the kids were friends, six- to ten-year-olds who played together around the neighborhood. They wore typical summer play clothes of jeans, T-shirts, sneakers, or whatever else the mothers allowed their youngsters to throw on. Donnie had on his usual knickers. It was midsummer 1929. The kids directed their cheering toward the two boys running intently toward them while balancing on the tracks.

"Keep goin', Donnie," yelled a friend. "You can take him!"

No problem beating this guy, thought Donald. He kept on running in perfect balance, like a fly on a clothesline. Sure enough, his competitor soon lost balance and staggered off the rail. Donald kept going a few more feet, stopped, then stepped off with ease. He had won again. He grinned as his friends went wild around him.

Indeed, this kind of competition was quite easy for him. Six-year-old Donald Lund was the best railroad track racer in the neighborhood. Even bigger kids had a hard time beating him as they tried to negotiate the hundred-foot rail race, without losing balance and stepping off the rail. The rules were simple: Two kids raced at once. Each one stood at the starting line, one foot on the rail and one foot inside on the same wooden tie. Someone said "Go!" Immediately both racers would leap on the rail and run along the top of it, as fast as they could, toward the marked-off finish line. The first one to lose balance and step off the rail would lose the race. If both retained their balance, the first one to reach the finish line would win. And nearly always, Donald won. He seldom had to go all the way to the finish line, because invariably the other racer would lose balance and step off. And

Donald knew why, but he never told them: they looked at their feet. They'd watch their steps, and boom! Right off the rail. Don never made that mistake, of course. He always looked way out at the track. His feet just went where they were supposed to. It was simple. But no way was he going to tell anyone his secret. After all, why train the competition?

The exception, of course, was his sister, Virginia. Don told her everything. Virginia tried the rail run, also found it easy, and after a few tries she could keep up with her little brother. But she didn't race him when other kids were around. She knew that if she bested her brother in front of others, it would make him angry. She also knew that taking advantage of his confidential disclosures would cause him to stop telling her everything. So she backed off and let him beat the other kids on his own. It was fun for him. Those were fun times.

This was one year after the Lund family had moved from the Matheson house on Detroit's East Side. Times had been good, the economy was booming, and Andrew was making excellent money as a welder at Detroit Edison. So he and Marguerite built a house on the West Side, at 12276 Sorrento. With the Mathesons' blessing, Andrew, Marguerite, Virginia, and Don moved to their new home and started fresh. Andrew was now the man in charge of the house. Marguerite had her own kitchen and made all her own homemaking decisions.

Virginia and Don made friends easily. The neighbors were friendly and supportive. The railroad, only about fifty yards from the Lund home, was a spur line that served a Ford Motor Company plant. It was only used by slow-moving freight trains, mostly at night. So the Lunds and the rest of the neighborhood generally felt the tracks posed little danger to the kids who played on them. No one had ever been hurt there, so no one worried about it. The last year had been good for the Lunds, and the future looked even brighter.

The family lived on Sorrento for three years, 1928–1931. Don enjoyed his young friends, most of whom lived on his same street and attended the same Parker Elementary School. Much of their play took place on vacant lots that dotted the neighborhood, including one next door to Don's house. The kids would build forts in the summertime out of dirt and scrap wood, throwing clumps of clay at one another from their homemade "ramparts."

In winter, they would flood the lot next door, and boys and girls from all over the neighborhood would skate throughout the daylight hours.

Don's friends called him "Tuffy," but he doesn't remember why. He also doesn't remember the content of special handwritten notes his teachers would give Virginia to bring home on occasion. Virginia knew the notes were about her little brother, but she never peeked. Her conscience wouldn't let her. Knowing right from wrong was something Virginia was proud of, and even a teacher's note wouldn't make her slip from duty's call. Neither Marguerite nor Andrew ever told Virginia what the notes said, nor did they discipline her brother about them. Their contents would forever remain a family mystery.

Then came the biggest day of Don's young life. It would last in his memory as one of the finest days he ever spent—Sunday, May 12, 1929.

It was around 9:30 in the morning. The family was sitting at the kitchen table, just finishing breakfast. Andy and Marguerite occupied their usual places at the ends, with Virginia and Don sitting at the sides. Their family table positions never varied, regardless of the meal being served.

Marguerite smiled at her son. "Your birthday's coming next week, isn't it?"

The boy looked at her and nodded.

"He's going to be six," said Virginia, "next Saturday!"

"So your father and I have a special birthday surprise for you, one week early." She beamed at her husband, who winked at her.

"Son, do you know who Babe Ruth is?" Andy asked with a smile.

Don's eyes flashed as he sat straight up and gripped the table with both hands. He practically shouted, "Babe Ruth? He's the greatest baseball player in the world! Everybody knows Babe Ruth!"

Indeed, everyone did know who Babe Ruth was. His name was a common word in homes throughout the country. Now he was in the zenith of his career as left fielder for the World Champion New York Yankees. For the past two years, the Yankees had dominated the baseball world, winning both the 1927 and 1928 World Series. As a matter of fact, the Yankees were

arguably the premier team in the American League, with a long
history of superiority. Many experts believed the 1927 Yankees
team was the best ever in the history of the game. And few would
question that Babe Ruth was the Yankees' dominant player. Many
would even say he nearly won the 1928 Series by himself. With
his famous left-handed swing, he pounded a record World Series
batting average of .625. Over the course of many years, wherever
he played in parks all around the American League, Ruth was
a magnet for baseball buffs. It didn't matter which local team
they favored. Fans of all ages converged on their respective home
fields when Ruth came to town. For many of them, seeing the
famous "Bambino" in action was just as important as watching
their favorite home team on the field. The Babe lived his own
legend. He was the master. And on this day, May 12, 1929, he
would be bringing his world-ruling New York Yankees to play
the Tigers in Detroit. Soon-to-be-six-year-old Don Lund was
going to be a part of that experience.

"How would you like to see Babe Ruth play?" said Andy.

His son jumped up, knocking his chair in a backward slide.
"Are you kidding, Dad? Are we going to the game today?" Don
could hardly contain himself. Although he repeatedly listened
to Tigers' games on the radio with his mother, he had never
attended a professional baseball game. But the radio broadcasts,
coupled with family talks about the games and conversations
with other neighborhood kids, gave him up-to-date knowledge.
He could quote team standings and player statistics. He could
"talk the talk" when it came to the national pastime, as well
as or better than any of the other kids. Consequently, he knew
the Yankees had come to town for a three-game contest against
Detroit. He also believed he was about to become the luckiest
kid in the entire city.

"Yep," said his dad, "I've got two tickets for today's game.
We'll be leaving in a couple of hours. So make sure you're cleaned
up and ready to go."

"Wow, Dad," the boy yelled, "Wow!" In a dash he was out
of the kitchen, up the stairs, and in his room. He was a lightning
streak of excitement, cleaning up and changing clothes faster and
better than he had ever done. Within ten minutes, he was back
downstairs. His hair was combed, his face was scrubbed, and
his Sunday-best shirt and pants hung nicely on his small frame.

He looked like he had just stepped out of a children's fashion magazine. He was as ready as a racehorse at the starting gate.

"OK, Dad," he yelled, "let's go!"

Andy smiled at his son as he grabbed his jacket and hat. He kissed Marguerite good-bye and headed out the door with the most excited kid on the block.

Two street rail car rides later, the pair found themselves in front of Navin Field, home of the Detroit Tigers. Named after Tigers' owner Frank Navin, the park was one of baseball's two second-oldest stadiums, sharing the honor with Boston's Fenway Park. Both opened their doors on April 20, 1912, and both hosted opening-day wins for their respective home teams.

Navin Field was a large square with rounded corners, featuring a double-decked grandstand around the infield. Bleachers nearly surrounded the outfield, although an opening between them in left-center field allowed a well-hit ball to shoot out into the street. A slugger like Ruth could park one in traffic, as others had done many times over the years. So here they were, father and son, celebrating the boy's sixth birthday at Navin Field. There was no happier kid in Detroit that day than Don Lund.

Their two seats were in the lower deck along the third base line, not far from the Tigers' dugout. They had arrived about an hour before the three o'clock game would start, in time to watch both teams take batting practice. Right away they noticed one remarkable difference between the Detroit and New York uniforms, beyond the home team's plain white outfits and the visiting Yankees' pin-striped grays. The Yankees players wore numbers on their backs, based upon the respective order in their batting lineup. Thus Babe Ruth, batting third, wore number three. This was the first year any major league team numbered its players. The Yankees began this practice for easy player identification. All other teams, including the Tigers, would eventually follow suit.

Don was as mesmerized as any kid would be watching his first professional baseball game. He studied the action each inning with rapt attention, yelling with everyone else at the hits, the catches, the put-outs, and the scores. He scarcely took his eyes off Ruth in left field, whose barrel shape and spindly legs set him apart from the other players. He marveled at the Babe's throwing ability. He shared the crowd's anticipation each time the Bambino stood at the plate awaiting the next pitch. He yelled, he cheered, and he jumped up and down for nine innings. When the game was over, he joined the crowd's overwhelming elation: their Tigers, their astonishing Detroit Tigers, had beaten the mighty New York Yankees, 9 to 7. This was a birthday present he would cherish for the rest of his days.

During those three years on Sorrento, there were many other things both Don and Virginia would later recall with fondness. Among these was the tapioca pudding their mother made from scratch. The pudding was kind of a family joke, because Marguerite was always forgetting some ingredient or another when she made it, which was frequently. But everyone in the family loved it, no matter how it turned out. They called it "puddy." It was the best dessert they ever had.

One particular skill Don learned in the vacant lot next door was the game of horseshoes. Somebody in the neighborhood set up a permanent pit. The adult men would pitch the shoes in the evenings and on Sunday afternoon. The kids would pitch after school. Learning the game of horseshoes was exceptionally exciting for Don. It was the first time he experienced playing with older boys, something he would continue to do as he got older and more talented as an athlete.

In 1929–1930, Don Lund was bigger and stronger than most of his six- and seven-year-old playmates. He never bullied them, but he was always their recognized leader. He could win nearly every game they played, nearly all the time. No one would ever dare throw a lump of clay at him as they defended their homemade "forts" in the vacant lots. He was known for catching it and throwing it right back. And a well-thrown lump of clay could hurt. So when it came to horseshoes, there was no contest at all among his own age group. Don was just about the only boy his age who could pitch a horseshoe more than thirty feet. As a result, he played with the older boys who could match his pitching skills. It was a strong developmental experience for him to play with older boys. It offered an opportunity for him to build his confidence in active competition among others.

From 1928 to 1931, in school, in neighborhood play, in contests such as rail racing and horseshoes, Don Lund grew as a boy, both physically and mentally. He recognized the fact that what seemed hard for others to do was fairly easy for him. He learned that competing with older boys was more challenging than competing with those his own age. At the same time, he learned to hold his confidence in check, since the older boys would win if he didn't try his best. He was never allowed to become too satisfied with himself. Bigger kids were good for his reality checks.

All those good times came crashing down in 1931. A national tragedy, the Great Depression, came into the Lund family's life. They were all affected, including Don, along with the rest of the country. The 1929 New York Stock Exchange crash started it all, but it took more than a year to affect the daily lives of all Americans. And no area of the United States was affected harder by the Great Depression than Detroit. Most people could no longer afford to buy cars, so the automobile companies nearly stopped production, discharged enormous numbers of workers, and virtually closed their doors. The era of good times and free spending was over. Books would be written about bankruptcies, bread lines, and beggars in the streets. Those who continued to work in non-automotive businesses had their wages cut in half. Detroit went from a booming, hard-working, freewheeling city to a town of needy and, in some cases, helpless people. It took almost two years, but the effects of the Great Depression on Detroit were devastating.

Andrew Lund was more fortunate in the beginning than most. As a Detroit Edison employee, Andy was not nearly as affected as his friends and neighbors on Detroit's West Side, since utilities were a high-demand industry. His wages remained intact, at least for a while. From time to time, Andy would help out a neighbor down on his luck by "loaning" him a couple of dollars, knowing he would never be paid back.

By 1931, however, even Andy and his family were in financial trouble. Andy's pay was cut several times, until he could no longer afford mortgage payments on the house. It became obvious that he and his family would soon be out of a place to live. The Lunds reluctantly turned back to the Mathesons for help. To their delight, John and Christina Matheson not only welcomed them back to live with them, they were actually anxious for them to return. They missed their grandchildren, Virginia and Don. They missed them terribly. For the Lunds, moving back to

Lycaste Avenue suddenly wasn't a defeat. The Mathesons wanted them and needed them. Moreover, their West Side home on Sorrento had been turning into a "doom and gloom" residence. The nearby railroad track seldom carried a train. The vacant lot next door was weedy and overgrown. And the house itself, with its impending foreclosure, was no longer enticing. The Lund family was eager to move back to the East Side. Happiness would welcome them back on Lycaste Avenue. They would once again be part of a supportive, extended family. They would live there, thrive there, and prosper there. Don and Virginia would grow from children to adults there. The year 1931 would prove to be the turning point year in all four of the Lund family members' lives.

Don would develop quickly. It wouldn't be long before people would marvel at his enormous physical skills. And they would admire his ability to handle himself at all times with good character and impeccable integrity. He seemed destined for athletics. Sports were all he talked about, all he wanted to do. Sports represented his dreams, his desires, and his future. Now, back on the East Side of Detroit, the former rail racer quickly began to acquire skills in the two things in life he wanted most: sports and healthy competition. And all he had to do to get these was venture out the front door of his house. His neighborhood had it all there for him. The neighborhood kids proved to be his performance network for fun, frolic, good times, and the best athletic competition he could possibly find.

6
Back at Lycaste

Don had lots of neighborhood playmates around his Lycaste Avenue home. With a knack for making friends through easy charm and a quick wit, he was a favorite with other neighborhood kids. They loved his penchant for never letting little things bother him the way others might be bothered. They were attracted to his particular style of humor, which focused on poking fun at situations, rather than at other kids. They readily made him their leader in choosing games to play, where to play them, and under what rules they were played. All this came naturally to him. He was at the center of neighborhood activities, and he loved every minute of it.

Don's Lycaste Avenue environs were mostly typical of an East Side Detroit locale of the 1930s. His particular neighborhood could best be described as blue-collar. Before the Great Depression, most of the workers earned livelihoods as laborers in the huge auto plants that dominated the nearby landscape. The people who lived there fully believed that the proximity of these manufacturing behemoths gave the Lycaste area an almost unique and special atmosphere. The auto plants were there first. The homes came later. The dynamics of social interdependence worked beautifully, providing mutual satisfaction for the companies, their workers, and the residents.

So close were these factories, Hudson Motorcar, Chrysler Assembly, and others, that one or more of them could be seen from every street corner on every block. The Detroit Edison Conner's Creek power station loomed over the whole scene, proudly displaying its enormous smokestacks. Termed affectionately as the "seven sisters," they belched continuous plumes of rich black smoke and coal soot hundreds of feet into the air, reminding everyone that the power that drove their lives was produced right before their eyes. The Great Depression slowed these dynamics greatly, of course. But the social dynamics of people supporting one another held fast, especially in those tough times.

For young Don Lund and his playmates, their neighborhood was wholesome and welcoming. It proved to be an exciting, happy place, where kids could romp in mutual security and grow up as they gave and accepted mutual personal challenges.

Don embraced it. This time of his life was more than just fun for him. It was a time for him to form solid relationships and a time for making his own self-image.

Friendships came easy to him. Don enjoyed being popular among girls as well as boys, and he vigorously joined and frequently led games that included both sexes. Certain games, like "kickball," which encouraged pushing and shoving, were mostly for boys, with a few exceptions for the hardier girls, such as Virginia Lund. Other games, like hide-and-seek, were played equally by boys and girls. For the most part, however, boys played with boys, and girls played with girls. Those girls who involved themselves in boys' games were those who demonstrated athletic ability and a certain "toughness," which allowed them to be included. Don never discriminated against, or purposely excluded, girls from any game. His was a performance judgment: you either "cut it" or you didn't. If you could cut it, you played. Fortunately for him, and for his peace around the house, Virginia could cut it.

His closest pals were Tommy Opper and Birch Williams, both of whom shared his passion for athletics. Sports were what they mostly talked about, what they did, what they wanted to do. They could recite baseball stats for pro players as if they did that for a living. They could talk for hours about other pro sports, football and hockey in particular.

Their heroes were varsity stars at Detroit Southeastern High School. These players, of course, lived in the same neighborhood as Don, Tommy, and Birch. All three boys thrilled to see the high school football games during the fall of each year, where they cheered with the crowd and rooted for a decisive Southeastern victory. These pre-teen years were especially valuable for all three as they palled around. Most importantly for each of them, the friendships they forged remained strong throughout their own school years at Southeastern. They would stay strong over many tests of time, separation, and career diversity, as each went forward to pursue his life's ambitions.

Tommy's favorite recess activity at the neighborhood elementary school was to toss a football around the playground with Don. Since Don could run a farther distance than Tommy could throw, he always ran a short pass pattern so Tommy could get it to him. When it was Don's turn to throw, Tommy would "go long," catch the ball on a dead run, then bring it back within his own range to return it. The two friends would do this nearly every school day. Tommy became a good long-ball receiver. Don became an accurate long-ball thrower. Both would fondly recall this game of football catch as one of the more fun pastimes of their young lives.

Birch Williams shared his friend Don's most memorable moment as a youngster in the Lycaste neighborhood. It happened at Mrs. Stafford's house, located directly across the street from the Mathesons'. All the kids liked Mrs. Stafford, as did their parents.

And for whatever reason, Mrs. Stafford took a special liking for this big kid with the big grin who lived across the street, Don Lund. He was her favorite, and she wasn't shy about letting other neighbors know it, especially Marguerite Lund. Mrs. Stafford would give him freshly baked cookies. Don would help her carry out the trash. She liked him, he liked her. That's the way it was. So it was no surprise when Mrs. Stafford came over to the Lund home to ask Marguerite if she could invite Don and one of his friends over for dinner.

"What's the occasion?" asked his mother.

"A very special visit from a very special person," responded Mrs. Stafford.

Hearing all this from the next room, Don and his friend Birch Williams listened intently as Mrs. Stafford explained how she and the famous baseball pitcher Lefty Grove were both from the same town, Lonaconing, Maryland.

Of course, everyone in Lonaconing knew everyone else, she said, and her parents were close friends of Lefty's parents. She went on to say that Lefty's team, the Philadelphia Athletics, was playing the Detroit Tigers this coming weekend, but that Lefty wasn't scheduled to pitch. So, being from the same town and all, she called Lefty and invited him to her home for dinner.

Lefty Grove accepted right away. Therefore, Mrs. Stafford wondered if Don and his friend in the next room would like to join them.

The boys' reaction was like a firecracker exploding on the Fourth of July, with "Wow!" and "Oh, boy!" yells at maximum volume. Birch ran home to ask his mother, who said yes right away. They couldn't believe it! They were going to have dinner with Lefty Grove, the best left-handed pitcher in the major leagues!

Don and Birch's special dinner took place the following Saturday night. Mrs. Stafford cooked a marvelous meal of meat loaf, mashed potatoes, greens, and peach pie for dessert.

The boys were dressed in their best Sunday clothes. Lefty was a big, rough-looking man who belied his rugged looks with a gentle personality. He was dressed in a gray suit, white shirt, and blue tie. The group talked baseball, with Lefty regaling them with anecdotes about batters he was facing around the league. At the end of the meal, Lefty, who had probably been asked in advance by Mrs. Stafford, produced a baseball. He signed the ball and gave it to Don. Birch didn't seem to mind that Don was the only one of them to get a ball, so Don was only too happy to accept it. Before long, though, he had a problem that almost drove him to tears. As the group continued to talk around the dinner table, Don couldn't just hold on to the ball or put it on the table. Instead he played with it, passing it lightly from hand to hand, back and forth. Most kids would naturally do that when someone gave them a ball.

But this wasn't just an ordinary baseball. It carried Lefty Grove's autograph on it. And that signature was fast disappearing under the hand manipulations of this excited blond-haired kid. Finally, Don looked at the ball in his hands. Lefty's signature was gone! Wiped away by playing with it! He was devastated and embarrassed. Everyone at the table stopped the conversation and looked at Don's terror-stricken face.

"What's wrong, Don?" asked Mrs. Stafford.

Don looked at her. Tears began to form but he bravely held them back. "Mr. Grove's signature's gone," he said. "I guess I rubbed it off."

"Gimmie back that ball for a minute," said Lefty. "Yep, she's gone, all right," he said, as he examined the ball. "But I'll take care of that right now." Then Lefty pulled out his pen, signed the ball once more, and gave it back to Don, who promised to treat it forever like the treasure it was.

This act was probably one of the few times in history when a ballplayer signed the same ball twice for the same person, at the same occasion. It also provided an interesting historical footnote. Lefty Grove, ultimately destined for Hall of Fame greatness, signed a baseball twice, and not just for a neighborhood kid. He signed it for a future major league player who would always remember him with reverence, gratitude, and complete respect.

And so, the neighborhood around Lycaste Avenue churned with positive and wholesome activities for the youthful Don Lund in the 1930s. He was a well-liked, dynamic, and forceful leader among his peers. In his mind, he had made it, so far. But he also noticed that many of the bigger kids in the neighborhood were gone during the summer daytimes. Where'd they go? What'd they do?

He ultimately found out through his mother, who summoned him one day to the kitchen. What she told him would expand his world beyond the Lycaste Avenue neighborhood. He would compete against and make friends with other kids from around the city. At the end of August 1934, ten-year-old Don Lund was about to join the Young Men's Christian Association.

7

Here Comes the Y!

Marguerite was standing at the sink, peeling potatoes, as her son walked in. She looked at his handsome little face. To her it was an angel's face, though she wouldn't tell him that. Surrounded by a mop of golden, hand-mussed hair, Don's face was dominated by a wide, toothy grin that never seemed to fade. He's so even tempered, she thought, he never gets angry. He doesn't pick on other kids, and he never gets in fights. But the kids around the neighborhood knew that her son wasn't one to be messed with. Andy helped his son in that regard by teaching him some self-defense tactics in their backyard. Marguerite was pleased that her boy was gentle. But she was also glad that he could be tough when he needed to be. Now it was time to give him the right experiences with other boys beyond the neighborhood.

Don's hazel eyes were focused on his mother, curiosity showing through them. He was wearing his typical play clothes: brown knickers, gray shirt, and sneakers. Her boy made her so proud, she thought. He was turning out just as she'd hoped. It was time to make him even better. Marguerite had been saving what little money she could all summer, just for this moment.

"Hi, Mom," he said, "you called?"

Marguerite feigned a stern look. "How well can you swim?" she asked.

"Aw, Mom, you know I can't swim at all," he answered. His eyes narrowed as he waited to see where this was going.

"As well you can't," said his mother, "and we're going to do something about that."

He looked at her standing in front of him at the sink. She was wearing her light blue housedress, covered by the white apron she always wore in the kitchen. She held a half-peeled potato in her left hand, the peeler in her right. As she spoke, she gestured with the peeler. He thought her swimming question was funny. "Tommy's dad told him last night he was going to haul him down to the river and throw him in it," he joked.

The idea was ludicrous, of course. The Detroit River, running nearby on the other side of Jefferson Avenue, was not for swimming. Its water might be dirty with runoff from the factories, but that wasn't the main problem. The river's strong current would sweep even the strongest swimmer far downstream from any starting point. For kids Don's age, jumping in and trying to swim in the Detroit River would be near suicide.

"Is that what Dad's gonna do to me?"

Marguerite laughed at her son's question. "Not today," she said, "but it's time you learned to swim. And to do other things, like play basketball on a real court. Son, it's time you joined the YMCA."

The eleven-year-old couldn't believe his luck. He knew the Y cost a lot of money to join, and he had no idea where his mother had come up with it. But he wasn't about to question this sudden stroke of fortune. "Wow!" was all he could say. "Wow!"

The next morning Don and his mother walked the six blocks from their house to the Hannah YMCA. The place was a huge red-brick and stone building at the corner of Jefferson Avenue and Garland Street. Every boy in the neighborhood looked toward the Hannah Y as the place to be for organized sports. The Y had classes in swimming, basketball, gymnastics, distance running, and weight lifting. Boys were grouped according to age levels. Instructors were competent, motivated, and dedicated to teaching athletics at all levels of ability among the boys they coached. Open seven days a week, the Hannah Y was a haven for eager youngsters who wanted to learn athletics and test their skills in competition with others their own age. The Y beckoned them. The Y fulfilled their competitive ambitions. The Y was the spot everyone sought for clean, wholesome, controlled, and honest athletic training.

One problem that everybody shared was the per-person annual fee for Y membership. Six dollars per year was the general rate, plus whatever it cost for gym shoes and other recreational items. And for everyone in the Great Depression year of 1934, six dollars was a lot of money to produce for recreation.

Nevertheless, Marguerite Lund had the six dollars in her purse as she and her son strode purposefully toward the

Hannah Y that morning. She had struggled to save every extra penny, nickel, and dime she could gather over the summer months, determined that her son was going to enjoy the wholesome benefits of the YMCA. Don was athletically skilled and highly competitive. Marguerite was committed to do everything in her power to give him the necessary and proper training. She had planned this for weeks.

The pair avoided the Garland side doorway, where members went in, and walked around to the front entrance on Jefferson. The Jefferson entrance was where overnight guests and others entered. It didn't take long for Marguerite to proudly enroll her son. With her hard-earned payment and the stroke of her signature, Don Lund became a member of the Hannah YMCA. He was about to start the most meaningful and rewarding stage of his young life, thanks to his mom.

Young Don's first task at the Y was to fulfill his mom's directive and learn how to swim. At first he was afraid of the water. He could outrun and out-hustle others of his age on land, but water was an equalizer. Size and strength weren't as important to successful swimming as they were for land games. However, it wasn't long before he overcame this fear, thanks to careful group instruction and patience from his swimming teachers. Soon the pool became a playground for him. By the time he was twelve, he could swim all the strokes, glide the length of the 25-yard pool under water, and perform flips off the diving board without fear. Later on, he was able to work as a lifeguard. Swimming, like the land games, came easy to him. The water was simply another source for good fun.

It didn't take long for Don to discover that the best offering at the Hannah Y was basketball. The court was regulation size and rigged for competition. Ten-foot-high baskets dominated each end of it. The highly polished oak floor held all the proper lines the game called for, and street shoes were forbidden on its surface. On the sides of the court were backboards and hoops used for shooting practice and pickup games. For every member who played there, the Hannah Y basketball gym was ideal.

The basketball court was also Don's "proving grounds" throughout his early teens. It was there where he learned to excel at making the right moves to get his shot, grab the rebound, set a defensive screen, and use his massive shoulders to gain advantage over others. But nobody deliberately taught him the moves. Like all the other kids in Y basketball, he learned by observation and imitation. If one boy, for instance, had a good dribbling style, the others would watch him and try to copy it. The same was true for anybody else who was good at some aspect of the game. He would be watched and emulated. The best copycats, therefore, became the better players. And those who could not only mimic but also improve upon what the better players did became themselves the best players. Don Lund emerged as one of the best.

One of the most influential instructors at the Hannah Y was a no-nonsense man named Brooke Marsteller. At about 5-feet-10 and 170 pounds, Marsteller was not a large man, but his body exuded the strength and poise of a professional bodybuilder, with rippling muscles accented by huge biceps and powerful shoulders. His short-cropped hair and laser-brown eyes rounded out the image of a man who could demand attention. And that's exactly what he got from everyone around him, members and staff included. When a kid heard "Hey, c'mere!" from Marsteller, there was no hesitation. The kid obeyed. On the other hand, Marsteller was fair to everyone in his charge. He listened before he spoke. He used common sense in judgment, and he treated the kids fairly. Parents considered him a role model. The kids, and especially Don Lund, looked up to him. And rightly so.

Marsteller exemplified the founding tenets of the YMCA, which mirrored other organizations also devoted to young people: a sound body was essential to a sound mind and a sound character. To get a sound body, you had to exercise, keep fit, and practice discipline. Discipline strengthened the mind, and as the mind grew strong, thus did the character. Marsteller taught these tenets every day, and no kid was a more eager pupil than Don Lund. He could hardly wait each week for Tuesdays, Thursdays, and Saturdays, the days he was allowed to go to the Y. Every time he went, Don would make the six-block trek into a game of sorts, by walking a block, running a block, walking a block, and so on, thus alternating his journey's pace until he reached the Garfield entrance. Once there, he threw himself into every activity that was open to him. He eagerly sought the strongest competition he could find. He grew rapidly from a raw-talented boy of eleven to a practiced, skillful young man. All under the watchful eyes of Brooke Marsteller.

As things progressed at the Y, Don was allowed to play and practice with older boys. Because of their advanced training, larger size, and additional experience, older boys offered more challenges for Don than did boys his own age. Moreover, competing with older boys was already natural for him, since he had been doing this around his neighborhood for years. In fact, he played at the Y with some of the same older boys he played with in the streets and alleys in his neighborhood. They accepted him with ease, no problem at all.

Young Don especially liked the interbranch basketball games between various YMCAs around the Detroit area. They were his first real taste of team competition, and he could play with the best of them. In fact, he was good enough, with his size, strength, agility, and speed, to make the difference for many Hannah Y victories. He was cheered by his teammates, endorsed by his proud parents, and admired by the younger kids. The Y had made his name a household word in the neighborhood.

There can't be any doubt that basketball was Don Lund's developmental sport. He learned it at the Hannah YMCA. Fortuitously, it all began with that call from his mother, who summoned him to her kitchen in August 1934, and launched his competitive career.

8
Dialogue

"So, how did you keep your humility," I asked, "considering all the attention you received as one of the best athletes for your age in the neighborhood?"

We were again sitting in his living room, the old coach draped in his favorite wingback chair, wearing a blue golf shirt with "Michigan Baseball" embroidered on the left breast, tan shorts, and his usual Sperry Top-Siders. Our meetings at his home were now common and comfortable for both of us. Fall was approaching, but the weather outside continued to be warm and sunny.

At my question, he raised his eyebrows. "Keep my humility?" He laughed, "They never let me be anything *but* humble. Not my parents, not Virginia, not Mr. Marsteller. And especially not the older guys at the Y. The minute anybody around me thought I was getting a big head, or something like that, they'd set me straight real quick. My dad was good at put-downs. My mom wouldn't tolerate self-praise. My sister was a neighborhood leader in her own right. She'd never tolerate a little brother with a big head. And the guys showed no mercy. No matter how good somebody thought he was, sure enough there'd be someone around the corner who'd be better. I wasn't taught to be humble. I was taught to be realistic." He grinned to himself as he remembered those earlier years. "That's just the way it was." He relaxed again.

"That's an amazing story about how your mom took you to the Y when you were eleven," I said.

His eyes softened as he answered, "I never figured out how she got the money, year after year. She only took me the first time. After that, she gave me the money and I signed up myself. But she and my dad would come to some of the games and sit with the others around the track above the court. They were always very supportive. So was Virginia."

I pressed on: "Why do you think the YMCA was so important to your parents? They sacrificed a lot to put you in there, every year for about five years. Why?"

His eyes darkened a little as he considered. "That's a good question," he said. "Maybe it's because they knew I was playing ball in the alleys and figured if I was at the Y, I'd be better off. Or maybe they checked out the programs at the Y and decided I should be playing under supervision. Or maybe it's a little of both. Anyway, I'm glad they did it."

"The Y was really good for you, wasn't it?"

He sat up straight. "Without question. Absolutely, without question. The Y was one of the best experiences of my life. I learned to play supervised ball there. I learned to play by the rules."

It was time to move on. The old coach was now in a perfect mood to reminisce in detail. I wouldn't waste his time. "Let's go back to when you were a kid in your Lycaste neighborhood, before you joined the Y. What do you remember about neighborhood play?"

His eyes narrowed as thoughts merged with memories. He smiled slightly, leaned back, and began to contemplate.

9

The Neighborhood Playground

Young Don's entire neighborhood was a playground. The kids never noticed the architecture of the houses. They paid little attention to the manicured lawns or the rainbows of flower beds that hugged the sides of each dwelling. Everyone's home vegetable garden was sacred to the daily lives of the families, so the kids avoided them when chasing a ball or just plain running around. What they eagerly sought, however, were the vacant lots, or the wide alleys behind certain homes, or the residential streets with the least traffic, or certain front porch steps that gave the best surface for rebounding a ball.

Nearly every block had a vacant lot. Those favored by the kids were the ones bordered on each side by a house. Corner lots were too open to contain a wayward ball from bounding into traffic, but had to be used as a last resort when no other lot was available. And the main game they all played on these parcels was football. There were no referees, no adults around to impose their wills on the conduct of the game, no yard markers, and no goal posts. Goal lines were marked with stones, loose boards, or anything else that lay around in the yard. The kids chose up sides and played the game. Arguments were settled among themselves. Actual fights were rare, because everyone knew that today's opponent could be tomorrow's teammate. For young Don Lund, these vacant lot football games were a gladiator's paradise. And because of his strength and size, Don was a principal gladiator.

Because of his size, he was always chosen by the other boys to play the line. The line was where you pushed and shoved. Where you knocked others down and got knocked down in return. Where you sidestepped, jumped over, dodged, evaded, and pounded over the kid in front of you. If you were quick enough on defense, you could break through and grab the ball, then run for your own touchdown. Don did that, lots of times.

To his credit, he never showcased his abilities or embarrassed those he bested on those vacant lots. They were his friends, his buddies. Of the things his parents and the Y taught him about playing sports, respect for the opponent was foremost.

Sometimes playing with a football at home could get a boy in trouble with neighbors or family. Kicking it around, for instance, might cause the football to land on a neighbor's front porch or, worse yet, in a neighbor's vegetable garden. And woe to the kid who broke a window pane! So football, with its unpredictable bounces, was usually played away from home. If there wasn't opportunity to use a vacant lot, kids needed to look for some-place else. Sometimes it was the nearby coal yard.

The men at the coal yard didn't mind too much if a few kids came over and just played football. As long as they stayed off the coal piles and away from the machinery, the boys could play without hassle from the yard workers. The only grief the kids would receive from coal yard play would, of course, come from their mothers, since coal yard play was black-coal dirty. Clothes, hair, skin, footballs, and everything else the boys brought with them to the coal yard would be covered with black dust. The kids thought it was fun. The harder they played, the dirtier they looked. Coal dust on the clothes was a badge of honor they all wore proudly, including Don. And he, for one, knew what was waiting for him when he got home. Marguerite would march him straight down to the basement and put him in the laundry tub. Don thought a bath in the laundry tub, with a half-dozen water changes from black to clear, was great fun. Marguerite, who cleaned up the mess, didn't like it at all. But she knew it was just boys playing a game they loved, so she reluctantly went along.

Other neighborhood playground spots were the alleys, where they played various games. There was one contest called "alley ball," a form of field-limiting baseball, wherein the batter was required to hit the ball straight down the alley for a safe hit. A ball hit in a yard or off a garage, whether it was caught or not, was an out. Virginia, a natural athlete like her brother, was good at alley ball. She was also good at "alley basketball." Hoops attached to garages in the alleys were common. Despite the stones, dirt, and uneven playing surface, alley basketball thrived in the neighborhood.

Another popular game for the more talented neighborhood kids had no particular name, but it involved hitting a baseball over a garage. The ball would be tossed up and hit over a garage by the batter, either from the alley or from a backyard. On the other side of the garage, one or more kids would try to catch the ball as it sailed over the roof. If the ball was caught, the batter was out. If the ball wasn't caught, the batter was awarded a base hit. This game, in fact, required more than average skill with a baseball bat. Garages had windows which could shatter, as well as wood siding which scuffed or dented readily. Not every family, therefore, would allow their garage to be used for this game. But when the neighborhood kids found one to use, they played with vigor.

One of Don's favorite around-the-house games was "step ball." Every neighborhood house had front porch steps. Most had three or four steps made from concrete or brick with squared-off outer edges on each step. The game used baseball terms and baseball scoring rules, but instead of using a bat, the "batter" would throw a baseball or a rubber ball against the steps, trying to rebound it back for base hits or a home run, depending upon the distance traveled by the ball. The other kids would stand behind the "batter" and try to catch the ball for an "out." The trick to "batting" was to throw the ball in such a way as to cause it to bounce off the squared outer edge of one of the steps, causing it to bounce outward a long way and avoid being caught. A ball bounced off the top or inner edge of a step would rebound poorly, so kids who could bounce the ball off the edges were quite successful at the game. Step ball was played by most of the children, including Don, Virginia, and their friends.

Then there was field baseball. Beyond the vacant lots, beyond the alleys, beyond the front porch steps and the streets in front of them, there were a few vacant neighborhood fields. Mowed by the City of Detroit to keep the weeds down, these fields were strong attractions for nine- to fifteen-year-old boys who wanted to throw, catch, and hit a baseball as far as they could. Of all the neighborhood games he played, Don delighted most in field baseball. He also took the professional game itself to heart. He studied the rules. He followed the daily progress of major league teams, noting especially the wins and losses of his favorite, the Detroit Tigers. He could quote the batting averages of the Tigers' starting lineup, plus those of other important players in both the American and National leagues. He formed opinions about the talents and prospects of prime players in both major leagues, which he shared freely with anyone who would listen. As a result, he played the game of baseball in his dreams.

The best example of Don's baseball commitment was his regular habit of watching a game played by older neighborhood boys or even neighborhood adults, then going home to grab a bat and imitate some of the more successful baseball swings he had just witnessed. His favorite spot for doing this was in front of the large window in his garage at home. He'd try to impersonate a successful player, watching his reflection as he swung the bat. He did this repeatedly, never tiring or getting bored. When he went to games, he didn't always pay attention to the overall action on the field. Sometimes he just studied the batters. He watched their moves, their routines, their stances at home plate. Then he'd go home and imitate them in front of that garage window, again and again.

All this brought Don two powerful baseball revelations. First, every player had specific, deliberate routines as they set up to the plate. Consequently, a batter's behavior might be predictable to an observant pitcher. Second, no matter what stance a batter took at the plate, no matter how high, how low, or how far back he held his bat as he waited for the pitch, his swing action when he hit the ball was precisely the same as that of other successful batters. Balance, motion, head position, follow through, they were all the same at the moment of impact. So who was he going to imitate? What style would be his own? The answer was simple. There was only one way to swing a bat properly to hit the ball. He would therefore develop his own comfortable style, practicing in front of his dad's garage window.

Those vacant neighborhood fields could have been where the phrase "pickup games" began. Boys, eager to play the game, would walk to the fields and pick up friends along the way. Once there, they'd pick up pieces of cardboard, old towels, small boards, and anything else they could find to fashion home plate, a pitcher's mound, and all three bases. They would choose sides, find a way to call the pitches, and go for it. They didn't need an umpire. They settled their own disagreements. They played with an abandon found when youth decide their own rules and handle disputes among themselves. Those who played those games cherished the experiences for the rest of their lives.

Since Don chiefly played with older boys, he was at first assigned to play in right field. Maybe they wanted to see what the younger kid could do in the outfield, or maybe they wanted to assign him to an outfield position that didn't see as much action with the preponderance of right-handed, full-swing batters. Nevertheless, the older boys wanted his bat at the plate, which he could swing as well as the best of his older friends. Besides, it didn't take them long to realize that Don Lund could catch a ball better than most. Soon they told him he could play whichever outfield position he'd like. He chose center field.

These neighborhood vacant baseball fields gave Don two basic lessons he would use to extreme advantage as long as he was associated with the game. First was to concentrate on developing one's own skills rather than trying to imitate others'. And second, for gaining an advantage, it helped to focus on peculiar traits of individual players. Strengths, weaknesses, and their routines could be studied and predicted. Throughout his baseball career, Don Lund would practice these concepts as a player, a coach, and a manager.

What's fascinating about the neighborhood playground, when considering today's organized sports programs, is that the games played by Don and his friends were self-directed. The kids themselves decided who would play a given position, what rules would be followed, and how a game would be scored. They settled their own arguments. They chose their own leaders. They played their own games. At that time there were no organized leagues, sponsored teams, or sports camps. There were no team uniforms or donated equipment. The neighborhood playground was completely self-directed.

Young Don Lund cut his competitive teeth in those neighborhood games. He learned how to play tough, how to play fair, and how to win. Now he was ready for something more organized. He would find that in junior high school.

10
Junior High

Ferdinand Foch, Marshal in the French Army and Supreme
Commander of Allied Forces during World War I, was one of
the world's great military heroes. To honor him, many places
around the world were named after Foch during the 1920s.
One of these places was the junior high school in Don's neighborhood. Standing next to Detroit's Southeastern High School,
Foch enrolled seventh-, eighth-, and ninth-grade students who
lived within a couple-mile radius, including the Lund house at
2183 Lycaste. Popularly known as Foch Junior High, or just
"Foch," the dark-red brick building had a rather plain façade.
No architectural adornments, other than the necessary windows
and doors, contributed to its design. It looked functional rather
than decorative; powerful rather than beautiful. The building
perfectly reflected the school's namesake, who was known for his
disdain of anything ornate. It housed four floors of classrooms
devoted to about 900 boys and girls. It was a place where girls
began to see themselves as young women. It was a venue for boys
to notice girls as something more than creatures to be avoided. It
was a site where gender attraction, at its most primitive stages,
fosters a strong desire to be socially acceptable to one's peers.
And no boy entering Foch Junior High became more conscious
of this than thirteen-year-old Don Lund when he examined
his clothes. For as long as he could remember, Don had worn
knickers. Knickers were loose pants that gathered just below the
knee, worn with long socks. Most boys around Detroit dressed
in them, starting around the age of four. However, their mothers
tended to change them into long pants as they moved through
elementary school, for many different reasons. Don, though,
continued to wear knickers right up through the sixth grade.
The truth was he liked them. They were loose and flexible. He
could play hard in them, which was how he mostly liked to play.
And after all, he thought, ballplayers wore them. That was good

enough for him. By the time he turned thirteen, Don was just about the only one among his friends who still wore knickers. But that never bothered him until he started to attend classes at Foch. He noticed his friends, the guys he chased around with, wearing long pants all the time, even after school. Now his knickers bothered him; for the first time in his life, Don became self-conscious about his appearance. He soon changed that by appealing to his mom, who responded right away. A few days later, Don casually sauntered into his seventh-grade homeroom wearing dark blue long pants and a checkered shirt. Everyone noticed him at once. Conversations stopped, one of his buddies gave a wolf whistle, and some of the girls eyed him as if seeing him for the first time. The scene was a Don Lund triumph; he never wore knickers again.

His three years at Foch were more fun for Don than they were scholarly. Homework was something he did as a necessary chore, not a relished activity. But he never placed himself in danger of flunking a test or failing a class. Marguerite saw to that. His mother seldom let him bounce into the house after school and glide to the kitchen refrigerator, his usual routine, without asking about his homework. She'd see that it was done before he went to bed.

Perhaps the best description of Don's three years studying English, mathematics, and social studies at Foch is that he "coasted" through them. Without seriously applying himself to the schoolwork, he was nevertheless able to grasp and retain enough of the lessons to keep himself in the upper 15 to 20 percent of his classes. That was fine with him. After all, academic classes weren't the only things Foch Junior High had to offer. There were other offerings that were far more important to this young, sports-minded athlete. One of these was swimming class.

Ralph Green was a constantly alert gym teacher who taught boys' swimming classes. One of his methods included dividing the boys into ability groupings. Those who were poor swimmers focused on things like treading water and learning fundamentals of swim strokes. Those who were good swimmers did pool laps, using different strokes as they swam. For convenience, the boys swam naked. Boy's school swimsuits were considered a home laundry nuisance at the time. Just the girls wore them in their own swimming classes, for the sake of modesty. Nearly twenty years would pass before boys would also be required to wear suits in swim class at their public school.

Don became a talented swimmer at Foch thanks to his learning at the Y. Starting at the intermediate level in the seventh grade, he rapidly progressed to the lofty post of lifeguard a year later. He loved swimming. He recognized swimming as a wholesome and challenging individual sport, and he was good at it. But he eventually decided that competitive swimming would not be for him. Instead he sought the challenges of team sports, with their dependence on uniting a whole group of people and combining their individual skills. It wasn't hard for him to learn to express his own energy through others. As early as the seventh grade, he could be described as a team player.

Swimming teacher Ralph Green became a school hero when Don was in the eighth grade at Foch. One of the boys in the class, Gordon Miller, was noticed missing. Someone yelled that Miller was lying motionless at the bottom of the pool, in the deep end. Immediately, Green jumped into the pool, swam down, and brought up the unconscious Miller to a hushed natatorium. Green began giving artificial respiration to the boy. After about thirty seconds, which seemed a whole lot longer to everyone watching, Miller began coughing up water and started to breathe on his own. His life saved, the boy was welcomed back by a thunderous chorus of shouts and cheers. The whole scene was an experience no one who witnessed it would ever forget. And Ralph Green, teacher and hero, was etched in the minds of Don and his classmates for the rest of their lives.

Gym class was another favorite for Don. The classes were taught by Paul Lampkin, a no-nonsense disciplinarian, whose classes in the boys' gym (girls had their own gym) tended to focus heavily on fundamentals. Don was right at home in this class. His hours of playing at the Y gave him a distinctive advantage over many of his classmates, plus he was bigger and taller than most of them. To him, gym class was a breeze.

Coach Lampkin had an interesting method of keeping the boys in line during his gym class. He carried a soccer ball with him at all times, which he'd throw with deadly accuracy at anyone who misbehaved. The boys always respected that soccer ball. No one wanted to leave gym class with a red mark on his butt. Fortunately for Don, he was seldom one of Lampkin's targets.

In his final year at Foch, Don was selected by Coach Lampkin to be on an interschool basketball team. The team would play other teams from junior highs around the city. Obviously, the coach picked the best players from his classes to be on the team, and Don was thrilled. With lots of school spirit behind them, the boys on the Foch basketball team played against the other schools with as much controlled intensity as junior high kids are capable of giving. Many of the boys they played against were friends from the Y, who lived in another school's service area. For Don, these games were a memorable start of his sports career.

Probably the most tangible and lasting thing that Don accomplished at Foch was something he made for his mom in a shop class. He fashioned a specially designed wood pole for stirring laundry. The laundry stick, as he called it, wasn't elaborate. It was about thirty inches long, made from a sturdy piece of oak, and flattened at one end to make it fairly easy to stir the wet clothes. At about a half-inch in diameter, the stick fit easily into Marguerite's hand. What prompted him to make it was noticing one day how his mother would sometimes reach in and stir the clothes with her hand, then quickly pull out her hand, red and sore from the hot water. He made up his mind to make the laundry stick as soon as he saw this. The result was a much-needed laundry tool, which his mom loved, and which also earned him honors in shop class. Don happily provided Marguerite with a useful household implement that she used for many years. But, like so many other things of Don's past, the laundry stick is long gone. What remains instead is a happy, sentimental, warm, and wonderful memory.

Marshal Foch Junior High School also opened up the appealing world of girls for Don. There soon came a time when girls stopped being those annoying creatures that slowed down neighborhood games, cried when they were upset, and generally presented an obstacle to fun with his male buddies. Instead, girls became attractive, appealing, interesting people. He saw they were far different from him, in the nicest ways. He discovered a shyness about him when it came to girls, an awkwardness he couldn't describe. Nevertheless, he decided one day, in his ninth grade year, to forge ahead with getting to know a girl. He chose one he thought to be the prettiest female in school, a friendly, outgoing girl named Virginia Stringer, who shared many of his same interests. After school Don would walk Virginia home, carry her school books, and talk sports with her. The two were never more than just good friends, but Don gained much from the experience. He noticed how girls saw the same things boys do, only differently. He realized firsthand that he couldn't fully understand how girls could see the same things so differently than he did, but he also recognized the fact that life was just that way. So thanks to Virginia Stringer, Don Lund was beginning to learn what it was like to associate with the opposite sex. And that was fortunate, because his next venture with girls would start within the halls of Southeastern High School, located right next to Foch, where he would meet and fall in love with a girl who would hang the moon for him.

11
Betty

"This meeting will now come to order!" deadpanned the speaker. Startled, all five of the other girls in the room abruptly stopped their conversations, stared momentarily at each other, then gaped with open mouths at their friend Betty Huff. Slim, five-and-a-half feet tall, with hazel eyes and shoulder-length black hair, Betty Huff commanded a peer presence that any girl in her late teens would envy. At that moment, however, Betty wore a face like the master of ceremonies at a funeral, and said, again, "This meeting will now come to ..." and she couldn't hold the face any longer. "Blaah!" she giggled and burst into hilarious laughter, which was immediately shared by her small group of high school best girlfriends. Once again, Betty "got 'em." They loved it.

The group was gathered at Betty's house this time. They met frequently after school, rotating among the members' homes. Although there was no formally elected leader, Betty took advantage of her home space to play the "call to order" joke. The six girls were popular, well adjusted, and academically successful students at Southeastern High School. They had found each other through mutual classes and school activities. One day they all spontaneously decided to form a club. They agreed to get together after classes at least once each week, at their various homes or at school. They all were extremely close friends, destined to remain so throughout their lives.

Betty was born Elizabeth Jayne Huff on December 15, 1922. Nobody, in her memory, had ever called her Elizabeth. She was always known as "Betty" or, sometimes, Betty Jayne. She was raised, along with her older brother Edward, by their mother in a house on Fairview, a block down from Foch Junior High and Southeastern High School. Betty had a natural gregarious tendency, which made her comfortable in groups of others both younger and older. She also had an infectious laugh, a lavish sense of humor, and an ability to show genuine interest in others. She wasn't just well liked, other kids were drawn to her.

The child Betty Huff spent her grade school years at St. Bernard Elementary School with other Roman Catholic boys and girls in her neighborhood. Unfortunately, her strongest single memory of being there was negative. One morning, when Betty was in the sixth grade, her teaching nun told the class she was leaving the classroom for a few minutes and that no one was to talk while she was gone. Naturally, Betty and many of the youngsters talked, until hushed to silence when some kid heard the nun coming back. The nun asked if anyone had talked during her absence. Betty raised her hand, looked around, and noticed to her dismay that hers was the only hand raised. Rather than praise Betty for telling the truth, the nun made her hold her hand in front of her, palm up. As Betty did so, the nun whacked her hand with a ruler and told everyone in the class how important it was to be obedient. Betty was humiliated. She never forgot the incident.

Moving to public school in the seventh grade, Betty spent her junior high years at Foch. She excelled in her classes, made lots of friends, and was promoted in good standing to South-eastern High. There she met Thelma Craig, destined to be her best friend.

Like Betty, Thelma was smart, beautiful, and very popular. She and Betty found a lot in common, quickly becoming trusted friends early in the tenth grade. Soon two more girls, Ruth Starkey and Gloria Bernard, made the group a constant foursome. And it wasn't long before an additional two popular and attractive young women joined the group, and their club of friends was formed. Six young women, enrolled in different grades, found a lot in common and just seemed to enjoy each other. The oldest of the six was a senior named Martha Jagger. Martha was a tall, charming brunette, who dated a tall, gregarious, and handsome classmate named Bob Selleck. Martha and Bob dated seriously in their senior year. The bond they forged would later lead to marriage, a successful real estate career for Bob in California, and three children: a daughter Marti and two sons, Bob Junior and Tom. Tom Selleck, handsome, athletic, and manly like his father, would go on to a gigantic career as an actor, movie star, and much-loved international celebrity.

Back in 1939, however, Martha was merely dating Bob Selleck. Bob was part of a small group of young men who were close friends and hung around together. Enrolled throughout all three high school grades, the boys all played sports and were extremely popular. Bob's best friend was Bob Gleffe, who later on would serve in the U.S. Army and acquire a wartime buddy named George Goebel. George would move on to become a famous comedian, while continuing his friendship with Bob Gleffe throughout both of their lives. Nevertheless, in 1939, Bob Gleffe and Bob Selleck were part of a close-knit core group of athletes at Southeastern High. Three of their number included basketball players George Hackman, an all-city standout, Harvey Pierce, a shooter who earned all-state honors, and Harvey Eckert, a playmaker whose combative style made him one of the most respected high school guards in the league. All five of them were seniors. The sixth member of the group, however, was a talented, three-sport sophomore who mixed in well with older players. His name was Don Lund.

Given the social dynamics of a large Detroit high school in the late 1930s, it would certainly be logical for these two highly visible and popular groups to find each other and become friends. That's exactly what happened.

It wasn't long before Betty Huff became attracted to Don Lund, despite his being a year behind her in school. Big, blond, handsome, and emotionally solid, Don was a respected starter on the football, basketball, and baseball teams, even though he was a tenth grader. Other girls talked about him in glowing terms. What's more, unlike some other athletes around school who were full of themselves, Don was a modest, outgoing guy whom everyone liked. Betty wondered how he would react to an "older" girl. That concern vanished when she learned that he had played sports and associated with older guys most of his life. She noticed that a lot of his friends were juniors and seniors. She saw him after games, hanging out with older teammates and friends at the Switzer Dairy, a favorite get-together spot for Southeastern students. It was clear to her that Don Lund was comfortable with everybody. She needn't worry about being an older girl in an upper high school grade.

Betty Huff and Don Lund were introduced at the Switzer Dairy in the late fall of 1939. Betty and Martha Jagger were relaxing there, waiting for Bob Selleck to show up with a buddy he said he was bringing. Bob's buddy turned out to be Don, the guy Betty was interested in. The two hit it off right away, for obvious and not-so-obvious reasons. Obviously, both Betty and Don were outgoing, friendly, and open-minded people. They both liked to talk about many things. Both of them liked sports. They were attractive, popular students. Not so obvious were subtleties only they could pick up from each other. Like a growing sense of trust. Or the knowledge that no matter how much they learned about each other, there would always be a strong desire to learn more.

Their dating throughout the 1939 school year was nearly always with groups of other students. Betty would attend Don's football, basketball, and baseball games, then join him and his teammates with her girlfriends at a school hangout like the Switzer Dairy. Sometimes the guys who had cars would let fellow students pile into their vehicles after a game, then drive out to Angelo's Restaurant at Nine Mile and Mack. Angelo's would always be crowded after a game, filled with exuberant Southeastern High youth. And if Southeastern won the game, Angelo's would be packed like a pickle jar. For the most part, everybody behaved themselves. These were happy times, building back up from the Great Depression. Any kids who caused trouble publicly would almost certainly face trouble at home, when word reached the parents.

Another popular gathering spot for students was the Vanity Ballroom on East Jefferson, which sponsored dancing on Friday nights. Being a good dancer, Betty had no lack of partners, and Don was only able to secure the first and last dances of the evening. The rest of the time, while Betty danced with different boys, Don would gather with friends to chat, dance with a few other girls, and, to his dismay, breathe in the smoke-filled air. The smoke was the only thing about the Vanity Ballroom he didn't like. A lot of kids smoked, even some of the athletes, but not Don. He didn't like the taste or the smell of cigarettes, but he put up with it just the same. He even endured the smoke at one of his favorite spots where just the guys hung out—Harry Gob's pool hall.

Sometimes after school Don and his friends would gather at Gob's to play nine ball or straight pool. Eventually they moved

Southeastern High School sweethearts Don Lund and
Betty Jayne Huff, 1939. *(Lund Family Collection)*

up to billiards, then to snooker. Snooker was a challenge, and
Don became quite good. He never played for money, though.
Nobody had money to spare in those days, especially for any
kind of gambling.

Betty and Don were always able to find a ride to their social
activities, mostly because they were popular and other students
wanted to be around them. In fact, they seldom needed to ask for
a ride. They particularly enjoyed double-dating with Bob Gleffe
and Thelma Craig. The four of them became best friends. Bob
and Thelma would also get married, then divorce several years
later. Even so, Don and Betty would remain close to each of them
for the rest of their lives. And they rode around in style, thanks
to Bob Gleffe's dad, who let his son drive the family four-door
sedan, a snazzy Hudson Terraplane. The places they went for
fun were easy to get to, thanks to that Terraplane.

Betty was more than just a popular and sought-after student
at Southeastern High. She was very much her own person. Raised
in a single-parent home, she learned the value of independence
even as a little girl. She saw the advantages of setting her own
goals and earning her own income. From early childhood she
discovered ways to forge ahead and achieve things on her own.
When she turned sixteen and could get working papers, she
enrolled in a modeling school. Soon Betty landed a modeling

job with the Annis Fur Company in downtown Detroit. Betty worked after school and on weekends, modeling fur coats and wraps in the store windows and on the shopping floor. The work gave her a modest income, which she shared at home, as well as the measure of independence she required. It also gave her added respect among her friends, and the additional admiration of Don Lund, who saw Betty as the most attractive, one-of-a-kind girl he would ever meet. She was his ideal woman. He loved her from their first meeting, and his love would never stop growing.

For Betty, falling in love with Don wasn't immediate. She had lots of friends; boys were always giving her attention. What made it happen for her, though, was Don's non-stop energy. She saw in him a young man who constantly strove to improve himself, who learned from his mistakes, who never blamed others for their weaknesses, and who delivered when he promised something. She had never met another boy who put together such a complete package. When she finally fell in love with him, she fell completely. She had found her mate. She would support him, comfort him, and love him without condition for the rest of her life.

12
Dialogue

"I'll tell you, those six girls were the best looking ones in the entire school." He looked right at me, absolutely serious.

"You wouldn't be slightly prejudiced here, would you, Coach?" I asked.

"Well, prejudiced toward Betty, I suppose, but I really mean it. All of them were positively beautiful."

We were again in his living room on another glorious late summer day in Ann Arbor. The old coach relaxed in his chair with legs crossed and his left arm curled over the top of the wingback. He wore long, dark blue trousers and a white short-sleeved Michigan logo shirt. White athletic socks merged with his usual Top-Siders. He seemed completely content. Sharing memories of Betty was obviously one of the things he treasured. I decided, however, to change the subject and move on.

"You said you didn't like the smoke-filled rooms in the places you and your friends went during high school," I said, "but so many people smoked cigarettes back then, even some of the guys you played sports with. But not you. Didn't you try it even once?"

He looked at me with a slight grin. "Yeah," he answered, "just once. Cured me forever."

I could sense a story coming on. I grinned with him. "Go on," I urged.

He shifted position, bringing his left arm down from the wingback. "It was a hot summer Sunday, and I do mean hot! My mom was at church. I was eight and Virginia was ten. We were in the backyard on Lycaste, lying on a blanket under an umbrella to keep out of the direct sun. Just the two of us having fun. There were also some of my grandparents' boarders out there, men smoking pipes and just sitting around. Virginia and I watched the men puff smoke and compared it to the way the railroad engines puffed. I guess we were kind of fascinated. Then we noticed another one of the boarders, a man named Joe Young, coming out of the house and smoking a large pipe. Joe was a friendly guy. Used to make Virginia and me laugh." He stopped and reflected on the memory.

I prompted him, "So what happened?"

"Well, just like that," the coach said, "Joe came over and said something like 'You two like the pipe?' And we said, 'Sure.' So he gave us his pipe and let us each take a bunch of puffs. Well, you can imagine what happened. Virginia and I both got sick, put a pail between us on the blanket, and took turns throwing up. Joe snatched back his pipe and took off. Then my mom came home from church. She played the piano every Sunday at Knox Presbyterian. I'll never forget the look on her face when she walked into our backyard and saw her two green-faced kids with that pail between them. She got excited, to put it mildly, and she said, 'I come home from the Good Lord and walk into this?' Oh, yeah, she really got excited. And I got really sick. That's why I never smoked again and never even liked the smell of cigarettes, cigars, or a pipe."

"What a story," I said. "Whatever happened to 'Mighty' Joe Young?"

"I don't know," he answered. "He never came back. Just disappeared, like the wind."

"Or the smoke," I retorted. We both laughed.

Moving on, I wanted to bring his memory back to high school athletics and his three years of competing in football, basketball, and baseball for Detroit Southeastern. The records show that Don Lund was truly a high school phenomenon. He was a prime competitor for all three of his sports teams all three years, and he captained all three squads in his senior year. In football, he ran over opponents, passed with needle-eye accuracy, and called the plays during the game. In basketball, he sparked both of the competing squads as well as the spectators with dazzling moves and a deadeye shot. In baseball, he energized his teams with mastery of all five things a successful ballplayer must do well: hit, hit with power, run, throw, and catch the ball. Don Lund was therefore celebrated as a stellar, all-around athlete throughout the public and private high schools in the city of Detroit. Plus, in addition to all that, he was overwhelmingly voted president of his senior class!

But I had to be careful when I interviewed him about what I considered to be his high school "glory" years. I knew he loved to talk about other athletes, but when it came to talking about himself he tended to clam up, often changing the subject quickly. Moreover, he had no use for flattery. Any compliments would have to be sincere and well-chosen. I decided to take an indirect approach.

"Coach," I began, "When you served as senior class president, what were some of the duties you performed?"

He thought a moment. "Not many, really. I think it was sort of an honorary title. Class officers didn't have any 'power' back then. The teachers ran everything. The one thing I had to do was give a speech at graduation."

"Do you remember much about your speech?"

"I don't remember anything I said," he answered, "but I do remember planning to say something funny at first, like 'Well, here we are after three years of hard study and total dedication to every class ...' but I didn't."

"Why not?"

"Because I had forgotten that our commencements were held in a church—St. Mark's Church in the neighborhood across from the YMCA. There was no way I was going to tell jokes in a church. So I scrapped the humor."

It was time to move on. "OK, Coach," I shifted, "let's talk about your high school sports. You started by going out for football as a sophomore under Coach Wayne Nestor. What can you recall about that?"

"I remember a lot about those years," he mused, "even the time when I missed a game ..."

13

Jungaleer Football

He prowled his defensive safety position with the boldness of a restless cat. He settled in, took a deep breath, and concentrated as the other team broke its huddle. The score was tied, with about a minute left in the game. Both teams were tired, though he personally felt energized. He was strong and eager. He was especially on edge because this was the season's big game. No one else on his high school team was more intent or more focused on winning tonight. He was vigilant. Like a predator.

"Set!" He watched their halfback call the play. "Hike one!" He noticed the halfback wiggling his right fingers, something he did before executing a pass play. "Hike two!" He saw the halfback grab the snap and run to his right. He also saw the other halfback dart left, pick up speed, and race toward him. He backpedaled fast, keeping the other guy in front of him, looking for the pass. It came, a soft spiral thrown a little high. Leaping forward, he charged just as the opposing halfback turned around toward the ball. He leaped and snagged the ball out of the receiver's hands as the crowd roared. He landed on the run, looking ahead toward the goal line. Charging like a runaway locomotive, he streaked down the sidelines. Nobody could catch him. He was going to win game and glory for the Southeastern Jungaleers! The crowd was screaming his name: "Mr. Lund! Mr. Lund! Why were they calling him that? Why ...?

"Mr. Lund!" His dream-bubble shattered. He blinked. His Latin teacher, Miss Margaret Sullivan, was calling him from her desk in front of the class. She was known to everybody as M.G. Sullivan, Latin Teacher. Behind her back, the students called her "Machine Gun," but the nickname bore no malice. M.G. was popular and respected.

Don Lund, first semester junior at Southeastern, stood up next to his back-row desk. "Yes, Miss Sullivan?" he asked politely.

The teacher looked at him with dark eyes and a frozen face. "Please recite from memory Julius Caesar's description of Gaul," she demanded. "In Latin, please."

Don looked around. Most of the other students were watching the teacher. "Uh ..." he murmured. "Uh, *Omnes Gallius, um ... Omnes Gallius est ...* divided into three parts."

M.G. looked hard at him. "That's enough," she said, "please sit down and see me after class."

For the rest of the class period, Don sat as his desk like a condemned prisoner. Finally, when all the other students had left, he walked timidly up to M.G. Sullivan's desk.

"You haven't been studying your lessons, Don," she admonished him. "You're smart enough, but you just haven't done the work. I'm giving you a failing grade in Latin this week."

"But Miss Sullivan," he argued, "if you give me a failing grade, I won't be able to play in this week's football game."

Her answer was not sympathetic. "That's something you might have considered, Don. Maybe you would have studied harder."

He looked at her, straightened to his full six-foot height, and said, "I'll study, Miss Sullivan, I promise." Then he left Machine Gun's room and headed quickly to Coach Wayne Nestor's office.

Nestor, a no-nonsense teacher from Michigan's Upper Peninsula, took the news calmly. He didn't say anything bad, and he didn't say anything good. He simply stated, "You'd better hit the books, son."

"Yes, Sir," Don responded and walked out to inhabit his worst dream: suspended from playing due to ineligibility.

His parents took the news calmly and Virginia, who excelled in languages, sensed her despondent brother needed support: "How about asking Aunt Arcola for help?"

Marguerite immediately jumped at the idea. Soon she arranged for her son to be tutored in Latin by her sister, Arcola Matheson. Arcola, a language teacher in the Detroit schools, happily agreed to help her nephew. She knew the young man was a family favorite. She also dearly loved her sister Marguerite. Fortunately, Aunt Arcola lived only a few blocks from the Lunds. Don walked faithfully to her house every night for a week, carrying his Latin homework under one arm while cradling a football in the other. Aunt Arcola never knew about the football. He would leave it on her front porch during the lesson. But her tutoring made a difference. He did his Latin homework. He studied hard. He practiced his Latin pronunciation. He felt he was ready. And the following Friday afternoon in Latin class, predictably, M.G. Sullivan called on him as the first student to perform. Don stood at his desk in the back row and recited the requested lines in flawless Latin. The entire class turned around in their seats. Was this really Don Lund who was speaking? Miss Sullivan beamed with approval. Aunt Arcola's star pupil would be playing football today!

As it turned out, his one-game suspension was actually a blessing in disguise. Don's thighs had taken a beating in the last game he had played, and he was sore, particularly on the inside of each thigh. He hadn't mentioned it to anyone, fearing the coaches might bench him. With the Latin suspension, he spent almost two weeks without hard strain on his legs, and he used the time to let them heal back into playing shape. At first, he merely walked back and forth to Aunt Arcola's house, carrying his book and the football. A couple of nights later he performed his "run a block, walk a block" routine. By the end of the week, he was running both ways. His thigh pain was gone. Machine Gun Sullivan, bless her heart, had actually done him a favor!

Don's sophomore year of football had been excellent training in game fundamentals. He was fully prepared for the roughness of the sport—basketball at the Y had taken care of that. With its lofty ideals and character-building practices, the YMCA was unmatched as a place for superb youth development, but its basketball courts were no place for kids who couldn't stand being shoved around. They played fair at the Y, but they played hard. The football gridiron was therefore an easy transition from contact sports at the Y, and Don quickly assimilated basic strategies. He learned to make clean, hard tackles. He found the most effective ways to use his enormous shoulders as he blocked and ran. Already adept at throwing a football for great distances, he practiced timing his throws to match the speed and path of the intended receiver. He learned significant techniques in punting for accuracy as well as distance. But most of all, he learned to read telltale movements of other players as they lined up in formation against him.

Studying other players for predictability was nothing new to him; after all, he started developing this knack as a kid while watching older boys play in their neighborhood games, so studying players was already a well-developed trait. In his first year as a Jungaleer, Don would be assigned to work out at several positions on both offence and defense, sometimes at end position or, because of his size, on the line. But once in a while he would be given a chance in the backfield, where he really liked to play. He even got to play in a few games, as a substitute halfback, and he performed well enough to gain respect as a player and win his sophomore football letter.

The 1938 Jungaleers finished in the middle of the rankings at season's end, but some members of the team played extremely well and earned special recognition. Halfback Pete Fonari ran most of the plays and was considered the best player on the team. Center Bud Rosteck had a good year. Backup halfback George Hickman, a basketball whiz who could rotate like a top while running through the line, helped win some games that year. But the coaches had their eyes on the big, blond sophomore who showed great all-around promise. He was a coach's dream— supreme talent, brains, brawn, toughness and desire. To Coach Wayne Nestor, Don Lund was his key to victory.

In his junior football year, Don blossomed out as a true triple threat around the Detroit East Side League, with his ability to punt, pass, and kick the ball better than most. On defense he played safety. On offense he played starting halfback, along with Claude (Dutch) Wise as the other starting halfback. Zeke Rosteck played center and defensive linebacker. All three won football letters that year, as did the other starters and a few substitute players.

It was in Don's senior year, 1940, where he earned his reputation as the best high school backfield player in the city of Detroit. Dominating every game he played for the Jungaleers that season, he was named by all three major Detroit newspapers to their all-city and all-state teams. He captained the team and called the plays on offense and defense. He also was named captain of the all-state team. He was photographed in action every week by the *Detroit News*, *Detroit Free Press*, or *Detroit Times*, and these images would grace the sports pages to the unabashed delight of Southeastern parents, students, faculty, and staff. Don's modesty about his celebrity, along with his natural likeability, led fellow classmates to elect him as their senior class president, without him campaigning for the job.

The team's biggest game that year, and the most memorable football contest of Don's high school career, was the Detroit City League East Side championship game against the archrival Hamtramck Cosmos. Hamtramck had the defending city champions, heavily favored to repeat, but the contest ended in a 32–7 upset victory for the Jungaleers. Most of the credit for the win was given by sportswriters, statisticians, and fans to Don Lund, who put on an amazing exhibition of football talent. As a defender, Don made most of the crucial tackles during both halves. On offense, he received the opening kickoff and most of the Cosmos' fourth-down punts running them for long gains. Calling the plays, he ran for two touchdowns and passed for a third. With well-timed blocks, he helped fellow halfback Dutch Wise run for two touchdowns. But the ultimate difference in the game was Don's passing attack. He was deadly accurate. He threw all over the field, forcing Hamtramck's defenders to spread out, which set up the Jungaleer running game. The lopsided final score was a tribute to Don. He personally refused to take any credit, which was typical. But everyone, from teammates to other students, from parents and family members, from friends to perfect strangers, all praised him lavishly. For the most part, Don brushed away the praise, with one exception. Betty, having graduated from Southeastern the year before and now working for General Motors, saw the game and told him how proud she was of him. Betty's opinion meant more to this big, young athlete than anything he ever saw, read, or heard.

Sure enough, the cheers of those Southeastern football fans Don dreamed about in M.G. Sullivan's Latin class became a reality. But they were nothing compared to the screams, shouts, and stamping feet of the excited crowds in the closed-in basketball gymnasium. Southeastern High School was considered by those who followed Detroit prep sports to be a "basketball school," no matter what other sports it offered, and the reputation was well deserved. Southeastern's basketball program was considered one of the finest in the city. It had a winning tradition and a renowned program under legendary coach Perry Deakin.

14

Don and Mr. Deakin

"Purple and White, fight, fight!
Purple and White, fight, fight!
Who fight?
We fight!
Purple and White, fight, fight!"

That familiar chant to Jungaleer fans rose to a deafening roar, reverberating off the walls, floor, and ceiling of Southeastern High's basketball gym. But this time, the yell from the standing-room-only crowd was most unusual.

Sure enough, Southeastern was playing against archrival Hamtramck, and sure enough, the Jungaleers were outpacing the Cosmos in a close game. But this particular chant, shouted at peak volume by the Jungaleer fans, had nothing to do with the game or even the close rivalry of the schools. In fact, the Hamtramck Cosmos fans were also clapping and cheering at the same time. This was most unusual. Because it was halftime, and there was no basketball action in the gym.

Instead, the crowd was seeing something that had never before occurred at Southeastern. Standing in the middle of the floor, dressed in his warm-up suit, was Jungaleer senior basketball captain Don Lund. Surrounding him were Andrew and Marguerite beaming with pride; Perry Deakin, Southeastern's basketball coach and athletic director; Floyd Stocum, Hamtramck's athletic director; Henry Collins, the Cosmos' basketball coach; Wayne Nestor, Southeastern's football and baseball coach; and Art Marcus, representing Southeastern's student athlete "S" Club. They were all there to celebrate "Don Lund Day" at Southeastern High School.

Such an honor was unprecedented and it hasn't been done for any Southeastern athlete since then. Arranged by Coach Perry Deakin, with support from the Hamtramck athletics staff, the half-time ceremony was a declaration of praise for seventeen-year-old Don Lund. He was presented with plaques from the "S" club, from the Hamtramck High School Varsity Club, and from Southeastern High School. Each presenter of a plaque spoke words of acclaim into a hand-held microphone. The silent crowd listened raptly to every word. The honoree, holding his plaques, stood modestly with his head down. Finally, Coach Deakin took the microphone:

> "What stands out in Lund above everything else, even his athletic ability, is his character. He is a role model for other boys on the team, and they all idolize him."

Coach Deakin handed Southeastern's plaque to Don, and that's when the crowd erupted:

> "Purple and White, fight, fight!
> Purple and White, fight, fight!
> Who fight?
> We fight!
> Purple and White, fight, fight!"

The booming noise quickly subsided when Don took the microphone. He spoke modestly, but with a strong voice. He thanked his parents and his coaches. He thanked his fellow Southeastern students. He thanked the students and teachers at Hamtramck High School. But most of all, he thanked his fellow teammates. He reminded everyone that no single athlete can win a team-sport game on his own. He credited every player who ever stood with him on a court or playing field. His remarks brought tears throughout the crowd. And when he finished speaking, the crowd didn't shout or roar. They applauded, loud and long, as the honoree and his presenters walked off the court. Don Lund Day, the first and last celebration of its kind at Southeastern High School, was a magnanimous gesture by Perry Deakin, acclaimed throughout Detroit as one of the greatest high school basketball coaches of his time. Newspapers and radio hailed the event, calling Don Lund the finest prep athlete in the entire city.

Afterward, his fame continued to spread. He was lionized by students and faculty in schools throughout Detroit and its

Don Lund Day, March 19, 1941. Southeastern High football coach
Wayne Nestor (*left*) and basketball coach Perry Deakin (*center*)
present Don with the certificate honoring him. (It was later
presented to him again at halftime.) No other Southeastern
athlete has been honored in this way. *(The Detroit News)*

suburbs. He was a young sports hero, recognized not only for
his three-sport accomplishments, but also for his impeccable
character. The highlight of it all was Don Lund Day, because he
was distinguished by the entire school. That all this took place
on the basketball court was especially meaningful, for Don Lund
was recognized as the best basketball player in Detroit's best
basketball school. And he'd worked hard to get there.

Basketball had been Don's "main" athletic experience going
into Southeastern High. He learned to play the game at the
YMCA, starting when he was eleven years old. With three "Ds"—
desire, dedication, and determination—he developed techniques
to use his weight and muscle to full advantage during a game. He
learned to apply his powerful shoulders to thwart the opponent's
attempt to grab a rebound. He acquired an accurate shot and,
more importantly, gained a skill for instantly deciding when to
shoot or when to pass the ball. Along the way to all this, at the
Hannah YMCA, he acquired that all-important fourth "D":

discipline. Practice at the Y turned his legs into coiled springs, which powered him in shot-blocking, rebounding, and tipping the ball to teammates. He sharpened his skills at ball-handling.

He practiced lay-ups, foul shots, long shots, short shots, dribbling, and passing. In games, he played with the best teams the "Y" could put together. Consequently, by the time he showed up for basketball tryouts, Don was already prepared to become a player for the Southeastern basketball squad and Coach Perry Deakin. And the Jungaleers, with a history of league dominance, were certainly ready for him.

Southeastern High was a basketball powerhouse in 1938–39. Sophomore Don Lund was a regular starter on the team, and he was frequently called upon to play different positions. Senior Pete Fornari was the team's star during the first half of that season, and when he graduated in January, the Jungaleers honored him by dedicating his final game to him. He was replaced for the rest of the season by Bob Gleffe. Rounding out the starting five were senior George Hackman, who earned all-city honors and was considered by many to be the best all-around player on the squad; Harvey Pierce, a deadly shooter who gathered all-city and all-state honors; and Harvey Eckert, a playmaker who led the team in assists. Together, they were a talented, cohesive team. Together, they were formidable. Together, they won the City High School Basketball Championship.

Don's biggest game in his first year came during a close contest between Southeastern and Eastern High, early in the season. The two teams had traded baskets and foul shots evenly throughout the game, and in the final seconds Eastern was ahead by two points. Just before the final buzzer, Pete Fornari launched a desperation shot from thirty feet away. It was high. But just as the ball hit the backboard and bounced wide, Don grabbed the rebound and scored as the buzzer sounded. The game finished in a tie. Southeastern went on to win all its other games that season.

The 1939 Metropolitan League Basketball Tournament was held as usual at the Detroit Naval Armory. Emerging victorious from the two preliminary games were two East Side high schools, Southeastern and Northeastern. They played for the championship. And for those who were there, that game was one of the most hard-fought and memorable contests in city tournament history. The teams traded points the entire game, finishing in a tie. Since championship games demanded a winner, they played overtime. The first overtime also produced a tie. The second overtime, another basket-trading session, was about to end when Northeastern called time out. Ten seconds remained on the clock. Coach Deakin looked at his tired players, decided on a substitution, and sent in Emil Hison for Bob Gleffe. Emil was a second-string senior who always gave 100 percent effort, though he didn't spend much game time on the court. However, Emil was like a caged cat this game. His was on his toes, eyes narrowed, face ready to explode. Deakin saw it. He sent Emil Hison in with seconds to go on the double-overtime clock. It turned out to be the best decision the coach could have made. As play resumed, Southeastern grabbed the ball. George Hackman bounce-passed it to Don Lund. Lund passed it to Harvey Eckert. The final seconds were ticking away. Eckert passed it to Emil Hison, who was moving unguarded toward his team's basket. Hison grabbed the ball and executed a simple, unchallenged layup off the backboard and into the hoop. Game over. Southeastern High School was the Detroit Metropolitan League Basketball Champion for 1939, and Emil Hison, coming off the bench, was the game hero. His simple layup would be the shot of his lifetime.

The post-game press interview included Coach Deakin, Emil Hison, and Don Lund, the game's leading scorer. Deakin praised his entire team. Lund praised Hison. Hison claimed he was in the right place at the right time. Victory was sweet. No Southeastern fan in the crowd would ever forget that 1939 Metro League Championship game.

The 1939–40 Jungaleer basketball season saw Don as the only returning starter from the previous year's city championship team. This left Don, in his junior year, the undisputed "senior" member of the team and the player whom coach Deakin would count on to be the squad's leader. Fortunately, the Southeastern High School athletic talent pool was large. The strong neighborhood YMCA program, plus enthusiastic, sports-minded encouragement from the athletes' parents, was a factor that gave Coach Deakin an excellent group of prospects. When players walked onto Southeastern's court for the first time, they arrived loaded with basketball skills, gained from hundreds of hours of practice and organized play at the YMCA. They understood the game's fundamentals. They

knew the moves. They showed up eager for Coach Deakin's fine
tuning, and ready for Don Lund's leadership.

Heading up the list of new players for the 1939–40 Jungaleers
was Bill Bauerle, a dead-shooting playmaker with court savvy
and a winning attitude. Tall, fast, and aggressive on the court,
Bauerle would prove to be perfectly matched with the talents of
Don Lund. The two would become close friends. Rounding out
the starting five that year were Charlie Clavana, whose jump
shot was a league phenomenon; Ray Robitaille, a playmaker
with enormous speed; and four rotating players, including Dick
Hansen, Gus Gorgus, Ray Zimmerman, and Zeke Rosteck. Making up the rest of the team were Roland Jump, Elmore Lundin,
Nick Trajchevich, Frank Zamboni, Fred Shedd, Lewis Parry, and
Joe Roberts.

The team played an excellent season. Don was team captain. Southeastern's hopes for repeating the league championship, however, were dashed with a loss to Highland Park in the
championship game. At season's end, both Don Lund and Bill
Bauerle were named to the All-City Squad, and Lund, according
to the press, was the dominant high school basketball player in
the city of Detroit.

Deakin's 1940–41 Jungaleers started another premier player,
Lewis Parry, who came off the bench and joined the starting five
in January when Bill Bauerle graduated. Parry had grown tre-
mendously since the previous year. Constant off-court practice,
combined with a fierce playing intensity, gave Lewis Parry the
talent to be a starter. Parry showed himself as a nothing-but-
net shooter, who played his forward position with a speed and
style that nicely complemented those same skills in teammate
Don Lund. Lund, team captain again, was designated a starting
guard, although he didn't always play that position. During several of the season's games, Don would be called upon to fulfill
critical assignments at other positions. Coach Deakin knew he
could count on his star to play anywhere on the court, and he
frequently called on him to do just that.

The rest of the starting five that year included guard John
Polance, center Jim (Pep) Wery, and a rotating forward rotating
among Louis (Flipper) DeFillip, Art Heymoss, or Ed Whittaker.
Of these three rotators, Flipper DeFillip was the most striking.
He stood a mere 5-feet-7-inches and weighed about 140 pounds,

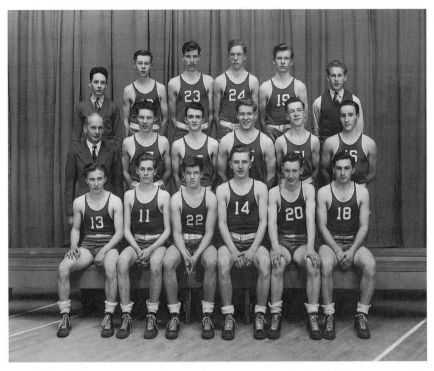

Southeastern High Jungaleers, Detroit City Basketball Champs, 1941.
Coach Perry Deakin is in the middle row, far left. Team captain
Don Lund stands three players from Deakin. Check out the
huge grin and the shoulders. (*Lund Family Collection*)

but he had amazing speed and outstanding dribbling skills. He
could also fake opposing players out of their socks, allowing
him to bullet-pass the ball to high scorers Lund or Parry. In
all, the 1940–41 Jungaleer squad was too much for the rest of
its competition. The team won all of its season games. These
seven highly skilled players went on to the Naval Armory, won
the preliminary game, and then won the Metropolitan League
Championship by defeating Detroit Central, 38–32.

Lewis Parry was named to the all-city squad. Don Lund,
the most highly touted prep athlete in Detroit, was named not
only to the all-city and all-state teams, he was also named their
captain.

By the end of the 1941 basketball season, seventeen-year-old
Don Lund had nothing to prove at Southeastern High School.

He had won three letters in football, three letters in basketball, two letters in baseball, had been named to all-city and all-state teams, and was looked upon as one of the most remarkable young athletes ever in Detroit. Everyone in the school thought he had it made, except for Don. Forget the past. Forget the honors. He had to continually prove his worth to himself. So he focused on another challenge in that spring of 1941. He set his sights on Southeastern's baseball program, where he had firmly established his mark, starting two years before.

15
Diamond Rivalry

Jumbo was on the mound. The big right-hander from Detroit's Eastern High School tried not to show concern with Southeastern runners on first and second. This was the biggest game of the 1939 season between these two chief rivals. As the next batter walked up to the plate, Jumbo turned away and looked around the outfield. They were playing at Belle Isle ball field, one of the nicest baseball facilities in the entire city, nestled within a beautiful island park in the Detroit River, just east of downtown. Although Belle Isle sported winding flower-lined pathways, a dance hall, an arboretum, a monumental fountain, decorative ponds, and a soft sand beach, Jumbo ignored thoughts of these marvels as he gazed around at his teammates. In fact, he practically ignored them. What held Jumbo's attention as he looked around, what really grabbed him at that moment, was grass. Lots of mowed grass. Mowed grass that carried way out beyond where his outfielders stood. Mowed grass that wasn't strategically bordered by fences. Mowed grass that therefore would allow a well-hit ball to bounce along like a terrified rabbit until an outfielder finally chased it down.

That's what Jumbo saw, and that's what Jumbo considered as he signaled his center fielder to move back a little. Then he turned around to face the guy at the plate, Southeastern's shortstop, who stood nervously waving his bat. Shouldn't be a problem, thought Jumbo. Might even hit into a double play. He glanced at the next batter waiting on deck and saw his nemesis from this year's basketball season, a tenth grader named Don Lund. Oh, yea, Jumbo thought. Lund. The guy he traded bruises with under the basket. The guy who backboarded that crazy last-second shot that won the game, put Southeastern in the championships, and knocked off Eastern High. He remembered Don Lund, for sure. But today they were playing baseball. Jumbo hadn't seen Lund play baseball, but after all, the kid was only a sophomore. He shouldn't be that much of a worry.

On deck, Don was carefully watching Jumbo Melkusch. He remembered that Jumbo was thought to be a nice guy. But he also remembered Jumbo as a guy who put aside that niceness when a game began. Jumbo was a fierce competitor. Don recalled some rib-jolting collisions with him on the basketball court. And as he thought about Jumbo, he also considered the traditional Southeastern High vs. Eastern High rivalry.

That rivalry was one of the most intense high school contentions in Detroit. But it wasn't because each school's students didn't like each other, or distrusted each other, or feared each other. To the contrary, they mostly knew each other well. All of them lived pretty much in the same geographical area. Their fathers worked in concert at the factories. Their mothers shopped at the same neighborhood grocery stores. They would see each other at their churches, the Y, and local playgrounds. As a result, any "school conflict" among them would doubtless be friendly, or at the very least tolerant. There was indeed a rivalry, however, and the cause of it was the system of boundary selection calculated by Detroit's public schools. The school board decreed that students who lived on one side of an established boundary went to a stipulated high school. Those who resided on the other side of it were assigned to the neighboring high school. Throughout the city, it wasn't unusual to see teenagers living across the street from one another walking to different high schools. As a result, the kids from each school assimilated school traditions, school spirit, school identities, and a sense of school independence. Even though some might live across the street from one another, these students became uncompromisingly loyal to their own high schools. The obvious result was emergence of strong rivalries. One of the strongest was between Eastern High School and the Southeastern Jungaleers. It was no coincidence that Don Lund and Jumbo Melkusch were competitors who knew each other well.

With two men on base, Don watched Jumbo pitch to his teammate. He studied the big right-hander, looking for throwing "giveaways" that might allow him to predict a certain pitch. And he saw one as he watched Jumbo heave his fastball, followed by his curve. Both pitches were wide of the plate for a 2–0 count on the batter. The third pitch was another fastball. Don noticed that before he threw it, Jumbo flicked his glove at the catcher. He didn't do that before he threw the curve. Don continued to watch. Jumbo flicked his glove and threw another fastball. The umpire called ball three. Jumbo held the ball and watched the catcher's sign. No glove flick. The curve ball missed, and the walk loaded the bases. Now it was Don's turn.

As he stood at the plate watching Jumbo and ignoring the catcher's carping comments, Don decided to take the first pitch and watch Jumbo throw it. Sure enough, Jumbo flicked his glove, and his fastball divided the plate for strike one. Don saw all he needed to see. Jumbo set himself. He flicked his glove.

His fastball came in about belt high, and Don was ready. He swung hard. The ball sailed out into deep left-center field. There was no outfielder in front of it, and no fence to stop it. It just kept bouncing away, while Southeastern's runners rounded the bases. That smash became the first grand slam home run Don Lund ever hit in competitive baseball. As Jumbo watched the ball continue to bounce out of sight while one of his outfielders scrambled after it, he might have thought that the Lund kid did it to him again, after that last-second basketball shot this past season. But he never complained about it then, or at anytime later. Jumbo Melkusch, the big right-hander, forever showed himself to be a big man, in every good sense of the term.

Don's next two seasons of Jungaleer baseball were pure fun for him. His respect and admiration for Wayne Nestor, his coach in both baseball and football, never wavered. There was one time, however, during the first few weeks of his sophomore baseball term, when Don was certain Coach Nestor make a bad decision. Nestor initially assigned him to second base, a position the young sophomore had never played. Don considered himself an outfielder. Without one word of complaint, though, he assumed second-base duties and proceeded to boot grounders, miss line shots to his right, and demonstrate his tendency to nearly always be out of position for the put-out throw. Fortunately, it didn't take Nestor long to question Don's assignment.

"What position do you like to play best, son?" Nestor asked.

"Outfield," said the big sophomore. "Center field is what I'm used to."

This photo of Southeastern High Baseball Captain Don Lund was prominent in the Sunday, April 6, 1941, edition of the *Detroit News'* Roto section. In fact, much of the Roto section that day was devoted to Don. The press called him the "best all-around athlete in the metropolitan area." (*The Detroit News*)

Nestor moved him to center field right away, and Don thrived. He never made a catching or throwing error as the Jungaleer center fielder. His fielding judgment placed him mostly under the ball as it descended, so he seldom had to dive for a catch. He had the strongest arm on the team and by far the best bat. Though Southeastern didn't win their league title during Don's three years in Jungaleer baseball, the team was always in the hunt. And when he received his varsity baseball letter in 1941, Don Lund became only the second, and ultimately the last, Southeastern High School athlete to earn nine letters. The only other one was legendary star Norm Daniels, who played football, basketball, and baseball for the Jungaleers during the mid-1920s. This comparison is more than merely interesting, however, because both men, Daniels and Lund, would go on to greatness at the University of Michigan. They would compete for the Wolverines in the same three sports, earning nine varsity letters and three freshman numerals each during their respective NCAA careers. Both athletes would join a very small list of the University of Michigan's three-sport athletes. They would be included within a select few to be honored as the best of the best, the finest of the fine, and the most worthy of respect among all those who ever wore the maize and blue.

When Don hung up his Jungaleer baseball uniform for the last time in June 1941, the act was merely a transition, rather than a completion. As a matter of fact, he hardly considered the Southeastern program, despite the excellent coaching of Wayne Nestor, as the foundation upon which his skills and his knowledge of the game were acquired. Instead, he credited the Detroit sandlots and the American Legion leagues for bringing him along. He didn't enter competitive baseball until he was fifteen, but he soon came to love the sport more than any other he played. Don Lund's baseball career began in the sandlots of Detroit, Michigan.

16

Detroit Sandlots

Maybe it was meeting Hall of Fame pitcher Lefty Grove when he was a kid that did it. Or perhaps it was watching Babe Ruth and Lou Gehrig play against the Tigers at Navin Field. But whatever served as the source of his main childhood dream, it focused him permanently on America's national pastime.

Don Lund's favorite sport, from the time of his earliest memory, has always been baseball. He loved everything about the game, especially the thrill of applying his bat against the unpredictable antics of a pitched ball. He welcomed the challenge of competing in the only sport he knew where the defense always controlled the ball. And he most certainly enjoyed the constant flux of individual player strategies during each game. Of course, he also enjoyed basketball and football, with their demands for power, speed, brute contact, and team synergy. He was, after all, a team player who enjoyed mixing his talents with others to form a cohesive, powerful unit. But baseball offered one thing the other sports he played didn't provide: the chance to go one-on-one against an opponent. Nothing in his sports world thrilled him more than beating a pitcher with a solid hit or running successfully against an opposing player trying to throw him out at a base. In baseball, he was forced to react with precision, making instant decisions as soon as the ball was put in play. There was no one else to run interference for him. When the ball came his way, he alone was in control of the outcome of his actions. That's why Don Lund put baseball first in his overall passion for sports. And that's also why, at the age of fifteen, in 1938, he couldn't wait for school to end in June, so he could move right into summer baseball and the popular Detroit sandlots.

Since amateur baseball in America was originally played during the nineteenth century on sandy lots, the term "sandlot" naturally came to mean any hometown baseball field where the organized, non-professional summer game was played. In

Detroit, the sandlot leagues were run by the Detroit Amateur Baseball Federation. Federation officials, most of them volunteers, managed game schedules, arranged for team sponsors, and coordinated hundreds of other volunteer workers. Skilled volunteers worked as managers, coaches, umpires, sponsor coordinators, scorekeepers, and support staff. The baseball fields themselves, owned and maintained by the Detroit Recreation Department, literally reflected the term *sandlots*. They were well-kept acres of dirt, marked by chalk lines to lay out the playing fields, with clumps of mowed weeds scattered randomly. Most popular among them was Northwestern Field, which sported five diamonds configured around a central makeup of bleacher seats. Each Sunday afternoon, spectators could enjoy up to five games at the same time. Northwestern #1 diamond was special on its own, being one of only two Detroit area sandlots to be landscaped like a big league ballpark, with infield grass and manicured outfield. Its twin was in Highland Park, the "City within the City," whose entire geography was bordered by Detroit. Other sandlots were established at Belle Isle, the famous park in the middle of the Detroit River, Mans and Jayne fields, which served the East Side, plus the West Side fields Stoepel and Butzell. Most avowed that Detroit's sandlots and sandlot leagues were among the finest in the country. Certainly the efforts of many dedicated Federation volunteers contributed to the success of the program. But one thing, one overriding factor that nourished Detroit's sandlot baseball like no other force, was sponsorship support from the city's business community. Sponsors furnished uniforms and equipment. Sponsors promoted the games. Sponsors provided trophies and team banquets. Sponsors were the backbone of the program.

There were, of course, advantages for the sponsor. Product identity, boosted by word-of-mouth as the teams pursued their schedules, resulted in more business for the company that sponsored a team. Sponsors figured to make more money than they spent, and that's exactly what happened. There was no shortage of local merchants, manufacturers, or service industries eager to invest in a sandlot team. The smaller shops and stores tended to sponsor class C and D teams, which played their games mostly in the local area, either on the East or West side fields. Don Lund, for instance, played his class C ball for teams sponsored by Viviano Florist and by O'Neil-Hoffner Fish Market, located on the East Side. However, class A and B teams, which competed at Northwestern Field and other places around Detroit, were sponsored by companies with broader appeal throughout the metro area. Year after year, class A teams would be sponsored by the major automobile companies and large local firms like the Altes, Pfiffer, and Goebel brewing companies. Sandlot team sponsorship was the sustaining element, along with city-employee efforts and volunteer dedication, that led to the program's national acclaim.

American baseball sandlots were known to be spawning beds for big league professional teams. In fact, most of our principal cities can boast of native-son major leaguers who honed their early skills on hometown sandlots. Detroit was certainly no exception. Sandlot baseball was a way of life for many Motor City families, some of whom went there for entertainment, or for unabashed love of baseball, or, in some cases, for fulfillment of athletic hopes and dreams. Sunday afternoons at Northwestern Field would be packed with players' relatives, neighbors, and friends in the stands. Young boys, who eagerly longed for the day when they could test their cleats in a sandlot game, sought out any spot they could find to watch and wonder. Others were there just to observe the sport they loved, played at different levels of skill. And there were still others who were there for business purposes: the major league scouts who studied, analyzed, and passed judgment on the players. Everybody in that huge, boisterous, excited Sunday crowd had their own special reasons for being there. Their focus was amateur baseball, played by husbands, fathers, sons, and grandsons.

Many major league ballplayers fine-tuned their early talents on the Detroit sandlots, after they first learned the game as high school kids. They were mentored by talented and committed coaches, most of whom saw themselves as character-building teachers before anything else. Not one of the big league players who came through Detroit's sandlots would deny that they emerged from an outstanding high school program. In fact, nearly all of them would be quick to credit their high schools for playing a critical role in their overall development. The high schools themselves, of course, would proudly remember these players in their respective honor rolls.

In addition to nurturing Don Lund, Detroit Southeastern also produced Mike Tresh, a highly skilled catcher who made a reputation for durability with the Chicago White Sox. Mike was the father of Tom Tresh, an all-star power hitter and Golden Glove winner for the New York Yankees.

Detroit Cooley High delivered catcher Joe Ginsberg, one of the most charismatic ballplayers ever to wear a major league uniform, and Milt Pappas, an all-star right-hander known as a control wizard throughout his ten-year big league career. Southwestern High generated catcher Stan Lopata, who had a great career with the Philadelphia Phillies and the Milwaukee Braves, plus Barney McCosky, a power-hitting star who produced a .312 batting average through thirteen years with the Detroit Tigers, Philadelphia Athletics, Cincinnati Reds, and Cleveland Indians. From Northwestern High came Harry Chiti, who signed with the Chicago Cubs at age seventeen and became an excellent knuckleball catcher; Hobie Landreth, another catcher who spent thirteen productive years in the big leagues with seven teams and was Casey Stengel's first pick for the expansion team New York Mets; and all-star outfielder Willie Horton, one of the most dangerous power hitters in the American League during his seventeen-year career and a favorite of the Detroit Tigers, who placed a statue of him in Comerica Park, along with other Tigers' legends.

Detroit Catholic Central High produced three major league pitchers through sandlot ball: Ray Herbert, a right-hander known for his durability over a sixteen-year career with the Detroit Tigers, Kansas City Athletics, Chicago White Sox, and Philadelphia Phillies; Art Houteman, another right-hander who signed with the Detroit Tigers right off the sandlots at age seventeen and had a stellar twelve-year big league career; and the incomparable left-hander Frank Tanana, who broke into the majors as American League Rookie Pitcher of the Year in 1974 with the California Angels, then went on to a twenty-year career as an all-star hurler who became known as one of the craftiest pitchers of his time.

Detroit Chadsey High produced infielder Johnny Lipon, who established himself as a winning minor league manager after his playing days with the Detroit Tigers. Detroit Eastern delivered Roy Cullenbine, whose ability to judge incoming pitches was so refined that he was able to draw more walks than most other players during his ten-year career in the majors. Roy could also swing the bat, twice hitting .300 and slamming twenty-four home runs in 1947 for the Detroit Tigers. One of the most notable major leaguers to come out of the Detroit Public Schools and the sandlots was Hall of Fame pitcher Hal Newhouser, from Wilber Wright High. A fiercely competitive left-hander, Hal was the dominant pitcher in the big leagues during the 1940s. He remains the only pitcher ever to receive two consecutive MVP awards.

Other Detroit metro area high schools also sent players to the big leagues through the Detroit sandlots. Most notable of these were Highland Park High and Hamtramck St. Ladislaw High, both of which represented cities located within the Detroit city limits, and both of which played sports within the Detroit Public Schools leagues. From Highland Park High came two big league left-handed pitchers: Ted Gray, a forkballer who starred as a WWII military pitcher before joining the Detroit Tigers and spending eight years with them as a dependable rotation mainstay; and all-star Billy Pierce, a league leader over a nineteen-year career with the Detroit Tigers, Chicago White Sox, and San Francisco Giants. Out of St. Ladislaw High emerged Steve Gromek, whose sixteen-year career with the Cleveland Indians and Detroit Tigers was highlighted by one landmark event after he won the fourth game of the 1948 World Series for Cleveland—he hugged teammate Larry Doby, who had hit the winning home run. The photograph of that hug, published by every major newspaper in the country, made great strides in the movement for racially integrating major league baseball. Also from St. Ladislaw High came Cass Michaels, an all-star infielder who played mostly for the Chicago White Sox during his twelve-year career, which was cut short at the age of twenty-eight when he was hit in the head by a pitched ball that fractured his skull and seriously impaired his vision.

A few other Detroit metro area high schools produced big league players through the Detroit sandlots. Ted Simmons, whose power, speed, hard playing, and defensive abilities made him a great all-star catcher for the St. Louis Cardinals, Milwaukee Brewers, and Atlanta Braves over a twenty-year stretch, came from Southfield High. Dick Radatz, whose blazing fastball made him one of the outstanding relief pitchers of the game in his years with the Boston Red Sox, Cleveland Indians, Chicago Cubs, Montreal Expos, and Detroit Tigers, was a product of Berkley High.

Two other major league players who established themselves on the Detroit sandlots, but didn't graduate from area high schools, are certainly worth recognition. The first is Reno Bertoia. Born in Italy but raised in Canada, Reno came from Windsor, Ontario, to light up the sandlot infields. His speed and fielding skills prompted the Detroit Tigers to hire him with a bonus in 1953. A popular player with the fans, Reno played for the Tigers and the Washington Senators before retiring after nine seasons.

The second player to brighten the Detroit sandlots who came from an out-of-state high school became a major league catcher and a baseball legend. His name, still honored throughout the Detroit area and renowned throughout the baseball world, is Bill Freehan. Bill came up to play the sandlots from Bishop Barry High School in St. Petersburg, Florida, where he was the most outstanding three-sport athlete in that school's history. He was recognized nationally in 1958–59 as a superb prep football quarterback and was being recruited by several major universities. Bill also played and loved baseball. He was raised in Royal Oak, Michigan, and he had many Detroit area friends. It was completely sensible to him to return to play in the summer leagues of Detroit's sandlots.

From there Bill accepted a baseball scholarship from the University of Michigan and played one year under Coach Don Lund, before accepting a huge bonus to play for the Detroit Tigers. During fifteen remarkable seasons, all with the Tigers, Bill Freehan was a dominant American League catcher. With eleven all-star appearances, seven of them as starter, numerous Gold Glove awards, and the accumulation of several major league milestones, this calm but intensely competitive team leader established a remarkable career behind home plate. By the time he retired in 1976, Bill held the major league records for most chances, most putouts, and highest fielding average for a catcher. He is without doubt one of the greatest baseball stars ever to emerge from the Detroit sandlots.

Don Lund's first exposure to Detroit's sandlots as a player came in 1938, through the highly organized American Legion program. Several Legion posts throughout Detroit sponsored a team open to fifteen-year-old boys. Starting positions were awarded to the best players who emerged from player tryouts, although the roster wasn't solely limited to the starting team. Team benches were often filled with others who didn't make the starting team, but showed desire and discipline. Effectively, American Legion baseball was a program steeped in fairness for all those who wanted to play.

Making the starting team was easy for Don. His reputation was beginning to grow, even after only one year of high school baseball, and he probably could have walked right into the lineup without going through the tryouts. But he reported for tryouts just the same and made the team without difficulty. He played in the outfield for Faust Post that year. The team finished somewhere in the middle of the standings, way behind the eventual winners from Roose-Vanker Post. The summer's experience with Faust gave him valuable seasoning, plus the chance to hone his ability to study other players and their nonverbal signals, especially pitchers.

The following summer, sixteen-year-old Don Lund started playing in the Detroit sandlot leagues, which were grouped according to age. Class E was for boys under sixteen, so he never played in that group. Class D, his sandlot debut, was primarily for sixteen-year-olds. Class C, where he preferred to play and quickly moved up to become a sandlot, was for college players coming back for the summer and talented high school players from around the city. Class A was for "old timers," former professional players who wanted to stay in the game or former college players, or even professionals assigned to play in the minor leagues. Class A games were the most favored by the crowds, for obvious reasons. Class C games were the most favored by the major league scouts, also for obvious reasons. Don played Class C ball throughout his high school years and during the summers when he would come back home between semesters at Michigan. He remembers his years in the Detroit sandlots as formative ones in his athletic career. His skills were never tested more than when he started playing Class C ball with older high school and college players. He was forced quickly to learn to hit a curve ball thrown by talented pitchers. His fielding was constantly provoked by hitters who knew how to place the ball. And he had to learn proper throws to cut off the runner or bounce the ball in to prevent a run from scoring. The sandlots were therefore Don's baseball cultivation grounds. They gave him maximum athletic challenges. They exposed him to players with enormous talents. They nurtured him. Finally, they matured him as a player who would one day embrace the sport of baseball as his lifelong vocation.

17
Dialogue

"Boy, those were some years with some great guys," he said. The old coach sat relaxed in his reverie, right hand on his right knee, left arm draped over the top of his wingback chair. His relaxed face showed a slight smile. His eyes wandered. "But you know," he mused, "it wasn't just baseball I thought about all the time. Other sports were there, too."

"Oh?" I asked.

"Well," he took his arm down from the top of the chair and focused on me, "when it was football season, we concentrated just on football. We forgot about baseball, or any other sport. Same thing with basketball. When you played one sport, you forgot about the others."

I looked at him, thought for a moment, and said, "You remind me of that song from *Finian's Rainbow* when Og, the leprechaun, sings 'When I'm not near the girl I love, I love the girl I'm near.' In your case, Coach, the line might be 'When I'm not playing the sport I love, I love the sport I'm playing.'"

He grinned. "Yes, that's about right. There's so much to learn and concentrate on when you play a given sport. You put your bat and glove in the closet each fall, grab the football, and move on. That's just the way it goes."

"And you had some fine coaching in high school," I noted.

He grinned. "The best in the city, I think. You can't count my Uncle Ken; he coached in Plymouth. Wayne Nestor coached me in two sports; Perry Deakin in one. But I'll never forget my senior prom. Betty was working and could afford to buy her own dress. I had to scrape together what money I had from working at the gas station to rent my tux. A couple of days before the prom, Coach Deakin asked me if it would be all right if he bought a corsage for me to give to Betty. I told him I thought that would be just fine. So he bought it and gave it to me on prom day. How about that? Believe me, Betty and I were awfully proud of that corsage. I'll always be thankful to Coach Deakin for a lot of things, but that one gesture put him over the top!"

I watched him blink a couple of times as he remembered. Time to change the subject. "I can't help thinking about Bill Freehan, coming back up here to dominate the sandlots the way he did," I said. That got his attention.

"Bill was a dominant player," he answered. "Just a natural take-charge guy."

"Want to talk about him?" I offered.

He leaned forward, placed his elbows on the arms of his chair, clasped his hands together, and smiled broadly. This was going to be good. In an eager voice, he said, "Sure." The exchange began.

"What's your first thought about Bill Freehan?"
DL: "He was the best I ever coached."

"The best athlete?"
DL: "Just the best, period. I mean, Bill had it all. Great talent. Great character. Great desire. A brilliant mind. Knew all the league batters as well as they knew themselves. A born leader. Played hard to win, hated to lose. All that and still a nice guy. A perfect gentleman. Solid as you'll find. He still keeps himself in shape, you know."

"How did you first hear about him?"
DL: "Word of mouth. Word got around the sandlots. Bill was known as a football star from Florida. But here he was in Detroit, playing ball at Northwestern Field. Everybody talked about how good he was. I remember the story about John McHale, who used to be president of the Tigers, sitting in the stands at Northwestern in 1959. At the time he was working in Montreal and he had flown to Detroit to scout some infielder. His pilot, a friend of his, was watching the games with him. McHale turned to his pilot and asked, 'Where's that catcher everyone's talking about?' The pilot said, 'I don't know about any catcher, John, but take a look at that kid playing first base.' McHale looked. The kid playing first base was Bill Freehan. When Bill wasn't catching, the team wanted to keep his bat in the lineup, so they put him at first base. He played well there, too."

"When did you first meet him?"
DL: "In the spring of 1959, my first year coaching at Michigan. We were on a spring trip to Florida State in Tallahassee, Florida. Bill and his dad came by to meet Charlie Maher, Western Michigan's coach. I saw them meeting and went over and introduced myself. I met his dad, too—wonderful guy named Ashley; everybody called him Ash. Betty and I got to know Ash and Bill's mother, Helen, quite well. We became close friends."

"What do you remember about recruiting Bill?"
DL: "Well, I was recruiting several players in '59, so I spent a lot of time at the sandlots. There were four guys I was really interested in besides Bill, and as it turned out, they were all playing together on the same team with Bill, and as it turned out further, all five of them, including Bill, ended up coming to Michigan and playing together on my team in 1961. How about that? Their sandlot team was sponsored by Lundquist Insurance."

"LUND-quist?"
DL: "Yes," he laughed, "heck of a coincidence. By the way, that was a heck of a team. They won the Federation National Championship two years in a row before five of them came to Michigan. Best sandlot Class D team in the whole country. An amazing bunch of talent. My best recruited class."

"Do you remember much about those four who came from their sandlot team together with Bill?"
DL: "Sure. Great kids who turned out successful. You don't forget guys like that. Let's see ... there was Dick Honig at shortstop. Good bat, great instincts. Nice on the double play. After graduation, he coached freshman basketball and baseball here at Michigan, then founded a local company called Honig's Whistle Stop, which distributes sports-officiating equipment all around the world. Dick himself became a Big 10 referee. He was voted the best of them all. He refereed a national championship game, he was that good. I still see Dick a lot. We're good friends. Then there was Denny Spalla, who played the outfield. He could run like a deer. Saved our bacon lots of times with his glove and bat. He's now in the corporate real estate business in Minneapolis, doing very well. Then came Jim Steckley. He played second base

for Lundquist, but when he came to Michigan I moved him to the outfield to take advantage of his strong arm. I remember his great attitude and team spirit. Everybody liked him. Jim went on to a prosperous career in management consulting. The fourth guy was my best left-hand pitcher, Fritz Fisher. He came to the sandlots out of high school from Adrian, Michigan. He won a lot of games for us. After graduation in 1964, Fritz spent a year with the Tigers before they sent him down to Knoxville in a switch for Joe Sparma. When I heard about it, I called the general manager in Knoxville and told him about Fritz and how good he was. Let me tell you, that Knoxville guy couldn't have been happier. I thought he was going to jump through the phone! Anyway, it wasn't long before Fritz was recruited out of baseball and into the banking business in Toledo. Obviously, I wasn't the only one who knew just how smart Fritz was."

"That's amazing. Four sandlot players, all on the same championship team with Bill Freehan, all joining him in coming to Michigan to play for you. That's quite a coup, Coach."
DL: "You bet it was. Plus, we won the Big 10 Championship that year," he grinned. "But my whole team was great, not just the five who played for Lundquist. There were others who also made great contributions that year. I'll never forget any of them."

"And Bill Freehan was your standout player?"
DL: "No question about it. You know, he batted .585 in the league that year. A Big 10 record that's approaching fifty years and still standing. How about that?"

"Bill was obviously getting a lot of offers from other colleges. How did you get him to commit to Michigan?"
DL: "You're right about lots of offers. Bill wanted to play both football and baseball in college, and he had it narrowed down to two schools—Notre Dame and Michigan. Notre Dame was offering him a football scholarship while allowing him to play baseball; we were looking at a baseball scholarship for him, with the option of playing football. Bill's decision came down, in the end, to school policy as explained by the coach. Notre Dame told Bill he would be required to play spring football and then join up with the baseball team. I told him that Michigan

didn't require spring football if you were already participating in another spring sport. That did it for him. Then, of course, he starred here in football as an end."

"He played only one year at Michigan, and then he accepted a huge bonus from the Detroit Tigers and left for the big leagues. How did you feel about that?"
DL: "I was grateful for the one year and the Big 10 Championship." He grinned and then he turned serious. "Let's be realistic. Lots of teams were after him, offering the same kind of money. Bill's dad, Ash, came to me and told me it was like they were all under siege. Bill came to Michigan instead of going right to the big leagues from the sandlots because he wanted to get a college degree. The education was important to him. I told Ash, and I also told Bill, that I understood completely. Bill Freehan was destined for a career in pro ball, and it made perfect sense to go for the advantages. So he went to the Tigers with my blessing. By the way, Bill and his dad agreed that he wouldn't spend a penny of that bonus money until he graduated from Michigan. And Bill was true to his word, which comes as no surprise. He took classes at nights and during the off-season at our Dearborn campus until he got his degree. You can't believe how proud I was of him. And how proud Ash and Helen were."

"He's like a son to you, isn't he?"
DL: "Yes."

"The Michigan baseball program has retired five numbers during its entire history: Ray Fisher's, yours, Moby Benedict's, Jim Abbott's, and Bill Freehan's. Isn't that right?"
DL: "That's right, but I think they're thinking about retiring a couple more numbers."*

"What was Bill's number when he played Michigan baseball?"
DL: "He wore number 14."

---

* The university retired Jim Abbott's number in 2009.

"But the University retired number 11 for him, his Tigers' number. Why would they do that?"
DL: "I don't really know. Maybe they just felt he was more identified with the number 11, which he wore as he got famous. Bill never said anything about the number mixup to me; he was just honored that the university did it. And, let me tell you, if it's OK with him, it's OK with me."

"When you consider it, it's pretty amazing; retiring the number of a player who only competed one year. Can you think of any other college player, in any sport, who had that same kind of impact on his school as Bill Freehan?"
DL: "No. There's nobody else like Bill. To me, he's one of a kind."

"He belongs in the Hall of Fame at Cooperstown, doesn't he?"
DL: "I can't understand why he isn't there. Maybe someday, somebody will make it happen. After all, it took a lot of years for them to name Hal Newhouser. Bill deserves it."

I decided to move on. "Let's go into your own college years. I'm sure you had several universities that were after you. What made you decide to go to Michigan?"

His expression again became serious, and he straightened up in his chair. "You're right. I was lucky enough to be able to look at other schools. But there was never any question about Michigan. My whole family wanted me to go to Michigan. My high school coaches wanted me to go to Michigan. Many of my friends were already in Ann Arbor. And Betty wanted me to go to Michigan. Her opinion meant a lot. But when you get right down to it, I personally wanted to go to Michigan. I wanted to go there and be a part of all that tradition. Notre Dame was in the running for a while, because it's a great school. But then someone told me a story that happened years ago: Notre Dame contacted Fielding Yost and asked him to teach them the game of football. And Yost went to South Bend and did it. When I heard that, my decision was easy. It was Michigan all the way."

"Let's get into that," I said. "Let's talk about your years as a player for the Michigan Wolverines ..."

18

Meeting the Wolverines

"You're sitting here with your mouth open," Andy Lund whispered.

Seated at the table next to him, Don whispered back to his father, "Dad, this is really something. I've never seen anything like it!"

The two were attending the University of Michigan Football Bust in the ballroom of downtown Detroit's Statler Hotel. A member of the U-M Club of Detroit, which annually sponsored the event, had picked them up at home and brought them in his car. Don and Andy were there as guests of the University of Michigan Club of Detroit, along with other acclaimed Detroit area high school football seniors. It was the evening of December 4, 1940, six days after Tom Harmon had been named the sixth winner of the Heisman Trophy and six days before he would travel to New York City to receive it. The room was filled with Michigan football devotees, all of them male. (Women would not become active in college athletic celebrations anywhere in the country for many years.)

Detroit Club members and their guests, newspaper reporters, Michigan coaches and staff, plus the entire 25-man team roster of players were all there to celebrate the University's football program. Each graduating letter winner was to receive the highly coveted "M" ring, presented exclusively by the Detroit Club. The high-ceilinged ballroom of the Statler, with its crystal chandeliers, paneled walls, and brocade drapes, was an impressive setting for the event. Damask linens covered the tables. Waiters wore black-tie uniforms, and they served the meal on elaborately monogrammed Statler Hotel china. All attendees, dressed in suits and ties, were seated in groups of eight at round tables, with the University contingent gathered at one end of the room. Sophomore, junior, and senior letter winners on the team occupied separate tables accordingly. Coaches and selected

Detroit Club dignitaries were located next to the speaker's platform. The only University football notable not present was Athletic Director and Michigan legend Fielding Yost, who was ill at home in Ann Arbor.

Don was thrilled by the whole scene. He had never attended this kind of ceremonial dinner, although he had heard about the Michigan "Bust" and its impact on those who played football for the Wolverines. His host had told them about additional Michigan Busts that were given by other U-M alumni groups, but that the Detroit Bust was the only one held close enough to allow players to attend. As he looked around the room, Don was impressed by everything he witnessed: the setting, the ambience, the dignity of the moment, the wholesome behavior of everyone present, and the happy expressions on faces everywhere. As the after-dinner program began, he glanced again at the grin on his dad's face, sat back in his chair, and took it all in.

First on the program was Detroit Club member and chairman of the 1940 Bust, Louis Hyde. After some introductory remarks, Mr. Hyde announced five awards that were being tendered to the legendary Fielding Yost. Two of the most prominent of these were an honorary life membership in the Detroit Club and a special "M" ring, the first ever to be given to someone other than a graduating Michigan senior.

Following Mr. Hyde, Detroit Club president Glen Coulter presented the seniors with their rings. As each senior received his ring, he spoke a few words of appreciation to the audience. The final two seniors to receive their rings were team captain Forest Evashevski, followed by MVP and Heisman Trophy winner Tom Harmon. Evashevski brought a few tears with his remarks about not wanting to leave Michigan. He spoke about his father, who four years before had told him he wanted to see his son receive the "M" ring, but couldn't because he was ill at home. Then he introduced next year's team captain, fullback Bob Westfall, who received a generous round of applause.

When it was Tom Harmon's turn to speak, he received a standing ovation. Tom, who was often called "TD" by his teammates, began by kidding about the Minnesota football team, stating that in three years at Michigan he was never able to play in a win against the Golden Gophers. "But I know we'll get 'em someday," he grinned as the crowd laughed (in fact, it wasn't until three years later, during Don's junior year at Michigan, when the Wolverines finally beat Minnesota in Michigan Stadium, 49–6). Harmon then presented thirty-eight gold-plated footballs, engraved with the words "TD's All-American" and the All-American football logo, to friends, coaches, teammates, and others he designated as his "All-American Team." Everybody appreciated his creative and generous gifts.

Finally, Coach Fritz Crisler stood and went to the lectern. The crowd went silent. Crisler spoke slowly and deliberately, in a strong and authoritative voice. He spoke of Yost and his legacy in the Michigan tradition; he expressed pride in the Michigan program and its emphasis on character development; he thanked his coaching staff. He finished by talking about his players and their importance to the university as students worthy of highest respect and admiration. When he concluded, the silence remained for a moment. Then the room erupted with cheers and applause as the entire crowd jumped to its feet. For Don Lund and many others in the room that night the reaction to Crisler's speech was the most enthusiastic they had ever seen. Afterward, Don and his dad were able to meet some of the players, including Harmon, Evashevski, and Westfall, before the team boarded the bus to return to Ann Arbor. On the ride home, father and son spoke about the evening in glowing terms. The next morning they read in the *Detroit Free Press* that the Bust was "the largest and most successful of its kind in U-M Club of Detroit history." Certainly, Andy and Don agreed, the 1940 Michigan Football Bust was truly a night to remember.

The next spring Don was visited at home by Notre Dame Head Football Coach Frank Leahy. Leahy was forthright, personally impressive, friendly, and polite. He promised only an excellent education at Notre Dame, nothing more, and Don and his parents were impressed. They decided to accept the coach's invitation to visit the campus in South Bend.

Don and his dad drove down together. They arrived to see the historic campus bustling with college-age men who crisscrossed walkways with determination and haste. University buildings were caressed on all sides by flowering trees and bushes, eagerly sprouting myriad colors as they welcomed the warm spring sunshine. In front of many private homes around the area, spring flowers lined gardens and sidewalks. Notre Dame was beautiful in a sea of moving colors.

Don and his dad met several of the athletics department staff and were shown around the sports facilities. They spent at least an hour in Notre Dame Stadium. In sum, their visit had been cordial, informative, and fun. Notre Dame was definitely a place to consider. However, after many discussions about the issue with family, friends, and his high school coaches, Don decided against South Bend. He concluded that, for as long as he could recall, there was only one college for him and it was located in Ann Arbor. He picked up his application from the high school office and sent it in. Two weeks later, by the end of April, he received his acceptance.

Don was contacted by two other out-of-state schools that spring, Yale and Northwestern. The Yale contact came through a phone call from a man in the admissions department. The caller informed Don that Yale was interested in him for their football program, but that he would have to attend classes at a preparatory school in order to qualify for enrollment. Don said no. The Northwestern contact came by a personal visit from Otto Graham, a sophomore tailback on the team who was visiting various high school prospects on behalf of Wildcats' head coach Lynn Waldorf. Graham would go on to memberships in the NCAA Hall of Fame as a Northwestern tailback and the NFL Hall of Fame as quarterback for the Cleveland Browns. But in the spring of 1941, Otto Graham was a tailback with the Wildcats and also playing basketball and thinking about a professional career in either sport. Graham's visit with the Lunds on Lycaste was interesting, and Otto himself was delightful. But his views on Northwestern were pretty much limited to the two sports he played. In talking together after Graham left, Don and his parents felt they really weren't given much overall perspective about the university itself. They decided to pass on Northwestern.

Michigan State College contacted Don through one of their exceptional football alumni, John Pringle. John was an All-American Spartan in 1938 and had established himself as a successful businessman in the greater Detroit area. Pringle had several talks with the Lund family about the Spartans, and he took Don out to dinner one night. The talks were cordial, and Don was impressed by John Pringle. Michigan State was also the school his friend Bob Gleffe was attending. Nevertheless, Don decided that Michigan State and East Lansing, despite the college's premier reputation, were not for him. He decided not to pursue it further.

Through the spring, up into the middle of May and Don's eighteenth birthday, no one from the University of Michigan's athletic department had contacted him. He wasn't concerned, though; he knew he could merely show up for freshman football and they'd accept him. The only question in his mind was paying for things on campus, including tuition. But he figured he could work three jobs if necessary. He was resourceful. He'd get by.

The contact came around the fourth week in May, through a former Southeastern High athlete and neighborhood friend named Don Brewer. Brewer had gone to the University of Michigan after high school and played shortstop under Coach Ray Fisher. After getting his Michigan degree, he returned to his old Detroit neighborhood and purchased a gas station on Jefferson Avenue. Naturally, much of Brewer's trade came from his home neighborhood, as did his station's employees. Bob Gleffe, who grew up next door to the Brewer home, worked there. Occasionally Don would come around and help him out. Don Brewer, of course, was a consummate Wolverines fan.

Brewer seemed to be always talking around the gas station about Michigan sports. He proudly displayed a U-M pennant and photos of his Michigan baseball teammates. He bragged about the Wolverines to his customers, and to everyone else who happened to visit his station. Don Brewer was also a well-known and much respected member of the Southeastern High community who came from an excellent family. His father, Clarence E. Brewer, was director of the City of Detroit Recreation Commission. One day in early May 1941, Don Brewer dropped by the Lund home and asked Marguerite if he could speak with her son. When Don appeared, Brewer said, "Don, I've been talking about you to my former coach at Michigan, Ray Fisher. Ray wants to meet you, and I'd like to take you to Ann Arbor and show you around. How about it?"

Don didn't even glance at his mom for approval before he fairly shouted, "Sure!" Then he looked at her and saw her smile. A week later, Brewer drove him to Ann Arbor on a baseball game day.

When they arrived on Michigan's campus, the two made their way directly to the main offices of the Athletic Department, right next to Yost Field House. There, they met a few baseball staff members before going over to the nearby baseball stadium, eager to watch the game. They weren't disappointed. Not only did the Wolverines win, they won triumphantly, through a colossal exhibition of hitting, running, and fielding by outfielder Dick Wakefield. Wakefield was the star of the day, capturing attention not only with his talent, but also with his outlandish personality. He seemed to be continually grinning over something happening in the game. His banter with teammates pepped up the dugout. He was the flame on the candle throughout the game. On that day, Don Lund was more impressed by one player than he had ever imagined he could be. There was no question in his mind about his future as a Wolverine. After the game, he met with Ray Fisher, who was as impressive as any coach in his memory. Ray had no pretensions. He talked straight on with no exaggerations. Don saw Coach Fisher as a man who would be hard to please but fair, which would make him work hard but also make him learn. He sensed that this coach would work with his players, helping them build their strengths and overcome their weaknesses. Ray Fisher, Don surmised, was his kind of coach.

By late August Don was informed by the Detroit U-M Club that he would receive a tuition scholarship at Michigan. He wouldn't have to work multiple jobs. He could earn a college degree and play sports for the Wolverines. There was nothing in his life he wanted more than to make that fall trip to Ann Arbor. He was on the way to his dreams.

19
The Entering Freshman

The sleek, black 1934 Ford rode smoothly but not fast enough this morning. In fact, ninety miles an hour wouldn't suffice for the big, blond eighteen-year-old college freshman in the back seat. It was mid-September 1941. Don Lund was on his way to Ann Arbor and his first year at the University of Michigan. Armed with letters from the admissions office, from student housing, and from the Athletics Department, he couldn't wait to get there. Forcing himself to relax, however, he sat back and enjoyed the ride.

His parents were in the front seat, with Andy driving and Marguerite sitting beside him. Marguerite's mood was exactly the opposite of her son's. He was leaving home for the first time in his eighteen years; her emotions ranged between feeling happy for him and sad for herself. She remembered how she had felt the same way when Andy gave her baby Donald his first haircut. As she believed back then, a part of her was inadvertently being removed. She sighed to herself, sat back, and quietly watched the passing scenery.

Andy, on the other hand, was totally enjoying himself as he drove through the countryside. He loved his 1934 Ford Fordor Sedan V8. Virginia had purchased it in 1940 from the original owner for an excellent price and then gave it to her dad so the family could again have its own transportation. To Andy, Virginia's gift was a true blessing. His previous car, a 1928 Chrysler, had to be put up on blocks in the garage on Lycaste during the Great Depression because Andy no longer had the money to operate it. Then the Detroit climate and weather changes had deteriorated the car so thoroughly it became inoperable. And so, like many other automobiles of the Depression era, Andy's 1928 Chrysler had been hauled away, simply to become part of a landfill. Now, thanks to Virginia, Andy was delighted with his "new" car and quite happy with things in general. Best of all, his son was going to college at a fine university. Andy Lund was indeed enjoying this family drive to Ann Arbor.

The morning sun chased the Lunds as their 1934 Ford carried them southwest out of Detroit and toward Ann Arbor, following Michigan Avenue nearly all the way. Their route initially coursed right through downtown Dearborn, home of Henry Ford and the Ford Motor Company. Dearborn appeared replete with Ford cars everywhere the Lunds looked. Fords meandered in front of them, behind them, and coming toward them on the opposite side of traffic. Andy realized he fit right in. His car belonged there. He drove through the village of Dearborn as if he held the mortgage on it.

Their journey continued through rolling fields of fenced farmland, stocked with herds of beef cattle and milking cows. Farmers could be seen pitching hay from overstuffed wagons into the upper lofts of their barns. Here and there, horses slowly trod their pastures and kissed the lush grass. All three travelers marveled at the tranquil charm of southeastern Michigan's rural countryside.

Soon they arrived in the village of Ypsilanti, named after a hero in the Greek war for independence. With a population of about 12,000, Ypsilanti was home to Michigan State Normal College, renowned for its teacher preparation, and also for being the first state-supported college in the country to admit women undergraduates.

The Lunds followed Michigan Avenue right into downtown Ypsilanti, where they slowed down at North Huron Street, right in front of Haab's Restaurant. Renowned for its prime steaks, Haab's was considered by many to be the premier dining spot in the entire area. For the Lunds, Haab's was their landmark for turning right on North Huron. For the next four or five blocks on Huron, the three were treated to some of the most beautiful and stately mansions they could imagine, many of them built during the nineteenth century. They were owned by prominent families who had chosen Huron Street to display their wealth through elaborate architecture. Don and his family had never been inside houses like these; they could only speculate about what lay behind those opulent front doors. Soon they came to Cross St. and turned left. Cross marked the east boundary of Michigan State Normal's campus for about a mile, and then it merged into

Washtenaw Avenue. Washtenaw would guide them the rest of the way through Ypsilanti and into the town of Ann Arbor.

As the family drove on, they reminisced about Ypsilanti's famous teacher's college and, in particular, their connection to it through Marguerite's brother, Ken Matheson. Ken had graduated from Michigan State Normal with a degree in education. He then became a teacher and coach at Plymouth High School, located in the quaint village of Plymouth, about 30 miles west of Detroit. Over the years, Don's Uncle Ken had visited his family frequently. Each of his visits was a special occasion for Don. Ken would always bring a ball, or a bat, or shoulder pads, or some other piece of athletic equipment as a gift. Naturally, Don's neighborhood popularity rose each time Uncle Ken visited. When the kids played a game, Don was often able to supply the equipment they used.

Thinking about his brother-in-law, Andy called to Don in the back seat, "Hey, Son, do you remember your first visit here, when you were little and we lived on the West Side? When your Uncle Ben drove us here to visit Uncle Ken when Ken was a student?"

Marguerite answered for her son, saying, "Dear, how could he possibly forget that time?"

Indeed, Don vividly remembered the time his father's brother, Ben Lund, drove the family to Ypsilanti. Ben had dropped off the family, parked his car, and left little Don alone in it. Ben had carefully set the hand brake, since the car was parked facing downhill at the top of a steep hill. Undaunted by being alone in the car, Don sought to amuse himself by playing "driver" behind the steering wheel. It didn't take the boy long to find the parking brake and accidentally release it, which caused the car to start rolling downhill. Fortunately, Uncle Ben saw what was happening, ran to his car, jumped in, and stopped it. Don thought the whole thing was hilarious. Ben breathed a sigh of relief. The rest of the family was stunned and grateful for the rescue.

Don smiled at the recollection. "Sure I remember, Dad. Would you like me to take over the driving?"

They all laughed together as they departed Ypsilanti and crossed into Ann Arbor, steering toward Michigan's campus and Don's new home for a year, a men's dormitory called West Quadrangle.

Don was assigned to Chicago House, one of the areas of "West Quad" that, like other living zones within the huge residence hall, was named so students could identify with a smaller and more homespun atmosphere. He was given room sixteen and paired with another Southeastern High graduate named Bob McPherson. Bob was also an entering freshman, but he was three years out of high school and, in fact, had been in the same Southeastern class as Virginia Lund. McPherson subsequently enrolled at the University of Michigan after working to save enough money to attend. He planned to study architecture. Don, of course, was delighted to room with him. The two became fast friends.

Don's first week at Michigan was filled with the necessary requirements for matriculating as a member of the incoming freshman class of 1941–1942. First of these was registration for his courses. All class registrations were held in Waterman Gymnasium, the men's facility for physical education classes. "Waterman" as it was popularly termed was originally built in 1894 through a matching funds gift of $20,000 from wealthy Detroit attorney and sports enthusiast Joshua W. Waterman. The building was a gray block structure that sported a 248-foot-by-90 foot wood-floor gym under a 60-foot ceiling. Around the gym's perimeter flowed an elevated rubber-surfaced running track. Each corner of the track held large open areas, used for student meetings or physical education classes. Adjacent to the gym was a connecting, five-story structure that housed locker rooms and faculty offices. During Waterman's first six years, women were only allowed to use the gym on selected mornings, but by the turn of the twentieth century, argument for a women's physical education building was very strong. After all, they reasoned, Michigan became the first public university in the United States to admit women as medical students on an equal basis with men in 1870. Therefore, it must also take a national leadership role in providing gender equity in other areas. President James B. Angell and several of the university's regents took up the cause. Ultimately, one of the regents, Levi Barbour, personally came up with the solution.

Barbour purchased a plot of land next to Waterman Gym for $25,000 and donated it to the university for construction of a women's gymnasium. "Barbour," as it was called, was completed in 1902 and had similar architecture to Waterman, but was devoted exclusively to women's physical education. In later years, Regent Barbour would give an additional $100,000 for construction of a women's dormitory named in memory of his mother, Betsy Barbour. Although both gyms were used seven days each week, only Waterman hosted class registration. It was Waterman where Don went to sign up in September 1941. It was also Waterman where he would spend much of his freshman year, taking physical education courses required for graduation.

Class registration at Waterman was looked upon by some students as a controlled frenzy. The entire gym floor was jammed with tables, each of them dutifully proctored by a staff worker. On each table were attendance cards for particular classes, limited to the number of students portioned for each class. For instance, if a freshman English class was scheduled to meet from 8–9 AM on Monday, Wednesday, and Friday, and its student roll was limited to 20, there would be 20 attendance cards for that class on the given registration table. When the 20 cards had been selected, the class would become "closed." Other students who wanted to take the freshman English course would have to select a separate card for a different class, hoping they could do so before that class became closed. Unfortunately, the system caused stress for students because all were assigned arbitrary registration times. University officials reasoned that staggered registration times made perfect sense for logistics, for if the entire student body showed up at the same time, the scene would be chaotic. Mandated registration at different times was considered a simple solution. However, the practice resulted in some later students finding their classes closed by earlier registrants. They were thus forced to scramble from table to table to find the class they needed, regardless of the scheduled meeting time. That's why some students called registration at Waterman Gym a controlled frenzy. There was also a popular registration joke that held that the term *maize and blue* didn't only identify the university's colors, it also referred to the *maze* students negotiated through Waterman's registration tables, and the *blue* you felt if you couldn't get into all the classes you needed.

Despite those widely circulated "warnings" about class registration, Don had no trouble signing up at Waterman for his courses. In fact, he had only a few minor registration problems throughout his entire undergraduate program. He went through the maze each time with comparative ease, considering himself lucky.

After he registered for classes, followed up on his athletic scholarship, and filed the various required forms for entering freshmen, Don focused on showing up for athletics. He walked the approximate mile from West Quadrangle to Yost Field House, quickening his pace with each step. He was excited. He couldn't wait to report for freshman football.

Yost Field House was built by its namesake, the famed coach of the Wolverines, Fielding H. Yost. At first reluctant to let the structure be named after him, Yost finally succumbed to widespread encouragement. Yost designed the brick-and-steel building to last 100 years. Events ranging from concerts to basketball games were held in it throughout the year. Next to Michigan Stadium, Yost Field House was the brick-and-mortar pride of Michigan athletics and the place where Don Lund was told to report for freshman football.

Don joined the group of players gathered in the middle of the cavernous arena and introduced himself. Those he met were mostly young men who, like himself, had established strong reputations on their high school gridirons. He also met a few walk-on players, men who just liked to play the game. He heard one guy say he only wanted to play on the same field Harmon did. That in itself, thought Don, was a good reason for being here. Eventually the freshman coaches came in and ordered everyone to gather at one end of the floor. There, another man approached them. He was heavy set, with broad shoulders and a barrel chest. He walked deliberately, carrying a subtle air of authority. He introduced himself as Wally Weber, the freshman football coach. Don was impressed by the man. Coach Weber spent about twenty minutes talking about the Michigan tradition and about freshman football. The squad wouldn't square off against another team in a game, except among themselves on one of the practice fields. Freshmen weren't eligible for intercollegiate competition. They would, however, scrimmage with the varsity each week. That was an important part of freshman training. When he finished, Coach Weber asked the newcomers to break off into smaller groups, according to the positions they were trying out for. "Linemen over there," he shouted as he pointed to his left. "Ends over there," pointing to his right.

Don thought he'd try out for tailback. That was his high school position, and he felt he might be good enough to get noticed if he played there.

"Tailbacks over here," shouted Weber, and Don started to move with them. Weber looked right at him. "Not so fast, Southeastern. You're a fullback!"

Don grinned to himself. He had heard that Coach Weber liked to call guys by their high schools, instead of their names. "How about that," he thought as he stepped back into the large group, "he called me Southeastern. He knows who I am!"

20
Freshman Fervor

It was mid-morning on Monday, December 8, 1941. The Michigan Union, a huge, red-bricked campus landmark devoted to leisure activities of male students, was oddly quiet. Nobody occupied the basement bowling alley. The billiards and games rooms, the lounges, the reading rooms, the offices, and all the conference areas were empty. Even the corridors were deserted. Any casual Michigan Union visitor walking in and viewing this scene would have been surprised by the tomblike atmosphere. But the surprise would end when the visitor walked into the cafeteria on the first level.

Normally arranged to serve about three hundred men at sittings for breakfast, lunch, and dinner, the cafeteria on the morning of this particular day was packed. People were sitting at tables, perched on counter tops, or simply standing around the room. Don Lund was there, standing off to one side of the room with some of his football buddies. The room was quiet. Everyone knew that something terrible had happened yesterday, and all attention was focused on the several loudspeakers placed around the room. When the radio broadcast began, no one moved as the President of the United States began to speak:

"Yesterday, December 7, 1941—a date which will live in infamy—the United States of America was suddenly and deliberately attacked by naval and air forces of the Empire of Japan."

The air in the room remained still until the president finished and the radio was turned off. Then the uproar began. Cries of outrage, shouts of anger, and invectives of resentment filled the room. Men vowed to enlist in the military right away. College could be postponed. The only alternative was to join up and fight back. Emotions ruled as everyone emerged from the Michigan

Union cafeteria and scattered throughout the building or moved out elsewhere on campus.

For the next few days, the main topic of nearly every discussion in and out of the classroom was the Japanese attack at Pearl Harbor. Men throughout Michigan's campus were determined to join the military. But none were more determined than those students who wore the maize and blue athletic uniforms. They considered themselves warriors. They were fit, able, competent, and ready. Among them was Don Lund, determined to fight for his country right along with the rest of them.

It wasn't long before national draft and enlistment procedures were established. Men on college campuses throughout the country left school to join the military ranks. Others, including Don and several of his friends, wanted to finish their academic year and join up during the coming summer. Don's parents agreed that finishing his freshman year at Michigan made good sense, so he continued to enroll in classes and play on the freshman teams.

His football experience under Coach Weber in the fall of 1941 had been mostly a good lesson in humility. The freshmen, ineligible for NCAA competition, were relegated each week to scrimmaging the varsity team. And the varsity players, experienced and eager for game-ready practice, were not about to take it easy on the first-year players. Playing fullback, Don would often be tackled before he could run or throw the ball, due to the varsity defensive line charging over less-experienced freshmen. When he played defensive halfback, he would often be blocked out or knocked down before he could make a tackle. All this was frustrating to him, despite frequent encouraging comments by Coach Weber. There were times when he remarked to others that his best friend was the turf on the practice field. But he never missed a practice, never complained, and never failed to give 100 percent effort.

One major upside of freshman football for Don was meeting and getting to know teammate Bob Chappuis. A speedster and good passer with natural ability and excellent instincts, Bob had been the star athlete at DeVilbiss High School in Toledo, Ohio. He was also the reason Don was assigned to the fullback position by Coach Weber. Weber wanted Chappuis to play tailback. The two athletes combined extremely well in the backfield. Moreover, they started a friendship that would continue throughout their lives. They would go on to play football together as sophomores at Michigan, then Bob would serve in the military until after the war, returning to the Wolverines in 1946. Bob Chappuis would become a football legend the next year, earning All-American honors, placing a strong second behind Notre Dame's Johnny Lujack for the Heisman Trophy, and starring along with Bump Elliott in the 49–0 Rose Bowl blowout over the University of Southern California. Don Lund would often remark, throughout the years, that he never knew a better man than Bob Chappuis, on or off the football field.

The freshman basketball program was much less strenuous for Don than was football under Wally Weber. Not only were freshmen ineligible for NCAA contests, they also didn't have to scrimmage against the varsity. As a matter of fact, the freshmen basketball squad really didn't have much to do except show up for practice at the intramural building and run drills five days a week. That doesn't mean they weren't serious about practicing. They drilled hard and tried to beat each other in shooting, rebounding, passing, and moving the ball around. Laziness wasn't tolerated; neither was fooling around on the court or doing anything that wasn't in keeping with fundamentals, such as trying to get away with taking too many steps in a layup shot.

There was no on-court nonsense in freshman basketball at Michigan. The squad was coached by Ray Fisher, Michigan's head baseball coach, whose first love was America's national pastime. Although Ray would make sure the players performed at their best level on the court, he would often allow their conversation during breaks to turn to baseball. For instance, it wasn't unusual for Ray to whistle a stop in court play and demonstrate how to execute a bounce pass, then call a break and demonstrate how to throw a breaking curve ball as the guys stood around and watched.

Right from the start Don Lund idolized Ray Fisher. He liked Ray's easygoing style and his ability to let you know that nothing got by him. Ray seemed to have his own campus intelligence network. One day he said to a player who attended a campus party over the weekend, "Did you intend to marry that keg?" The player had only drunk a few glasses, but everyone was amazed that Ray knew what he did, since the coach was out of town that very weekend! Ray also had a superb ability to search for and point out performance weaknesses, no matter which athlete or what sport he was watching. The freshman basketball players eagerly listened to his analysis of the varsity teams and their opponents after a game. His cogent remarks, combined with detailed demonstrations, gave Ray's players valuable insights for correcting their own weaknesses.

For Don, the most important aspect of his freshman basketball season was getting exposure to Coach Ray Fisher. In Ray, Don saw a consummate baseball man who would teach him about the game he loved most. Ray would become his mentor throughout his career as a Wolverine and, in fact, throughout his life until Ray's death. The two would get to know each other well and become close friends. There would never be resentment between them. They would never have arguments or harsh words. Their relationship would always be special.

One day on a visit home during Don's freshman year his dad asked him, "What do you think of Coach Fisher?"

Don grinned and said, "He's a Latin teacher, Dad. And do you remember M.G. Sullivan? Anyone who teaches Latin sure knows a lot more than I do!"

One of the first things Don had to do in his freshman year was find a job. His scholarship paid the sixty-dollar-per-semester tuition, but he was responsible for all other costs. These included room and board at West Quadrangle, books and supplies, living expenses, and a little pocket money. Campus slogans were tossed around, like "Without the dough, you'll live quite low" or, more appropriately, around the athletes, "No money gives you a Spartan life!" The double meaning was clear.

Don wasted little time finding work, since his family had no financial resources to help him. His first job was in the West Quad cafeteria. He did everything from washing dishes to cleaning tables. But daytime classes plus football practice restricted him to only a few hours of cafeteria work. He needed to find something else. He needed a night job. By mid-October he found it.

Edwards Brothers Printing Company, a large producer of textbooks and catalogs for colleges and universities, was one of the most well-known and well-run businesses in Ann Arbor. Owned and run by a prominent local family, Edwards Brothers supported the community in many ways, one of them being a policy to hire and train employees from the surrounding area.

Students were encouraged to work there, providing they could show a desire to work hard, a willingness to learn various aspects of the printing trade, and discipline enough to show up on time and do the job with few mistakes. When Don presented himself for an interview, he was hired on the spot. They liked his "can-do" attitude; he liked the 7 PM to 11 PM hours. For the next four years, Don worked for Edwards Brothers, earning enough money to sustain his college expenses. Although he performed various tasks, his main duty involved cleaning linotype and getting it ready to be inserted in the ever-waiting plates. Though his job might be considered menial, Don didn't see it that way. The printing process at Edwards Brothers was highly organized, efficient, and labor demanding. He was part of a production team, just like he was part of a football team. The missions were similar: prepare, execute, and deliver what's expected. He was used to that kind of process, and he welcomed it.

When freshman basketball season ended, Don went directly into spring football practice. Spring football was required for all players, and the freshmen were particularly excited about it. This would be the first time they'd merge with the varsity players. It would also be their first exposure to Michigan's famed coach Fritz Crisler, whom Don remembered for the stirring speech he witnessed at the Michigan Football Bust. Crisler's remarks were memorable. Don couldn't wait to meet him.

One thing Don noticed right away when he reported for spring football was that several of his freshmen teammates weren't there. The coaches explained that these men were serving in the military, as were several of last year's varsity players. Crisler spoke to their absence when he addressed the assembled players. He talked about honor and tradition; about duty to the job you have to do, whether on the battlefield or the football field. He talked about devotion to yourself, your family, your school, your country, and your God. When he finished, there was complete silence for a moment. Then, with a flourish and a wave, he shouted, "Now go and get in your positions!" Thirty men scrambled in frenzy.

The best part of spring football for freshman Don Lund was finally becoming a part of the Michigan Wolverines. The program was embedded with history, traditions, and legends established by men whose stories echoed through the minds of everyone who ever attended a game in that great stadium. Don belonged to it now. He could sense it in the sincerity of Coach Crisler's words. He would be a warrior, first for his country, then for the university which bonded him for life.

The next best part of spring football was when it ended. The baseball diamond beckoned.

Freshman baseball was practically a breeze for Don Lund and his teammates. They couldn't play any games, of course. They could only work out in their positions and take turns in batting practice. For the most part they were ignored by the varsity baseball players. Coach Fisher gave them individual attention to improve their skills, and showed extreme interest in their progress. And as he showed them on the basketball court, Ray wouldn't accept anything but an athlete's best effort when on the field or at the plate. Nevertheless, freshman baseball was nothing but repeated drills for the players. For Don, baseball practice was something he did because he was dedicated to do so. But soon his first year at Michigan would be over. He would move on to the summer months, maybe to play some sandlot ball. He wanted to return to Michigan; he was committed to that goal. But he didn't know when he'd be back, or even if he would ever be back. One thing was out there waiting for him, and he intended to pursue it hard. Those fateful words kept going through his mind:

"Yesterday, December 7, 1941—a date which will live in infamy ..."

21
The Biggest Disappointment

"Come over here, son," said the doctor. "Sit down." Don did as he was told. He sat down. Didn't say a word. The doctor looked to be in his forties, with brush-cut light brown hair, pointed nose, square jaw, tiny ears, and dark brown eyes that seemed to pierce right through your brain. He was about medium height, medium build, and looked to be in pretty good shape. He wore a white coat over a white shirt and black trousers. He wasn't smiling. "Wait here a minute while I find your X-rays."

Don waited nervously. He wondered why they had pulled him out of line after they checked his knees for reflexes, and then taken him to be X-rayed. As he looked around the cavernous room filled with about three hundred nearly naked men, standing in a line that meandered around the room, he thought about his situation. He was at his draft board headquarters, on the corner of Jefferson and Mt. Elliott in Detroit, being processed voluntarily for induction into the U.S. Army.

It was the summer of 1942. Determined to join the military along with the rest of his buddies, Don had first sought out Michigan football legend Harry Kipke, who ran the navy's V-5 rocket program on the Ann Arbor campus. Kipke had been sympathetic but not very encouraging. His program was filled with the maximum number of candidates allowed. The same was true of the navy's V-12 program, also headquartered in Ann Arbor. In fact, all military enlistment programs that had been available during the school year had closed by the time classes finished in June. The only prospect that now existed for Don to join the military would be his own draft board. So here he was, going through his army physical exam, annoyed that he was being singled out for some kind of special unknown problem, and waiting for a doctor to pass judgment on him.

He gazed around the processing facility. The line of men moved slowly through a series of randomly placed examination booths, each one staffed by a doctor and devoted to a particular specialty. One stop checked for pulse and heart rate; another examined bone structure; another checked for abnormalities. The one that checked for hernia drew comments and snide remarks from some of the guys in line. Don remembered one man being pulled out because his feet were too big for the largest army-issued boots. Some men, Don among them, had been pulled out for further specialized testing, such as X-ray or a thorough dental check. The best description of the entire scene at the draft board that morning would be a highly organized, methodical, and efficient human processing system. There was no levity. The whole thing was aimed toward a specific goal. And to everyone present in that large room, the goal was extremely clear.

The doctor returned and sat in a folding chair across from Don. He still wasn't smiling. "Have you ever had pain in your knees when you run?" he asked.

"Never," said Don.

The doctor looked right through him. "How about jumping?"

Don looked right back. "No, Sir. I can grab a basketball right off the backboard above the rim with no pain at all."

For the first time the doctor showed a slight smile. "You play basketball?"

Don came right back, "Yes, Sir. And baseball. And football."

"Football," said the doctor. "You're big enough to play the line, where you bend your knees a lot. Ever get sore doing that?"

"No, Sir," said Don, "I'm not a lineman."

The doctor was relentless. "What about just kneeling down, or sitting down with your knees bent for a long period?"

Uh-oh, Don thought. Here it comes. "Well, Doctor, whenever I sit in a theatre with my legs bent, after a while my knees start hurting and I have to get up and stretch. But it's no big thing."

The doctor stared at him until Don started to squirm. "Young man," he said finally, "it may not be a big thing to you, but it's a big thing to the Army. And since it's obvious to me that you're here trying to get into the service rather than get out of it, I'm going to take the time to tell you just why it's a big thing to the Army."

Don looked at him with a startled expression and stunned attention.

"Son," the doctor intoned, "you have what's known as Osgood-Schlatter Disease. You've probably had it since you were about ten years old and started to grow fast while you played all those sports. Osgood-Schlatter is a swelling and soreness in the knee area that affects mostly boys who play strenuous sports between the ages of ten and fifteen, when they have growth spurts. Most of them complain of pain when they run or jump hard, and they're given treatment. In your case, for some reason, you never had pain, so you weren't treated for the disease. This resulted in permanent growths on cartilage and bone just below your knees." He pointed to Don's knees with their large growths just below the kneecaps. They had looked that way to him for years.

"But, Doctor," said Don, "my knees don't bother me when I play sports, and I get knocked around all the time and land hard on them when I play football. Why would they bother me in the Army?"

"Because," the doctor said quickly, "in the Army you'd have to crawl on your knees, walk on your knees, and sometimes rest on your knees for hours at a time. You couldn't do that. You'd know what I mean if you tried to play the line in football or tried being a catcher in baseball. You'd really be hurting because you'd be bending your knees all the time."

Don felt like he'd just been sucker-punched in the gut. His shoulders slumped as he sat there, feeling like the loser in a lop-sided boxing match. He couldn't talk. He could hardly breathe. He wanted to find a hole and disappear.

The doctor slowly stood up and placed his hand on Don's shoulder. "Don't take it so hard, son. Go back to school. Make something of yourself."

Don walked back home, head down, hands in his pockets, slouching all the way. For the first time in his life he had failed to achieve something that was really important to him. What would people think of him, he thought. A big, strong guy like him who could jump and run with the best of them was unfit to fight for America? This was absurd. This was ridiculous. This was unfair.

"Whoever told you life was fair?" His mother's eyes drilled right through him.

He had expected sympathy, or relief, or at least some kind of understanding for his feelings of rejection. He wasn't prepared for her to respond that way. The two were seated across from each other in the Lycaste Avenue kitchen, which served as Marguerite's domain as well as the center of household activities. He had just finished telling her about his morning at the draft board.

"Well, life isn't always fair," she went on. "Life is a series of ups and downs; of pluses and minuses; of wins and losses. Let me ask you, Don, when you lose a game, do you feel like a loser?"

"No," he said, "I just want to play 'em again." He thought about that. Losing wasn't a permanent thing. It was merely a setback. He'd lost this morning at the draft board, but it wasn't the end of his life. His mom was right. He wasn't a loser. He would never consider himself a loser. "You're right, Mom," he said finally, "I've been looking at this the wrong way. I guess the best thing for me to do is put this morning behind me and just move on."

Marguerite stood up, went around the table, and hugged her son. "That's my boy," she said, "follow the doctor's advice. Go make something of yourself."

22

Hello, Varsity!

He could hardly believe it. Around the room's perimeter were tables burdened with steaks, pork chops, ham, and several varieties of potatoes, bowls of garden vegetables, milk, coffee, soft drinks, and enough desserts to satisfy a sweet tooth forever. All you could eat and everything free! The coaches called it Training Table; he called it the ultimate feast.

Don was making his first dinnertime visit to the Anderson Room in the Michigan Union, known by many as the Training Table Room. He was there along with several other varsity football players, all of them viewing the sumptuous banquet before them. His fellow sophomores shared the amazement by gaping in awe. The upperclassmen, used to all this, simply strode in and began filling their plates. Eventually, Don and his classmates did the same. What a great way to start football, he thought. What a great way to begin the season! Tomorrow he would begin the rugged, two-week preseason varsity football practice, designed to get the players in shape for the 1942 season.

When he had arrived in Ann Arbor the previous day, he looked up his friend and freshman roommate, Bob McPherson. Bob was an architecture major, and also a member of the professional architecture fraternity Alpha Rho Chi. When the two had moved out of Chicago House the previous June, Bob promised to find a room for Don at his fraternity house on the corner of State and Madison. Finding Bob true to his word, Don thankfully moved in as the guest of his friend. He would stay at the Alpha Rho Chi house for a couple of months, until he was asked to join Phi Delta Theta, an internationally renowned social fraternity. As soon as he became a member, he moved into the Phi Delta Theta house at 1437 Washtenaw. He would live there for the rest of his sophomore year.

True to its mission of getting the varsity players ready for the playing field, the two-week preseason training session was deliberately severe. The players practiced in the morning, showered, changed, had lunch, and then came back to practice in the afternoon, Monday through Friday. All this would be interspersed with sessions devoted to the team's playing strategies, learning the plays, and building the cohesive unit that would become Michigan's football team for the season. This preseason system was called "Two-a-Days." College and university football programs throughout the country routinely followed the same plan. For the most part, the varsity players at Michigan accepted it with a positive outlook as they prepared for the 1942 season. It was something that just had to be done, they believed, in order to field a winning team. They liked certain things about the regimen, such as the three-meal-a-day training table (changed to only one meal when the season began), plus the building of team spirit and a sense of camaraderie. One thing they didn't like was returning after lunch and donning the same wet and muddy practice pants they had taken off in the morning. But everyone got used to it as they plunged into each day's routine. For Don, however, the whole preseason sophomore experience was welcome. He put it in the right perspective. He had no trouble comparing it to the mundane, second-class existence of last year's freshman squad. There had been no training table; there were no games to prepare for. No one sympathized when the varsity team ground them into the practice turf. Coach Wally Weber, with sheer force generated by his commanding personality, made them feel important as football players. That, plus the chance to meet outstanding men like Bob Chappuis, Bob Wiese, and many others had made the experience worthwhile. And he did, after all, receive freshman numerals in his three sports. In sum, his freshman athletics year had been a learning laboratory, just as the university intended it to be. But now that was past; he was a sophomore, receiving perks denied him last year.

So goodbye, freshmen. Hello, varsity!

Football at Michigan was practiced at Ferry Field, a 38-acre complex of outdoor arenas for football, baseball, track, tennis, and intramural sports. It was named after Dexter M. Ferry, head of Ferry Seed Company in Detroit, who purchased and donated the land to the university. Ferry also paid for construction of a ten-foot brick privacy wall along the roads bordering the property, plus small buildings for ticket windows and an elaborate wrought-iron gate designed by Albert Kahn. Yost Field House and the Athletics Administration Building bordered the east corner of Ferry Field, while the imposing Intramural Building rested on the north side. Any University of Michigan historian would refer to Ferry Field as the school's traditional sports facility, where legends were made and legendary feats were accomplished. For instance, it was the Ferry Field outdoor track that echoed the pounding feet of Jesse Owens as he set four world records at a Big 10 meet on May 25, 1935. It was in the baseball stadium at Ferry Field where Hall of Famer George Sisler played for the Wolverines under Hall of Fame Coach Branch Rickey. The Intramural Building at Ferry Field was where Director of Intramural Sports Earl Riskey invented the sport of paddleball in 1930. And it was Ferry Field where Michigan legend Fielding Yost coached his final home football game in a 37–0 rout over Wisconsin on November 6, 1926. Ferry Field embodied Michigan sports tradition, and this fact was uppermost in the mind of sophomore athlete Don Lund.

Don would sometimes arrive early for football practice in 1942 and walk around the grounds of Ferry Field by himself. He would stand at the edge of the football field, imagining the cheers of ghostly voices screaming from the past over a big play or a Wolverines' touchdown. Then he would gaze west, over the Ann Arbor Railroad tracks and its appropriately named Ferry Railroad Yard, and beyond open fields, where Michigan Stadium stood in silent majesty about a half-mile away. Yost designed, built, and named Michigan Stadium, though he never coached a game there. It opened in 1927, the year after Yost retired and became the university's athletic director. Knowing all of this, Don would be filled with nostalgia as he strolled around Ferry Field. It humbled him to be there, walking where so many of Michigan's greats had walked before.

Home football games in Ann Arbor were surrounded by excitement, which reached its peak on Saturday morning before the kickoff. Fraternities sometimes decorated the fronts of their houses, often having contests to select the best design. Students marched to the game in specific groups, such as fraternities, sororities, and members of special interest clubs. Townspeople hosted pregame cocktail parties in their homes. Passenger trains came in from Detroit, Grand Rapids, Toledo, and as far away as

Cleveland and Chicago. They would line up beside each other, on sidings within the Ann Arbor Railroad's Ferry Yard, built especially for football Saturdays. Train passengers trekked the quarter-mile distance to the stadium dressed in style. Women draped themselves in wool dresses, leather coats, fashionable hats, and leather walking boots that matched their purses and gloves. Men wore dark suits, ties, long wool coats, and expensive fedora hats. Their parade to the stadium was filled with playful good humor, fueled in part by partisan team emotions and in part by booze in pocket flasks. They all looked good and felt good. Their collective mission was clear: cheer for their "Champions of the West" and settle for nothing less than a win.

Combined with home game excitement on Saturdays was a little bit of pageantry, brought on in one instance by the Michigan Marching Band. Directed by esteemed music school professor William D. Revelli, the marching band was a proud fixture at Michigan games, especially when they performed during half-time. Revelli was a perfectionist who treated his band members like raw recruits under a drill sergeant. And they loved him for it. He also insisted on using a wide variety of instruments in the band, with brass, woodwinds, and percussion, making his halftime music sound like it came from a concert band. It was powerful, of course, but mellower than the bleating sound heard in typical brass bands of the time. Revelli would say, "I don't want a brass marching band that blows away the audience when it gives a concert. I want a concert band that marches." His approach was copied by many other college marching bands. William Revelli became the most revolutionary band director of his time and one of the most celebrated.

Another type of pageantry occurred in the pregame routine of the team itself. Right after a light workout on Friday afternoon, the team would shower, dress, and pile into cars for a twenty-minute ride to Barton Hills Country Club. Founded in 1920 as a golf club for wealthy Ann Arbor residents, Barton Hills was a high-class, low-profile facility located in secluded wooded hills just north of town. It offered privacy and excellent accommodations for housing the players, plus it provided a substantial food menu. Also, many of the Barton Hills' members were alumni of the University of Michigan, who had strong feelings about giving players and coaches nothing but the best pregame service. Don had never before been a guest at a country club. The first thing he wanted to do was check out the golf course. This late in the season the weather was cool, but there were still a few golfers on the course. Don casually walked over to the tenth tee and watched a foursome swing away. All four drove their tee shots successfully, right down the middle of the fairway. In fact, the golfers made the process look easy. This golf stuff looks pretty simple, he thought. Maybe someday I'll give it a try. Should be easy. Yea, right.

After dinner, the players relaxed around the clubhouse. Lights out came at 9 PM. After breakfast the next morning, the players would assemble in groups by position for sessions in their specialties with the assistant coaches. Biggie Munn would talk to the linemen. Benny Oosterbaan would chat with the ends. Earl Martenaeu spoke with the backfield, which included Don as a reserve fullback. They all talked about game strategy, potential problems, how to adjust to the opponent, and other game-related topics.

When it was time to leave, everyone climbed aboard cars for the trip to Michigan Stadium. They traveled by the same route every week: Barton Drive to Plymouth Road to Broadway to Fifth Avenue to Green Street to the stadium. The convivial atmosphere of yesterday afternoon's car trip to Barton Hills was absent on the Saturday morning ride. People standing along the route would see grim-faced gladiators, eyes front and intense. Most players were oblivious to the pageant they created. Once they were suited up in the locker room, Coach Crisler would speak to them with fire and passion, saying something like, "Who are they who would dare to come here and face Michigan?" Then the players, with adrenalin rushing and hearts pounding, would charge down the tunnel like a highly organized gang and burst onto the playing field, shouting and waving their arms. Crisler's pregame message must have worked in that first game of Don's varsity years, September 26, 1942. Michigan went into the game against Great Lakes Naval Station as overwhelming underdogs in front of the smallest crowd of the year, only 17,000 relatively quiet people. By game's end, though, at least 2,000 more fans had walked into the stands and joined the others, who were all standing, screaming, and shouting as the Wolverines pulled off an upset, beating Great Lakes 9–0.

Don Lund, the backup fullback from Detroit Southeastern High, was thrilled. The Wolverines had made him a believer. Go Blue!

The rest of Don's 1942 football season saw him getting into several games and doing fairly well on both sides of the ball. He played almost the entire Minnesota game in Minneapolis, after Bob Wiese was injured, and did well. At season's end, he was fairly satisfied with his performance and content with his contributions. The team finished 7–3 overall. Albert Wistert and Julius Franks were named All Americans. Don was awarded a letter.

The 1942–43 Michigan basketball season was filled with enthusiasm, fueled principally by the natural effervescence of head coach Bennie Oosterbaan. Playing guard, Don did well with his right-handed set shot from every angle around the key, making strong contributions each game. Don had learned to shoot one-handed for high school coach Perry Deakin. Under Deakin, Southeastern became the first Detroit Public High School basketball team to use the one-handed shot beyond the layup, and Don Lund had been its star performer.

Complementing the team at forward was Howard Wikel, a go-getter who could turn a game around with bursts of energy and accurate passing. Overall, Don's sophomore basketball season would be considered average, with a 10-8 total record. In the Big 10, however, the stats were better. Michigan went 8-4 in the conference. One of its proud achievements came in a game against the University of Illinois. Illinois was the Big 10 powerhouse that year, with its "Whiz Kids" and their star Andy Phillips. The Associated Press considered them the best team in the country. In the first half of their game against Michigan, they played as expected, trouncing the Wolverines and going into halftime with a 32–6 lead. In the second half, however, Michigan fought back with a vengeance. They doubled their rebounds, sank shots that had eluded them in the first half, and pressed the Whiz Kids until the Illinois lead was cut in half. The Illini won the game, 47–34, but it wasn't as easy a victory as the media had predicted. Coach Oosterbaan expressed everyone's thoughts after the game when he said, "You never lost confidence. You never gave up. You were Michigan!"

Don's 1943 sophomore baseball season was literally a wash-out. Many games were rained out for the Wolverines. Their Big 10 Conference record ended up with just three wins and two losses. The team's biggest disappointment that year was the rainout of an exhibition game between Michigan and the Detroit Tigers, scheduled at Ferry Field. Everyone just stood around and watched the rain varnish the whole scene. No one was able to joke about it at the time, or for several weeks afterward.

Don's greatest moment of that season came during the game against Illinois. The Fighting Illini had runners on base, and Don was playing shallow centerfield. When the batter smashed a long line drive in his direction, Don took off, running as hard as he could to get under it. As the ball came down, he reached up and caught it over his shoulder on the run, took one step and fired it to the infield, stopping the runners from advancing. That one step is what made the play work. Many players take two or even three steps after that kind of catch. Years later in the 1954 World Series, Willie Mays would do the same thing before a national television audience. One step after an over-the-shoulder grab in mid-stride, followed by a dead-on throw. The ball caught by Willie sailed over 450 feet in dead center field. Willie's performance would become immortalized as "the catch."

At season's end, Don was happy he got to know Coach Fisher quite well. A natural pessimist, Ray would say things like, "If we don't score five runs in the first inning, we could lose the game." He would say it with a poker face. It took a while for the guys to get it, but then they liked his style, which worked much better than the "rah-rah" optimism so many other coaches used. Also, Ray never swore; it wasn't his style. He had a favorite expression, though. When something didn't go right, he'd roll his eyes and say "Lord Almighty!" That was Ray Fisher. Don believed he had found his mentor. He didn't swear either.

23

Dialogue

We were once again in his living room. He lounged in his chair, dressed as usual. His full head of white hair casually tossed above his almost wrinkle-free face, combined with a natural white-toothed smile, challenged the fact that he was born in 1923. It was raining outside. One of those all-day, overcast, steady rains common to this area in late summer. We were both gazing wistfully at the persistent downpour.

I asked him, "Is this what it was like during your 1943 baseball season?"

He answered, still looking outside, "Oh, yea ... probably the wettest season I can remember. It drives you nuts, you know, not being able to play. That's what you're there for." He looked at me. "You come in. You dress. You look out and see that tarp on the infield. Then you just sit around and wait. Some guys could laugh about it. I couldn't."

"Well, Coach," I said, "at least you could look forward to playing summer sandlot ball."

He grinned. "That's not exactly true. I went to the sandlots, all right, but not to play. I had to make some money, so I took a job with the Billy Rogell Baseball League."

"Was that the league named after the Tigers' shortstop?" I asked. "The one who shared the keystone with Charlie Gehringer when they won the World Series in 1935?"

"The one and the same," he said. "Billy Rogell did a lot for Detroit, besides lending his name to the Baseball League. He served as a city councilman for many years."

"So what was your job?"
DL: "I was in charge of the baseball field at St. Clair Recreation Center on Fairview Avenue. I'd show up in the morning, get out the equipment, and make sure everything was ready when the kids started coming in to play."

"*Kids?*"

DL: "Youngsters around ten years old, up to about fourteen or so. They were organized into teams that played each other all over the city. It was an excellent program."

"*Did you coach or manage any of the teams?*"

DL: "Not then. Each team had its own manager, who also did some coaching. I just ran the field."

"*So what else did you do that summer?*"

DL: "I got married."

"*Married?*"

DL: "Yes. June 12, 1943. Best day of my life."

"*Was it planned? Was it sudden? Did your folks know about it?*"

DL: "No, yes, and no."

I laughed. So did he. "OK, Coach, tell me about it."

DL: "Well, there's not much to tell, really. It was a Saturday. I walked over to Betty's house in the morning. We started talking, and we just decided to get married that day. I was twenty, Betty was twenty-one, we didn't need permission, and we thought talking to our families beforehand would just muddy the waters. So we took a bus to Toledo and found a Justice of the Peace."

I was astounded. Don and Betty Lund had a storybook marriage that lasted more than fifty-four years. They were both products of the same neighborhood, extremely well-known and popular students at Southeastern High, and they would have been acquainted with hundreds of people who lived in their neighborhood. They could have had one of the largest weddings in the city! Yet they chose to elope without telling anyone. Admittedly, it was wartime. Social events were curtailed. With men entering the military and leaving girlfriends behind to wait, there was an ever-increasing rush to nuptials around the country. But Don wasn't going into the military. What, then? Large weddings, even small ones, weren't cheap. Neither of the families had cash to spare, nor did Don and Betty. Maybe financial concerns had been a factor. A sure bet would be that the two of them would never

Newlyweds Don and Betty Lund, 1943 (*Lund Family Collection*)

have considered placing a monetary burden on their parents. Who knows what actually went through their minds at the time? I decided to leave the whole matter of Don and Betty's marriage reasoning to speculation. After all, Betty was gone and couldn't enlighten things. I would just stay with the factual story.

I asked him, "What about the license? What about witnesses?"

"The license was easy to get," he said. "The war increased the number of marriages, so they made the procedures fairly simple. In fact, that was one of the reasons we chose Toledo instead of Detroit. Smaller town, less waiting. As far as the witness, we found people just standing around the Toledo courthouse. They seemed to be perfectly willing to be witnesses, so we chose this one guy. No problem at all.

"Did you spend the night together in Toledo?"
DL: "Oh, no. My folks and Betty's mother had no idea where we were. We took the bus right back to Detroit. She went home to her house, I went to mine."

"How long did you wait before you told your folks?"
DL: "We waited a few days. We told my folks first, then went to Betty's house and told her mother."

"What was their reaction?"
DL: "Surprise, at first, then acceptance. My folks liked Betty, so there was no problem of welcoming her to the family. Their only concern was that we didn't share the same religion. I was Protestant; Betty was Catholic. That wasn't going to change. Betty's mother, also being Catholic, actually made more of an issue of the religious difference. She made us promise to bring up any children we had in the Catholic faith. And we did. Our daughter Susan was raised Catholic."

"Once your secret was out, did you and Betty start living together right away?"
DL: "Oh, sure. We moved in with my mom and dad. I remember my mom treating Betty just like her own daughter. Welcomed her into the kitchen. Taught her to cook things the way I liked. And Betty fit right in, too. Helped with the laundry, housework, things like that."

"And that's how you spent the rest of the summer?"
DL: "Not quite. About a month after we were married, my Uncle Ken told us he was going to work for the rest of the summer at a youth camp up north. He invited Betty and me to move into his place while he was away. He had a house on Birkshire, off

Warren, about four or five miles from my dad's place. So we moved over there. It was nice."

I remembered the story about his Uncle Ken and the gifts of sports equipment he would bring to the house on Lycaste. But Marguerite's younger brother was more than just a relative bearing presents. He was, in fact, Kenneth "Beef" Matheson, a member of Eastern Michigan University's Hall of Fame and one of its greatest football players of the late 1920s, when the school was Michigan State Normal College. During the time he was bringing those gifts to his favorite nephew, Ken was athletic director at Plymouth High School in Plymouth, Michigan, where he also coached all the sports. Later on, Ken distinguished himself as an athletic director and coach in the Detroit Public School System. It's fair, then, to conclude that "Uncle Ken" was a primary influence in Don Lund's lifelong commitment to athletics. Ken was a three-sport coach. There is every reason to assume that he wholeheartedly encouraged his three-sport nephew.

"How long did you stay at your Uncle Ken's house?"
DL: "Just through the summer. Then I went to Ann Arbor for preseason football practice. Betty went back to live with my folks and continued to work as a secretary for General Motors. Before long, I found a place for us in Ann Arbor, a second-floor flat at 211 East Madison Street. It was owned by a nice family named Kerns who couldn't do enough for us. That house still stands today and looks pretty much the same."

"So Betty quit her job and moved to Ann Arbor. What then?"
DL: She found another job right away, as a secretary for Argus Camera on Fourth Street. They found out she had modeled for Annis Furs in Detroit, and they asked her to model for them in magazines. It was a nice job."

"How long did you live on Madison?"
DL: "Not too long. We found a bigger flat on the third floor of a house on Geddes for less money. It's no longer there. The university bought the land and tore it down to build a recreation center. But we liked living there. Sometimes it was a party place. Guys would bring over drinks and snacks and hang around. Our

daughter Susan was born in 1946 while we still lived there. I remember something about Susan as a baby there. She would rock her crib back and forth, making a grinding sound on the wood floor that could be heard at night from her third-floor bedroom, all over the building. We tried to pad the feet of the crib, but nothing worked. We laughed about it, but I'm sure it drove our neighbors crazy."

Once we began to talk about what happened in 1946, I decided to bring the conversation back. "Whoa, Coach," I said, "Let's not talk about Susan just yet. We still have your junior and senior Michigan years to cover."

"You're right," he answered, "and let me tell you, those were great years."

24

A New Image at the Old U

The ship stood majestically at its permanent mooring. More than six stories high, it accommodated several thousand men of the U.S. Navy and Marine Corps. It had no guns or other armament. There was no bridge, no bow, and no stern. Yet it was in fact a ship, according to the Navy in 1943. It had a name—West Quadrangle.

The University of Michigan campus that greeted Don Lund in September of 1943 had a far different image than the one he left three months before. The buildings were the same, of course, and the overall curriculum remained intact, except for a noticeable increase in math and science courses. Most of the student body was completely transformed from the year before, in three important ways. First, they were men from all economic and social strata from all around the country. Second, most appeared fit, trim, and in good physical condition. Third, they were all dressed in military uniforms. Some wore the traditional dark blue jumper and round white hat of U.S. Navy sailors; others were the U.S. Marine Corps green utility uniform. All of them were University of Michigan students, enrolled in the U.S. Navy V-12 College Training Program.

The V-12 Program was begun by the Navy in July 1943 as a means to increase its force of officers during World War II. The demand for college-educated manpower at that time was tremendous. The Navy would eventually commission over 5,500 ships, create numerous marine divisions, and build hundreds of naval land bases throughout the war theaters. Millions of men would be needed to fight the naval battles; thousands of competent officers would be needed to command them. Moreover, the draft age had been lowered to eighteen. That meant that colleges and universities around the nation would suffer an enormous loss of students and face possible collapse. The Navy needed college-educated men; the university needed full classrooms. Therefore, the V-12 program benefited both the Navy and the participating schools in a huge way. The federal government paid tuition and board to the school, plus fifty dollars per month to each V-12 student. The plan accepted those already enrolled in the Navy and Marine Corps college reserve programs, as well as enlisted men who were recommended by their commanding officers and high school graduates who passed a national qualifying test. All V-12 students were active duty sailors and Marines. They were subject to the strictest form of military discipline, and they were billeted in college dormitories that were designated as "ships," under the same commands and rules as their counterparts at sea.

There's no question that Don Lund experienced some feelings of envy toward those in military uniform, and perhaps he even felt slight pangs of guilt. One time, soon after his arrival on campus that fall, he confided his thinking to one of his marine pals.

"You must be kidding," said his friend, "I'd trade places with you in a minute. At night, you go home to your dream girl. I just go home to my dreams."

After that, Don never spoke to anyone about his thoughts on the subject. And nobody ever said anything to him about his 4-F rating, either. He enjoyed equal status as a student, and even more status as a flourishing three-sport athlete.

The first thing Don noticed when he reported to fall football practice was the absence of familiar faces and the appearance of new ones. Half the guys he played with the previous year were gone, including his buddy Bob Chappuis. In their places were sailors and marines, rugged athletes from other colleges and universities, including Big Ten Conference schools. It was no secret throughout the V-12 Program in America that the best athletes went out for intercollegiate sports, and that the Navy encouraged it. This, of course, produced a high level of college multi-sport competition throughout the country. It also represented the first time in NCAA history that an evening curfew for an athlete could be sanctioned through penalty of law. For junior Don Lund, Michigan athletics in 1943–44 would be both interesting and memorable.

Maybe it was a twist of fate that pitted two three-sport athletes, destined to be lifelong friends, against each other on the basketball court and the baseball field in 1943–44. Don Lund, of course, played for Michigan. Chalmers "Bump" Elliott played for Purdue as a V-12 marine. They didn't meet socially, even though they played the same positions in football, basketball, and baseball and certainly had plenty of chances to see each other in action. Nevertheless, they shared mutual honors in their respective schools that year. Each won three letters, each played for a Big Ten championship team in at least one sport, and each established himself as an outstanding athlete on his way to becoming a legend. Later on, Bump Elliott would muster out of the Marines and join his brother Pete at Michigan. There, he would establish himself as one of the University's Hall of Honor greats, as a football player, a head football coach, and an associate athletic director. Eventually, Bump Elliott and Don Lund would work together at Michigan, two former rivals who would become close and trusted friends for life.

Michigan football in 1943 was mostly a successful season. Ranked number three in the nation, the Wolverines compiled an overall 8-1 record. Their only loss came from a service team in Iowa City called "Iowa Pre-flight." They tied for the Big Ten conference Championship with Purdue (and Bump Elliott), whom they didn't play. For Don, however, the 1943 football season would give him rewards beyond the Saturday games. He formed enduring friendships with some very special V-12 athletes.

Elroy Hirsch was a football phenomenon from the University of Wisconsin. He was labeled "Crazy Legs" by a sportswriter from the *Chicago Daily News*, who publicly commented on Elroy's running style after he watched the sophomore Badger gallop for a touchdown against Great Lakes Naval Station in 1942. He would be known as "Crazy Legs Hirsch" for the rest of his life, and he would wear the nickname with pride. Football was Elroy's main sport. After the war, he went back to Wisconsin and became its preeminent gridiron legend. He then went on to become one of the greatest professional football stars in NFL history, playing for the Los Angeles Rams as the first-ever full-time "flanker," or wide receiver. At Michigan in 1943, however, he played four sports: football, basketball, baseball, and track. He won letters that year in all four, becoming the only man in the history of Michigan athletics to do so. Don's most memorable football game with Hirsch was when they shared the same backfield against Elroy's alma mater, Wisconsin. The Wolverines crushed the Badgers in Michigan Stadium, 27–0. Over the years, Elroy wanted to forget about that game. Don would never let him.

Mervin (Merv) Pregulman was an outstanding tackle for the Wolverines in 1943, earning All-American honors as a senior. After graduation and military service, Merv accepted an NFL draft and played forty-seven professional games before retiring in 1949. He went on to a successful career in the steel industry. Although Don remembers Merv as the "piece of rock who converted to steel," he also recalls the man himself. In addition to his football credits, which include memberships in the University of Michigan Hall of Honor and the College Sports Hall of Fame, Merv is known for philanthropy toward his alma mater. Don Lund considers Merv Pregulman to be All-American in every meaningful definition of the term.

Tremendous speed and power earned fullback Bill Daley All-American honors in 1943, against some of the strongest defensive lines in college football. He averaged almost seven yards per carry, and scored fifty-seven points in the five games he played. He was also named to the all-conference team. Since Don also played fullback for the Wolverines along with Bob Wiese, he related well to Bill. To him, Bill Daley was a mentor, a friend, and a football player who excelled when it counted.

Voted the most valuable player by his teammates that year was Bob Wiese, though he played in only three complete games that year and was only a junior. Bob was a sparkplug for the squad, always urging his teammates, always emerging as a natural leader, and always performing with tenacity on the field. Next year the team would vote him captain. No player carried more respect than Bob Wiese.

There were two unfortunate circumstances that affected returning football players in 1943. Julius Franks, All-American right guard for the Wolverines who played in all ten games the last season, and Tom Kuzma, principal left halfback for the 1942 squad, did not return. Both men, in separate cases, contracted tuberculosis during the 1943 summer. They spent six months in recovery at University of Michigan Hospital, much missed by the whole team. Both of them eventually recovered completely. Tom became a successful sales representative. Julius had a renowned career as a dentist in Grand Rapids, Michigan. Both men and their families became lasting friends of Don and Betty Lund.

Benny Oosterbaan was in his fifth year as Michigan's head basketball coach in 1943–44. Even at that time, he was famous in Ann Arbor, a three-sport, nine-letter winner considered by many to be the greatest athlete ever to wear the maize and blue. Benny was immensely respected by all who knew him for his fierce loyalty to the University of Michigan and its athletic traditions. He was also admired for his ability to analyze any game he played, coached, or observed, no matter what sport was involved. Like Fritz Crisler, Benny shared the same dedication to building good character, the same focus on winning with honor, and the same sense of pride in representing the university. But Benny was different from Fritz in other ways. Whereas Fritz was austere and sometimes aloof with his players, Benny was informal and friendly. While Fritz worked with red and blue pencils on a clipboard, Benny worked with gestures. While Fritz could bring out tears, Benny brought out grins. The players revered Crisler and called him "Coach." They loved Oosterbaan and called him "Benny." So it's not hard to imagine head basketball coach Benny Oosterbaan's approach to his team in 1944. "Here's how we'll do it, men, now: just go out and beat 'em."

Don Lund played guard in most of his basketball games that year; the others he jumped and played center. Elroy Hirsch had a reliable jump shot and played the forward slot. When the team traveled, they used two methods of transportation. The coach, the assistants, and the non-military players traveled by train and usually stayed overnight. The sailors and marines, regulated by a 48-hour curfew, went in cars and drove back to their West Quad ship after the game. Both arrangements were acceptable to all, without reservation. That's just the way it had to be. The biggest win that season was against Illinois, 52–45. The biggest loss was a two-point struggle, 44–46, against Purdue. The final conference standings showed Michigan in sixth place, a disappointing finish for Don and his teammates. But that was nothing compared to the disappointment the team felt a few months later, when the conference final standings for all sports in the Big Ten came out. The basketball team was the only one in all nine sports played by the University of Michigan that did not win the Conference Championship.

While Fritz Crisler might be formal and Benny Oosterbaan could be casual, head baseball coach Ray Fisher would be right between them. Everybody called him "Ray," but Coach Fisher had the ability to maintain intensity and distance as a teacher and mentor, while at the same time showing high personal interest in his players.

It wasn't unusual for Fisher to be seen one minute showing a pitcher how to throw, then seen the next minute chasing around practice fly balls with the outfielders. Don considered Ray Fisher a serious, hands-on type of coach, much like his high school coach Wayne Nestor. Ray also had good credibility as a former big league pitcher. His comments weren't taken lightly, especially by his junior class center fielder from Detroit Southeastern. In fact, Don idolized his baseball coach. To him, Ray Fisher was his ticket to becoming a well-rounded player. All Don needed to do was pay attention to Ray and work as hard as he could; the rest would fall into place.

Michigan won the Conference baseball championship in 1944, thanks to smart fielding and booming bats. Sixteen Wolverines hit over .300 that year. Don's most memorable performance, one that made the newspapers and earned him NCAA stardom, happened in the fourth inning of the second doubleheader game for the Western Conference championship against Purdue. Elroy Hirsch was pitching for the Wolverines. The Boilermakers had men at first and second base, with two outs. Batter Ray Murphy took Hirsch's first pitch for a ball, then hit a long line drive to left center field. Don raced to his right; the Michigan left fielder, Bill Gregor, ran straight back. It looked as if the two might collide. As the ball was looming toward them, Don hesitated, ready to let Gregor make the catch. But Bill didn't go for it. He stopped. Don was forced to lunge for the ball, and he was out of position to get his glove in front of it. He only had one way to make the grab. Reaching out with his bare right hand, he snagged the ball and held on to it, closing out the inning for the Wolverines. The stands erupted. Bill Gregor stood open-mouthed in disbelief. As Don trotted toward the dugout, his catch was given the highest compliment: there, on the mound, was Elroy Hirsch on his knees.

Captains all, champions all, 1944. Baseball acting captain
Don Lund jokes with five other Wolverines' captains. Left to right
are Phil Marcellus of Rockford, Illinois, golf; Charles Fries of Ann
Arbor, swimming; Bob Hume of Canonsburgh, Pennsylvania, track;
Alden C. "Jinx" Johnson of Grand Rapids, tennis; and John Greene
of Pittsburgh, Pennsylvania, wrestling. After this photo was taken,
Lund went on to lead Michigan to a win over Purdue and the
Western Conference Title. The other five captains pictured here
also presided over conference championships. Absent because of
military service is football captain Paul White, who helped his
team capture a first-place tie with Purdue. In 1943–44, the
Wolverines won the conference title in every sport except basketball.
(*Bentley Historical Library, The University of Michigan*)

He was lifting his arms up and down in a supplicating salute,
grinning from ear to ear!

Don's overall experience on campus in 1943–44 was one he
would always cherish. He played on two of Michigan's eight
conference championship teams, making him an integral part of
the greatest sports year in Wolverine history. In addition, tremendous contributions came to Ann Arbor through the sailors and

marines enrolled in the V-12 Program. They provided talented athletes from all around the country, which in turn increased the level of sports competition. Michigan fielded its strongest teams ever. And Don Lund was quickly becoming a three-sport phenomenon. He looked with eagerness to his senior year, his final as an NCAA amateur. He felt he was in the best physical shape of his life. It wasn't hard for him to imagine that things could even get better; in his heart he knew they would. He could hardly wait for next football season.

25

From Amateur to Professional

They called him "Dead Earnest." He was an old guy, probably in his seventies, at least. He weighed exactly 179 pounds. His head was shaved bald. He didn't smile, he didn't frown; he didn't even blink. His open mouth produced no words. "Dead Earnest" was, in fact, stone cold dead. He was a cadaver, laid out on a dissecting table at the University of Michigan's gross anatomy laboratory, one of many bodies placed there for the purpose of providing direct knowledge of how a human being was put together. The small group of physical education majors was assigned to study him, dissect him, and learn from him. They picked out the "Dead Ernest" name in order to lighten up whatever morbidity anyone felt. Notwithstanding, they approached the task seriously. Everyone on that small dissecting team, including Don Lund, showed the professional demeanor expected of them. They all worked hard; they all passed the course.

Don remembered "Dead Ernest" as the bus carried Betty and him back to Ann Arbor in the fall of 1944. That anatomy class had been one of his most interesting ones, so far. He particularly liked the labs and their hands-on approach to education, rather than the philosophical lecture halls. That's how he intended to focus himself once he became a physical education teacher. After all, he thought, why waste time describing to some kid how a football bounces when it makes more sense to just throw the ball down and let the kid see for himself? Just like the anatomy class, he thought. All the textbook words and all the drawings of a particular muscle or tendon could never be as effective as seeing it and feeling it in your hand. He would never be a lecture-type teacher, he vowed. Show them how, let them try it, and then show again. Make them practice until they got it right. That would be his way in the classroom, in the gym, or on the field. "Dead Ernest" taught him that.

Andrew and Marguerite Lund enjoy the University of Michigan's serene campus on a Sunday in September 1944. Their son and daughter-in-law, Don and Betty, had taken them for a late afternoon stroll. They never let Don forget that he came from the working class. (*Lund Family Collection*)

Don had only ten months of study to go before graduation in June. Once armed with the degree, he knew he would have no trouble getting a job. In fact, the war had greatly diminished the supply of male teachers in all subjects, all over the country. Consequently, the education market cried out for replacements. A fellow student in one of his education classes jokingly boasted to Don that he could pin a map of the United States on a wall, throw a dart at it, and get a job wherever it landed. Don knew he wasn't far from wrong. In the coming months, he was looking forward to finishing his last year of classes. All his required coursework was finished; he had to take only elective courses for the hours he needed to get the degree. Bachelor of Science in Physical Education: the title sounded good.

So what was he going to do after graduation? His first choice was to play professional baseball, though he wasn't sure how good his chances were. There were only sixteen teams in the major leagues, plus hundreds of minor league teams fielding thousands of ballplayers. And the Triple-A clubs were so close in player talent to the big leagues that players sometimes went back and forth between the two leagues like kids playing musical chairs. He wouldn't mind playing Triple-A ball, he thought, providing he got a shot at the big leagues. Triple-A towns loved their baseball teams, sometimes to the point of becoming very upset if they lost a key player to the major league team who "grabbed" him during a hot season. On the other hand, some ballplayers made good careers through the Triple-A leagues, spending many years as the hometown favorite. And they made a fairly good living at it. Don had no doubt that playing baseball for a living would be ideal: doing exactly what you want to do, having fun, and making money doing it. All he needed was somebody to notice him enough to make an offer.

Then there were the other two sports he played, basketball and football. Basketball, the first game he played seriously as a kid, was easily ruled out. It was primarily an amateur sport. As much as he loved the thrill of playing on the court, with screaming fans only a few feet away, he couldn't see himself becoming a pro. There was no organized basketball league playing in the big cities in 1944.*

---

* The Basketball Association of America was founded in New York City in 1946. Three years later it merged with the National Basketball League to form the National Basketball Association.

He couldn't make a living at it. So that left football. Football was definitely a possibility. Many University of Michigan football stars, such as Benny Friedman, had gone on to phenomenal careers in the National Football League. Also, the NFL teams were located in major cities, drawing more fans every season. When the war ends, he thought, talented athletes will join the NFL. There were definitely good career opportunities for him in pro football, which was bound to erupt in nationwide popularity.

He also thought of another job possibility after graduation: coaching college sports. There were many men he could name who went on to the coaching ranks after getting their degrees. In fact, Michigan's Athletic Department was continually getting requests for coaching job referrals, and the Michigan head coaches didn't hesitate to recommend certain players for specific jobs. Don, as a three-sport athlete, had an even better chance to get coaching referrals than most of his fellow players. He would definitely consider college coaching.

As the bus meandered into Ann Arbor's city limits, Don turned to Betty and confided his thoughts to her. When he finished, he asked her, "What would you like to see me do?"

She answered, "Well, Honey, if you become a teacher or a coach, we could live in the same place and have stability for a lot of years. If you play pro sports, we might have to move around from team to team. On the other hand, if you play pro baseball, you could teach during the off-season and we'd make more money than if you just had one full-time job. But whatever you decide, I'll go along with it. It's your choice."

He looked at her and smiled. That was Betty, completely supportive. No wonder he couldn't wait to marry her last year. Betty was his equilibrium; his best friend in the whole world.

This past summer had gone quite well, even though he wasn't able to spend the time as he really wanted to. He would like to have joined Ray Fisher in the summer Northern League, a high-level amateur league in Vermont. Ray coached a team there; the competition was strong. Don knew he could have learned a lot by playing in that league and wished for the chance. It was not to be, however. The Northern League was cancelled in 1944 because of the war. So he and Betty had vacated the house on Madison, went back to Detroit, moving in with his folks on Lycaste. Soon Don joined the Detroit sandlot leagues at their

Class A level and played for a team sponsored by Paris Cleaners. He enjoyed it, but sandlot ball even at its most competitive level just didn't match up to what he had at Michigan. Sandlot ball didn't have batting practice; it didn't have warm-up times; it didn't have individual performance coaching. The players on each team simply showed up and started the game. However, the players were great guys and he knew many of them from earlier sandlot days. On the whole, the Class A sandlot experience was fun. It kept him in shape and he enjoyed it. After all, he was playing ball in his hometown. That in itself was a plus.

Another thing Don pursued as soon as he arrived back home in Detroit was employment, which he easily found again through the Billy Rogell Baseball League. This time he was assigned to manage Northeastern Field at the corner of Warren and East Grand Boulevard, performing the same duties as he did the year before at the St. Clair Recreation Center. He readied the playing field, prepared and laid out the equipment, and made sure everything was ready before the first bunch of kids showed up. In June a pleasant experience happened, which made his job exceptionally worthwhile. One day a young man showed up and introduced himself as Cass Kwietniewski (he pronounced it "Viet-noov-ski" from Hamtramck. He was about six feet tall, showed a trim and muscular 175 pounds, and wore a faded baseball cap over light brown hair. His clothes included khaki pants, white short-sleeve shirt, and black high-topped sneakers. He sported an easy smile. He said he was seventeen, but he looked and acted much older. Don liked him right away.

Cass told him that he was under contract to the Chicago White Sox as an infielder. He was home for a while, expecting to be called up anytime. He needed to work out, and he wondered if Don would be willing to hit some balls to him and maybe even throw him some pitches before the teams arrived. Don eagerly agreed. And so they began a morning ritual for several weeks before Cass was ordered to report to the White Sox. Don would hit grounders to Cass all around the infield, trying his hardest to get the ball past him. Cass gobbled up everything, making the effort look easy. Don would hit short fly balls to left field; Cass was always under them. And when Cass stood at the plate, he hit every strike-zone pitch Don threw. When they weren't working out they talked baseball. They became friends, even though their only time spent together was at Northeastern Field. Don enjoyed every minute of the time he spent with Cass Kwietniewski.

Don's reverie about the summer months ended when the bus pulled up in front of the Michigan Union on State Street. He and Betty retrieved their luggage, three suitcases that contained practically everything they owned. They walked about four blocks east, past the Michigan League, a social activities building for women students, and arrived at their newly acquired apartment. Located near the corner of Geddes and Washtenaw, their living quarters comprised the entire third floor of a large house. It was completely furnished and not very expensive to rent. Both of them liked the location close to central campus and Don's classes. They also appreciated being far away from railroad noise and the clatter of freight trains, a complication they had to endure every night when they lived on Madison, about one hundred yards from the tracks.

Now, instead of being jolted by train whistles in the mornings, they were often greeted by beautiful carillon music emanating from the Burton Tower. The tower, a campus landmark named after a former university president, was also about one hundred yards away. The whole scene was nice for them. They were comfortable, happy, and looking forward to Don's senior year.

Don was admittedly the standout player on the 1944 football squad, particularly on defense. Voted by his teammates as "Most Valuable Player" at season's end, Don could look back with satisfaction on many circumstances that made the team special to him. They finished second to Ohio State, which played one less game than the Wolverines, but beat them by four points in a brutal struggle at Columbus. Some of the season games brought smiles as he remembered them. At the time Coach Crisler put him in at center against Marquette, he had never played center, but he played well, except for the first time Michigan had to punt the ball on fourth down. Don hiked the ball on one bounce to the kicker, who fortunately caught it and got the kick away safely. Michigan won the game, 14–0, but still the guys ribbed him about his "bounce pass" for the rest of the season.

Don finally found his chance to start at fullback when team captain Bob Wiese was transferred elsewhere for further naval training. Before that, he and Wiese had alternated between the center and fullback spots. Don and quarterback Joe Ponsetto

Newly elected Michigan football captains Don Lund, fullback, and Joe Ponsetto, quarterback, pose near the end of the season in November 1944. They replaced team captain Bob Wiese, who was called up for military service. Note the leather helmets and a lack of face guards or heavy padding. Also note Don's wedding ring. He never took it off. (*The Ann Arbor News*)

were named co-captains, and Don played the rest of the year at fullback. The team eventually finished with an overall 8-2 in the conference.

One of the most heartwarming aspects of the season had been the return of Howard H. Mehaffey to the line at left guard. Howard had first joined Wolverine football as a blocking fullback in 1938, gaining fame in the Ohio State game by taking out four OSU players at once, while Tom Harmon ran for a touchdown. Then trouble came to him in the next year. He contracted osteomyelitis in one of his legs and began a five-year battle against the disease. Most predicted that Mehaffey would never play football again. But Howard was determined. He remained on the

Don Lund's lifelong number was 33. He not only wore it at
Michigan, he also carried it at Detroit Southeastern High, as he's
shown above scoring a touchdown against Hamtramck in 1940.
The University of Michigan retired his baseball number, 33, in 1999.
(*Bentley Historical Library, The University of Michigan*)

perimeter of Michigan football, working as a spotter for radio
broadcasts of the games, all the time working hard in therapy.
Finally, during the 1944 season, Mehaffey began working out
with the team, wearing a specially designed aluminum leg brace.
When Coach Crisler finally allowed him to play, Mehaffey was
cheered by everyone as a shining example of courage and commitment. Howard Mehaffey was twenty-six years old when he
took the field again, in front of a mass of wartime fans who
adored their heroes. His counterpart on the team, right guard
Quentin Sickels, was seventeen. That remarkable nine-year age
difference between two linemen remains unique in Michigan
gridiron history. Howard Mehaffey went on to a distinguished
career as a dentist, later becoming president of the Michigan
Public Health Association. He became active in the university's

Don Lund posing as one of Michigan's basketball captains in 1945.
This was the only Michigan team in all seven sports during the
1944–45 season that did not win the Big Ten title.
(*Bentley Historical Library, The University of Michigan*)

alumni association, eventually serving on its volunteer Board of
Governors. He will always be revered as one of the most coura-
geous athletes to wear the maize and blue. Don Lund, the team's
MVP, would never forget him.

With the end of the football season, about a dozen members
of the team showed up at Yost Field House and reported to Coach
Bennie Oosterbaan for positions on the 1944–45 basketball
team. Even though a couple of games had already been played,
the final starting squad had not yet been selected. Bennie had
been waiting for the footballers to arrive. It didn't take him long

to make his selections; about half the prospects were cut within a couple of days. Don was picked to start as a guard. His best game that year was against Iowa, when he was leading scorer in the victory. The team wasn't a formidable contender that year, even though some improvements had been made from the previous year. Coach Oosterbaan made one striking change, though. There was no overall team captain. Instead, different players were named as "captain" for a particular game. Every starter served at least one game as a captain, and Don was captain for several games. As a result, no single player could claim the title as Michigan's basketball captain for 1944–45, but a lot of guys were co-captains. Nobody really knows why Bennie chose to organize the team that way. Maybe it was just his method of adding interest to a humdrum season, wherein the players gave their best efforts but couldn't seem to win many games. Don enjoyed his last basketball season, though, compiling many fine memories of friendships made through court competition. When he received his third basketball letter, with one more to go in baseball to make a clean sweep of nine letters in three sports, the local press called him Michigan's most versatile athlete. When a reporter asked him what he thought of the term, he simply laughed. "Did you say Michigan's most versatile athlete?" he asked. "Take a look at the man who's coaching our basketball team, then try to call me that. His name is Bennie Oosterbaan!"

The 1945 Wolverine baseball season marked the turning point in Don Lund's aspirations. He was the team captain; he was having his best year ever as a player, and the team was a cinch to capture its second Big Ten championship in a row. He no longer doubted that someone in professional baseball would notice him. All those thoughts about playing pro football, coaching, or full-time teaching were cast aside by the ultimate highs he found on the baseball diamond. When he put on that uniform and ran out to center field, he was like a little kid on a romp. Baseball was fun, not work. He was completely consumed.

The 1945 National Football League draft was held on April 8. The Chicago Bears drafted Don Lund in the first round. Don was initially surprised and immensely flattered. The Bears were a great team; they were owned and managed by George Halas, one of the founding fathers of the professional league. Being drafted by them was a great honor. Some of his friends urged

Head Baseball Coach Ray Fisher (*left*) and team captain
Don Lund prepare for the 1945 season. Michigan would
win the Big Ten title. (*The Ann Arbor News*)

him to accept it. The Bears ran his type of offense, they said;
he could be a star for them. His parents and Betty were non-
committal, wanting only the best for him; it had to be his own
decision. Ultimately it came down to one question: What did
he really want to do? Football was challenging, and he liked to
play it, but it didn't give him the same kind of special high he
felt in baseball. He liked the intensity of one-on-one when he
squared off against a pitcher. On the other hand, football had
presented him with a bona fide offer; nobody in pro baseball
had contacted him yet. But what did he really want to do? He
finally had to admit it to himself: he wanted to play baseball.
So Don turned down the Chicago Bears, expressing profound
thanks for their interest and confidence in him. The Bears were

gracious, as expected. Don Lund, first round draft pick, would never earn his livelihood in professional football.

Toward the end of April, Don started getting contacts from major league teams. One of the more interesting came from a Detroit Tigers' scout named Wish Eagen. Wish invited him to a Saturday game between the Tigers and the Chicago White Sox, telling him they would arrive early, watch the teams warm up, and meet some of the Tigers' players. Naturally, Don was eager.

As he was walking along the infield sidelines during batting practice at Briggs Stadium, Don recognized a familiar White Sox player, who was standing near the visitors' dugout fingering a couple of bats. It was Cass Kwietniewski, Chicago's regular second baseman. He had changed his name to Cass Michaels. Don walked over and said hello, and Cass remembered him right away from their practice sessions the previous summer at Northeastern Field. He greeted Don enthusiastically. Small talk quickly turned to Don's obvious question: "How do you like playing for the White Sox?"

Cass turned serious. "I owe the White Sox everything," he said. "They've really been good to me, ever since I got out of high school. The guys on the team are all right, too. I'm the youngest one playing regular, and they treat me like an equal. Good bunch of guys. I'm happy."

After a few more pleasantries, they parted, and Don walked back to join Wish Eagen in the stands. Wish didn't ask him about his random visits with players before the game, but the first time Cass came up to bat, Wish said to him: "You see that guy at the plate? He's from Detroit. He wishes he played for the Tigers." Don couldn't believe the Detroit scout had said that. Maybe Wish knows something I don't, he thought. Or maybe he's just saying that to impress me. Either way, Wish Eagen was wrong about Cass Michaels.

Don's final game day with the Wolverines was a double header against the Wisconsin Badgers. His performance was outstanding. In the first game, he produced three hits in four at-bats, one of them a home run. He slapped three hits out of five at-bats in the second game. His fielding was flawless. Michigan won both games without ever losing the lead. Don's final season tally showed him leading the team in RBIs with a batting average of .291. He had championed the squad all year. After the second game, he was standing in front of the Michigan bench chatting with his teammates when he was approached by a man who emerged from the stands. He introduced himself as George Sisler.

George Sisler! Don thought he must be dreaming. There was only one George Sisler: probably the best first baseman ever. Hall of Famer. Mechanical engineering grad from Michigan who played during college for Branch Rickey back around 1912–14. George Sisler! Wow!

Don tried not to show his awe at meeting one of the most famous big league ballplayers of all time. "Hi, Mr. Sisler, I'm glad to meet you." He could hardly contain himself.

Sisler explained he was visiting Ann Arbor specifically to watch Don play, and he was most impressed. He said he was now working on special assignments for Brooklyn Dodgers' owner Branch Rickey, his college coach and friend for many years. He wondered if Don would be willing to go with him to New York, to work out a little with the Dodgers and meet Mr. Rickey. He would like them to leave on Sunday. Don immediately said yes, and promised to meet George in front of Ann Arbor's Michigan Central Railroad Depot. Sisler congratulated him again on his day's performance, shook his hand, and walked away. Don was practically leaping out of his socks as he watched the legend leave.

26
Turning Professional

The midday sun was trying to peek around Brooklyn, New York's downtown buildings as two men walked determinedly along a sidewalk on Montague Street. One of them was George Sisler, fifty-five years old, a baseball legend, and six-year member of the Hall of Fame. The other was twenty-two-year-old Don Lund, eager, confident, and hopeful of a professional career in his chosen sport. Sisler wore a dark gray suit, white shirt, red tie, and a black fedora hat. Don was hatless, and the dark blue suit he wore over a white shirt and yellow tie was the only one he owned. It was Monday, June 11, 1945. They headed for a date with Don's destiny: 215 Montague, headquarters of the Brooklyn Dodgers and the office of owner/general manager Branch Rickey.

Their journey had started yesterday at the majestic Michigan Central Railroad Depot in Ann Arbor. Constructed of gray granite block in the American Romanesque style, the impressive depot was opened in 1886 with great ceremony from railroad dignitaries, townspeople, and University of Michigan officials. Inside the building, stained glass windows tucked high in the granite walls allowed the sun to paint its rays in rainbows. A highly polished red oak ceiling loomed overhead. At the north end of the lobby, an open mezzanine where passengers could buy sandwiches and refreshments seemed to hover between floor and ceiling. It was a familiar place to Don Lund. He and Betty would sometimes stroll around Ann Arbor on weekends, often ending up at the Michigan Central Depot to sit and watch the trains. Now, on this warm Sunday morning, he wished Betty had accompanied him to the train station. She had warmly declined, however, preferring instead to say goodbye at home and not wanting a lonely walk back to campus. He completely understood her feelings, but he missed her just the same.

As he approached the depot, Don grinned at the typical frenzied activities of incoming travelers. Many of them arrived in cars or pickup trucks of the 1920s or 1930s, since automobile production had stopped when the war began, and hadn't yet resumed to any great extent. The men in the crowd wore dark suits and hats, a study in sartorial consistency. Women and children were dressed tastefully in muted colors. All were scurrying about, hauling suitcases and travel valises, saying their good-byes to loved ones remaining behind in the cars, and making for the center entrance door as fast as they could. The entire scene, to Don, was an amusing one of constant motion, until he noticed one man standing alone next to the front door. George Sisler waved him over and welcomed him.

The two spent their waiting time by sipping soft drinks in the upper mezzanine inside the depot. Sisler explained their rail route, which took them north to Detroit, then south through Windsor, Ontario, and finally east through Canada to New York City. They would arrive that evening at Grand Central Station, and then spend the night at the St. George Hotel in Brooklyn. The plan called for Don to spend the next morning working out with the Dodgers at Ebbets Field. After that, he would go downtown with Sisler to meet with Mr. Rickey.

As the steam engine pulled its train of cars through the fertile landscape of southeastern Canada, Don marveled at the tranquil scene unfolding continually out his window. Corn fields showed foot-high early June sprouts; wheat, oats, and barley spread out everywhere in three-inch-high rows of thirsty grain. Here and there, cattle farms and horse ranches displayed their grazing animals. Don again wished Betty could be with him to share such beauty.

During the trip, Don easily formed a bond with George Sisler. The University of Michigan offered common experiences, though separated by a generation, and some of their conversations focused on mutual memories of the Ann Arbor campus. But their main topic was baseball. George's stories of his playing days made the long trip seem much shorter, especially when he talked about his contemporaries, such as Babe Ruth, Ty Cobb, Eddie Collins, Rogers Hornsby, and many others. Don was enthralled the whole time. Eventually, the conversation turned to Branch Rickey. Don already knew that Mr. Rickey had strong emotional ties to Ann Arbor, having coached baseball there and earning his law degree from the university. He also knew that Mr. Rickey founded the major league system of minor league "farm" clubs, making him one of the great innovators of the professional game. What he didn't know, though, was what kind of individual Mr. Rickey actually was. He asked George to tell him about the personal side of this fabled man who ran the Brooklyn Dodgers, knowing that he would probably hear glowing praise from someone who not only played for Mr. Rickey, but who also was a very close friend of his. And indeed George Sisler was lavish in praising Mr. Rickey, especially when it came to the man's deep religious convictions and high moral standards. It was a fact, said George, that Mr. Rickey was a Wesleyan Methodist who practiced his faith. Among other things, Mr. Rickey believed that Sunday was reserved for the Lord. He stayed home with his family on Sunday. He didn't conduct business on that day, and he never attended Sunday ballgames. Even during his playing and coaching years, Mr. Rickey stayed home on Sundays, much to the consternation of some of those with whom he worked. Don agreed with George that anyone who was that true to his principles was worthy of deep respect. Then George said something else about Branch Rickey that really got Don's attention. Mr. Rickey, he stated, believed that major league baseball was missing out on a vast pool of talent that now played in the many Negro leagues around the country. He felt the game of professional baseball would be vastly improved if that talent could be tapped. Moreover, he firmly believed that exclusion of an entire race of people in any human undertaking was morally wrong. Consequently, Mr. Rickey's favorite American president was the Great Emancipator, Abraham Lincoln. Sisler went on to say that Mr. Rickey had been intent on hiring one or more black players into the Dodgers' organization for quite some time and had won over these same feelings from the other two Dodgers' owners. He was now probably only a couple months away from making it happen.* After hearing all this about Branch Rickey, Don was totally impressed. He couldn't wait to meet the man who was doing so much to improve the game he loved.

The rest of the trip to Brooklyn went smoothly. At nine o'clock Monday morning, Don found his way to Ebbets Field

---

* In fact, Branch Rickey signed Jackie Robinson to a major league contract on August 28, 1945.

and presented himself to player/manager Leo Durocher, who had been told by the front office that Don was a prospect of interest, and that he should be allowed to work out with the team that morning. Durocher greeted him cordially, then turned him over to one of the coaches to get Don suited up in a practice uniform and ready for the morning's workout.

Don's time with the team that morning went extremely well, in his opinion. Shagging fly balls with the rest of the guys, he caught everything that came his way. When they let him have a turn at batting practice, he gave a good accounting, even hitting one into the lower left-field stands. The best part of the morning, though, was meeting and talking with some of the players. Second baseman Eddie Stanky was the first player to walk over and introduce himself when Don emerged from the dugout to start his workout. Stanky in turn introduced outfielder Goody Rosen. Rosen escorted him to the outfield, where he met Luis Olmo and Dixie Walker, among others.

All the players he met were great guys, in his opinion. He was pleased with the workout. Now he was ready to meet Mr. Rickey.

After a quick lunch at a diner near the ballpark, Don and George walked briskly toward Branch Rickey's office at 215 Montague. Neither man spoke as they neared their destination. Don's thoughts were focused on the bonus money he would ask for, provided he was offered a contract. Would $7,000 be out of line? Would Mr. Rickey just laugh at that figure? What about George Sisler? Would George be embarrassed if I asked for that much? He decided to just see how the conversation went. Maybe ask for less, rather than look greedy.

The building that housed Mr. Rickey's office was quite plain in appearance, much like the other office dwellings on the block. Since George had been there many times, he led the way up two flights of stairs to the second floor, then over to a frosted-window door with "Brooklyn Dodgers Baseball Company" stenciled on it in gold-colored letters. They entered and were greeted warmly by the pleasant smile of Branch Rickey's longtime executive secretary, Jane Ann Jones. Jane was short, pretty, and smartly dressed in a navy blue dress. Her dark brown hair was short and curly, just covering her ears. She appeared to be in her mid-thirties. Don saw a lot of intelligence in her eyes.

Dodgers rookie outfielder Don Lund, 1945. Is he thinking
about that signing bonus? (*Brooklyn Dodgers Archives*)

"Hello, Mr. Sisler. Hello, Mr. Lund," she said. "Did you have
a pleasant trip from Ann Arbor?"

"Yes, we did, Jane," George answered, "and we also had a
nice morning with the team. Is Mr. Rickey expecting us?"

Jane pointed toward the partially open door behind her. "He
sure is. Please go right in."

Branch Rickey stood up and walked around to the front
of his desk as George and Don walked in. Standing about six
feet tall and carrying a soft 200 pounds, he looked rumpled in
a wrinkled white shirt and blue polka dot tie. Big horn-rimmed
glasses covered half his face. There were streaks of gray in his

casually combed black hair. The crease in his dark gray pants meandered down to his dull black shoes. Compared to the only other sports executive Don knew, the sartorially tidy Fritz Crisler, this man looked sloppy. He made up for it, though, with his welcoming grin and friendly style. His smile was punctuated by a large, unlit cigar that stood straight out from the right corner of his mouth. Don was actually impressed. He had expected Mr. Rickey to be somewhat flamboyant, to have an ornate office filled with memorabilia. What he found was just the opposite. Rickey was impressive in his manner, not his dress. And he worked out of an everyday, ordinary office. His desk was large, but plain. His gray suit coat dangled on a simple wooden coat tree in the corner behind the desk. On the wall behind him were three photos: one of Abraham Lincoln, one of Leo Durocher, and one of George Sisler. The windows behind the desk faced Montague Street. On the wall across from his desk hung the most impressive piece in the entire office: a large blackboard that contained the team names for the entire Dodgers organization, including all the minor league farm clubs. A couple of small office chairs sat in front of the desk; a large upholstered chair stood to one side. To a visitor, Branch Rickey's office would be clearly seen as a place to simply conduct business.

Stepping forward from his desk, Rickey said a big hello to both of them and eagerly pumped their hands. He guided Don to the upholstered chair, motioned for George to sit in one of the other chairs, then went around his desk and slid comfortably into his chair. There was no need to "break the ice." Rapport was immediate.

Their conversation quickly became focused on memories of Ann Arbor and the University of Michigan. Rickey talked about his law school years and the good times he enjoyed coaching Wolverine baseball, speaking fondly of his campus days. He praised George Sisler until the Hall of Famer began to turn red around his ears. Sisler in turn spoke in glowing terms about his education at Michigan. They all laughed when Rickey said, "Just think, George, if it turned out you couldn't hit the ball past the mound, you could have been a mechanical engineer!"

And then Rickey turned serious. "I'm sure you know you're here because we want you to play for the Brooklyn Dodgers," he said to Don. "I'm also sure you've put some figures together in your head. So tell me, son, what do you have in mind?"

Don froze at the question, forgetting all his previous thoughts about the subject of money. Without thinking, he blurted out, "I want a seventy-five hundred dollar bonus and a major league contract." He couldn't believe he had said that. He felt stupid. Then he couldn't believe Mr. Rickey's response.

"OK. We'll give you your bonus check right now. Your pay will be six hundred a month. But we want you back here, ready to play in three weeks. You'll report on July third." Rickey extended his hand, and the shocked young nine-letter winner simply grinned and shook it. The rest of their conversation was a blur to him. He signed the contract. On his way out, Jane Ann Jones handed him a check made out to him for seven thousand five hundred dollars.

George had arranged for him to fly back to Ann Arbor the next morning, rather than take the train. As they headed back to the St. George Hotel, Don couldn't help wondering about Mr. Rickey's immediate acceptance of his bonus demand. Maybe he should have asked for more, he thought. Just maybe …

He had no way of knowing that in just a little over two months, Branch Rickey would sign Jackie Robinson to a contract that would revolutionize the entire world of big league baseball. And he would pay Jackie a bonus amounting to less than half of that which he had just issued to Don Lund.

The following morning George Sisler said goodbye to Don at LaGuardia Airport. "You're a credit to Michigan, Don. Let's hope yesterday was the start of a great career for you."

Don pumped the Hall of Famer's hand. "I hope so, too, George. Thanks for being so nice." With that, the two parted and Don went into the LaGuardia terminal to face his first flight in an airplane. He would be flying on American Airlines, nonstop between New York and Detroit. After checking in at the ticket counter, he grabbed an American Airlines brochure and sat down to read it while he waited for the plane. The more he read, the more excited he became. In about four hours after takeoff, he'd be landing at Detroit City Airport. Talk about fast travel! The plane would be a Douglas DC-3, reliable and safe, the type our military used during the war. It cruised at 170 miles per hour. How about that?

As he walked with the other passengers across the tarmac, Don noticed the sleek lines of the waiting DC-3, painted silver with "American Airlines" lettered in dark blue along the fuselage. To him, the plane seemed ready to pounce in the air. It crouched with its tail down on one wheel, while two powerful engines atop broad wings stood on two wheels just below the cockpit. Kind of like a defensive tackle, he thought, anticipating the snap in a three-point stance. After boarding, Don found himself in a window seat near the back of the cockpit, behind the right wing, perfect for viewing the countryside, he thought. When he heard the right engine start to come alive, he looked out to see a flash of flame and dark smoke bursting from the rear of the engine, combined with a deep roar as the pistons engaged and the propeller turned. He was so startled he almost bounded from his seat. Then he noticed that no one else on the plane seemed at all concerned. He looked back out the window and saw the engine running smoothly with no smoke trailing from it, although its power was slightly shaking the plane and its noise was almost deafening. As the left engine started the same way, Don realized that the flash and initial smoke were expected and relaxed with the rest of the passengers. The plane taxied to the runway and took off with ease.

The flight to Detroit was smooth. Even the constant engine drone soon became merely background noise and went unnoticed. Don was able to look down on the same pastoral scenes he witnessed a couple of days before from the train window, marveling at the different perspective from high above. When they flew above downtown Detroit, his gaze focused on the tallest building, the Penobscot, and then on Belle Isle with its famous bridge named after World War II General Douglas MacArthur. He fondly remembered his high school baseball games as he picked out the aerial view of Belle Isle's ball fields.

But a few minutes later, when the plane descended for its approach over Detroit's East Side to the city airport at Connor and Gratiot, Don was thrilled at what he saw: his old neighborhood and his parent's house on Lycaste! It wasn't hard to spot. The Edison smokestacks loomed up like seven huge cannons, belching smoke in a straight line toward the river. Using them as a vantage point, he simply allowed his eyes to wander around the nearby area until they zoomed right in and found his boyhood home. He couldn't wait to tell his folks!

The landing seemed effortless, just a couple of loud chirps as the main wheels touched down, followed by a third as the rear wheel settled. During the short taxi to the terminal, Don reflected on his three-day trip and felt extremely pleased. He was now one of the Brooklyn Dodgers. He had in his pocket the largest check he had ever seen. He had a degree and irreplaceable memories from Michigan, and he was married to the finest woman he'd ever met. He was never happier than right now, he realized, and things could only get better.

The short bus ride to Lycaste Avenue brought tears of pride and hearty congratulations from Marguerite and Andy, followed by one of the best home-cooked dinners Don had put away in a long time. Then he took the long bus ride to Ann Arbor, where another home-cooked dinner waited with Betty at the Geddes Avenue apartment. Once there, he swept her in his arms. Their reunion was better than superb, Don remembered more than sixty years later.

Over the next twenty days, Don and Betty made arrangements to transition from Ann Arbor to New York. Since Don was confident he could find work somewhere on campus after the end of the major league season, they decided to keep the Geddes apartment. Moreover, Argus Camera had promised Betty her old job back whenever she wanted it. There was more than enough incentive to return to Ann Arbor in the fall.

Around the end of June, a reporter from the *Ann Arbor News* came around to inquire about Don's contract status, and he then followed up with a nice article about Don's signing with former Wolverine coach Branch Rickey. The piece went on to review Don's three-sport, nine-letter achievements both at Michigan and Southeastern. Don and Betty were happy with what the reporter wrote; many of their friends clipped out the article and gave it to them. They all considered it a fine tribute to Don's illustrious college and prep career.

On June 29, the couple went to New York by train, with tickets provided by the Dodgers. They checked into the St. George Hotel and went apartment hunting, finding a small furnished place near Ebbets Field in only one day. By July 3, an extremely

Betty frequently posed with an Argus camera for magazine
ads when she worked for the company in Ann Arbor.
This photo was taken in 1944. (*Argus Corporation*)

excited Don Lund was more than eager to start his career. He
showed up early, found his locker, dressed in the uniform hanging
in it (it fit fine), and just hung around as players arrived. Eddie
Stanky remembered him; so did Goody Rosen and Luis Olmo.
He had a nice chat with a right-handed pitcher named Clyde
King, who seemed to have a lot of baseball savvy, and whom he
liked immediately. Manager Durocher frowned his way into the
locker room and went right into his office, calling Don in a few
minutes later. "You're a college kid, aren't you?"

Don nodded. "Yes, Sir, Michigan."

Durocher didn't smile. "Well, let's see what you can do. We'll try to get you in a few games this week."

As Don walked out of Durocher's office, he remembered he hadn't played in nearly a month. Was he ready to step right in?

As it turned out, he wasn't ready. The layoff between his last Michigan game and now had taken too much off his edge at the plate. And he didn't step right in, either. Durocher made him sit most of the time that first week. He went to the plate four times, producing three outs and drawing a base on balls. The only redeeming factor was getting some dugout chatter time with some of the other players.

At the end of the week, Mr. Rickey approached him after a game and said, "Don, it's obvious to Leo and me that you could use some more seasoning. We're sending you to St. Paul right away. Maybe we should have started you there in the first place."

Don agreed. "Thanks, Mr. Rickey, I'll get packed."

It didn't take long for Don and Betty to quit the Brooklyn apartment. They didn't have many possessions, and they didn't have a lease to worry about. Now they knew what the landlord meant when he told them he wasn't about to make a ballplayer sign a lease; he had said it wasn't worth it. Players were always coming and going. So off the couple went to St. Paul, Minnesota, to join the Triple-A league St. Paul Saints. Train tickets were furnished by the Dodgers. It was the middle of July 1945.

By the time they arrived in St. Paul, Don was actually looking forward to joining the team. After all, he knew he wasn't stepping down much in terms of competition. Triple-A ball was nearly as good as the major leagues, thanks to there being lots of fine ballplayers in the country and only sixteen big league teams. Besides, the Saints were a top-quality team, and in the hunt for the league title this year.

Finding a place to stay proved easy, thanks to a couple named Lester and Margaret Anderson. Les worked in the Education School at the University of Minnesota. He was also doing graduate work in Ann Arbor that summer, and he and Margaret thought that tenants in their home would offer company to Margaret in her husband's absence. So they advertised, the Lunds responded, and the deal was made. Afterward, Margaret told them, "I wasn't very happy with the idea of renting to a ball-player, but when I saw the two of you walking down the block holding hands, I knew you were all right." As a matter of fact, the Andersons and the Lunds would become very close friends for many years. Even during that first summer in St. Paul, Margaret Anderson trusted her tenants enough to let them babysit while she visited Les in Ann Arbor. Over the years, she would grow close to this ballplayer and his wife, like her own family.

Don played out the rest of the 1945 season with the Saints, hitting .265 and playing defense like he owned every blade of grass in right field. His one home run was a crusher in the center-field upper seats. He would have had a second, but the ball sailed high above the left field bleachers, hit a sign atop the Coliseum Bowling Alley next door, and bounced back onto the field for a ground-rule double, driving in a run but keeping him at second base. The Saints won the game. One thing that happened that year, which greatly matured him for the professional game, came by way of friendly advice from the Saints' long-time catcher Buddy Lewis. Not to be confused with the Washington Senators' John Kelly (Buddy) Lewis, who was having a great year at third base in the nation's capital, the Saints' Buddy Lewis was a career Triple-A catcher who knew more about game strategy than most players in general, even big leaguers.

One day, when the Saints were ahead by nine runs with the game close to ending, Don stole third base.

Afterward, Lewis called him aside and said, "When you stole that base with the game wrapped up, you rubbed it in to 'em. This ain't like college, Don, where you play about sixteen games and go all out every time or the coach gives you hell. This season plays 154 games. You'll see these guys a lot. And they got memories like elephants. Rub it in like that, and the next time they see you at the plate, they'll put you on your ass!"

Don felt like a door had just been opened. He couldn't believe how naive he was. He couldn't thank Buddy Lewis enough, knowing that the catcher was going out of his way to show him the kind of friendship a lot of other players wouldn't. He would never forget Buddy's counsel. You just didn't show up your fellow professionals; you treated them with respect. Besides, someday you might be playing with them as teammates. Meeting Buddy

Lewis this early in his career, he thought, was an absolute stroke of luck!

Don's most memorable event that summer, though, had nothing to do with baseball. He and Betty were walking around their St. Paul neighborhood one evening after dinner. The Saints had won that day, Don had gone two for four, and he was feeling pretty good.

Betty held his hand as she started a random conversation. "It's pretty nice in this town, just the two of us, isn't it?"

He allowed that it was.

"Only there aren't two of us."

"Huh?" He looked at her, "What's that?"

"There are three of us."

"Who's visiting?"

Betty stopped and looked up at him. "Nobody's visiting, Honey. There are three of us because I'm going to have a baby!"

Don wasn't sure he'd heard right. Then it sunk in, and he practically fell down, he was so happy. "Wow!" He was speechless. All he could say, with a grin as wide as the sidewalk they stood on, was "Wow!"

The baby was due at the end of March, which would be during spring training. Don was sure he could work out a short break for the trip back home and the delivery.

When the season ended, the couple moved back to their Geddes Road apartment in Ann Arbor. True to its word, Argus Camera had Betty's secretarial job waiting for her.

Don didn't have to look far on campus to find a job. In fact, he didn't have to look around at all. One of the first things he did was stroll over to the Intramural Building just to see if some of his friends were there. He hadn't been through the front door more than a few steps when IM director Earl Riskey called out to him, "Hey, Don, got a minute?" The legendary paddleball inventor then proceeded to hire Don on the spot, as a swimming pool lifeguard and program supervisor. He was much needed, Riskey said, because the V-12 sailors used the pool in shifts all day. Someone from the university was needed to serve their needs. Don accepted immediately and started work that morning. The job was fun, and somewhat challenging.

The V-12 Program mandated swimming, regardless if the sailors liked it or not. And many of them didn't like it, so they would find other things to do, such as stacking towels. Some would even try to hide out behind benches or crates, like the freshman he found one day sitting on the floor behind a bench. He recognized him as a first-year member of the football team. "You OK?" Don asked him. "I'm Don Lund. I work here."

"Pete Elliott," the freshman said. "I'm in the V-12 unit, but I just went through a tough football practice, and I honestly don't feel like jumping in that pool."

Just then, Don saw a chief petty officer walk in through the door. Don ran over to him. "Hey, Chief," he said, "can you spare a minute? I'd like you to approve these new towels we just got in." As he followed the chief into the locker room, Don stole a glance over his shoulder and saw Pete Elliott disappear into the pool. He didn't know it then, but Pete Elliott would go on to muster out of the V-12 Program and remain at the university. Competing all four years, he would become the most lettered athlete ever produced at Michigan, winning 12 letters overall in football, basketball, and golf. Pete and Don would become close, lifelong friends. And Don, always the kidder, would never let Pete forget about that time in the IM Building when he saved a certain sailor's hide.

27
Dialogue

"That's a good story about you and Pete Elliott at the IM Building," I said. "I'll bet you two still have some laughs over that one."

The old coach grinned. "Oh, yes. We rib each other all the time. He's got some good ones on me, too."

"Like what?"

"You'll have to ask him."

I knew better than to pursue that one. We were in his kitchen this time, sitting at a glass-topped table that could easily serve four for lunch. The food preparation area featured a U-shaped counter that extended around two walls and jutted out into the middle of the room. The refrigerator and other major appliances ran along the opposite wall, completing the rectangular space. The room itself was gleaming and spotless, like the rest of the place. The man wouldn't put up with anything less, probably because Betty had been that way. He liked to say she trained him well. Tucked in a corner was a built-in desk, which he used for paying bills and keeping up with correspondence. He didn't have a computer; he didn't want one, either. He still frequently received requests for his baseball card and his signature, coming from all around the world. The fan would usually include a stamped, return envelope, to guarantee Don's sending it back. Sometimes the return envelope wouldn't have a postage stamp on it. That didn't matter to Don; he just put his own stamp on it and mailed the signed card back. No big deal.

I returned to the subject: "You're still pretty close to Pete Elliott and his brother Bump, aren't you?"

"Absolutely," he said. "There's nobody else like them, and there's no set of brothers better than them, either. You know, they played together at Michigan in 1946, but then they played against each other when Bump coached Michigan and Pete coached Illinois. They both raised fine families; I could go on and on about Bump and Pete."

"Didn't Bump play on the Purdue baseball team that lost the conference championship to Michigan in 1944, the game where you made that bare-handed catch?"
DL: "Yes, but I didn't know him then. Bump says he saw the catch, though. He says if he had been the batter, I wouldn't have a hand left."

We both laughed. I changed the subject.

"Coach, you finished up your years at Michigan earning nine letters and three freshman numerals. You were a team captain in all three sports. You worked in a printing factory all four years at night to pay expenses, and you earned enough credits to get your degree and graduate on time. To me, that's amazing!"
DL: "Well, don't be amazed. A lot of people worked and went to school at the same time. Many also played sports. Remember, all of us had come through the Depression with our families. We were taught to survive. I just did what I had to do, like lots of others in those years."

"OK, but you can't deny you excelled. The records prove it. Take, for instance, the nine letters you earned. Today's players can earn a letter by virtue of participation and working hard for the team all season, regardless of playing time on the field. Was it that way for you?"
DL: "No. Fritz Crisler was tough about awarding letters. You had to play a minimum number of minutes or score points to get a letter. It really meant something. Same thing when Bump coached. When Bo Schembechler came here, he changed all that with a different philosophy. I wouldn't say that either system was better, just different. Bo put his players first; so did Fritz. But each coach had his own separate style."

"Let's move on to Don Lund, the college graduate turning pro baseball player in June 1945. You had to feel pretty good about yourself back then."
DL: "Well, I don't know about that. They say feeling good about yourself can lead to trouble. I guess I felt OK, though. By the

way, I missed graduation, since I was in New York at the time. They mailed my degree to me later."

"Are you saying you got a mail-order degree from the University of Michigan?"
That got a big laugh, and a "Yea, right!" from the coach. I went on.

"That was quite a summer for you. From Ann Arbor to Brooklyn to St. Paul, where Betty tells you she's pregnant, then back to Ann Arbor. Full circle in a couple of months. And you kept up your game performance."
DL: "I really liked St. Paul. Great fans, great people. They told me I fit it with my Nordic looks—you know, blond hair, blue eyes, stuff like that. One funny thing I remember was when we played Minneapolis, we'd dress in our own locker room, then hop on the bus in our uniforms and go across the river to play the game. They'd do the same thing. We never saw each other's visitors' lockers!"

"So, back in Ann Arbor, you work at the Intramural Building, Betty works at Argus Camera, the war ends, you have lots of good friends to enjoy during the off-season, and pretty soon it's time for spring training. Are you ready to talk about that?"
DL: "I'm ready to talk about the whole year. Nineteen forty-six was, well, it was the most unusual year for Betty and me you'd ever imagine. It started with the Dodgers' spring training in Daytona Beach, Florida ..."

28
Here Comes Susan!

"Excuse me, please! Whoops, sorry! Pardon me!" He couldn't believe how many people were in the corridors. What's more, he couldn't believe how big the maternity floor was. It was March 20, 1946. Don was in Detroit's St. Joseph Hospital, fresh off the plane from spring training in Daytona Beach. He was searching for Betty and his newborn daughter, walking fast and swerving around the white-clad nurses, various support staff, and visitors who scurried about as they took advantage of the limited visiting hours. Just as he squeezed between a pair of guys who seemed to be moving too slowly in front of him, he heard, "Don, where are you going?" It was Betty's voice.

He looked back to the open doorway he had just passed. There she was, propped up in a bed, holding a bundle in her arms and grinning at him. He practically leaped into her room.

As he looked at Betty holding their infant girl, Don was nearly overwhelmed with emotion. Betty had just undergone nearly twenty-three hours of labor and delivery. She wore no makeup, her hair wasn't combed, and the large hospital bed made her seem like a tiny bundle of cloth holding an even tinier bundle of blanket. But he had never seen anything more beautiful, more enchanting, than his dark-haired woman with those familiar sparkling eyes, who smiled with a look of love that said it all. He kissed her tenderly as a small tear rolled down his cheek. He tried to speak, but the words weren't there. He could only return her loving gaze.

Finally, Betty broke the spell. "Would you like to see your daughter?" She carefully removed the baby's blanket.

Don was again awestruck; he still couldn't speak. Betty handed up his daughter as Don's heart filled with emotions he had never experienced. Now he knew what it felt like to have a child. There was no question in his mind that this tiny baby girl, soon to become a child, then to become a teenager, then to become an adult, would occupy his most precious thoughts for as long as he drew breath. As he held his daughter in his left arm, he carefully examined her. Then he smiled. His emotions escalated, replaced by that special sense of pride and happiness known by new fathers around the world. He and Betty had created a jewel!

"Yep," he chuckled, "She's got all her fingers and toes; I guess we can keep her."

Betty laughed with him as he gently handed back the baby. "Remember how we agreed to name the baby Susan if it turned out to be a girl?" she asked. "Do you still like that name?"

"Susan it is," he answered. Then he gazed at his daughter's sleeping face. "How about that name, little girl?" The baby yawned, stretched her arms, and Susan Elizabeth Lund, nine pounds, seven ounces and nineteen inches long, said hello to her parents.

Don stayed with Betty and Susan until visiting hours were over. They would be released in about a week. The plan was for them to spend a few weeks with Andy and Marguerite on Lycaste, then travel to join Don after spring training, when he got settled in for the regular season. Meanwhile, he had to get back to Daytona Beach. So far, he thought, things had been going quite well.

Thankfully, they had been able to sublet their Geddes Road apartment for the summer. They enjoyed that third-floor place, and they hadn't wanted to let it go. It was spacious, it was close to Michigan's campus and its cultural life, it was owned and operated by nice resident landlords, the rent was reasonable, and most of their friends lived nearby. Besides, they planned to come back in the fall, since Earl Riskey had invited Don to return to his off-season job at the Intramural Building.

The sub-tenants were a wholesome couple named George and Norma Kiesel. George was a native Detroiter and an All-City center from Northwestern High School who had joined Don at Michigan in 1941. The two of them became friends during freshman football, where eating mud and getting knocked around by the varsity was a way of life. Both earned freshman football numerals, followed by sophomore football letters the following season. Then their paths separated; Don stayed at Michigan, while George enlisted in the Marine Corps. George mustered out in 1946, married Norma, and returned to the University of Michigan to finish his degree in education and play football for the Wolverines.

It hadn't taken long for George to hook up with his old pal Don Lund. He and Norma were quite happy to sublet the Lunds' apartment through the spring and summer of 1946. George would earn his education degree and then move on to a successful career in the Jackson, Michigan, public schools as a teacher, a football coach, and as principal of Jackson Parkside High School. George and Norma Kiesel would remain lifelong friends with Don and Betty.

Don had to get back to the Dodgers' spring training. So he took Betty and the baby to his parents' house on Lycaste, where they would wait until he sent for them to join him in Brooklyn. Two days of railroad rides, first on the C&O, whose motto was "Never a ripple on a glass of water," and then on SAL's "Orange Blossom Special" brought him back to Daytona Beach. When he checked in at camp, he noticed how out of shape he was.

This was his first time since Foch Junior High that playing baseball hadn't been preceded by playing basketball and football. He was a three-sport athlete; that's how he stayed in shape all year around. Sure, he had run laps and exercised every day at the IM building, but that wasn't the same as the intense team competition played at Michigan's Division 1 level. He missed that in a big way. Now he was reduced to playing only one sport, albeit his favorite. So he set his mind to work harder than he ever had before. It might be a long spring.

The first thing Don noticed as training camp began was that the Dodgers' team spirit was extremely high, thanks to several star players coming back from military service. Shortstop Pee Wee Reese was returning from three years in the Navy; outfielder Gene Hermanski was back from the V-12 Program; and outfielder Pete Reiser came back after two years in the Army. These guys would make a difference, Don thought. The returning servicemen were bringing spring training back to the high level it was before the war.

Don had no trouble getting to know his teammates. Eddie Stanky, known by the baseball world as "the Brat," was nice to everybody, especially the newcomers. Babe Herman, who had replaced Don in right field last season at Ebbets Field, laughingly recalled how he had let a ball go through his legs near the wall, then turned around for the bounce and let the ball come back through his legs again. "I wish I had your glove," said Babe. "And I wish I had your bat," Don retorted. Babe's hitting had made him famous. He still holds Dodgers' records that may never be broken.

Don also got to know some of the other new players, particularly outfielder Carl Furillo and catcher Bruce Edwards. One guy Don really liked was shortstop Gene Mauch. The two of them roomed together throughout spring training, and Don learned much from Gene about game strategy. He didn't know it at the time, but Gene Mauch would go on to a renowned career as a major league manager, becoming famous for his bench strategy that stressed the "little things." And his roommate Don Lund would someday put what he learned from Gene into good use, when he himself would became a successful coach and manager.

At the end of spring training, Durocher divided the squad into A and B teams for playing the New York Yankees, who were also divided into teams A and B. The teams played each other in a series of "road games" in various small cities and towns along the way up the East Coast to New York. The A teams played each other in the more populous stops along the way; the B teams, riding other trains, competed at whistle stops.

Don was on Durocher's B team, where he expected to be. He had struggled at the plate throughout spring training, even though his fielding had been flawless. Durocher carped to him about his batting from time to time, saying things like, "They teach you that swing in college?" Early in spring training, one of the outfielders told Don that Durocher didn't like college players. Don figured there was nothing he could do about that, even if it was true. He decided not to let it bother him.

As soon as he arrived back in New York, Don was optioned back to the St. Paul Saints. Undaunted, he showed up in Minnesota and jumped right into the lineup. He was cheered by fans who remembered him from last season. He was happy to be back. He sent for Betty and Susan. He found a place for them to live on Wabeshaw Street, a one-room apartment at the cheapest price he could find, $20 a month. He should have kept looking.

Although the apartment was clean and convenient to the ballpark, it was way too small for more than one person to occupy. The double bed took up much of the space. The kitchen consisted of a sink and shelves along one wall. The size of the bathroom would allow him to simultaneously shower and brush his teeth at the sink. Nevertheless, he figured the three of them could get by until he found a bigger place. After all, the rent was a steal. So off he went to the St. Paul depot to await the train from Detroit. When it arrived, Betty stepped down as one of the first passengers off. She carried Susan in her right arm. Don rushed toward her, feeling like a teenager with wings. He had missed them terribly.

As he hurried closer, he noticed Betty's smile and her familiar flashing eyes. The baby was awake. The woman next to his wife seemed to be walking awfully close to her, he thought. Plus, she was looking his way. So he glanced back at her; then he looked again and gasped. Walking in step next to Betty, his mother was grinning like a grand-slam game winner!

On the way home, Marguerite confirmed that she had been concerned about Betty bringing baby Susan all by herself to St. Paul. Andy agreed it would be better if Marguerite went along, so arrangements were made. Plans called for Don's mother to stay for about two weeks, all the while helping Betty with the infant. Of course, no one had told Don about this before he rented the miniature apartment. He therefore wasn't too anxious to show it to them.

Much to his relief, neither woman complained when they entered the place, much beyond a gasp from Betty and an "Oh, my!" from his mom. Susan couldn't have cared less. Anyway, life became somewhat bearable for them in that cramped place on Wabeshaw Street, even if Don, Betty, and Marguerite had to share the same bed, each taking turns to crawl up and soothe the nighttime woes of a baby girl. Don took to getting up in the wee hours to walk over to the ballpark and look for a night watchman to let him in early. If that worked, he'd curl up somewhere and snooze.

The first thing Betty purchased was a used four-wheel baby buggy. It wasn't long before one wheel fell off somewhere and disappeared, but the determined Betty pushed her baby around anyway, balancing the buggy on three wheels. The neighbors admired her for it. Nevertheless, it took Marguerite only three days to tire of living like a sardine. She anxiously told them she needed to get back to Andy. Her son and daughter-in-law sympathetically agreed. So after a tearful farewell at the train depot, Marguerite went back to her husband, leaving Don and Betty with fond memories and a lifetime of hilarious stories about the "Cramped Camp on Wabeshaw Street."

Around the middle of July, Don received a call from Branch Rickey, telling him he was being transferred to the San Diego Padres. Tickets were being held for him at the train station. After quick good-byes, the Lunds headed west to the fabled sunshine of California. They got as far as Cheyenne, Wyoming, before a railroad employees' strike stopped them in (or on) their tracks.

Things weren't too bad on the train until their second day of waiting. Then everyone became claustrophobic. Even though the porters were nice and their fellow passengers were fairly patient, Don and Betty simply had to get out and walk around. Around noon, they found a little restaurant not too far from the tracks and had roast beef sandwiches, which tasted a little strange but were also being consumed by several other patrons. They dismissed any concerns, finished lunch, and went back to the train. They didn't get sick until that evening.

All that night it was back and forth to the restroom for both of them. Don told someone he needed to get better in order to feel like dying, but the joke was wasted when he immediately jumped toward the toilet. Betty held up like the trooper she was, but the food poisoning took its toll on both of them. They stayed in bed most of the next day, while several women passengers took turns looking after Susan. They didn't recover until about twenty-four hours after they ate those sandwiches. The only good thing was when they finally were able to get out of bed, the railroad strike was over and the train was chugging them toward Los Angeles, where they would meet the Padres on the road, playing the Los Angeles Angels and the Hollywood Stars.

After checking into the hotel where the Padres were staying, Don took a bus to Wrigley Field, home of the Hollywood Stars, and joined his team. Over the next five games against the Stars and the Padres, he played in the lineup several times and gave a good accounting, especially on defense. He felt he was making a contribution to the team.

On a game-off day, Don and Betty decided to take Susan on a bus tour of Hollywood, to see the sights they had only read about. One of the tour stops was the famous Hollywood Bowl, where celebrities performed, and where the Los Angeles Philharmonic Orchestra played to sellout crowds. As they strolled around, Betty became aware that Susan needed a diaper change. They looked around and saw that the only appropriately level spot to lay Susan down to be changed, other than the bare ground, was the stage itself. So that's where she changed the diaper.

Years later, Susan would be talking to a friend who had just returned from a vacation in Hollywood. "We went to the Hollywood Bowl," her friend said, "and we saw the Bob Hope Show. It was terrific."

"I was at the Hollywood Bowl one time," Susan answered. "As a matter of fact, I was onstage."

Her friend looked incredulous. "Were you performing?"

Susan grinned, "Oh, yea. And it must have been pretty good, too, because they changed my diapers!"

After the final game with the Angels in that series, the Padres went back to San Diego. Don immediately sought leads for renting an apartment, since the team wouldn't pay for more than a couple of days in a hotel room. The best approach, he decided, was to take a taxi around town. He, Betty, and the baby hailed a cab and told the driver just to drive around.

"Don't you have a destination?" the driver asked.

"Well, we're looking for an apartment to rent," said Betty. "We thought we'd just ride around town and look things over."

The driver pulled over to the curb, stopped the taxi, and said, "I have an apartment for rent. It's big enough for the three of you. Would you like to see it?" Don said they would. Two hours later, they were tenants of the taxi driver, who turned out to be a strong Padres fan. No charge for the taxi ride, plus a slight break on the rent. The Lunds moved in that evening.

For the next month, Don played in the outfield for the Padres, living out the "good-field, no-hit" blues at first, but knocking in a few runs from time to time. He enjoyed playing under Manager Pepper Martin, whom he saw as a solid, good guy. Martin was a couple of years into retirement from his playing days with the St. Louis Cardinals. All the players knew Pepper as a former World

Series whiz, who played both infield and outfield positions for the Cardinals over a thirteen-year career, plus pitched for them in his early years. Pepper Martin carried a lot of respect from everyone on the team.

One day during practice, Martin called him over and told him that Bill Starr, the team's owner and general manager, wanted to see him. Don looked forward to the meeting. He knew that the Brooklyn-born Starr was a good friend of Mr. Rickey's, and that both men shared some of the same visions for the future of baseball. In fact, Don had heard rumors that Bill Starr was also interested in tapping Negro League talent to improve overall competition.* Don went quickly to the general manager's office and was invited in. Starr stayed seated behind his desk and looked at Don with expressionless eyes and a polite smile.

Don stood in front of the desk. "Hello, Mr. Starr. You wanted to see me?"

"Sure, Don," he said. "Pack your stuff and get ready to move. Mr. Rickey called. He's sending you to Fort Worth. Your tickets are already at the train station."

"OK," Don answered. He turned around and walked out.

Within two hours, the three Lunds were on a train heading to Fort Worth, Texas. Don only knew a few things about the Fort Worth Panthers. They were one of Mr. Rickey's flagship minor league teams. The great Rogers Hornsby had managed them before the war. They played at LaGrave Field, one of the best facilities in the minor leagues, and this year they had a fence-busting centerfielder named Duke Snider. The closer the train brought his family to Fort Worth, the more Don looked forward to joining the Panthers. This could be his chance to get his game back.

The train brought them smoothly to Fort Worth, and it didn't take long for Don, Betty, and Susan to find their prepaid hotel and check in for the night. The next morning Don reported to LaGrave Field, and before he could even find a uniform, one of the coaches called him over. "Are you Don Lund?" Don nodded, and the coach said, "We just got word from Mr. Rickey that you're being sent to Mobile. You're supposed to be on

---

* In 1948, Bill Starr hired catcher John Richey to play for the Padres as the first African-American to play in the Pacific Coast League.

the afternoon train to Little Rock, where you'll meet the team. Tickets are waiting for you. OK?"

Don's eyes darkened as he stared at the coach. "I'm being sent right now to Mobile, Alabama? But I just got here."

The coach stared right back. "Don't blame me, Don. I'm only the messenger."

Don shook the coach's hand. "You're right. Sorry. I'm on my way." He left the stadium, picked up a shocked Betty and his baby daughter, and headed for the railroad. So far this year he had been optioned to the Pacific Coast League, the Texas League, and now the Southern League. Though Don felt badly about treating his family like a bouncing ball, he wasn't angry, especially since Betty was completely supportive. He understood what "under contract" meant. All he really wanted to do was play baseball at the highest level he could achieve. If the next step was Mobile, so be it.

The Mobile Bears had a history of strong competition in the Southern Association, which this year had been classified as a Double-A League. The talent was better than average this season, due to returning veterans on their way up who were optioned there for seasoning, plus some older players on their way down who still demonstrated enough savvy and skills to play at that level. The team played all their home games in Hartwell Field, a better-than-average 5,000-seat stadium located midtown on Virginia Street. The team was managed by Al Todd, a former catcher with eleven years playing for the Phillies, Pirates, Dodgers, and Cubs.

Don and Betty were lucky in finding a place to stay in Mobile, thanks to the good graces of Cliff and Stanna Dapper. Cliff was just coming off a brilliant war-years career as a catcher for the Dodgers. His assignment as Mobile's catcher probably meant the end of his big-league days; the huge talent guys were mustering out. Cliff was the sort of player who just loved the game. Mobile was fine with him. Cliff and Don quickly became friends, and it wasn't long before Betty Lund and Stanna Dapper completed the foursome. Soon the equation became obvious—the Lunds needed a place to stay and the Dappers had lots of extra room where they lived.

The arrangement was almost perfect—only the notorious Mobile bug hordes interfered with their domestic lives. In fact, none of them had ever seen such a preponderance of the insect world, most of which showed little respect for window screens or sink traps. One day Stanna pulled back the covers on her bed and found the sheet covered with ants. Her screams brought help from Cliff and Don. Anyway, they all put up with the bugs as best they could, and Don and Cliff played out the rest of the season as starting-lineup Bears. Near the end of that season, they played a game in Hartwell Field that was to be the most disastrous of Don's entire playing career.

They were playing against the Atlanta Crackers on a warm September Mobile evening. The game was being broadcast over ticker tape in Atlanta, by a young and highly talented radio personality named Ernie Harwell, who would eventually be elected to baseball's Hall of Fame. Ernie was one of the great talents in sports broadcasting whose creative comments could actually make his listeners sense the reality of the game, even though he personally wasn't there. The ticker tape was all he had, and he handled it better than most. This contest, however, would challenge even Ernie's imaginative talents.

It lasted through twenty-one innings of evenly matched baseball and, because of the city's evening curfew, ended with the score tied at four. There was no winner; the fans were left hanging in a baseball limbo. For those listening in Atlanta, Ernie Harwell let them down gently with his remarkable banter. In Mobile, however, thousands of discouraged people noisily left Hartwell Field, frustrated and feeling cheated by the way the game ended. For them, it was not a happy day. And for the Bears' right fielder, his game was doomed from the start, when Manager Todd assigned him the lead-off batter slot. He had never batted in that rotation, not even in high school. He didn't feel ready for it, and unfortunately, he proved it.

Don played the entire game and went 0 for10 at the plate that day. In addition to that humiliation, he was charged with an error when his throw behind the wide-running batter at first base was missed by the first baseman. The runner advanced to second and eventually scored to tie the game. Afterward, to top off an already miserable day, Manager Todd completely blamed Don (accusing him of trying a "tricky" play), rather than the first baseman who should have caught Don's easy throw. "Tricky play my ass! Don't ever try anything tricky again," said Todd.

Don's eyes darkened and he swallowed hard. He took a deep breath. "OK," he said and walked away. He couldn't wait to get out of that stadium and put his worst game behind him.

The final game of Don's 1946 season was played against the Crackers at Stiller Field in Atlanta. Also known as Ponce de Leon Ball Park, Stiller Field was considered one of the finest in the minor leagues. Don liked playing there because of the park's unique outfield. Unlike any other pro baseball stadium, a huge magnolia tree rested 462 feet from home plate and dominated center field. Any ball bouncing off the tree was in fair play; any ball hit into the tree was a home run. So far only Babe Ruth had homered into that tree, launching his bomb during a Yankees' barnstorming trip in 1925. Don would have loved to match that, as did every other slugger who ever stood at the Spiller Field plate.*

As the season ended, Betty and Susan took the train from Mobile, joining Don in Atlanta for the rail ride back to Detroit. Don had purchased a light brown suit for the trip back home, feeling like he ought to splurge on something to make him feel good after having gone through such a disastrous season. His new suit was a perfect contrast to Betty's light blue summer dress. At least he was going home in style, or so he thought. When they arrived at Detroit's Michigan Central Depot, Don carried baby Susan in his right arm as they walked from the tracks through the enormous depot lobby. He noticed a small group of people walking toward them, led by a beaming man he recognized as Detroit Mayor Edward Jeffries. Mayor Jeffries stopped abruptly in front of them, tipped his hat to Betty, and said to Don with a huge smile, "Ah, the joys of fatherhood!" Without waiting for a reply, the mayor and his entourage moved on.

Don looked at Betty. "What was that all about?" he asked.

"Look at your arm, Honey," Betty answered.

He looked at the arm that held his sleeping baby daughter. Susan had wet her diaper. His new suit now sported a huge dark spot on the right sleeve. He looked at the spot, looked at Betty, and then burst out in the biggest laugh he'd had since spring

---

* Several years later, Eddie Matthews became only the second player ever to hit a home run in that tree.

training. "I thought Mayor Jeffries stopped because he recognized me," he roared. "It turns out Susan's the big star here!"

Betty laughed with him. "Welcome home, Honey. You're my big star, anyway!"

Back in Ann Arbor, Don and Betty regained their Geddes Road apartment from George and Norma Kiesel, and Don resumed his duties at the IM Building under Earl Riskey. Just before the start of the basketball season, he received news that pleased him enormously. Michigan had just hired a head basketball coach to replace Bennie Oosterbaan, who was taking over for Athletic Director Fritz Crisler as head football coach. His name was Osborne (Ozzie) Cowles.

Ozzie had just spent the past ten years running the Dartmouth basketball program. He was eager to take on the Michigan job, especially since freshmen could now compete. Michigan was renowned for attracting some of the finest athletes from Detroit, whose high schools made national basketball headlines. Ozzie knew he could win with the Wolverines. He also knew about Don Lund's basketball history in Ann Arbor. It didn't take long before Ozzie was able to find Don and ask him for help with team practices, along with his other duties. Don quickly accepted. After all, the basketball practices were held in the IM Building. It was easy for him to do both jobs. More importantly, the 1946–47 team had a player roster that included some people he wanted to get to know better. Two of these were the Elliott brothers, Bump and Pete. They had just finished the 1946 football season, where Bump played right halfback and Pete played quarterback. Both were quickly on their way to becoming Michigan icons.

Pete Elliott was a starting guard. Bump wasn't a starter, but he was good enough to get into several games. Football was Bump's prime sport, and he was the first one to admit that. Nevertheless, Bump was a fierce competitor in any contest. No one took him for granted. Another standout on the team that year was guard Bob Harrison from Toledo, who would move on to a stellar nine-year career in the NBA. Another guy, one of the friendliest on the team, was Hal Morrill. Hal was a gifted athlete from Flint who also played first base for the Wolverines. He gave a whole lot of ignition to the basketball team, even during practice. Don liked Hal Morrill immediately. They would become lifelong friends.

Don got along quite well with Coach Ozzie Cowles, even though Cowles was known for certain kinds of stunts that some might consider strange. For instance, Cowles didn't like to use the bounce pass. He considered it too awkward for the taller players to handle, even though other teams used it effectively. He also made the team shoot underhand foul shots. Many of the players had a hard time getting used to that. But it was the pregame meal that established Ozzie Cowles' strange reputation.

The starters ate steaks. The non-starters ate hamburgers. The players laughed about it, especially the Elliott brothers. Bump wasn't a starter and was served hamburger. Pete got the steak. The two of them kidded each other about it. Ozzie was also known to try to increase game attendance by personally selling tickets outside Yost Field House. No other Michigan coach ever did that. Finally, Ozzie had his own special way of protesting other school's basketball courts that didn't have lights bright enough for him. So he would put sunglasses on himself and all the players as they practiced in the opponents' gym. The tactic seldom worked, but always got some catcalls from the fans. One rival college newspaper compared him to the famed circus promoter P.T. Barnum. Of all the Big Ten basketball coaches of the time, Ozzie Cowles was almost certainly the most colorful character. Don Lund would never forget him.

29
Dialogue

"Zero-for-ten in twenty-one innings! Plus being charged with someone else's error. Plus being unfairly criticized by your manager. That's the ultimate definition of having a bad game!"

We were relaxing in metal-trimmed patio chairs on the large wood deck that adorns the back of Don's condo. A mature oak tree in front of us stretched its leaves to hinder the sun's late afternoon rays and furnish us with shade. We looked out on a two-acre meadow of freshly mowed grass, which was surrounded by other perfectly matched condos and a small pond that contained a sprouting fountain. Only the constant noise from the fountain's shower broke the stillness of the scene. The old coach sat back with his hands folded against his chest, enjoying the tranquility.

After a few moments, he turned his head toward me and smiled. "Oh, yeah," he said, "that was some game, all right. As a matter of fact, I'd tell that story to some of my Michigan players from to time to time, whenever one of them thought he had a bad game. Sort of put things in perspective."

"You must have felt awful at the time, especially after what Todd said to you. How long did it take you to get over it?"
DL: "I'd say about twenty-two minutes."

"Really?"
DL: "That's about how long it took for me to get home and pick up the baby. Susan looked at me and just grinned. I melted right away."

"Susan would have been about five months old at the time?"
DL: "That's right."

"How do you remember her as a baby?"
DL: "Susan was a happy baby, always looking around and smiling. Betty had a lot to do with that. Betty was so attentive. The

neighborhoods we lived in that year were pretty noisy. Sometimes you couldn't even hear the radio over the sounds outside,
but all Susan had to do was give out a quiet whimper from her
crib in the next room, and Betty would hear it. She surprised me
many times by jumping up and running to Susan's crib, when I
hadn't heard the baby at all. Betty really took care of her. I can't
remember a single time when Betty handed me a crying baby.
She was a devoted mother."

"And Susan was a happy baby?"
DL: "A happy baby, a happy child, a happy adult. Susan always
had a positive attitude. Made friends easily. Now she's a mom
herself, with super kids. Susan and her husband, Bruce Allison,
live right here in Ann Arbor—lucky for me."

"Let's get back to 1946, your first full year in professional base-
ball. You went to spring training cold. That is, you didn't play
your other two sports for the first time since you were a kid. It's
fair to say you were probably out of shape."
DL: "That's right."

"Then right in the middle of spring training, you had to go back
to Detroit because Betty had the baby. When you returned to
Florida, your training was at least a week behind the others."
DL: "That's also right."

"Plus, the competition for your outfield position was dramati-
cally increased due to experienced players returning from the
service."
DL: "Right again."

"Finally, you were bounced around from team to team like a
pinball. You were never able to get settled into any kind of con-
sistency. All this led up to that 21 inning, 0-for-10 nightmare in
Mobile, thanks to conditions mostly beyond your control."
DL: "That's right, but what's your point?"

"Nineteen forty-six was a lousy year for Don Lund."
DL: "That's wrong."

"You're calling it a good year?"
DL: "Yes."

"All right, Coach. Now it's your turn. Why do you think 1946 was a good year?"

DL: "Because I had my little girl. Susan completed Betty and me. Nothing else ever came close to giving me such happiness. Because of her, 1946 was a fantastic year."

"You're right, of course. Nobody would argue against the impact Susan had, but I'm talking about your professional baseball year. Most players would consider that a lousy year."

DL: "Well, I'm not going to do that."

"OK ...?"

DL: "I mean, I'm simply not a complainer. Never have been, never will be. I always try to calculate the pluses, not the minuses. For instance, there were some guys I met that year who taught me a lot: Pepper Martin, for one, and Gene Mauch, plus lots of others."

"But what about the way Branch Rickey moved you around so much, never letting you settle in? Or managers who gave you a hard time? Or just the plain circumstances which held you back that year?"

DL: "Look, there's nobody I'd ever blame for anything but myself. I'm the one who had to face the pitchers, not Mr. Rickey. I'm the one who had to suit up and play the game. Sure, they moved me around, but they counted on me to perform. I'd like to think I gave it my best shot. You know, I'm sort of sick and tired of reading about people who try to explain away their troubles by transferring blame to others. I mean, they'll fault their parents, their teachers, their former friends, their neighbors, even their coaches—anybody and everybody except themselves. They blame what they saw on television, or what they read in magazines or comic books. It's ridiculous. They should start by looking in the mirror."

"Are you talking about sports people writing their autobiographies?"

DL: "Not just sports people. Entertainers, politicians, even corporate types who write about themselves. Don't get me wrong, though, I've read a lot of excellent autobiographies by outstanding people, people who give credit to others for helping them succeed and take proper blame for their own mistakes. I've also read books by those who take all the credit and transfer all the blame. For some reason" [he grins], "those seem to be the ones I never quite finish."

So, if you're going to find fault with anybody for your baseball troubles in 1946, you'll look in the mirror?"
DL: [Chuckling] "Well, at my age I'm not sure I want to look in the mirror. Maybe I won't like what I see. Hey, do you remember that comedian Flip Wilson?"

"I sure do. Very funny guy."
DL: "Well, he had a line that really hits at that whole transfer-of-blame thing. He would put an innocent look on his face, and yell, 'The Devil made me do it!' How about that?"

"Right on. But seriously, Coach, you had to be discouraged after that season, no matter who's to blame. Anybody would be dispirited. How did you honestly feel about your first professional year?"
DL: "You know, somebody once said that when you're down and out, there's nowhere to go but up. I never felt down and out, and I never felt personally discouraged or let down. But I did have some catching up to do, and I knew I had the skills to do it. I just put that season behind me and looked forward to next spring."

"So that leads us to 1947."
DL: "Oh, yes. Things came together. Good things started to happen to me that year."

30

From Montreal to the Pennant

The morning sun was already starting to blaze its way across the municipal maze of Havana, Cuba, as Don Lund strolled among the sidewalk swarms of people. He felt like the stranger he was among these rushing crowds, but the feeling was not unpleasant. He couldn't understand the chorus of Spanish surrounding him, although the people seemed friendly and courteous as he passed by. He noticed a myriad of racial and ethnic backgrounds. Havana seemed as cosmopolitan to him as New York City and just as bustling. Busy people walked purposefully toward some predetermined destination. A few were in pairs, but most were striding along by themselves, faces determined, seemingly focused on reaching wherever they intended to be. There was no pushing or shoving as bus travelers boarded the coaches. Those who caught his eye smiled back at him. So Don quickly became comfortable as he sauntered toward the ballpark. He hardly noticed the slight tug on the right leg of his trousers.

"Hey, mister, you my friend."

Don looked down. The boy couldn't have been more than six years old. T-shirt soiled with dust; wrinkled shorts so full of mud and dirt it was hard to tell their original color; no shoes; dark hair, coal-black eyes; grimy face. A street urchin.

The boy grinned up at him. "Hey, mister, you my friend. Gimme five cents!"

Don smiled down at him. "You speak English, little fella?"

The boy's grin widened. "Hey, mister, you my friend. Gimme five cents."

Don quickly guessed that this phrase might be the extent of the boy's English vocabulary. He looked around. People kept walking right on by, paying no attention. Children begging for food or money might be commonplace here, he thought. So he reached into his pocket, found a quarter, and gave it to the boy, who grabbed it quickly and ran off without another word. Don straightened up and looked through the crowd. He could see more urchins heading his way. Time to move out. He quickened his pace toward Gran Stadium, the new spring training home of the Brooklyn Dodgers. It was Tuesday, March 4, 1947.

Don had reported to spring training the week before, but not as a member of the forty-man Dodgers' roster. He had been assigned instead to the Montreal Royals, the Dodgers' premier Triple-A farm club. Both teams trained in Havana. At first he thought his consignment to Montreal was due solely to his mediocre performance the previous year, but when he showed up for training, he found out that, yes, Mr. Rickey thought Don might need additional seasoning, but he also learned that there were a lot of experienced outfielders who had returned from the service last year and played for Dodgers' farm teams, who deserved a closer look. Their posting to the major league camp made sense in that regard, so Don was squeezed out and sent to the Royals.

Even so, Don wasn't upset by the move. He knew that Triple-A ball was closely competitive with the big leagues, and Montreal was last year's International League champion and winner of the Junior World series. There was no doubt the Dodger roster was a short step up for a player who performed well with the Royals. So he set himself up for spring training with the same typical enthusiasm he'd had throughout his three-sport career. The returning veterans called such an attitude "Gung-ho." Well, he thought, if that's what they call it, then that's what I am: "Gung-ho."

Royals Manager Clay Hopper was first to greet Don when he arrived at training camp. The meeting was pleasant. Hopper had a quick grin and an easy laugh, was liked and respected by the players, and enjoyed being considered a tactful leader who knew how to combine speed and power in his lineups. He had also been known as a trusted manager by Mr. Rickey for over twenty years. Don liked him. He knew that Hopper was going to give him playing time—and sure enough, he was in the lineup almost immediately, playing with some of the most interesting guys he'd ever met. One of them was Jackie Robinson.

Jackie was certainly one of the best talents Don had met so far. As he roamed the keystone at second base, Jackie's skills were boosted by an almost unbelievably quick lateral movement, which made it seem as if the ball was actually seeking his glove. However, Jackie's tenure at second base was short. Dodgers manager Leo Durocher sent word for him to train at first base, which started a rumor among the Montreal squad that Durocher intended to move Jackie up to the Dodgers for the regular season. Since Eddie Stanky had a lock on second base for Brooklyn, moving Jackie to first base made sense.

Jackie had no problem with the move. He was the type of player who'd be comfortable playing any infield position. Or, Don thought, playing anywhere on the field, he was that good. Don was also impressed by Jackie's base running, which was fast and deceptive. One day, while waiting in the on-deck circle, Don watched Jackie hit a short line drive to left field, normally a single that would be snatched by the left fielder and thrown to second base to hold the runner on first. But Jackie took a huge turn at first and stopped. The left fielder, seeing a chance to catch the runner off first base, threw to the first baseman. Jackie jumped for second the instant the ball came out of the left fielder's hand, and he slid into the base before the first baseman could make the putout throw. For anyone else, that base-running feat would have been considered magnificent. For Robinson, it was typical.

Don found Jackie to be a solid guy personally. Their common ground was that they had played sports other than baseball. The two of them enjoyed reminiscing about Jackie's playing days at UCLA and Don's experiences at Michigan. Both of them earned letters in every sport they played, in every year they played them. Jackie was a hero to the crowds during spring training. Gran Stadium was home to thousands of Cuban baseball fans who were used to watching racially integrated games; the Cuban League had been racially integrated in 1900. This year, Jackie Robinson was the crowd favorite. Their cheers of approval over his superb performances on the field would resound throughout the stadium.

Don liked to kid him about it. "How come I don't get that kind of crowd reaction?" he'd joke. "What am I doing wrong?"

Jackie would grin back and say something like, "Get in line, you're next."

Other players Don got to know that spring included Marv Rackley, an outfielder from South Carolina who also befriended Robinson, which some of the other southerners on the team didn't like. Don never saw any racism in Marv. In fact, Marv was one of those players who always seemed to take the good side. He was easy to like.

Another friend Don made that spring was Earl Naylor, an outfielder from Kansas City. Earl was a few years older than Don and had some experience with the Phillies before joining the Dodgers' organization in 1946. The two of them decided to hang around together on off days, and they frequently went into downtown Havana to see the sights. On one of their jaunts, while jostling along on a crowded sidewalk, Earl spotted a popcorn vendor. "My treat, Don," he said. They struggled their way to the vendor and ordered popcorn. Earl reached in his pocket to pay the vendor. "Sonofagun," he said, "my wallet's gone!" His pocket had been picked. Don paid for the popcorn, and Earl grumbled all the way back to the team's dormitories.

Another player on the Montreal roster Don got to know pretty well was a first baseman named Chuck Connors. Chuck had just come off one season of pro basketball with the Boston Celtics, where he had logged himself in trivia lore by becoming the first pro player to break the backboard while shooting. It happened during a pregame warm-up in Boston Garden. Chuck was an outgoing and very likable man. At 6-feet-5-inches, he was noticed everywhere he went, on or off the field. He and Don would often exchange stories about their sports experiences. Both were multi-sport athletes, a common ground for conversations, and both shared the same love for baseball as their main sport.

One of the most remarkable incidents in spring training that year involved Chuck Connors, and though it wasn't very funny at the time, Chuck was able to joke about it afterward. It happened before practice on a particular hot and muggy Havana morning. The team had sandwiches and cold milk waiting for the players, set out on tables in front of the stands. Connors had a couple of sandwiches and then proceeded to wash them down with repeated drinks of milk. He was putting away the milk so fast that some players noticed. Connors stopped between gulps, winked, and said, "for a growing boy." Then he tossed down a couple more drinks. The team took the field. Connors danced around first base a little, took a few throws, then collapsed. Players carried him off the diamond where he soon revived, emptied his stomach, and sat out the rest of practice. Don admired him for the good-natured way he took the forthcoming barbs.

Chuck Connors would go on to play in the minor leagues until MGM discovered him playing in a Los Angeles ballpark. Then he would enjoy a remarkable career in movies and television, most notably playing a heroic character named Lucas McCain, "The Rifleman."

There was another Royals teammate Don especially liked. Spider Jorgensen, a third baseman from Folsom, California, was a heads-up peppery player on the field and fun to be around. Spider was a natural right-hander who batted left. He and Don would often talk about batting strategies as they watched others take their swings in practice. Spider had a special knack for picking out strengths and weaknesses as he watched others play, and Don felt he learned from him. What he didn't know at the time was that Spider would eventually wind up using his keen observation skills to great advantage as a successful scout for the Chicago Cubs for more than twenty years. Nevertheless, Don enjoyed those discussions with Spider, particularly since they helped hone his own ability to judge other players. He would use these skills to great advantage in later years.

A nice thing happened to Don one day in early March, following an exhibition game between the Dodgers and Royals. Stadium promoters had arranged for World Heavyweight Champion Joe Louis to put on a boxing exhibition in Gran Stadium after the game. The Brown Bomber had just arrived in Cuba to prepare for a December title defense against Jersey Joe Walcott.

Joe Louis knew the Havana fans loved him, so an exhibition after the game, with fans already in place in their seats, would be no problem. So the ring was set up in the infield with bleachers for about one hundred spectators spread around it. The ballplayers had enough time to shower quickly and change into street clothes before settling into ringside bleacher seats. An announcer provided plenty of patter and chatter before, during, and after the event, which sounded kind of funny through the reverberating echo of Gran Stadium's sound system: "And now ['and now, and ow, an' owww'] the Heavyweight ['weight, ate, aaate'] Champion ['ampion, eon, eonnn']..." Joe put on an entertaining boxing demonstration using two separate sparring partners. When it was over, he climbed through the ropes and walked down the stairs wearing a dark red robe. He wasn't mobbed by the crowd, which remained in the stands, or by the ballplayers who kept the silent code of courtesy professional athletes tend to give one another.

Louis was easy to approach, and Jackie Robinson was one of the first to do so, with Don following close behind. After some pleasantries, Jackie introduced Don to Joe Louis: "Champ, this is Don Lund from Detroit."

Don offered his hand, and Joe shook it with his still-taped fingers.

"Detroit, you say," said the champion. "You play sports there?"

"Yep," answered Don, "since I was a kid."

The Champ grinned. "Best sports town in the world."

The conversation then turned back to include Jackie. The three continued to talk for a while, and then Joe left, with a parting word to Don: "Say hello to Detroit for me."

As they walked away, Don said to Jackie, "Nice guy."

Jackie responded, "Yea."

The best part of spring training in Cuba for Don Lund was the fact that he completely turned around his playing performance from the year before. He became focused. His confidence level rose every day as his bat practically leaped at the ball. Hitting in either the fourth, fifth, or sixth spot in the lineup, his batting average quickly rose to over .300. Home runs thundered. Singles, doubles, even a couple of triples put him in the lead at the plate, right up there with Robinson. In the outfield, he was superb—no errors. He made hard catches look easy. He felt relaxed and self-assured. He also knew he was being noticed.

The Royals played all their spring training games against the Dodgers in Gran Stadium, a one-year-old spectacular showplace that held 35,000 spectators. Don appreciated the Cuban fans, who swarmed to the stadium like ants attacking chocolate cake. Those who could afford a ticket packed the seats without a vacancy; others milled around outside to catch information about the game any way they could.

From his right field spot, Don saw the huge, mostly male crowds as a study in black and white. The men wore white shirts and dark, mostly black trousers, like a noisy army in matching uniforms. What the fans lacked in color, however, they made up for in exuberance. They shouted, cheered, yelled, and stamped their feet, sometimes making the entire facility, including the ground underneath, rumble and tremble. Much like, Don imagined, those famous Flatbush Faithful fans devoted to their marvelous "Bums" at Ebbets Field. But there was one difference between American baseball crowds and the fans in Gran Stadium.

The Cubans didn't "boo" over something they didn't like, they whistled. A short "tweet-tweet" was the standard sound for showing displeasure. And when thousands of fans went "tweet-tweet," the whistles overflowed eardrums. That took some getting used to. Throughout spring training Don continued to slam the ball around and patrol both right and left fields like he held the lease on them. Once a fan came up to him after a game and held out one of his home run balls and a pen for his signature. Don was in top form—feeling good; feeling ready.

Spring training broke up shortly after the end of March. The Royals and Dodgers sailed from Havana to Florida, then took the train up the coast to New York. Notably missing was Dodgers Manager Leo Durocher. An ugly public rift had been brewing between Durocher and New York Yankees' owner Larry MacPhail, each accusing the other of involvement in gambling. In Durocher's case, MacPhail's accusations were at least partially true. Finally, MacPhail prevailed upon baseball commissioner Albert "Happy" Chandler to suspend Durocher from the game for one year on the charge of "associating with known gamblers."

Durocher did not travel north with the team, much to the surprise of his players. One of his coaches, Clyde Sukeforth, agreed to manage the Dodgers on a temporary basis, until Mr. Rickey could replace Durocher. The final game of the exhibition season was held at Ebbets Field on Friday, April 11, four days before opening day of the regular season. All spring Don had been on a production roll. He was tuned. He was supremely confident. His big moment came in the second inning of that game, during his first time at bat.

Ralph Branca was on the mound for the Dodgers. He had established himself as the team's ace starter with stellar performances during spring training. Branca showed confidence, as if he somehow knew he was on his way to an All-Star slot and a career high 21-game season. He had thrown smoke in the first inning, fanning two batters and making the third one pop out to Dodgers' catcher Bruce Edwards. In this inning so far, the first Royals batter grounded out to Eddie Stanky. Batting fifth, Jackie Robinson knocked a stand-up double down the left field line and was standing with both feet on second base.

It was now time for the sixth Royals' batter—Don Lund. He strode quickly to the batter's box, nodded at Edwards, set himself with one bat tap on the plate and a casual lift of the bat over his right shoulder, caught the "hit" sign from the third-base coach, and settled in with his darkened eyes on the pitcher. Branca served a curve above the letters for a called ball one. Don knew the smoke was coming next. He had seen Branca follow his breaking ball with a fast one many times. Besides, his speed was working, and Edwards was the type of catcher to make him throw it. Branca stretched, checked Robinson's lead at second, reached back, and let the ball rip.

Don watched it come in low and outside, just above his knees. Fastball. He could practically see the sweet spot of his bat meet the ball. He knew it was gone. Half way to first base, he slowed as he watched the ball sail into the upper deck above left center field. Dixie Walker, playing center, just turned around and watched it. Left fielder Pete Reiser did the same. Don continued around the bases, and as he came to third, he saw Jackie Robinson, who'd just scored, waiting to congratulate him. He'd never felt more of an emotional high than he did at that moment. Fortunately, a family friend captured the scene. Don would treasure that picture for the rest of his life.

Soon after the game, word came from Mr. Rickey that three Montreal players would stay in Brooklyn and join the 28-man Dodgers' roster: Spider Jorgensen, Jackie Robinson, and Don Lund. All three were told to report the next morning to sign their contracts at the Dodgers' offices on Montague Street.

Don tried to play down his excitement when he called Betty in Detroit right after he received word. "I'm signing with the Dodgers tomorrow morning," he told her. "Bring Susan as soon as you can. We'll need to find a place to live." Betty yelled with delight and informed his parents, who each had to take the phone and congratulate him with typical parental pride. Eventually he was able to tell them about the just-completed game that, he thought,

Don Lund is greeted at the plate by teammate Jackie Robinson, after hitting a home run for the Montreal Royals in an exhibition game against the Brooklyn Dodgers at Ebbets Field, April 11, 1947. The next day the Dodgers bought Don's and Jackie's contracts, along with that of third baseman Spider Jorgensen, in a landmark signing. Jackie didn't just break the color barrier in major league baseball, he pulverized it. All three players debuted with the Dodgers on April 15, 1947. (*Lund Family Collection*)

might have triggered his move up to the Dodgers. The next day he would learn that Mr. Rickey had actually been closely following his progress all spring. His performance in the last exhibition game was a plus, but not the only deciding factor.

Jackie, Spider, and Don had agreed to arrive together the next morning, Saturday, April 12. As they approached, a hoard of press reporters swarmed on the sidewalk outside 215 Montague. They had apparently been given press releases and were well aware of the impact of Jackie's signing. Questions like "How's it feel to be in the big leagues?" were hurled as the trio made their way into the building, but the press was polite and let them through.

Mr. Rickey and interim manager Clyde Sukeforth were there, along with Jane Ann Jones, and the contracts were signed by all three.

"Welcome aboard, men," smiled the Dodgers' owner. Then he turned to Don and Spider. "Jackie's going to have to face that bunch of wolves down there," he stated, "but you two don't. Before we let 'em in, why don't you go on down the back way?"

They did. Don and Spider Jorgensen escaped down the alley without saying a word. They both knew that Jackie was about to face a pile of challenges. And they also believed that if Jackie held on, the game of major league baseball would change forever.

Spider Jorgensen and Jackie Robinson were put in the Dodgers' starting lineup right from opening day, with Spider playing third base and Jackie at first. Don Lund, Gene Hermanski, and the other outfielders were assigned behind starters Pete Reiser in left, Dixie Walker in center, and Carl Furillo in right field. After the second game, Burt Shotton replaced Clyde Sukeforth, who resumed coaching duties. Shotton was mild mannered and respected. He also was a long-standing friend of Branch Rickey, dating all the way back to their mutual stint with the St. Louis Cardinals. Since Rickey didn't work on Sundays, Shotton had substituted for him as the Cardinals' Sunday manager. The two were trusted pals.

The biggest trait about Burt Shotton was that he always wore a suit and hat in his managerial role instead of a baseball uniform. Moreover, he seldom appeared on the field during a game. A coach, rather than Shotton, would present the lineup to the umpire beforehand. Nevertheless, Burt Shotton would prove to be the right kind of person to level the emotions of a team that was poised to make baseball history.

As predicted, Jackie's troubles as major league baseball's first African-American started from day one. Even some of his own teammates shunned him, or gave him whistles and "cat calls" whenever he took his turn at bat. Don felt sorry for him and did what he could to ease any situation among teammates that could cause Jackie emotional or physical harm. Burt Shotton, with his easy-going manner, eventually put an end to any outward displays of racism among his players. Don admired Burt for that, but not nearly as much as he admired Jackie Robinson. He had never seen such courage or restraint displayed by any man.

Jackie never argued, never complained, never even raised his voice. He took all the abuse with class. Reporters couldn't bait him. Neither could the opposing teams, who tried with remarks like "Hey Jackie! I fucked your wife last night!" Whatever was said, Jackie stood above all of it, resolute, confident, ready to play every day.

By season's end, Jackie Robinson would show them all by being named Rookie of the Year. Over time, Don Lund would be asked to name the greatest baseball player he'd ever met. His answer was always the same, and not just because the man was his friend or that he once had played on the same team with him, or that the man's athletic skills were superb. His answer would always focus on one thing: the character of the man. To him, Jackie Robinson was the greatest man with whom he ever played the game of baseball.

For the first month of the 1947 Dodger season, Don didn't see much action. The outfield starters were playing well and the team was off to a good start. He felt good, though, and his batting was as productive as it had been in spring training. Somebody must have noticed him, he surmised, because at the end of thirty days he made the cut to the twenty-five-man roster. But about the third week in May, during a road trip to Pittsburg, Don was called in to see Manager Shotton. "Don, you're just not playing much, and that's got to frustrate you, especially since you're practicing well," said Shotton.

Don didn't answer. He wondered where this was going.

"So I talked to Mr. Rickey and he agrees you need playing time."

Don still didn't answer. His gut tightened.

"We're sending you to St. Paul right away."

So that's it, he thought. His eyes darkened; he took a deep breath. "OK, Burt," he said evenly. "I appreciate the consideration. Thanks a lot, and good luck." He walked out of Shotton's office with mixed feelings. On one side, nobody wants to be sent back to the minors; on the other, St. Paul was definitely not banishment. The Saints were as good as it gets in the minor leagues. Besides, he really did need playing time.

Finding accommodations for Betty and Susan in St. Paul turned out to be easy, thanks to the Saints' first baseman John Douglas. John and his wife Nancy had been staying in a house owned by Dick Siebert, an eleven-year major leaguer who had retired from the Athletics in 1945 and was soon to become a legendary baseball coach at the University of Minnesota. Siebert wasn't in town this summer. John asked Don if he would like to move his family in and split the rent. The house was certainly big enough, and Don said yes right away. Betty was happy for the company.

But Don was not happy, and Herman Franks was the reason. Franks was the player/manager of the Saints who played catcher and who managed in the Leo Durocher style: whatever it took to win was OK. That included intimidation, flashing spikes, and throwing at a batter. As much as Don rejected that approach, his problem with Franks was simply that Franks wasn't playing him, and he wouldn't explain why. Don pretty much rode the bench all during June and July, feeling useless.

True to his nature, though, he never complained to Franks or talked behind the manager's back. He just gathered butt splinters, day after day. Then in August, Franks left the team to resume his playing career with the Philadelphia Athletics. The new manager, Curt Davis, hired by Mr. Rickey specifically to manage the Saints, was a gift from heaven as far as Don Lund was concerned.

On the second day after his arrival, Davis pulled him aside. "Don, you're supposed to be playing here, not wasting your time in the dugout. I'm putting you in the lineup right away." With that comment, Davis opened the door to the proverbial lion's cage, and Don sprang into dominance. He ruled for the Saints throughout the remaining games that season. The sound

1947 St. Paul Saints. Don Lund stands in the second row, third
from right. He did so well the Dodgers recalled him after the
St. Paul season ended. His bat helped Brooklyn win the pennant.
He was ineligible to play in the World Series though, because
he joined the squad after September 1. He watched from the
stands as Brooklyn took the Yankees to seven games
before losing. (*Lund Family Collection*)

of his bat echoed throughout the stands every day, causing local
newspapers to write headlines like "Where Have You Been, Don
Lund?" His hits won games. Singles, doubles, triples, they were
there when it counted. His best day at the plate was an awesome
one-man performance on the road against the Toledo Mud Hens
at Swayne Field. He blasted three home runs and hit a double
that missed another home run by inches. Don Lund became
the hometown hero of St. Paul, Minnesota. At season's end in
September, the three Lunds boarded the train to Detroit, and a
small crowd of fans saw them off in a chorus of well wishes.
"Thank you, Don!" was heard many times.

Don grinned and said to Betty, "Thank you is right; thank
you, Curt Davis!"

Back in Detroit, the family settled in on Lycaste with Andy
and Marguerite. Don was planning to contact the Detroit Recreation Department to see about a school-year job. A phone call

from Jane Ann Jones in New York changed everything: "Mr. Rickey would like to speak with you," she said.

The man himself came on the line and got right to the point. "Don, I want you to join the Dodgers right away in Chicago. Wait a minute. Check that. They only play day games in Chicago. You'll never get there in time. Join the team in St. Louis. Miss Jones will have tickets waiting for you at the train station."

Don only had time to say, "Yes, Sir. Thanks," before Rickey hung up. He was on his way back to the big leagues. Someone must have told them about his performance with the Saints. Did he owe another debt to Curt Davis?

In St. Louis, Don sat out the first game on the bench. He took his three swings of batting practice before the second game, hitting a couple through the infield and putting one in the left field seats. His swing felt good.

In the middle of the second game, Shotton called on him to pinch hit. "See if you can hit one like you did in batting practice," he said.

Don walked out toward the on-deck circle and heard his name announced as he stretched and warmed up. The Cardinals' pitcher was left-hander Howie Pollet, a twenty-one-game winner last year who had some control problems earlier this season but was coming on strong near the end. The Cardinals' catcher was Joe Garagiola, a natural sparkplug who would later become one of the wittiest and most-sought-after retired major leaguers in the entertainment business. It was impossible not to like Joe Garagiola.

Pollet's first pitch was low, for a ball. His second pitch was a mid-thigh inside fastball. Don blasted it into the seats, about fifty feet from where his practice ball had landed. As he returned to the dugout after circling the bases and accepting congratulations from his teammates, he sat down with a smile. He had just hit his first home run as a major league ballplayer. One of the guys would put it another way after the game: "Lund, you broke the ol' cherry!" He felt like he could conquer the world.

The Dodgers were racing toward the pennant and Don was called on to help them, sometimes as a left field starter, and other times as a pinch-hitter. He came through. His best effort came against the Pirates in Forbes Field, which the Dodgers won 3–1. Don scored two of those three runs for Brooklyn, one of them a monster home run that soared over "Greenberg's Gardens," the left field wall named in honor of right-hand power hitter Hank Greenberg. Hank had joined the team this season at first base after sixteen magnificent years with the Detroit Tigers. He was playing his final year in the major leagues. The fans loved him.

Don continued to help the Dodgers with his bat, right up to the day they won the National League Pennant. He finished the season with an official twenty times at bat, his average sitting at .300 after the final game. But that would be all. Don was not allowed to compete in the World Series, because of the MLB rule that a player must be on the roster prior to September 1 in order to be eligible for the series. Don had been called up a few days after that, so he was relegated to being a spectator if he wished to hang around. No problem there. The World Series pitted the Dodgers against the American League Champion Yankees, a "New York" contest. All games would be played in Ebbets Field and Yankee Stadium. Don and Betty could see them all, from right behind the Dodgers' dugout. Neither of them would even consider missing the series, which started on September 30, even though they'd have to pay October's rent. It was more than worth it.

Great news came from back home immediately after the Dodgers won the pennant. Don's sister Virginia had just been married to the love of her life, Bill Lyle, who worked in the offices of Chrysler Corporation. The newlyweds planned to honeymoon in New York and attend the World Series. To Don and Betty, who had to miss Virginia and Bill's wedding because of Don's playing commitments, this would be an opportunity to spend dedicated time with them. Don quickly arranged for game tickets and made reservations for the Lyles at the St. George Hotel. Then they received another bit of good news. After talking with Betty, their landlord had agreed to prorate their rent to a daily charge until the end of the series.

Things were working out nicely. And they would continue to do so, as the two couples attended the games and saw the sights of New York City. They particularly enjoyed having dinner at Toots Shor's place on Fifty-First Street. Photos of famous celebrities filled the walls, many of them in poses with the restaurant's equally famous proprietor. Toots himself stopped by their table and expressed his regrets that Don wasn't playing. Don merely responded with a smile and a thank you. Betty, Virginia, and Bill beamed with pleasure at Don being recognized by Toots Shor. The four of them would long remember that particular dinner.

The Dodgers lost the World Series in seven games, and Don watched every one of them with mixed feelings. Naturally, he was a partisan fan for the Dodgers, being under contract to them. Moreover, he admired Branch Rickey for many reasons. He also felt kinship with his friends in the Dodgers' lineup. Against this, however, was his proclivity to study the game without judgment as he saw it played before him. While others in the stands might scream at an umpire's call, Don would instead mull over what the call meant in terms of playing strategy. Simply put, Don Lund the spectator was more objective than Don Lund the player. There were only two exceptions: the Michigan Wolverines and the Detroit Tigers. He was absolutely nuts about the Maize and Blue for many reasons, and the Tigers were his boyhood craze. Beyond these two, he could be passionless.

Don would keep two prime memories of the 1947 World Series. Game four, held October 3 at Ebbets Field, was the most remarkable. It was almost the first no-hitter ever pitched in a series game. Yankees' starter Bill Bevens, whose record included two no-hit games in the minor leagues, was on the mound. This game Bevens hurled eight and two-thirds innings of no-hit ball, even though he had given up a series' record of ten walks. Two of those walks, Al Gionfriddo and Eddie Miksis, were on base for Brooklyn with two outs in the bottom of the ninth inning. The Yankees were hanging on to a 2–1 lead. Don watched with interest as Dodgers' manager Burt Shotton called Eddie Stanky back to the dugout. Shotton sent in another right-handed hitter, Cookie Lavagetto, to face the right-handed pitcher Bevens.

Don could think of two possible reasons why Shotton would do that. First, Stanky had finished the season with his lowest batting average (.252) since joining the Dodgers. Plus, Bevens seemed to have his number this game. Second, Lavagetto looked very good in batting practice, and he had a way of crowding the plate that might draw a third walk. Sure enough, the first pitch to Cookie was curved low and outside for a ball. But the second pitch, an outside fastball, put Cookie Lavagetto forever in the books of baseball lore. Cookie smacked it into the right-field corner, scoring Gianfriddo and Miksis to spoil the no-hitter and win the game for Brooklyn. It was to be Lavagetto's final hit as a major leaguer, but game four of that World Series would always be known as "The Cookie Game."

Don's second major World Series impression was an appreciation for the amazing talents of Yankees' legend Joe DiMaggio. Joe seemed to glide over the outfield, with a grace and style that set him apart from other fielders who would charge madly and dive for the catch. Don witnessed two great catches, made in succession at Ebbets Field in game three that placed Joe DiMaggio permanently in his memory. First was a parallel-to-the-ground stretch grab of a deep line drive by Gene Hermanski. DiMaggio snagged it with full extension of his glove, then rolled to the right center wall, leaped up and held aloft his ball-filled glove. Hermanski was robbed of sure extra bases. The next Brooklyn batter popped a short blooper over Yankees' shortstop Phil Rizzuto. DiMaggio swooped in and made a one-handed catch above his shoe tops for the out. He made that amazing grab look easy. However, there was one time when Don saw the Yankee Clipper lose his normal unruffled composure.

In game five, Joe hit a screaming line drive down the left field line, a sure double on its way. The Dodgers' left fielder Al Gionfriddo ran like a panicked rabbit and reached out his gloved right hand to pull in the ball right in front of the bullpen. Joe saw Gianfriddo's miracle catch and stopped running just as he neared second base. In a rare show of anger, DiMaggio kicked the base path dirt and sent up a cloud of dust about three feet high. He was roundly jeered by the Brooklyn partisans. Don, though, saw DiMaggio's demonstration as only a measure of the man's competitiveness. Joe DiMaggio in fact was a gentleman, known not only as an exceptional ballplayer, but also as a modest guy who kept his composure both on and off the field.

After the World Series, Don, Betty, and Susan returned to Detroit while Virginia and Bill remained a few extra days to enjoy their honeymoon in New York City. The 1947 baseball season was over. Had Don Lund played in the World Series, he would have earned a minimum $4,081.00. And who knows what his involvement might have produced? Don thought about that, wishing he could have suited up. But he didn't dwell on what might have been. On the contrary, he ended the season with profound gratitude toward two people: Curt Davis for putting him on the field in St. Paul and Branch Rickey for giving him the chance to make his first mark in the sport that held his heart.

31
Meet Me in St. Louis!

"Have you ever thought about selling life insurance?"

Don blinked at the question. He was sitting in the living room of the Phi Delta Theta house in Ann Arbor, with his friend and fraternity brother Bob Ufer. It was Monday, November 10, 1947, one month after he, Betty, and Susan had returned home from the World Series.

The train ride from New York back to Detroit was productive as well as enjoyable. It gave them concentrated time to examine their situation as a family, to realistically think about what they wanted at this time in their lives. Their first decision was easy: they'd spend the off-season months on Lycaste with Andy and Marguerite, who had plenty of room and wanted them there. The chance to be with Susan, their only grandchild, was just one of their reasons. So no problem there. The next decision, which involved spending some of their savings, was more difficult. They had little choice: they needed their own transportation. Families, even those with meager incomes, didn't just ride around in buses and streetcars in the automobile capital of the world. They filled their garages and packed the streets with favorite cars. So Don and Betty made up their minds on the train trip back to Detroit. They would move in with Don's folks, and they would buy their first car.

Don had no trouble finding a car he liked and could afford. His friends recommended a Pontiac dealer in the Detroit suburb of Ferndale by the name of George Higgins. George sold cars to baseball players throughout the country. Known as a nice guy who talked plain and looked a man straight in the eye, he related well with professional athletes. Don bought a 1947 Pontiac from George Higgins, closing the deal soon after he walked into the showroom. A four-door sedan, the car was a beauty in light gray with dark gray upholstery. It was the first major asset Don Lund ever owned, and it was brand new. He could now take his family around in style. No more buses or streetcars. No more Greyhounds to Ann Arbor. His new car was a home run; a touchdown; a game-winning basket. He absolutely loved it.

All this led up to November 10, 1947. Don had driven to Ann Arbor to see some of his buddies on Michigan's football team, including Bob Chappuis and Bump Elliott. Michigan had battered the Hoosiers from Indiana University two days before in Michigan Stadium, 35–0, and was undefeated with only two more games remaining on the schedule. The team was being touted by the press as the "Mad Magicians" because the backfield could baffle their opponents with ball-handling skills that defied logic. Their trick was to make it look like they were always running the same play, but to move the ball around so randomly and fast that the other team couldn't tell who the ball carrier was going to be. The play always started with the same snap to fullback Jack Wiesenburger. Jack would flip it, pass it, hand it off, or lateral it to either Bob or Bump, starting left and right tailbacks, or to quarterback Howard Yerges. One of them would then run it, pass it, or advance the ball some other way, which might include getting it back to Jack.

Although these play variations were well conceived and executed with perfect timing, they appeared to be "razzle-dazzle" from the stands. But they worked, as people said, "like magic." Bob Chappuis and Bump Elliott were the backfield's most visible "magicians." Don hadn't seen either of them or his other friends on the team since last season. He knew he'd be able to find them in the afternoon, and he was looking forward to it.

This morning, however, he was visiting the Phi Delta Theta house for a chat with his good friend and fraternity brother Bob Ufer. Ufer had been the dominant member of his Michigan track team. As a freshman, he established eight school records, and then went on to set a new world record in the 440 yard run at a Big Ten meet in 1942. After graduation, Bob joined Penn Mutual Life Insurance Company as a sales representative and quickly became Penn's rising star.

By 1947, Bob was also enjoying limelight as a local radio broadcasting firecracker for Michigan football games. His exciting personality, his forthright speaking, and his Wolverine-biased play-by-play were drawing Maize and Blue fans by the thousands. Despite all this, however, he still wanted some objective credibility. Ufer's biased style could attract listeners only so far, and Bob knew this. To keep them, he needed authoritative comments from someone the fans would respect, someone they looked up to, someone who loved Michigan as much as Bob did, someone, he decided, like Don Lund. So Ufer asked Don to join him in the broadcast booth, which was like asking a kid if he'd like to have an ice-cream cone. Don jumped at the chance, of course. He was a natural analyst in all three of his playing sports; commenting on Michigan football would be a cinch. The two of them, Bob Ufer and Don Lund, would become a popular Wolverines' radio football team for the next thirty-four years.

Ufer noticed Don blink at his question. So he asked again, "Have you ever thought about selling life insurance?"

This time Don answered. "Me, sell life insurance? Come on, Bob."

Ufer then explained how selling life insurance was quite lucrative, since salesmen received residual commissions on policies they sold. He went on to say that Don should have no trouble doing the job, since he already knew a lot of people in Detroit. He would easily find prospective customers in his hometown. Besides, Ufer added, Penn Mutual had an excellent sales training program, and they wouldn't mind if he played baseball and only sold full-time during his winter off-season. Don wasn't quite sure about all this, until Bob pointed out, "After all, Lundo, what have you got to lose by trying it?"

Don agreed with that logic and said yes.

A few days later Don showed up at the downtown Detroit offices of Penn Mutual. Ufer had set up a job interview for him. Don met managers, salesmen, even an actuary, and all went well; he was hired. His sales training program consisted of acquiring product knowledge, sales fundamentals, and customer contact training acquired through accompanying experienced salesmen on their daily rounds.

Finally, Don was asked to make a list of family and local personal friends he could contact as prospective customers. He couldn't do it. Nobody he knew, including his family, had money for life insurance. He would have to call on strangers. So his sales manager helped him make a list of prospects from Detroit's business community, most of whom were people who were specifically placed in a "forget it" file by other salesmen.

They were men who simply refused to talk to insurance salesmen, or they were executives highly sheltered by secretaries who
protected their bosses with the fierceness of meat-starved German
shepherds. Or they were people who emphatically declined to
buy life insurance, time after time. They were all included on
Don's list. He went to work. Three of the first five people he
telephoned, all businessmen, agreed to see him within the next
two days.

His manager couldn't believe it. "You're gonna set us on fire,"
he bragged. "We're gonna be callin' you Mister Impossible!"

His first prospect was the owner of a company that manu-
factured auto parts for Chrysler Corporation. On his way to
the call, Don mentally recounted the features and benefits of a
particular whole-life policy he intended to present. He decided to
push whole-life's guaranteed death benefit and guaranteed cash
value as benefits a successful business executive would certainly
go for. After all, he reasoned, the word *guarantee* was something
the prospect seldom heard. He'd stress it in his presentation.

The secretary greeted him by name as he walked in the
prospect's office suite, which surprised Don. She led him to the
owner's closed door, knocked gently, and opened it. Don stepped
in, to be greeted by an effusive man in his mid-thirties, whose
outstretched hand fairly leaped from his right side to greet him.
He was thin, about six feet tall, with black hair and a pencil
moustache. He wore a dark gray suit, white shirt, dark blue tie.
His all-teeth smile and bright eyes made Don wonder which of
them was really the customer. With this guy's attitude, it was
hard for him to figure out why other salesmen had put him on
a "forget it" list.

"So you're Don Lund?"

Don smiled as he answered, "Yes, Sir. Don Lund from Penn
Mutual."

The man motioned Don to a chair as he sat down behind his
large walnut desk. "Of course you are," the man smiled. "You're
also Don Lund from Southeastern High, right? And Michigan.
And now with the Brooklyn Dodgers?"

Don wasn't sure where this was going. "That's me," he
acknowledged.

The man never broke his toothy grin. "Well, I'm tickled you're
here, Don. My son's at Foch. He'll start Southeastern next year.

His favorite sport's baseball, and you're a big hero of his. Tell me, what's it like to play in the big leagues?"

Don politely answered his questions for more than an hour. They talked about guys he played with. They talked about Michigan football. They talked about Southeastern High. The man never stopped showing his teeth.

Finally, Don asked, "Have you ever thought about life insurance for yourself?"

The man's smile broke a little. "Life insurance? Hell, yes, I've thought of it. My wife's cousin sells for Prudential. He's got me so insured I'm worth ten times more dead than alive. Whenever I see him coming, I head for the nearest closet! Didn't I tell you that when you called?"

Don's eyes darkened, but he kept his composure. "No, you didn't," he responded, and stood. "I guess I'd better get going."

The man reached in his desk drawer and pulled out a baseball. "Before you go, Don, would you autograph this ball for my son?"

Don signed the ball. On his way out, the secretary said, "Good-bye, Mr. Lund. By the way, it's freezing rain outside."

For the next month, he faced more than a few similar reactions from other prospects who considered him a hometown luminary. One automotive spring manufacturer was so excited to meet Don he escorted him around the entire plant to meet his workers and sign a few baseballs—but at least the man signed up for a whole life policy.

Eventually, Don forced himself to face the fact that he wasn't cut out to be a life insurance salesman. Too many people he met simply refused to see him as someone other than a sports star. It wasn't important that he didn't consider himself a celebrity. Others did, especially those who worked outside the realm of sports but believed themselves to be dedicated fans. They meant well, but they made him an uneasy salesman. To reach his hoped-for comfort level, Don became convinced that he needed to leave the insurance business and avoid any other livelihood not related to sports. Thanks to Bob Ufer, Don saw his future more clearly; he decided to work exclusively in the field of athletics for the rest of his lifelong career.

It didn't take him long to hook up with the Detroit public schools' high school sports program as a part-time substitute physical education teacher. He also became a referee for city league football and basketball games. On Michigan football Saturdays, he joined Bob Ufer in the broadcast booth. Bob's bluster and Don's cogent comments brought their listening audience right into the action all through the Wolverines' undefeated season and their 49–0 romp over Southern California in the Rose Bowl. When the Associated Press awarded Michigan the national championship in a post-season poll, Don joined his "Mad Magician" friends in their many celebrations. His only disappointment came when his pal and former teammate Bob Chappius placed second in the Heisman Trophy selection, behind winner John Lujack of Notre Dame. Otherwise, his 1947–48 off-season months with family, friends, and sports-related jobs were completely satisfactory.

Around the second week of February, Don received a letter from the Dodgers addressed to all player personnel. It stated that 1948 spring training would be held in the Dominican Republic. It also covered directions and logistics for players to get there, including the fact that Don would be flying out of Detroit City Airport. At dinner that night, he and Betty showed the letter to his parents.

Andy said, "Who's that dictator down there, the one who massacred all those Haitians about ten years ago?"

Betty answered, "His name's Rafael Trujillo. I went to the library and looked it up after I read the letter."

Andy looked at Don. "Son, I'll bet this Trujillo guy is paying the Dodgers a truckload of money to train down there. But it could be rough. Do you think you'll be safe?"

Don assured his family he'd be OK. Betty told them that the United States supported Trujillo, not because of his politics, but because he was Latin America's leading anti-communist. It was in Trujillo's best interest to keep the Dodgers free from harm. Betty added her own belief that the dictator was paying a lot of money to the Dodgers in order to get them to train in his country. She went on to point out, however, that Branch Rickey was only one of three Dodgers' owners. Whereas Mr. Rickey ran team operations, the other two were more involved with financial matters. Therefore, the decision to train in the Dominican Republic was probably made by the group of three. With that, the family was satisfied. Don would go to the Dominican Republic with their blessings.

Getting ready for spring training was easy. Don was in excellent shape, due to daily workouts in various school gymnasiums. He would run the indoor tracks, practice wind sprints on the basketball floors, and keep his throwing arm in shape by playing catch with high school coaches. Betty carefully watched his diet at home; he did the same at work. His weight and muscle tone stayed pretty much at his playing level. The only physical thing he really needed was total immersion back in the game; he would get that in Santo Domingo. There would be no physical exam by the team. No special inoculations were required. The water over there was safe to drink. All Don had to do was show up not later than Sunday, February 29, one leap year day before the 1948 major league baseball season officially began.

The tiring flight to Santo Domingo was quickly forgotten as Don comfortably merged into spring training as a regular member of the Dodgers' team. He took pleasure in getting back to the cordial give-and-take camaraderie with friends and fellow players. He also welcomed the times he could stand at the plate, eagerly trying to test his 34-ounce bat, one-on-one, against the pitching of Ralph Branca, Joe Hatten, and Preacher Roe.

Branca had an arsenal of throws that could move the ball up, down, or sideways like a striking rattlesnake. Opposite to Branca's style was Roe, who could deal enough junk over the plate to make the batter jump and fan the air. And then there was Hatten, who cannoned the ball hard enough to make the battleship *Missouri* jealous, but whose control problems could cause some batters to sign up for life insurance.

All three posed an array of challenges to the entire squad at spring training. Don was always eager to face them. Moreover, he became somewhat content with his performance in the outfield. His ability to get the jump on a ball for an easy catch had not diminished over the winter, nor had his timing or his throwing accuracy. But, like so many other professional athletes, he was never satisfied. He drove himself hard every day, always pushing his own threshold. No matter what it took, he told himself, he was determined to be one of those twenty-eight guys who made the cut and headed up to Ebbets Field.

Most obvious to Don and the rest of his teammates that spring were the extensive personnel changes being made. Team leadership, player assignments, and the addition of one very talented catcher were prominent.

Foremost was the return of manager Leo Durocher. Fresh from completing his one-year forced suspension, Durocher showed up in Santo Domingo direct from Hollywood with his wife of two months in tow, actress Laraine Day. Miss Day, as Laraine liked to be called, had been in movies for more than ten years. Though never a major movie star, she had appeared in films with such leading men as Ronald Reagan, Lionel Barrymore, Cary Grant, and Edward G. Robinson. A practicing Mormon from a prominent Utah family, Laraine neither drank nor smoked, had a wholesome outlook toward others, and tended to approach things that sparked her interest with unbridled enthusiasm. This included baseball. As a matter of fact, Laraine Day would soon be known as "The First Lady of Baseball." She was especially nice to the players, who all thought she presented a perfect public contrast to her husband.

With Laraine that spring was her close friend, actress Gail Patrick. Gail had just announced her retirement from movie acting. She was spending a few weeks with Laraine in Santo Domingo on vacation, after which she intended to shift her career into movie producing. The players liked Gail Patrick because she showed high interest in the sport, attended the inter-squad games, and always wore a big smile wherever she went.

Both Laraine and Gail were fun to be around and were seen as delightful additions to the Dodgers' camp. Plus, they used their Hollywood influence to have first-run movies shipped from Los Angeles to Santo Domingo. There were several evenings when players, coaches, staff, and even Durocher would gather at the movie house with Laraine and Gail to watch the latest release from Tinsel Town. One player who never missed these was Don Lund.

From the first day of spring training through the next four weeks, Durocher and the Dodgers focused a lot of their attention on the infield. First, it was necessary to move Jackie Robinson over to second base, his normal position, in order to make the best use of Jackie's defensive talents. The past year Jackie had covered first base, mainly because Eddie Stanky was having a great year at second. Even though Jackie had been named 1947

Rookie of the Year, everyone knew that first base was not Robinson's most comfortable position.

Now it was 1948. Branch Rickey decided it was time to make the move. So on March 6 All-Star Stanky was traded to the Boston Braves and Jackie replaced him at second. This, of course, left first base open. Don Lund and the others wondered what Durocher would do. It didn't take him long. On March 7, Gil Hodges, last year's catcher, was moved over to first base. Hodges was a four-sport high school seven-letter winner who could play any infield position. First base would now be his. That left the catcher's spot open. The players wondered what Durocher would do.

Again, it didn't take him long. This time, though, the new catcher didn't come from the established squad. He came from the Negro Leagues. The same day that Gil Hodges trotted out to take ownership of first base, the whole squad watched as a light-skinned African-American put on the pads and strode purposefully to take his position behind the plate. His name was Roy Campanella. At 5-feet-8-inches and 200 pounds, Campanella was built like a fireplug, yet he moved with great speed and agility.

Don practically stared at him because the new catcher wore number 33, Don's old Michigan numerals. Later, Campanella would switch to number 56, then to his career number 39. But Don's first impression of Campanella, wearing his Wolverines' number, couldn't have been more positive. Right then he decided to get to know the Dodgers' catcher better. And so did a lot of other players. Roy Campanella, with his wide grin and magnetic personality, quickly became one of the most popular men on the roster.

Don's biggest impression about Santo Domingo was the extent to which Dominican Republicans showed their love for baseball. More than 14,000 screaming fans paid to pack the stadium, Estadio Quisqueya, every day the Dodgers took the field. Amateur teams of all skill levels played each other year around. Even young boys played the game in the streets, sometimes using cut-down broom handles for bats, taped-up old balls, and anything they could find to use as bases. All this reminded Don of those vacant lot games in his old Detroit neighborhood. If it weren't for Uncle Ken Matheson and his gifts of equipment, he thought, he and the other kids might have also used cut-up broomsticks. And that probably would have been OK.

One incident happened during the first couple of spring training weeks that could have turned serious. Don and a small group of his teammate friends were walking around and looking for something to do after practice one day. There were six of them: Don, Pee Wee Reese, Gil Hodges, infielder Gene Mauch, outfielder Dick Whitman, and pitcher Clyde King. They spotted an open playground with a cement basketball court and a couple of iron hoops. One of them took off and came back with a basketball. They played a few games and then decided to come back every day. It was fun.

These basketball games were also rough. The players were highly competitive, finely tuned athletes. When they played anything, they played to win. It didn't matter that they fooled around on cracked pavement, wore street clothes, or had no referees to enforce rules. They played to a standing crowd of neighborhood kids, teenagers, and adults. They played hard. They were in their glory. Don Lund and Gil Hodges were the standouts, both having played as amateurs in organized leagues, both having been basketball team captains, and both being large men. Don considered Gil Hodges one of the nicest players he'd ever met. In fact, he counted all five of the others in this post-practice group as good friends.

However, two things happened that broke up the games. First, when Don went up for a rebound one day, he accidentally body-slammed Dick Whitman. Whitman lay on the cement for a while with his wind knocked out. When he recovered, the game broke up and the guys went back to their hotel. Second, while the whole group was diving for a loose ball, Gene Mauch accidentally thumped Pee Wee Reese on his throwing-arm shoulder. Pee Wee grabbed his right arm and writhed in agony for a minute or so. That was it for the entire group. They canceled any future basketball play and quietly walked off the court. Thankfully, Pee Wee was as good as ever after a couple of days with the trainer. Durocher never found out about the incident.

A funny thing happened to Betty Lund during spring training that year, which involved the Dodgers but had nothing to do with Don. On Friday night, March 19, Betty was in Ann Arbor with some girlfriends to see the new movie *Easter Parade*, starring Judy Garland. Marguerite was watching Susan back home in Detroit. It was a nice break for Betty to get away the day before Susan's second birthday. Just before the movie began, a *Fox Movietone News* segment was shown entitled "The Brooklyn Dodgers Train in the Dominican Republic." Some of it featured the team working out on the field, but more than one scene displayed various players having a good time in local cantinas, with drinks piled high and dancing girls performing in scanty costumes. To Betty's relief, her husband wasn't among the players being portrayed. Nevertheless, she had carefully described to her friends that spring training in Santo Domingo was hot, lonely, and stifling to the players. Now they were seeing something quite the opposite. Later, on their way out of the theater, they all laughed about the *Movietone* scenes. Betty put up with some good-natured kidding, and after a while she had to agree the segment had been funny. But would she tell Andy and Marguerite about it when she got home? Not a chance, she said to herself. And she didn't.

The end of spring training in Santo Domingo saw Don making the cut and going back to New York with the team. On the way, the Dodgers stopped for one night in Vero Beach, Florida, to see Dodgertown, which was just getting started and would be ready for them by the following spring. Then they barnstormed up north in various towns like Birmingham, Alabama, and Knoxville, Tennessee, playing local teams or just giving inter-squad exhibitions. Finally, the team arrived in Brooklyn a few days before opening day at Ebbets Field. Betty had driven the Pontiac from Detroit, along with Susan and a girlfriend who shared the driving. The Lunds, grateful to be together again, settled into a small Brooklyn apartment.

For the first half of the season, Don played in twenty-five games, rotating between left and right field. His hitting had not established the groove he was looking for. In his own mind, he thought he might be trying too hard at the plate, tensing too much, trying for the seats. He was determined to relax a little more and see if that would help.

Monday, June 28, was an off-day for the Dodgers. The weekend had not gone well, considering back-to-back losses to the Cardinals. Don was home that evening, reading the daily newspaper. Susan was playing in her crib. Betty was in the kitchen, washing dishes. As he read the sports pages, Don was grousing a little about his lack of playing time. Resting on the bench was bad enough, he mused, but sitting there watching your team lose was awful. Maybe if he talked to ... Suddenly his eyes caught the headline of a small article near the bottom of the page: "Dodgers Deal Lund to Browns." He blinked. Then he read two paragraphs that said the St. Louis Browns had picked him up on waivers from the Dodgers. The announcement had been made that morning.

"Honey," he called to Betty, "come here and look at this. It says I've been sold to the Browns."

Betty read the article; she read it again. "You mean they sell you, and this is how you find out about it?"

"I guess so," he answered. "I'd better call the Dodgers' front office and see what's going on." He ran down the stairs and out the door to the phone booth at the curb. He was glad that Jane Ann Jones was still at her desk on Montague Street. She answered on the first ring.

"I'm sorry you had to find out about this the way you did, Don," she told him. "I wanted to call you this morning, but you don't have a phone. I pretty much had to wait until you contacted me." She urged Don to call the Browns right away, and she gave him the phone number of the Browns' general manager Bill DeWitt. When Don placed the call, Bill DeWitt answered, "Yes?"

"Mr. DeWitt, this is Don Lund. I just learned you've picked up my contract."

DeWitt: "Yes."

Don could almost feel the icicles on the phone line. "Mr. DeWitt, I want you to know I'll get there just as soon as I can."

DeWitt: "Your contract says you have forty-eight hours to get from one club to another."

Don responded, "Okay, I'll be ..."

The line was dead. Bill DeWitt had broken the connection.

Don called the Dodgers' front office and confirmed travel arrangements. He would be on the morning flight to St. Louis. He then went back upstairs to their apartment and told Betty about his phone conversations. They agreed that Betty and Susan would take the train back to Detroit and wait until Don was settled in St. Louis. That left only the Pontiac to consider, and Don's pal Bob Chappuis brought a stroke of luck.

Bob just happened to be in Brooklyn that day with his father, Sylvan. The two had traveled to New York to meet Branch Rickey, owner and general manager of the newly franchised Brooklyn Dodgers football team. Ever the entrepreneur, Rickey wanted to expand his sports empire into football. He obviously thought a franchise in the All-America Football Conference was an ideal way for him to do it. He named his team the Brooklyn Dodgers. There was no connection between Rickey's team and the defunct Brooklyn Dodgers of the National Football League (1930–1943). Why Rickey chose the name was anybody's guess. Some thought he wanted only Dodgers to play home games in Ebbets Field, no matter what the sport. In any case, Rickey formed his team in part by purchasing the rights to players already drafted by other AAFC teams. Bob Chappuis was one of these. Bob had been drafted by the Detroit Lions while he was still in the military in 1945, but nothing came of that. In 1948, following his All-American senior season at Michigan, Bob was drafted by the AAFC champion Cleveland Browns. Subsequently, the Browns allowed Rickey to purchase his draft option. And so it was that Bob Chappuis, whose college football fame included the cover of *Time* magazine, signed a professional football contract with the Brooklyn Dodgers on June 28. One year later, the team would fold after a losing season. Bob would play another year in pro football before starting a highly successful career in labor relations.

"Hey, Bob," Don was on the pay phone. "I'm being sent to the St. Louis Browns, and I have to be on the plane tomorrow morning. Betty's taking the train back to Detroit. I've got my car here, and I was wondering ..."

True to his character, Bob Chappuis volunteered his help before Don could finish his sentence. He and his father would drive the Pontiac back home. Don was grateful to have such a good friend. With that, all the arrangements for his St. Louis transfer, though hastily done, were in place. He was ready to hop a plane.

The next morning Betty and Don said good-bye at the curb in front of their vacated apartment as two taxis stood by. One would drive him to LaGuardia airport. The other would take Betty and Susan to Grand Central Station. As they parted, Betty kissed him and said, "Remember that musical we saw a couple of years ago that starred Judy Garland?"

Don smiled. "Sure. *Meet Me in St. Louis.* Kind of appropriate, isn't it?"

Betty went on, "That title song, 'Meet me in St. Louie, Louie,'" she sang, "Meet me at the fair ..." Then, "How about if I change the words: 'Meet me in St. Louie, Donnie...'"

He laughed, and then sang, "Meet me at the park ..." Soon Don boarded an Eastern Airlines DC-3 for St. Louis. During the flight he would sometimes gaze out the window, watch the clouds go by, and sing in his mind, "Meet me in St. Louie, Betty ..."

As the plane touched down and its rear wheel settled, Don felt a wistful sense of history to be landing at St. Louis's Lambert Field. He'd heard that Theodore Roosevelt took the first presidential airplane ride from this spot.* A more important milestone occurred here just before Don's fourth birthday, as his mother had told him many times. On May 12, 1927, Charles Lindbergh took off from Lambert Field in his "Spirit of St. Louis" on his way to becoming the first solo pilot to cross the Atlantic Ocean. Don was moved; he wished Betty could share this landing with him.

Don caught a taxi from the airport to Sportsman's Park, home field to both the American League Browns and the National League St. Louis Cardinals. Since the playing field was used by both teams, Sportsman's Park was one of the most utilized game facilities in the major leagues. As if that weren't enough, the All-Star game would be played here on July 13. Fans were going to wear out the turnstiles.

Don was no stranger to Sportsman's Park, of course. The last time he showed up here he was wearing the Dodgers' uniform. And the biggest thing he remembered about those games was the stifling and unrelenting heat that smothered everyone, especially the players in their wool uniforms. Some outfielders swore that the reason the grass was so green in Sportsman's Park was because it was constantly watered by player sweat. Don chuckled when he thought of the various player peeves around the place,

---

* On October 11, 1910, Roosevelt flew out of Kinloch Airfield, later to become Lambert Field, St. Louis.

especially those involving sweat-slippery bats, waterlogged base-balls, or itches in certain places. If nothing else, Sportsman's Park was a popular target for ballplayer grumps and grouches. That, thought Don, was part of the stadium's charm.

He quickly found the Browns' locker room. He wasn't sur-prised to find a few players, the team trainer, and the equipment staff present; the first game of a three-day home stand against the Chicago White Sox was tonight. It was mid-afternoon and players were starting to drift in. Don walked over to a player about his size and introduced himself. It turned out the player was Whitey Platt, a six-year veteran outfielder who had spent his first three seasons in Chicago with both the Cubs and the White Sox.

"You're from the Dodgers?" Whitey grinned. "Welcome to the big leagues!"

Don laughed at Whitey's reference to the traditional rivalry between the two major leagues.

"By the way," Whitey added, "you know the Cardinals' locker room is over on the other side, behind their dugout, right?"

Don acknowledged that he knew.

Whitey said. "I checked it out. Ours is better!"

Don laughed again. Then he asked Whitey if he could recom-mend a place for him to stay until he found a more permanent home for his family. Whitey recommended the Fairgrounds Hotel on the corner of Natural Bridge and Spring avenues. It was close to Sportsman's Park and fairly reasonable. He added that a lot of ballplayers used the Fairgrounds Hotel for temporary housing until their families arrived. Some single players even lived there. Stan Musial, for instance, called it home for several years.

Don thanked Whitey, left the stadium, and walked over to the Fairgrounds Hotel, where he checked into a single room. Three days later, Betty and Susan arrived with the Pontiac. The next day, Friday, July 2, they found a flat close enough to the stadium for Don to walk there. On Saturday morning, they moved into the apartment. Don phoned Bob Chappuis at his father's place in Toledo to thank him for driving his car back home from New York.

"You're welcome," said his friend, "Dad and I really enjoyed your car. It rides great at ninety miles an hour!"

That was Chappuis; ever the kidder—at least Don hoped he was kidding. They were settled into their apartment by Saturday night. Betty wondered if they would enjoy St. Louis as much as other places they had lived. Don said they probably would, but they'd have to get used to the heat. The next day was Sunday, July 4. Everyone seemed to be celebrating with backyard bar-beques. Everyone, that is, but Don and Betty Lund. While Betty strollered Susan around the block to see the neighborhood, Don and the rest of the St. Louis Browns were in Union Station, boarding a train to Chicago for the start of a twenty-two-day road trip.

Don played in forty-five games the rest of the 1948 season with the St. Louis Browns. He batted 161 times, hit 3 home runs, drove in 25 runs, and finished with a batting average of .248. His fielding was flawless at 1.000. He was the only outfielder on the team who played more than thirty games and never made an error.

In more than one game, he stood out as a dominant player, and there were some memorable moments. In a game against Ted Williams and the Boston Red Sox in August, Boston scored six runs in the first inning. The Browns came back right away against the left-handed pitching of Mel Parnell and loaded the bases. Then Don took his first turn at the plate. On Parnell's third pitch, he smacked a triple to left center field, scoring all three runners. He ran home on a single, and St. Louis took the lead, 7–6. Two innings later, the Red Sox replaced Parnell with a right-hander. When Don's turn at bat came and he started for the on-deck circle, Browns' manager Zack Taylor (no connection to America's twelfth President) called him back to the dugout. Zack was a firm believer in the theory that right-handed hitters do best against left-handed pitching, and vice-versa. So Zack replaced Don with a left-handed hitter. The Browns went on to lose the game while their right-handed triple hitter, who was responsible for four runs, rode the bench.

Don made some good friends on the Browns' squad that year. One was Ned Garver, a rookie right-handed pitcher. Ned was a bright guy who had a sinking fastball that made batters swing for the seats, only to twist like a pretzel as they fanned the air. Ned was also unusual for a pitcher because he was good at

Game winners, St. Louis Browns, 1948. Victorious pitcher
Cliff Fannin is surrounded by the three players who provided
his winning offensive muscle. (*left to right*) Outfielder Whitey Platt,
Fannin, first baseman Hank Arft, and outfielder Don Lund.
(*Lund Family Collection*)

the plate. Often the Browns used him to pinch-hit, and he just
as often came through. Ned Garver proved to be much more
than just a rookie pitcher, and he was also a trifle superstitious.
When he was on the mound, he always wanted to receive the
ball back from the third baseman after an out. His teammates
obliged, of course. After all, some of them carried superstitions
much more bizarre than that. Another friend was third baseman
Bob Dillinger. Bob liked to tell jokes and kid around. Everyone
liked his sense of humor.

One day, just before a home game at Sportsman's Park,
Dillinger pointed to the infield and said to a group of players,
"Just look down that left field line; look at that third base area.
We use it; the Cardinals use it; everybody in town, probably even

the dogs, use it. You're looking at a gravel pit. There's no way I'm gonna get in front of a ball hit there. Lose some teeth or break my jaw!" Then he proceeded to get in front of every ball hit to him, fielding it perfectly off the nicely groomed third base area. After he made the last put-out in one inning, Dillinger came back to the dugout, flashed his teeth and said, "Still got 'em!"

There were also some interesting times on road trips. Like when outfielder Paul Lehner brought his wife along on a two-week jaunt in the second half of August. As the team was boarding the train in Union Station on August 16, Lehner and his wife were saying good-bye. Don was part of a small group of players standing nearby on the platform.

Lehner said they'd be back on September 2. She said she'd miss him terribly. He said she ought to come along. She said she had nothing to wear for the trip. He said not to worry; they'd buy clothes along the way. She said OK.

Don watched as they boarded the train arm-in-arm, oblivious to the grins of nearby teammates. No one said a word about the marital road trip arrangement until six days later, on August 24. The Browns went to Washington, D.C., for a three-game stint against the Senators.

During the first game at Griffith Stadium, Manager Taylor said to Paul, "Hey, Lehner, grab your glove and get out there."

Paul looked around. He had left his glove in the visitors' locker room, which could only be reached in this particular stadium by returning through the Senators' dugout. Highly embarrassed, he confessed his mistake to Taylor.

The manager glared at him. "How about that, Lehner! You remember to bring your wife along, but you can't even remember to bring your own glove on the field?"

Lehner walked back through the Senators' dugout to retrieve his glove, all the time looking like a forlorn puppy with his tail between his legs.

On a later road trip, Don witnessed one of the most amazing scenes he had ever seen. It happened on Monday, September 13, in Cleveland. The Browns had taken a pasting from the Indians over the weekend, losing three games out of the two doubleheaders played. The fourth game, the second of Sunday's doubleheader, had been called in the late innings because of a mandated Sunday curfew. The score had been tied at three, which meant the game must be replayed the next day. The Browns would have to stay over one more night.

Outfielder Dick Kokos, who hit the tying run for St. Louis, took a lot of good-natured kidding: "Hey, Kokos ... why didn't you close your eyes before the pitch and we'd be outta here!" Or: "If it weren't for you, we'd be havin' a beer on the train!" Kokos laughed at the barbs right along with his teammates. He was that kind of guy.

Anyway, Don's amazing scene came during the rescheduled game on Monday afternoon. He could hardly believe the overflowing stands. Here it was, a Monday afternoon and Cleveland Municipal Stadium was packed with people to its entire 78,000 capacity. They were cheering, shouting, chanting, screaming; creating noise that must have carried across Lake Erie into Canada. The fans wore so many different colors that Sherwin-Williams probably sent a scout. Don, roaming his left-field spot, was thrilled. He knew the stands were jammed because of two factors: Indians' owner Bill Veeck, whose skill at promoting baseball was unequaled, and the plain fact that Cleveland was in the hunt for the American League pennant. Those screaming, yelling, colorful, partisan fans wanted their "Tribe" to sweep the four-game series by winning this one. It wasn't to be. The Browns won, 3–2. Don felt sorry for the disappointed multitude—for about two seconds. That's how long it took for him to refocus on tomorrow's game in Philadelphia.

In 1948, Don also arrived at the Baseball Hall of Fame, and he showed up in grand style. During the All-Star game break, the Browns played the Philadelphia Phillies in Cooperstown, New York, at the Hall of Fame Stadium. Don was the star of the game. He hit one of the longest home runs of his career, and then followed with a base hit that won the game. For many years to come, he and Betty would kid their friends about Don making it to the Hall of Fame. The memory was marvelous.

After the season, Don and Betty drove the Pontiac back to Detroit with Susan. On the way, they decided to look for their own apartment. It was time they found some independence, they decided. So that's the first thing they did after they arrived.

32
From a Tiger to a Mud Hen

Susan Lund is two-and-a-half years old in mid-October 1948. She's rambunctious, precocious, a bouncy blond ball of energy. Her constant question "Why?" requires answers patiently given. Betty is also convinced that Susan must expand her social experiences beyond her parents and grandparents. She needs playmates. So she and Don looked for an apartment in a neighborhood that had lots of kids. After several days, they found one on the far east side of Detroit, at Seven Mile and Moross. The whole area is stocked with two-, three-, and four-year-olds, plus lots of other youngsters ranging upward through the teens. It proves to be ideal for the naturally convivial Susan Lund.

Don immediately found work in Detroit's public schools as a substitute teacher. He worked at all levels, from K–12, mostly in physical education classes. From time to time the schools would call him to assist in other academic classes. Then he'd have to rely heavily on a teacher's notes, or when notes weren't provided, simply ask the class to spend the period studying a particular lesson. At times he just "baby-sat" and monitored class decorum. There were a few occasions when he'd be called to work at an "ungraded" school. These were schools for wayward kids, troubled youngsters, or simply children who needed special academic attention.

One time Don walked into his classroom assignment at an ungraded school, only to be confronted by a group of teenagers standing near the teacher's desk. One of the bigger boys said, "Hey, mister, what if we ganged up on you?"

Don went up to him and put his face about an inch from the boy's nose. He shouted, "Who's gonna be first?"

With a look of panic, the boy turned around and found his seat. The others followed. "Man, your eyes changed," said the boy.

Don looked at the class. "Yea, they tend to do that." The rest of the class period sailed smoothly.

Don's other source of income came from officiating at football and basketball games under the Michigan High School Athletic Association. He worked games throughout southeastern Michigan, from as far north as Flint and Port Huron, to as far south as Ann Arbor and Washtenaw County. In addition, he officiated for the Roman Catholic Archdiocese of Detroit. On Fridays he'd referee a Detroit City League game in the afternoon, and then a suburban game that night. On Sundays he'd work a Catholic high school game.

One fringe benefit to all this was getting together with the other referees following the games. The men would swap stories, exchange strategies, and generally support each other as they discussed tough calls they made. Don looked forward to these meetings, especially when it came to "war stories." A memorable one was told by a guy who had just finished refereeing a football game in Royal Oak: "This coach was ranting and raving, jumping up and down, screaming bloody murder, so I asked him, as calm as I could, 'Would you like me to call you an ambulance for the heart attack you're gonna have?' You should have seen him. He calmed right down and walked away. I should become a psychiatrist!"

In the middle of February, Don went to the AAA office and picked up a routing for San Bernadino, California, where the St. Louis Browns were headed for spring training. He figured the drive out there with Betty and Susan would take about a week. A couple of days later, while he was working out in a high school gym after classes, one of the teachers hurried up to him.

"Hey, Don, it's great you're going to play right here in town!"

Don looked at the man's serious expression. "What do you mean?" he asked.

The teacher stared at him incredulously. "You don't know? You've been traded to the Tigers; says it right here in this morning's *Free Press*."

Don took the offered sports page and read a small column headlined: "Tigers Get Detroit's Lund." The Detroit Tigers had purchased his contract from the Browns. He thanked the teacher, quickly showered and dressed, then walked to the principal's office to use the phone. He was astonished. For the second straight time the only way he had learned about his being traded was through a newspaper article. His call to the Tigers' front office at Briggs Stadium confirmed that he now belonged to the Tigers, and that he was expected for spring training in Lakeland, Florida, on March 1. Don practically ran from the principal's office to his Pontiac outside. The Detroit Tigers! His hometown team and his favorite! He couldn't wait to get home and tell Betty about their good fortune. Tomorrow he'd go back to the AAA office and get a routing to Lakeland.

Lakeland, Florida, was a sleepy town in central Florida, located in equally sleepy Polk County. It was surrounded by grain farms, orange groves, and miles of raw land. If you ventured a few miles out of town, you'd find oranges, palmettos, oranges, pine trees, oranges, and freshwater lakes filled with alligators. Polk County, and consequently Lakeland, was dry. If you wanted a drink you'd have to join the Elks Club. If you were a major league baseball club looking for a place where your players probably couldn't get into trouble, Lakeland would be splendid. And if you also wanted a first-class field where you could get your players ready for the big league season, Lakeland's Henley Field was ideal. Named after Clare Henley, a local druggist and baseball promoter, the stadium had a superbly conditioned playing field. As a matter of fact, Henley was the jewel of the Grapefruit League, thanks to the loving care of one man, Claude Warren.

Claude destroyed any stereotype for a head groundskeeper in a small-town baseball field. His nearly six foot tall, 150-pound frame was impeccably dressed in starched shirts and creased pants. A dark fedora sheltered his clean-shaven face from the incessant Florida sun. His eyes looked through large, horn-rimmed glasses. Claude spoke with a soft Southern drawl that hid a stern, no-nonsense approach to his job. Some said he made personal friends with every blade of grass. Claude's rule was simple: "Don't mess up Henley Field unless you're playing the game." And he meant it. One time Don and three of his teammates started to play "pepper," a practice game of ball control with the bat, usually involving players standing a few feet from each other. They tried to play it behind home plate. Claude chased them off. No one argued. They all knew Henley Field was Claude's "baby." Thanks to him, every team in the league looked forward to playing games at Henley Field.

Claude Warren would go on to become Lakeland's recreation director and retire thirty years later as one of the town's most beloved citizens.

A covered, wood-bench seating bowl for about 2,000 fans stretched around Henley's infield. The entrance façade was classic Florida stucco; it sported ticket booths on either side of the central gates. The Tigers were there simply because in 1929 Clare Henley told team owner Frank Navin that Lakeland was the best place for spring training. Navin agreed, so excepting the WWII years, Henley had been spring home for the Tigers since then. Eventually, the Tigers would build their own facility at an abandoned military air base just north of Lakeland. They'd call it "Tigertown." Their new stadium would be named after Lakeland's popular recreation director at the time, Joker Marchant.

The Lunds found a small apartment outside of Lakeland on Highway 98. It was old, but clean; the kitchen was barely large enough for the stove and fridge, but at least the windows were screened; the place would be OK for a month. Renting next to them was a sportswriter for the *Flint Journal* named M.B. Cossman. He asked Don to call him Morey when they met outside their apartment building.

Morey recognized him. "I saw you refereeing a basketball game at Flint Central in January."

Don grinned. "How'd I do?"

Morey grinned back. "You did just fine; Central won."

Morey Cossman was an interesting character. Back in Flint he sold pots and pans because sportswriting didn't pay him enough. Don Lund, teacher and referee during the winter months, connected right away. Morey mentioned Don in some of his columns; Don paved the way for some of Morey's interviews. The two got along famously.

The Tigers had a new manager this year. Red Rolfe had directed the team's farm system in 1948. With the departure of Steve O'Neill for health reasons, Rolfe was picked for the helm. He brought an impressive pedigree with him, including seven years as regular third baseman for the Yankees during their World Championship years. Red Rolfe was a clear contrast to Steve O'Neill. O'Neill was effervescent; Rolfe was laid-back. O'Neill was outspoken in public; Rolfe kept his opinions to himself. O'Neill was outgoing with the players; Rolfe was aloof. Only a few similarities between the two of them existed, such as a history of health problems. The previous year there were a few times when O'Neill couldn't leave the dugout because of pain in his legs. Rolfe suffered from stomach ulcers during his playing years, and he showed up for spring training this year with a severe case of colitis. O'Neill needed time off to recuperate; Rolfe just didn't feel good much of the time. Nevertheless, Rolfe stepped in with authority.

Don merged right in as a new Tigers' outfielder. He was happy to see Dick Wakefield again and pleased to note that Dick hadn't lost his quick wit and raucous sense of humor. Pat Mullin, Johnny Groth, Hoot Evers, and Vic Wertz were all superb guys who made him feel welcome right away. Only one of the coaches, Dick Bartell, caused a problem. One time Bartell decided to run the outfielders especially hard while hitting fungo fly balls. He ruthlessly hit to the far right, the far left, deep to center, short in, or anywhere else he could make the fielders run themselves out trying to make the catch. At the same time, Bartell kept his face in a constant frown. He seemed to be trying to make a point, but he didn't speak, so nobody knew what it was. Finally, Rolfe saw what was going on and walked over, telling Bartell to stop. Bartell just dropped the fungo bat and walked away. The players shared some choice words among themselves. They avoided Bartell as much as they could until training camp ended.

The Tigers played other Florida-training teams in an alliance known as the Grapefruit League. Teams from both the American and National Leagues would travel to meet them at Henley Field. Accordingly, the Tigers would travel to other Florida towns like Sarasota, Tampa, Plant City, Clearwater, and St. Petersburg. The competition wasn't nearly as fierce as the regular season. Managers would try different strategies, move players around in the batting order, shift outfielders, and test various game plans. Winning the games wasn't as important as working properly to field the best team on opening day. Don played well enough to make the twenty-eight-man squad as the team broke camp and headed north to Detroit. Betty was quite happy to know they could stay in their own apartment in Detroit, rather than have to set up a temporary home in who-knows-where. She and her husband had no way of knowing at the time, but Don Lund was destined to stay in the Detroit Tigers' organization for the rest of his active career in professional baseball.

On the way up from Lakeland, the Tigers stopped off in Pittsburgh for an exhibition with the Pirates at Forbes Field. It was the third week in April, that time of year when the weather calls for sweaters and raincoats. As the team left Pittsburgh's Union Station, they headed for taxis to take them to the Schenley Hotel. Don was one of the last to hail a cab, so was Manager Rolfe. They climbed in the same one. On the way, Don tried to initiate a conversation. He decided to avoid any topic about baseball or the team, which might be awkward for both of them. Instead, he remembered that Rolfe graduated from Dartmouth and coached basketball at Yale. Don, of course, played basketball at Michigan. Rolfe was receptive and talkative. He mentioned that the only professional basketball team he coached, the Toronto Huskies, lasted just one year before they folded for financial reasons. After his first season, he was out of a job. Beyond that, Rolfe was happy with his college basketball years. He added that someday he'd like to return to Dartmouth in some capacity.* When they arrived at the Schenley Hotel, Don reached for his wallet to pay his half of the fare. Rolfe told him to put his money away, the ride was on the Tigers. Don walked away feeling good about the new manager, who also knew something about basketball.

The exhibition game at Forbes Field was canceled by the weather and a tarp covered the infield, so the Tigers practiced at the University of Pittsburgh's football field, Pitt Stadium. This proud home of the Pittsburgh Panthers was a solid, above-ground, fully enclosed oval that stood about sixty feet high and housed 56,000 fans. It was built to keep noise in—great for a football game, weird for baseball practice. You didn't just hear the crack of a fungo bat, you heard it echo over and over, as the sound bounced around the stands. Don actually caught a ball before the sound reverberation of the hit died down. The practice session was bizarre, but fun for all that day at Pitt Stadium.

---

* Rolfe later served as Dartmouth's athletic director. Red Rolfe Field there is named for him.

Tuesday, April 19, was a spectacular home Opening Day
for the Tigers. Mild weather was crowned by the bright rays of
a lonely sun in a cloudless blue sky. More than 54,000 excited
fans streamed into Briggs Stadium with dreams of victory over
the Chicago White Sox, and they weren't disappointed, thanks
to the hitting exhibition of outfielder Johnny Groth. In Detroit's
5–1 win, Groth hit two home runs. The second of these brought
everyone in the stadium, including both teams, to their feet,
because it was inside the park. A right-handed hitter, Groth
reached out for an outside curve ball and blooped it down the
right-field line. The ball was called fair by the first base umpire
as Chicago outfielder Pat Seerey, who had been playing Groth
in short left center field, raced for the ball like a hound after a
rabbit. The ball landed, bounced a couple of times, and then
stopped dead in the corner. Second baseman Cass Michaels
also scrambled after it. Groth's legs were churning, his arms
were pumping like pistons, he was kicking up a dust cloud that
shadowed him around the bases. By the time Seerey barehanded
the ball off the ground and threw, Groth was already sliding into
home plate. The sellout crowd went wild. For them, Opening
Day in Detroit couldn't be better.

Don got into some games during the first thirty days, but he
wasn't playing enough to make him feel he was contributing to
the team. On the road, he roomed with third baseman George
Kell, one of the best roommates he ever had. Kell was smart
beyond the baseball field. He talked expertly on many subjects.
He made anyone he met feel comfortable, whether they were
five years old or fifty. He had a natural charm in social groups
and a relaxing sense of humor. All this, plus tremendous athletic
skills, made George Kell a player's player.

Near the end of that first month, while the Tigers were on
the road against the Washington Senators, Rolfe called Don into
his hotel room. "Here's what's happening," he told him. "We're
going to send you to Toledo. But you might be coming back if
this deal we're working on for Wakefield goes through. If it does,
you'll come back here pretty quick."

Don didn't say anything, he just nodded.

Rolfe went on, "In the meantime, the rule says we have to
trim down to twenty-five players in a couple of days. The other

two guys will know who they are by the end of the day. You should get ready to go to Toledo. Good luck."

Don thanked Rolfe and shook his hand. He soon found his locker, cleaned it out, and then went home to Betty and Susan. Later that day, the Tigers announced that Don Lund was being sent to the Toledo Mud Hens, Saul Rogovin was optioned to the Buffalo Bisons, and Jimmy Outlaw was announcing his retirement from the game.

Betty was actually upbeat over Don's news that he hadn't made the thirty-day cut. It was only about a two-hour drive to Toledo from where they lived. Don could commute in the Pontiac; she and Susan would continue to live in Detroit. As for Don's feelings, the disappointment about not making the Tigers roster quickly wore off. He wasn't one to carry negative thoughts for long. Besides, he thought, the Mud Hens were a Triple-A team in the American Association. The competition was almost as good as the big leagues. Besides, he thought, I can live home and commute to Toledo. Besides, he thought, I might be called right back up to Detroit. Besides … he shrugged. Maybe he'd just show up tomorrow and see what happens.

The Mud Hens played their home games at Swayne Field, corner of Monroe Street and Detroit Avenue, in downtown Toledo. The stands held room for 10,000 spectators. Sometimes they were filled. What the team lacked in crowd appeal, however, it made up in spirit, determination, and hard play. Responsible for this was the Mud Hens' newly acquired manager, Eddie Mayo.

Eddie was just retired from several years in the Tigers' infield. His nickname in his earlier playing days was "Hot Shot," and he lived up to every letter of it. Eddie's enthusiasm was infectious; his smile seemed welded to his face; he didn't mince his words when he talked to a player. He was, in fact, a player's kind of manager. Eddie Mayo intended to take his 1949 Toledo Mud Hens from a bottom-of-the-league, publicly unappreciated team to one that demanded respect whenever and wherever it played. He wanted to light a fire under his team. And the spark to ignite it stepped right into his office on Friday, May 20.

Don Lund, grinning like a kid with his favorite candy bar, presented himself as the newest Mud Hen. He was ready for his first game. Eddie Mayo complied by sending him in to pinch hit in the third inning. Don hit a screaming double on the first pitch thrown to him in Swayne Field. In the second game, the bases were loaded in the fifth inning. Mayo called down, "Grab a bat, Lund." Don strode up, took his stance, and hit the second pitch for a grand-slam home run. The crowd exploded, and Don was on his way to a great season. He played with electricity. His glove was a vacuum cleaner; his arm caused runners to stop advancing on hits that otherwise meant extra bases. His bat became a cannon.

There was one home game, in fact, when his bat made the nation's sports pages. On his first trip to the plate, he hit the second pitch for a home run into the left-field stands. On his next trip, he again hit the second pitch for the left-field stands and a home run. His third trip produced another second-pitch home run, practically in the same spot in the left-field stands. This time, as he trotted back to the Mud Hens' dugout and sat down, the guys went crazy with praise. When Don's fourth time came to bat, the game was pretty much put away for Toledo. The first two pitches came wide and away for called balls; he swung and missed the third pitch. The fourth pitch came right toward the middle of the plate, belt-high. Don felt the sweet spot of his bat make contact, and he saw the ball sail toward left center field. As he rounded first base, he watched it hit the wall a few inches below the rail and bounce back about twenty feet. The center fielder caught the rebound and, in one motion, launched a dead-on throw to first base. Don scrambled back just in time. The game ended with Don still on first base, but also with a nice win for the Mud Hens. His bat had made the difference. A few inches from four home runs in four times at bat.

Don contributed more to the team that year than just his hitting. His matter-of-fact, never-cut-the-pie attitude on the field made him a favorite with the fans. Lively, supportive crowds choked the Swayne outfield stands. They'd cheer him even when he made an easy catch. *Toledo Blade* sports writers picked up on this and sought to interview him before and after home games. Don Lund was, in the words of one reporter, "good copy." By the end of the season, Don's batting average was .298. He'd hit seventeen home runs and led the team in runs batted in (RBIs). He was idolized by the Toledo fans and considered a local celebrity.

Now all he needed to do was spend an enjoyable winter teaching in Detroit and waiting for the Tigers to summon him back. That, after all, is what he really wanted. But first there came a chance to earn extra money and have fun at the same time.

Shortly after the Mud Hen's last game, Don received a call from his friend George Kell. Kell told him that he and Dizzy Trout were organizing a "barnstorming" tour for some of the Tigers' players, now on their own time, to play against home teams in several towns across Michigan's Upper Peninsula. It would be ten days of fun, plus a good chance to make a few extra bucks. Some of Don's friends, such as Johnny Lipon and Virgil Trucks, were going. Kell asked if Don would like to join them. He didn't hesitate; he was in.

About a dozen Tigers and one Mud Hen outfielder (who considered himself a Tiger) swept in and out of small towns in the Upper Peninsula. They cruised through dots on the map with names like Watersmeet and Negaunee; they played town teams in Bruce Crossing and Marquette. Some of the teams were organized into amateur leagues, while others hurriedly scrounged up some local citizens for a day of fun with pro players.

Hardly anyone took the games seriously, and that included the big league barnstormers. One time Dizzy Trout had the public address announcer tell the crowd that the next batter was none other than the "Famous Bambino himself, Babe Ruth." As the crowd laughed, Trout emerged from the Tigers dugout with a large pillow stuffed into his shirt and an exaggerated stride to the plate. Few noticed that "Ruth" was batting right-handed (the real one batted left), and nobody cared. With his cap pulled down to his eyebrows and a scowl that would have petrified Dracula, Trout extended his bat toward center field bleachers. He waggled the bat just enough for the fans to pick out the "Babe's" target. To everyone's delight, Trout was going to replicate Ruth's famous "calling his shot" home run during the third game of the 1932 World Series. The crowd went silent. The pitcher set himself and eyeballed the batter with a face that would have bluffed the best poker player in Las Vegas.

Then he threw a medium-fast, nothing-on-it ball right at the middle of the plate, belt-high. The "Babe" pounded it. Everyone stared at the soaring ball, and then gasped as it seemed to steer toward center field, sailing right where "Ruth" had pointed.

When it hit the dividing wall just below the designated spot, the crowd erupted in cheers, yells, and applause. Trout ran around the bases with his flopping pillow. All three outfielders scrambled for the ball like the Keystone Cops trying to catch Buster Keaton. They kicked it around and just couldn't seem to come up with it. Finally, one of them threw it into the stands as Trout crossed the plate. The immortal "Babe Ruth" had scored again! And fun-loving Dizzy Trout added another notch to his popular legend.

After the tour, Don resumed his substitute teaching and officiating jobs. As weeks passed, he began to anticipate word from the Tigers about bringing him back up. With the productive year he just had in Toledo, he thought there was ample reason for them to bring him to Lakeland as a major leaguer for 1950s spring camp. He waited patiently until the middle of January. Then he decided to act. He remembered those two times he read about his professional fate in the newspaper. It was time to become aggressive. So he went to the Tigers' front offices at Briggs Stadium to meet with general manager Billy Evans.

Evans had over twenty-five years experience in the American League, mostly as an umpire. He was considered one of the best ever to make the calls behind the plate. He was also one of the few umpires ever to fight Ty Cobb under the stands in front of both teams (he lost). One day he would be enshrined in the Hall of Fame. He was entering his fourth year as general manager for the Tigers, presiding over a team that finished in second place over the past two years.

Evans' most dramatic move thus far with Detroit, one that made him some enemies, was selling aging superstar Hank Greenberg to the Pittsburgh Pirates. Some fans wanted his head. As Don walked into his office, Evans jumped up and eagerly shook his hand. Like greeting an old friend, Don thought. Or maybe like a fox greeting its next meal in the henhouse. He couldn't tell which. Evans looked young for his sixty-six years. He stood a little over six feet, weighed about 170 pounds, and dressed like an ad for proper office wear—dark gray suit, white shirt, red tie, and cufflinks. His long nose presided over a bright set of teeth and a prominent, square jaw. He smiled broadly as they both sat on facing chairs. Their talk started easy as it rambled over baseball subjects, ending with Don's fruitful last year with the

Dad with four-year-old Susan at Toledo Mud Hens' spring training in Bartow, Florida. Only one of Susan's stuffed menagerie had a name. "Little Bear" takes its rightful spot next to its owner. (*Lund Family Collection*)

Mud Hens. Finally, Don told Evans, "I think it's time you and Detroit repurchase my contract."

Evans demurred. "I'm afraid we can't do that, Don. There's a rule that says if a team sells you outright to an affiliate, it can't reacquire you unless you first go through the unrestricted draft. And we certainly don't want to lose you through the unrestricted draft."

Don's stomach tightened. Sells you outright to an affiliate? Had he heard Evans properly? His eyes darkened as he asked Evans: "You didn't option me to Toledo with the possibility of bringing me back if a deal with Dick Wakefield went through? That's what Red Rolfe told me."

Evans became serious. "We couldn't option you, Don. You had already been optioned three times; that's the maximum right now. We sold you to Toledo. That's where you'll be this year."

Don's shoulders slumped. "I guess I didn't understand, Mr. Evans."

Evans was sympathetic. "I'm sorry you didn't, Don, but cheer up; have another good year. You'll be back, I know it."

With that, their meeting ended and Don headed home. Red Rolfe had either lied to him about the possibility of being brought back up from Toledo, or else he didn't have the right information. Don respected the Tigers' team manager, and chose to believe the latter. But he still wasn't satisfied. Rolfe told him one thing; Evans told him another. He decided to appeal his case to Baseball Commissioner Happy Chandler. He would take it to him personally.

Don rode the bus from Detroit to Cincinnati and entered the lobby of the building that housed the headquarters of Major League Baseball. He didn't have an appointment. He didn't want one. He didn't want to be told by some "gatekeeper" that Mr. Chandler wasn't available. So he waited in the lobby, hoping for a chance to meet the commissioner as he left for the day.

In about two hours, one of the elevators ejected a tall, trim man who walked with a purposeful stride. He wore a dark gray, double-breasted suit over a white shirt and blue checkered tie. His dark hair was parted straight back in the middle of his head. He had a large nose, thin lips, thick eyebrows, and brown eyes, all of which combined nicely into a handsome man. Don recognized him from photos he'd seen. He was the Commissioner of Baseball.

Albert Benjamin "Happy" Chandler was baseball's second commissioner. Following the death in 1944 of Kenesaw Mountain Landis, Chandler was elected unanimously by the sixteen team owners. He had just completed one six-year term as a U.S. senator from Kentucky. He had no plans to run again. Prior to that, Chandler served four years as Kentucky's governor. He had been forty-seven years old and ready for more challenges. Now, five years later, he had established himself as a controversial leader, frequently going against the will of many club owners. For instance, he ignored a 15–1 negative vote by the owners and paved the way for Jackie Robinson's remarkable career.

Moreover, Chandler became known as a player's advocate. He set a minimum $5,000 annual major league player's salary. He supported a new player pension plan. And he suspended Dodgers' manager Leo Durocher for the 1947 season, because of Durocher's suspicious gambling activities. Don felt that Commissioner

Chandler would at least listen to him. He counted on a fair shake from the man who had done a lot for the players.

Don jumped up as he saw Happy Chandler emerge alone from the elevator. He approached cautiously, but with confidence. "Mr. Chandler, I'm Don Lund. I'm with the Tigers' organization. I wonder if I could talk to you about my contract."

Chandler was receptive. Don told him the details of his move from Detroit to Triple-A Toledo and his recent meeting with Billy Evans. They went up to the commissioner's office, where Chandler looked up the rule cited by Evans. "It says right here, Don, if you're sold outright by your big league team to one of its farm teams, they can't reacquire you unless you go into the unrestricted draft. And you tell me they won't let that happen."

Don took his eyes off the rule book. "Yes."

Chandler closed the book slowly and sighed. "That's it then, Don. I'm afraid I can't help you."

Don thanked him and headed for the door.

Chandler called to him as he opened it. "Good luck, Don; have a great year in Toledo. I really mean that."

On the bus back to Detroit, Don had mixed feelings. He wasn't pleased with having no chance to return to the Tigers this year, despite his strong performance last season, but he had enjoyed meeting Happy Chandler, a man who obviously sympathized with the plights of players who lived and worked by the whims of club owners. Maybe Chandler would eventually make a difference in the system. Don had no way of knowing, of course, that the owners would not rehire Happy Chandler the following year.

Back in Detroit, Don waited out the remainder of the off-season winter months. He continued his work in teaching and officiating. Eventually he forced himself to accept his contract situation. After all, he reasoned, he was first and foremost a professional baseball player. He would play for an excellent Triple-A team in Toledo. He was young and strong; he still had lots to prove.

33

Triple-A Transition

His Toledo Mud Hens contract arrived just after the 1950 New Year's celebrations faded away. The first thing Don noticed was the salary it offered. One thousand a month, for four and a half months. He was shocked. This was less than a laborer with an eighth-grade education and no skills was making at the Chrysler plant. For him, it was the biggest pay cut since he signed with the Dodgers in 1945.

Betty wanted her husband to visit the Tigers' home office before he signed the document, so he made an appointment to see Muddy Ruel, the Detroit Tigers' farm director. Muddy had authority over minor league players' contracts throughout the Tigers' farm system, including the Toledo team. On the way to his appointment, Don tried to lighten his mood. He thought of the irony over seeing Muddy about the Mud Hens. A joke. But not right now. He needed to be respectful. So he thought about the man he was meeting.

From 1915 through 1934, Herold D. "Muddy" Ruel enjoyed twenty seasons as one of the toughest and most durable catchers in the American League. During that time, he also earned a law degree, was admitted to the bar by the U.S. Supreme Court, and became an expert on laws affecting baseball. After that he spent the next ten years as a coach for the White Sox, followed by one year as Commissioner Happy Chandler's assistant. Then he managed the St. Louis Browns in 1947, the year before Don played for them under manager Zack Taylor. Now he ran the Tigers' farm system under general manager Billy Evans. Don hadn't met Muddy Ruel. He figured, though, that anyone with that kind of baseball background would certainly be willing to hear his story, so he looked forward to seeing Ruel, the man who could beef his salary back up to a respectable amount.

Don was quickly ushered into Muddy's plain, old-wood office. The place reeked of pipe smoke. So did the man who greeted him with a big smile and a soft voice. The cause of the smoke was a glowing briar in his left hand. He was indeed Muddy Ruel, but he didn't fit one's typical image of the tough catcher who snagged Walter Johnson's incredibly fast pitches. You'd expect to see a big guy with hands like frying pans, but the man saying hello wasn't very tall, wasn't very heavy, and wasn't very muscular. The only thing that gave him away as one of the great catchers of his time was his handshake. He could have crushed granite; Don was glad he didn't try. Muddy was dressed in a light gray wool suit, white shirt, and blue tie. His close-cropped gray hair topped a long face with a prominent nose, stern brown eyes, and dark bushy brows. His demeanor was friendly; his attitude was all business. Muddy slowly puffed his pipe as Don presented his expectations for a higher salary. He'd had a pretty good season last year. He finished by asking Muddy to reconsider.

"I'm sorry, Don, I really am," said Ruel, "but I just can't find you more money." He told Don that even though the Toledo Club was part of the Tigers' organization, it was financially independent. The entire payroll was dependent on Mud Hens sales of tickets, food and beverages, and promotional items. He went on to say things like Don was one of the highest paid on the team. No two players received the same compensation. The only way a player in Triple A ball could make more money was to move up to a major league team. Ruel was pleasant when he said this, and he appeared to respect Don's feelings. Don was grateful for that. When they parted, he thanked Ruel for his time. Muddy wished him a successful season.

On the way back home, Don clearly saw how he and other professional baseball players serve at the whim of powerful club owners. They can be traded around from team to team. They can be arbitrarily moved up and down between major and minor league clubs. Their families might be displaced at a moment's notice. They have no pensions, no fringe benefits, no employment rights at all—unless, of course, a player is talented enough to be among the very best. Players are paid on performance. Superstars are paid the most. Don Lund wasn't a superstar. So what makes us, he asked himself, me and all those other ballplayers in the minor leagues—me and the thousands of guys who ride rusty buses and compete for as little as twenty-five bucks a game in the lower leagues—what makes us continue to play?

The answer was as clear as his own name: it's love for the sport, he admitted. We inhale it like the breath of life. We thrill at the "crack" of a well-turned piece of northern white ash slamming into a horsehide-covered ball; or the "smack" of a ball as it hits a leather glove. Especially if we're the ones doing the "cracking" and the "smacking." Our national pastime, played at the highest levels, is addictive to those who play it. Let's face it, he thought. I'm addicted and I'm chasing a dream. That's why I signed that contract in front of Muddy Ruel. That's why I'm going to play as hard for the Toledo Mud Hens as I would for the Dodgers or the Tigers. I'm just like all those other guys who suit up every day all over the country. Baseball is in my blood; if I have to, I'll bleed for it.

On March 1, he reported to Mud Hens spring training in Bartow, Florida.

Bartow, located in Polk County about twenty miles from where the Tigers trained in Lakeland, will strongly be remembered by Mud Hens players who trained there. Bartow was a nice enough city. The townsfolk were especially pleasant. The town was clean and decent, fairly free of crime. But so were a lot of Florida towns where spring training took place, including those hosting other Triple-A teams. With only sixteen big league teams, the major leagues couldn't hold all the quality players in the game. Triple-A was only a small step, and in some cases like Toledo, a half-step from the majors in terms of talent. So spring training towns were fairly matched equally among major and Triple-A league teams. This was true for the Mud Hens. But the players wouldn't remember Bartow for its niceties. They would remember it for its smells.

West of town, the phosphate mines were the biggest in the United States. Mining activity filled the surrounding miles of air with acrid smells of its byproducts, including ammonia. The atmosphere didn't make breathing uncomfortable, but its pungency was unmistakable. Worse was the sulfur odor in the water. "Hold your nose when you drink it" was one of the first phrases a newcomer learned. Getting used to it was easy for some, hard for others. It took the Lunds about a week. Mud Hens players, however, never got used to showering in that stinky water. They'd walk out after every practice smelling like rotten eggs. "Whew!" became the most clearly understood word in their vocabulary.

That was the one big, lasting ballplayer memory about Bartow, Florida: the stink.

Another place, located a few miles east of Bartow, held a real delight for players with cars. Lake Wales, Florida, boasted an optical-illusion place called Spook Hill. One of Don's friends on the team told him about it, so he decided to check it out with Betty and Susan. He drove to Lake Wales and started up Spook Hill. Following directions, he stopped the car about halfway up and put it in neutral. The car amazingly rolled uphill instead of backward. Word about Spook Hill in Lake Wales got around, and every Mud Hens player eventually tried it out before spring training ended.

Don easily made the Mud Hens starting lineup in right field. He felt good as he rode the train back up north with the team. Betty and Susan took the car in an automobile caravan of players' families. Don could hardly wait for Opening Day.

The 1950 and 1951 baseball seasons saw Don Lund settle in as a solid Triple-A starting outfielder for the Toledo Mud Hens. During the off-seasons, he was able to boost his income through teaching every day in the Detroit public schools, and also by officiating football and basketball games after school, at night, and on weekends. Susan continued to be a low-maintenance, ever-smiling and happy child as she grew into her fifth year. Susan went to bed with a smile and woke up with a smile. Since her parents never used baby talk with her, she spoke in cogent sentences. She loved to watch *Howdy Doody* and ride her tricycle in front of the house. Like most kids at age five, Susan Lund had no enemies. Happily, Susan would continue that trait through her adult years.

Don was a popular player in Toledo, liked as much for his open friendliness with the fans and the press as for his record on the field. His performance was above average, but the team itself in 1951–1952 was solidly average. Jack Tighe managed them. Tighe had spent his entire playing and managerial career in the minor leagues, except for a couple of months as a Tigers' coach in 1942. He was liked by his players, mostly because he didn't show much of a temper, and he didn't seem to take himself too seriously. He also liked to sing.

One of Tighe's favorite pastimes was crooning with the guys in the clubhouse. Jack loved barbershop songs like "Sweet Adeline" and "Down by the Old Mill Stream." He'd get those who joined him to harmonize with his tenor renditions. Sometimes the entire clubhouse sang along. Don wasn't much for singing, but he never hesitated to join the spirit of the moment. One time he stood up on a bench and announced: "Men, Jack and the guys are gonna sing for us now. A cappella. Also without music!"

Don liked Jack Tighe and played hard for him.

The best, most career-boosting contact Don Lund ever made as a professional baseball player happened right there in Toledo in 1950. He had the great fortune of getting to know the Mud Hens' Business Manager Jim Campbell.

James Arthur "Jim" Campbell was born in 1924 and grew up in Huron, Ohio, a little town on the shore of Lake Erie just east of Sandusky. His mom was the town postmaster. His dad was a Great Lakes freighter captain. As a kid, Jim liked to stand on the shore with his playmates and proudly watch his father's ship go by. Little Jim Campbell thought his dad was a maritime hero. As he grew up, so did big Jim Campbell. At Huron High School, he played football, basketball, baseball, and he pole vaulted on the track team. Known for his sharp wit and his devotion to baseball trivia, Jim had lots of friends and was considered a natural leader.

Campbell's favorite team growing up had been the New York Yankees, but that changed when he was sixteen and the 1940 Cleveland Indians came alive. The Indians had four players who were tearing up the competition: Bob Feller, with his blazing fastball, had thrown a no-hitter on Opening Day; another right-hander, "Chief" Mel Harder, was winning games with style; the bats of infielders Lou Boudreau and Ken Keltner were scoring runs. The Indians came close to winning the American League pennant that year. They settled for second place. The Tigers beat them out with their own superstars: pitching ace Bobo Newsome, outfielders Hank Greenberg and Barney McCosky, and second baseman Charlie Gheringer. When that happened, sixteen-year-old Jim Campbell became a Detroit Tigers' fan for life.

While still in high school, Jim entertained the idea of going to the University of Michigan. One of his uncles had been the

football team physician for several years, so he visited Ann Arbor
one day without an official invitation, appearing unannounced at
Yost Field House. Freshman football coach Wally Weber agreed
to see him. Weber wasn't too encouraging. Jim went away feeling
he'd be nothing better than a tackling dummy and a bench rider
if he went out for Michigan football. He'd be better off staying
in Ohio. He had a lot of friends at Ohio State, so the Buckeyes
would be his choice. However, by the time he graduated from
high school in 1942, America was at war. College would have
to wait.

Jim Campbell spent nearly four years with the U.S. Navy until
the war ended. Then he enrolled at Ohio State, played baseball,
became a dedicated Buckeye, and graduated in four years with
a business degree in 1949, at the age of twenty-five. Campbell
decided to work in professional baseball, so he contacted John
McHale, director of Minor League Operations for the Detroit
Tigers. McHale, a former Tigers' player who married the Detroit
team owner's daughter Patty Briggs, was so impressed with
Campbell he hired him during the interview. Campbell was tough,
McHale reasoned, and he appeared to be a problem-solver type.
And right now the Detroit Tigers had a problem with their farm
team in Thomasville, Georgia. The Thomasville Tigers were a
low-level minor league outfit that played in the Florida-Georgia
League Class D circuit. They had lost their business manager for
some reason unknown to McHale, and there were only vague
financial reports being sent to Detroit. Thomasville needed a
business manager; Jim Campbell was McHale's man.

Campbell's introduction to the Thomasville Tigers was a
baptism of fire. Literally. As he arrived on his first morning, fire
was breaking out in the clubhouse. Firemen couldn't contain
the blaze. Training equipment, uniforms, printed programs,
receipts, and financial records were all lost. Luckily, no one was
injured. The field and bleacher stands were saved. So were the
grounds tools. Jim Campbell, brand-new business manager, had
to immediately rebuild from the ashes. He did it quickly and
cost-efficiently. One year later McHale moved Jim to the Detroit
Tigers' top farm club—the AAA Toledo Mud Hens. That's where
he met right fielder Don Lund, in April of 1950.

Their first meeting, on the sidewalk outside Swayne Field,
was a humorous chance encounter. Don was wearing dark blue

trousers and a dark yellow shirt. Maize and blue. Campbell was wearing an Ohio State tie. Jim recognized Don as one of the players and grinned: "Are we scraping the bottom of the barrel and letting Michigan players on this fabulous field?"

Don grinned right back: "Is this fabulous field really in Ohio?" And that, as the cliché proclaims, was the start of a beautiful relationship.

On June 27, 1950, Don played in one of the most memorable games of his career. He was the second most important player that day in a Mud Hens' perfect game win over the Indianapolis Indians. The most important was, of course, pitcher Marlin Stuart. Marlin retired twenty-seven men in a row, chiefly by throwing screwballs and knucklers. His feat was the first and only time a perfect game had been thrown anywhere in the city of Toledo. It wouldn't have happened without Don Lund. In the sixth inning, Indianapolis pitcher Elmer Riddle punched a sinking line drive to right field. It looked and sounded like a sure base hit. Don charged, stretched, and picked the ball off his shoe tops for an inning-saving catch.

The instant Don caught the ball, everyone in the park sensed that this particular play would make the difference. It turned out they were right. No other Indians' batter was able to challenge first base. Don also drove in the winning run in the Mud Hens' 1–0 victory. Stuart was beside himself in thanking his right fielder. As one of Don's friends joked later, "Marlin would have adopted you. Or married you. Or nominated you for president. Anything, man, anything."

The Mud Hens' trainer was a gentle, unassuming, and friendly man named Charles A. Foley. Everybody called him "Doc." He wasn't a medical doctor; he was just good at what he did, so nobody cared about his formal training. Doc Foley stood nearly six feet and carried about 170 lean and muscular pounds. He typically dressed casually, in slacks, T-shirt, and white gym shoes. Large, thick eyeglasses dominated the upper part of his narrow face. There was no style to his dark, bushy hair; it just piled up on top of his head like a soft clump of weeds. Foley was popular with the team, mostly because he showed genuine concern for their aches and pains. His hands were strong enough to remove most muscle cramps and kinks. He took his time. No one complained about waiting their turn.

Doc was never known to treat women at Swayne Field, except for one time. Her name was Betty Lund. The accident happened after a game, when Betty was walking out of the stadium with her husband. She didn't see the broken bottle in front of a coke machine. She was wearing open-toed shoes. The cut was deep and bleeding hard, so Don practically carried Betty to Doc Foley's training area.

"You'll need stitches, Betty," said the trainer. "I'll patch you up as well as I can. But you'll have to go to the hospital right away from here." Foley applied pressure bandages and gauze wrap. Betty's foot looked like it belonged in the tomb scene of an Egyptian movie. But Foley's bandaging stopped the bleeding, and in less than an hour Betty's injured foot was stitched properly by an emergency room doctor. Doc Foley came through big time for Betty, but more than that, Foley didn't demean her by telling her to stop wearing open-toed shoes around a ballpark. Don would never forget Doc Foley's ultimate kindness.

Then there was the case of the "foul-ball pigeon." During the late innings of a night game at Swayne Field, Don rammed a hard drive deep down the left field line. The swing felt good to him. If it stayed fair, the ball would soon be bouncing toward the smokestack beyond the fence. Don started toward first base, because he knew the ball was hit too high and hard for the left fielder to grab. He watched it sail about three feet inside the line; a sure homer. Then suddenly the ball stopped in midair.

From Don's perspective, it looked like the ball split in two halves, one falling to the left into the stands, the other falling to the right on the grass. Don stopped on first base as the left fielder reached down and picked up, then held up, the bloodied remains of a pigeon. The bird had collided with the ball and the bird was dead. The ball was foul; strike one. The crowd groaned. Don strode back to the plate with his head down.

"Hey, Lund," a spectator yelled, "you got a hunting license?" That got some laughs. Later on in the dugout one of the players said to Don, "I sure wouldn't want to be the guy who had to pick up that pigeon with all the blood on it." Another one chimed in, "Oh yea? How'd you like to be the guy in the stands who caught the ball?"

"Toledo Times Night" was held at Swayne Field late on July 31, 1951. The Mud Hens hosted the Kansas City Blues, a

Triple-A farm team of the New York Yankees. Most of the Toledo team, including their starting right fielder from the University of Michigan, expected this to be just a routine game against a team that wasn't exactly blowing apart its competition. In fact, they expected to win this night. They weren't aware, until just before game time, that the Blues were starting a nineteen-year-old outfielder from Oklahoma, recently sent down by the Yankees for some seasoning. The kid's name was Mickey Mantle. Nobody on the Mud Hens staff, including players and coaches, had heard of him. Nor had anybody else in town—that included fans, print media, and broadcasters. But all of them were about to see the most astonishing one-man exhibition of baseball they would ever witness. Don could hardly believe his eyes as he watched it happen.

Mantle went five-for-five in that game, hitting the cycle: a single, a double, a triple, and a home run. In his fifth time at bat, he hit another home run. He flew around the bases like one of those mule deer from his home state being chased by coyotes. His feet didn't seem to touch the ground. Mickey Mantle gave much more than a demonstration of how to hit a round ball with a round bat that night; he also gave a demonstration in maximum human speed on a ball diamond. Don knew he had witnessed some special magic that night, performed in a Triple-A baseball setting that nearly rivaled the big leagues. Like everyone else at that game, he was overwhelmed by the enormous talent of a rookie from Oklahoma named Mickey Mantle. The Yankees recalled him back to New York the next day.

Toledo finished out of contention for the post-season tournaments in 1951. Their final game of the season was Don Lund's last performance in a Mud Hens uniform.

34
Dialogue

He was quiet now. His mood was pensive. We had just finished another typically animated conversation, this time about his years with the Toledo Mud Hens. He'd left no doubt about his being happy there. Toledo was, in his opinion, one of America's nicely wholesome small cities. The people were more than just casually friendly; they showed genuine interest in each other. Strangers would strike up a conversation while waiting for a city bus. Or riding an elevator. Or waiting for the game to start at Swayne Field. Most who visited Toledo, Ohio, departed with good impressions. Don Lund was one of them.

We were in his living room. The old coach was slouched in his wingback chair; head back, fingers laced together against his chest, legs straight out in front His eyes were focused casually on the space in front of him. I asked him what he was thinking about.

"Lots of ballplayers made a career out of the minor leagues," he said, "and they did quite well. Some of them became home-town celebrities."

Our dialogue began:

"But they still chased the dream of being a major leaguer."
DL: "Oh, sure. We all did. But there were thousands of guys in the minors. And every level had its own group of leagues. Toledo was class Triple-A. There was also class Double-A; class A; and then classes B, C, D; right on down. They all played professional ball."

"Thousands of men chasing the dream, and only sixteen major league teams."
DL: "And each team had a twenty-five-man roster. Do the math."

"That's 400 players. Thousands of men hoping to get one of those 400 spots."
DL: "Uh huh. And also thousands of men doing what they have a talent for, plus doing what they love to do."

"For peanuts."
DL: "Sure. Like I said before, it's just pure love of the game that makes you do it. That, plus the mental and physical challenges of competing at the highest level you can. Besides, back then, it was easy to find off-season work. I taught school. Others went back to the family farm, or they sold cars, or painted houses. I remember an infielder in Mobile who could take apart a car engine and put it back together blindfolded. He would have made a lot of money doing that full-time, but he wanted to play baseball."

"What about today? Now Major League Baseball has thirty teams. There are those who say that the level of big league baseball we see today, because of expansion, is about the same as Triple-A ball about the time you played, simply because the top Triple-A players can now move up more easily."
DL: "Well, I don't agree with that. So many things are different now. Athletes stay in shape year around. Trainers show them how to do it. They can play winter ball. Careers can be extended by players who take care of themselves. Besides, it isn't right to make comparisons between eras. You can't say that so-and-so of today is better than so-and-so of yesterday, and back it up with anything but opinion. It doesn't matter if you use a computer to spit out all kinds of figures and stats. Unless you can put the real Detroit Tigers of 1968 against the real New York Yankees of 1927, unless you can put the real Joe Louis in his prime against the real Muhammad Ali in his prime, or the real 1950 Sam Snead against the real Tiger Woods ... Unless you can do that, you can only speculate. You're just playing around with sports ideas. That's why I'd never agree that today's baseball level of play is any better or worse than when I played."

"But the money's better now."
DL: "Yes. It's better today in all pro sports."

"Millionaires are playing baseball."
DL: "And football, basketball, golf, tennis, and so on."

"Do you think today's athletes, including baseball players, are overpaid?"
DL: "Absolutely not."

"But some of them are making millions upon millions ..."
DL: "That's right. And for every single one of those multi-millionaires there are hundreds of minor league players who struggle to get by, hoping for their big break."

"They stay and play in the minors."
DL: "Yes."

"For the love of the game."
DL: "And for the love of playing it. Don't forget what I said about making minor league ball a career. It can be exciting. Some of those minor league towns love their baseball teams. Lots of players can't walk around town without being stopped several times for autographs. Many of them are guys who'll never play in the majors. But they still enjoy celebrity in their hometowns; they earn fairly decent money, and they'll probably be offered a good job when they retire—all because they can play baseball."

He sits on the edge of his chair. I can sense the adrenalin running. When he talks about other people, he becomes much more animated than when he talks about himself. Minor league players are as much a part of his life as the legends he played with. He identifies with struggling ballplayers because he's been there. There's no bitterness in his eyes as he talks about them, just understanding and empathy. I'd hit one of his hot buttons when I mentioned "chasing the dream." Time to move on.

"Coach, let's talk for a minute about your three years with Toledo. We've covered the overall picture. Are there any specific instances you remember that had any kind of impact on the rest of your career?"
DL: "Getting to know Jim Campbell had a great impact on me."

"Anything else?"

DL: "Well, now that you ask, there were a couple of things," he grinned. "During the '49 season we were on the road, and a bunch of us—I think maybe four or five—were too hyped to just go back to the hotel after the game that night. So we went out for some beer and sandwiches. Nobody misbehaved; nobody got drunk or anything like that. We were just having a good time. Then somebody noticed we only had a few minutes before the midnight curfew. So we all ran like mad back to the hotel and got there less than five minutes after twelve. Manager Eddie Mayo was in the lobby when we walked in. He greeted us with a big smile like we were long-lost brothers and told us we better get up to our rooms. Well, next day at the team meeting, Mayo said something like: 'The following players will be fined twenty-five dollars for missing curfew.' Then he reads off our names. I learned a lesson from that one. Twenty-five dollars was a lot of money to me then. At least we didn't have to pay it until the end of the season."

"You mentioned there was another impact situation."

DL: "Oh, right. I don't know if this was an impact thing, but I remember it pretty well. The 1950 Tigers almost won the pennant. They lost out by three games. During the off-season I was back in Detroit, teaching, when I got an invitation to a team party one night. While I was there, Ted Lyons, one of the coaches, said to me that he wished I had been on the team instead of in Toledo. He said I would have made the difference. I started to laugh, but he said he was serious. Lyons was a good pitcher for the White Sox before he started coaching at Detroit. He wasn't known as a B.S.'er. I thanked him. Didn't know what else to say. Later I told Betty about it, and then I put it aside."

"Did you think Lyons was right?"

DL: "No. More of that opinion stuff we talked about. I wasn't on the team. Mere speculation. Nice of him to say it, though."

"Do you have any more comments on your years with the Mud Hens? How about that Kansas City game when Mickey Mantle did it all?"

DL: "That was the best baseball performance I ever saw. It's kind of nice to know I played against Mantle in both the major and minor leagues. One time he robbed me of a possible home run."

"When was that?"
DL: "In 1953, when I was with the Tigers and we were playing the Yankees in Yankee Stadium. All three of the outfielders were playing me straight away. I hit a long drive to deep left center field. I thought it might be gone, because it felt good when I hit it. I was rounding first when I saw Mantle jump up next to the wall and grab it about six inches above the rail. He must have run like a deer, because he covered a lot of ground to make that catch."

"Did you ever get to know him?"
DL: "Sure, but only as a player. Before games, stuff like that. We never socialized. Mantle was a friendly guy."

"I suppose when someone mentions the words Mickey and baseball in the same sentence, Mantle is the first one who comes to mind."
DL: "Not to me."

"Oh?
DL: "Mickey Mantle was named after another famous Mickey. Mickey Cochrane."

"Hall of Fame catcher for the Tigers."
DL: "That's right. Cochrane actually came to the Tigers in 1934, as a player-manager. Right away he led them to two consecutive world championships, in '34 and '35."

"Mantle was named after Cochrane? How much alike were they?"
DL: "They were both exceptional ballplayers. They both were key figures on championship teams. The big difference was in their personalities. Mantle was easy-going; Cochrane wasn't. They called Cochrane 'Black Mike' because of his strong temper. *Black* wasn't a racist term. It referred to his mood. When the Tigers lost, watch out: Cochrane might tear up the locker room. Mickey Mantle would never do that."

"So when you think of great ballplayers named 'Mickey,' those two come to mind."
DL: "I also played against Mickey Vernon."

"Legend of the Washington Senators?"
DL: "He played with other teams, but he made his mark with the Senators. He batted left and could hit to any field. Kept us all on our toes. Vernon won the batting title when I played against him in 1953. He'd won it before, in 1946. Great first baseman. Nice guy, too."

"Mantle, Cochrane, and Vernon. Three major league Mickeys to think about."
DL: "Think about two more."

"Who else?"
DL: "We can't overlook Mickey Stanley."

"You're thinking about the 1968 World Series."
DL: "Right. Mickey Stanley was not just a talented athlete; he was also a versatile athlete. I saw him play in the minors when I was Tigers' farm director. Mickey would fool around during practice, playing different positions, all just for fun. I saw how he could scoop up a ground ball. Very impressive guy."

"What did you think when manager Mayo Smith played him at shortstop during the World Series?"
DL: "One of the smartest moves Mayo made that year. His best player, Al Kaline, was injured a couple of weeks before the season ended. By that time, though, the Tigers had already clinched the pennant. Mayo figured Al would be ready for the Series. But he had several season games left to play, none of which would affect the team's first-place standing, so he decided to experiment. He knew about Stanley's pregame fooling around in the infield. So he asked him to play nine games of the final season at shortstop. Then, when Series time came, Mayo took Stanley out of center field and put him at shortstop in order to keep his bat in the lineup. He moved Jim Northrup from right to center field so that Kaline could play right field. Willie Horton continued on in left field."

"And the Tigers won the pennant."
DL: "Amen."

"How do you think Mickey felt about being moved to shortstop?"
DL: "Well, you have to understand Mickey Stanley a little bit. He was buddies with everybody. Never gave anyone a hard time. Plus, he showed he liked to experiment fielding grounders in the infield. Mayo could have asked him to play catcher and Mickey would have done it. He's that kind of a team player."

"But how hard is it to change positions from the outfield to the infield at the major league level?"
DL: "It's tough enough for someone with Stanley's versatility, next to impossible for others. Remember, Mickey had never before played the infield in his professional career. Plus, this is the World Series we're talking about. What Mayo Smith did was one of the gutsiest moves in World Series' history. And what Mickey Stanley did in response to it was amazing. By the way, Mickey Stanley also won a Golden Glove that year."

"Amazing is right. By the way, you said there were two more. Who's the other Mickey?"
DL: "Mickey Lolich."

"The Tigers' renowned left-hander, hero of the 1968 World Series."
DL: "That's him. Super guy, too. I remember being down on the field at Tiger Stadium during my front office days, watching Mickey work out. He was throwing fastballs that made the pop in the catcher's mitt echo all around the empty stands. I walked up to him, thinking I'd kid him a little, and I moved my right hand like a snake toward the catcher. 'Can you make the ball do that?' No way did I think he'd take me seriously. Mickey said, 'Sure,' and threw the ball. It zigzagged just like I moved my hand. The ball went 'whoop!' right into the catcher's mitt for a perfect strike. Mickey grinned and winked. I grinned back and walked away shaking my head."

"You've always liked Mickey Lolich, haven't you?"
DL: "You bet. As much for what he's been in retirement as for what he was as a player. Mickey has always been a credit to the game, on and off the field. Still has that great laugh."

"I remember Lolich jumping into Bill Freehan's arms when the Tigers won the pennant in '68."
DL: "One of baseball's great moments."

I pointed out to him that three out of his five most memorable "Mickeys" just happened to be former Detroit Tigers' players. Could he be slightly prejudiced? The old coach merely grinned. I changed the subject.

"Why don't we move on to your 1952 year? You ready for that?"
DL: "Sure. Nineteen fifty-two brought me back to the Tigers. It started when the Mud Hens were sold and our Triple-A Tigers franchise moved to Buffalo, New York ..."

35

Back to the Majors

"Honey, we're going to Buffalo!" Don had just hung up the phone. He was standing in the living room of their Detroit apartment at Seven Mile and Moross. Betty came in from the kitchen. "The Tigers sold the Mud Hens franchise," he told her, "and bought the Buffalo Bisons franchise. The whole team is moving."

Betty stared at him. "And just think," she laughed, "they called you personally about it. You didn't have to read it in the paper!"

He gathered her in his arms. "Yes, how about that?"

The Bisons met for spring training in Bartow, Florida, right where Don and Betty had been last year. This time they rented a place in Lakeland, sharing a house with Viola and Bob Mavis. Bob, or "Bobby," or "Mave-eye" as some called him, was a career minor leaguer who had appeared in only one game in the major leagues. On September 17, 1949, he was a pinch-runner for the Tigers against New York in Yankee Stadium. Mavis subsequently went back to Toledo, and then moved with the team to Buffalo in 1952. He was an extremely popular player with an infectious laugh, who seldom became upset. Bob Mavis was a superb infielder, a heads-up base runner, and an outstanding base-hit type batsman who seldom hit below .300. History would record him as a perfect example of the high-quality talent that dominated the minor leagues, before the major leagues expanded to more teams. To his ultimate credit, Bob Mavis stayed dedicated for life to the game he loved, knowing he would probably never move beyond Triple-A ball. This year, 1952, he became one of Don Lund's closest friends.

House-sharing in Lakeland was beneficial to both families and lots of fun. Don and Bob drove to and from Bartow each day, leaving Betty and Viola with a car, usually the Lund's. Karen Mavis was an ideal playmate for Susan. Although nine-year-old

Karen was almost three years older, she treated Susan as an equal. Both girls were gentle, happy, and well-adjusted, so their play together tended to be more relaxed than rambunctious. Their mothers seldom worried about the two of them getting into trouble. Among the four adults, Viola was the most entertaining. Her sense of humor gave them all some comic relief from the day-to-day routines. Once, when Don and Bob were due back from a road trip, Viola said to Betty, "Let's put up the toilet seats before they get here; they'll think we've had visitors!"

Don breezed through spring training and easily found a starting spot in the Bisons' outfield. Wind sprints and chasing fungos brought his speed back. He wasn't the fastest man on the team, but he certainly wasn't the slowest. He watched his diet. He worked on his timing. By the time he left with the team for Buffalo, he felt as strong as ever. He was confident he was ready. He firmly believed he would have a good season with the Buffalo Bisons.

Finding a place to stay in Buffalo was the first major challenge for nearly everybody on the team. The players had pulled roots from Toledo after they found out about the move to New York. Some had friends in the area and were staying with them temporarily; others crowded into local hotels until they could find something more permanent. The Lunds were planning to live at the Princeton Apartments. But that changed with one fortuitous phone call to the Andersons.

Betty had kept in touch with Margaret Anderson ever since their first meeting in St. Paul nearly eight years before. She and Don rented part of the Andersons' house during the 1945 baseball season. While Don was endearing himself to the Saints' fans as a game-breaking outfielder, Lester Anderson was on the University of Minnesota Education faculty and finishing up his master's degree in Ann Arbor. Since then, Lester had moved to the University of Buffalo as dean of men. Betty and Margaret had kept up correspondence throughout all of this and, as a result, the Lunds and Andersons still maintained their close friendship, so one of the first things Betty did when she and Don arrived in Buffalo was call the Andersons, who immediately invited them for dinner.

Lester and Margaret lived in Eggertsville, a pleasant suburb of Buffalo. They enjoyed a spacious, early American-style house, fixed among other large homes on a tree-lined street. The neighborhood flowed with solid, middle-class ambience. Don was impressed with the place, and he told as much to Lester during dinner conversation.

"I'm glad you like the house," said his host. "How would you like to live here this summer?"

Don looked at Betty. "We couldn't impose on you like that," he said. "We plan to stay in Buffalo."

Lester continued, "You wouldn't be imposing at all. As a matter of fact, Margaret and I intend to get a place on the lake. This house will be vacant. You'd be doing us a favor. I'll make the rent low enough just to cover taxes and insurance. You keep the place up. Fair enough?"

Don and Betty couldn't say no to that kind of a deal. A week later, they moved into the Anderson home. "Here I am," Don told Betty, "a minor league ballplayer living like I own the team. What would Mom and Dad say to all this?" He didn't have to wait long to find out.

Marguerite and Andy were there within a week. They loved the place. Next came other friends from Detroit and Ann Arbor. It hadn't taken long for word to get around that the Lunds lived in a visitor-friendly home. Local company included friends from the team, especially Bob, Viola, and Karen Mavis. Even business manager Jim Campbell dropped by one day. Jim and Don saw each other nearly every day the Bisons played at home in Offermann Stadium. They were quickly cementing a close friendship.

When he first saw the Anderson's house, Jim joked, "Are we paying you too much?" Don answered by pulling his pants pockets inside-out. Over the course of the summer, the Lunds had a constant supply of guests. Someone remarked that their front door had more wear on it than the batwings of an Old West saloon. And, of course, Susan was the star. With her blond hair, blue eyes, and sweet disposition, the six-year-old grabbed everyone's attention. Yet she never let it spoil her, much to her parents' delight. Other children might have been turned inward by all the adult recognition; Susan Lund wasn't.

One of Susan's friends that year was a little neighborhood girl named Jackie. Jackie talked with a pronounced lisp. One day Jackie called on the phone and Betty picked it up. "Ith Thoothan there?" Jackie asked.

Betty said, "I'm sorry, Jackie; Susan's taking a nap."

Jackie responded, "Mitheth Lund, how do you know ith me?"

Betty and Don kept that one as a crack-up private joke for many years.

Camaraderie among the Bisons' players was especially keen. It probably formed as one result of wholesale change when the team moved nine hundred miles from Toledo. Everyone moved into a new residence. They played in a different home stadium, in a different league, against different teams. They also worked for a fresh baseball club. The Bisons were free from the near-bankruptcy doldrums of past years and were now thriving under the tutelage of new business manager Jim Campbell, so camaraderie thrived, and several players made special contributions to it. One of these was catcher Ed Mordarski, who boosted road trips each morning at breakfast by reporting the day's sports news. Mordarski made it his personal mission to rise early and read all the morning papers he could find. Then he'd regale his teammates with tidbits, trivia, and gossip about the latest events, mostly about sports. Someone suggested to Ed that he swap places with one of the prominent radio newscasters. "I might do that," said the Bisons' catcher, "but it wouldn't work out. Sure, I could read the news all right, but that guy who took my job probably couldn't hit a basketball with a tennis racquet!"

Don was having a first-rate season at bat with the Bisons. Offermann Stadium was known as a hitter's ballpark; the left-field wall was 321 feet. Right-field distance was 297 feet. It was also cozy around the plate for a batter. The fans were perched not more than thirty-five feet behind the plate, and nearly all of them were local, vocal, and highly partisan Buffalo New Yorkers—a great situation for the hometown sluggers, deadly for visitors who succumbed to the jeers. Don loved it. He ranged between a .306 and .355 average, never made an error in the outfield, and became a popular crowd favorite with his ready laugh and his willingness to sign pregame autographs.

Then he was assigned to the infield. He shouldn't have been playing the infield, but manager Jack Tighe, determined to pack his lineup with strong bats. He moved Don to first base so that George Lerchen could take his place in right field. Lerchen had joined the Bisons in early June, after playing fourteen games with the Tigers. Tighe wanted Lerchen to play. The first baseman was struggling. Tighe reasoned that right fielder Lund would have more position flexibility than his other two starting outfielders, Frank Carswell and Bubba Phillips, so he made the switch.

Tighe couldn't know it at the time, but he picked the wrong guy. He should have chosen Phillips. Years later, Bubba Phillips would easily move from the outfield to play third base for the Chicago White Sox. Anyway, Don moved to first base. His biggest challenge was getting used to the first baseman's glove. It was longer and deeper than his own, and sometimes he couldn't feel the ball after he caught it. He had to look just to make sure. Naturally, he took some razzing during pregame workouts. Someone would catch a ball near Don, then make an exaggerated stare into his glove. Typical good-natured kidding, with lots of laughs all around. Fortunately, Don didn't do too badly and played just a few games at first base. Tighe brought back the starting first baseman, took out Lerchen, and sent Don back to his regular right-field position. But Jack Tighe's urge to switch came back only a few games later. Don was moved to third base.

Again, Tighe's motivation was keeping a hot batting order. The third baseman was struggling. Don was hitting the cover off the ball. Utility outfielder Bill Tuttle was looking good in batting practice, so Tighe made the switch.

At first Don felt as he did back in his sophomore year at Southeastern, when Coach Wayne Nestor started him out at second base: like a goat in a horse race, completely out of his element, thrown in to perform a task without any training. In practice he booted grounders. In his first game he played too deep, or too shallow. And he forgot a couple of times to run out for the cutoff throw from the outfielder. But he tried hard. And he learned. By his third game, Don Lund was probably the hardest-hitting but least confident third baseman in the International League.

His most anxious game while guarding third base was a potential no-hitter being thrown by Bisons' starter Wayne McLeland. Don was so concerned about spoiling Wayne's chances that he played on high alert, even between pitches. He prowled constantly. He wiped the sweat from his face with his sleeve. He smacked his glove with his fist. Once during ground throws between innings, where the first baseman tosses the ball on the ground to the infielders, Don's return throw was so hard it nearly knocked the first baseman off the bag. Don waved his glove in apology and tried to settle down. Unfortunately for McLeland, an opposing batter nailed a line-drive single to right field in the fourth inning, ending the no-hitter. Don wasn't happy about that, nor did he feel relieved; he would have done anything he could to support Wayne McLeland that day.

His most astounding third base performance took place in an away game against Ottawa. He made two throwing-flatfooted errors that allowed in two runs. He also drove in three runs. Final score: Buffalo, 3; Ottawa, 2. Don Lund had been solely responsible for the entire score of the game for both teams! Shortly after that, Tighe moved him back to right field.

Tighe switched Don one more time that year, in only one game, for only one half-inning. It proved to be one of the best managerial decisions he made that year. In another game against Ottawa, the Bisons were ahead by one run when Ottawa came to bat in the ninth inning. Their first batter smashed a ground ball single beyond second baseman Bob Mavis's reach, and then promptly stole second on the next pitch. The number two batter hit a clothesline drive deep to center field, which George Lerchen caught for the first out, while the runner advanced to third. That's when Manager Tighe made his change. Ottawa had one out, a fleet-footed runner with the tying run on third, and a left-hand hitter coming up who liked to hit to the opposite left field. In fact, he had already hit a couple deep to left earlier in the game.

Tighe sought insurance. He wanted Don Lund's strong throwing arm in left field, so he switched him there. He took out Frank Carswell. He sent Bubba Phillips to Don's place in right field, and kept Lerchen in center. When the batter came to the plate, the third base runner took a slight lead, while paying close attention to Ottawa manager Frank Skaff, who coached at third base. Don played fairly deep in left center. On the third pitch, the batter launched a deep fly ball to left field. The runner at third tagged the base and crouched like a coiled spring waiting to hurl himself toward home.

The instant Don made the catch, Frank Skaff launched his runner. Don took one step and heaved the ball toward an anxious Ed Mordarski at the plate. The ball took one hop and found

Mordarski's mitt belt-high. Everyone watched the slide, the tag, and the umpire's thumb as it shot toward the sky. The runner was out. Game over. Buffalo Bisons by one run. Jack Tighe took full credit in the papers. Don Lund shrugged off full credit from his teammates.

His greatest game at bat that year was on June 19 in Syracuse against the Syracuse Chiefs. Bob Keegan, the Chiefs' ace right-hander, was on the mound. Keegan had an unusually quick motion, which involved a short left-leg kick and a snap turn, with delivery coming straight over his right ear. He never varied this motion, no matter the type of pitch he threw, and he threw with control. Don greeted Keegan with a home run his first time at bat. He then proceeded to hit a double, a triple, and a single. Four times at bat, collecting the circuit. He tagged four out of the Bisons' nine hits, including the game-winning single. When the team walked off the train back in Buffalo, the first one to greet him was a smiling Jim Campbell.

But his most special and memorable game in 1952 had little to do with him personally, other than being a major support player. It was all about his teammate, right-handed pitcher Dick Marlowe. On August 15, about a month before his twenty-third birthday, Marlowe threw a nine-inning perfect game. It was the International League's first perfect game since 1910. Don made several put-outs and scored a run in Buffalo's 2–0 win, but his own performance meant little to him in light of Marlowe's achievement. To be part of a perfect game was more than enough personal reward.

One week later, he received a phone call from the Tigers' general manager, legendary Hall of Famer Charlie Gehringer. "We bought your contract," said Charlie. "We want you back here with us."

With his heart pounding, Don answered, "I'll be there as soon as I can, Charlie."

Gehringer said, "See you soon," and hung up.

At home Don grabbed his laughing wife by the waist and swung her around in their living room, much to the delight of a wide-eyed Susan. "I told him the same thing I told Bill DeWitt about getting there as soon as I could. Gehringer just said 'See you soon.'" He said to Betty, "What a great guy. Not anything like DeWitt, who quoted the terms of my contract to me. How about that? Detroit, here we come!"

His first at bat in Briggs Stadium that year was against the Boston Red Sox's fiery left-hander Mel Parnell. He swung at Parnell's first pitch and knocked out a base hit. A few games later, he hit four-for-four. He only played the final two weeks of the Tigers' 1952 season, but he hit over .300 and reestablished himself as a solid major leaguer. He could scarcely believe it: back in the big leagues, playing for his all-time favorite team, right here in his own hometown! He could barely wait for spring training in Lakeland.

36
Year of the Tiger

Take a month's winter vacation with your extended family. Everybody bring your kids. We'll all go to a pleasant spot in a warm climate near a lake. There'll be a park close by. We'll rent cabins, houses, and apartments near each other so the kids can play together.

If this sounds like a dream, or a travel agency's ultimate family vacation, it's not. It's the real thing for wives and children of major league ballplayers in spring training. It takes place in Florida, Arizona, or anywhere else the big league clubs train. Minor league teams don't usually train in attractive places like the big leagues do. Their budgets won't allow it. But the big leagues train in nice spots. Families live near each other; kids play together. New friends come and go as players switch from one team to another. It's like the military as far as making fast friendships. It only lasts for one month each year, a month's vacation for a major league regular player's family. The Lunds had theirs in 1953.

Don, Betty, and Susan moved into a bungalow in the Lake Morton complex of housing units, just west of Lakeland. They rented the upper half of the house; the lower half was taken by Jack and Beverly Tighe and their two sons, John (Tiger) and Bobby. Both boys were around Susan's age. They treated her like a sister and included her as an equal in whatever they did around the neighborhood. Jack still managed the Bisons, who trained a few miles south, in Bartow; he commuted every day. Don trained with the Tigers at Henley Field. The strongest friendship between these two families was shared by Betty Lund and Beverly Tighe. Every day Beverly tried to work on her seasonal tan by reclining on a chaise and reading under the blazing rays of the sun. Betty was less inclined for this, but she did it anyway. She enjoyed Beverly's ability to converse with intelligence and a sense of humor on all kinds of subjects.

Other Tigers' families rented in the same general area. They all hung out together nearly every day, with the fathers joining in for picnics or cookouts when they weren't at the ballpark. Most appealing about the Lake Morton Tigers families was the fact that they didn't merely stick to themselves as a closed group. Outsiders were welcome, including members of the press.

Joe and Rosie Falls were entertaining people who loved to tell stories about their native New York. In 1953, Joe was the Detroit bureau chief of the Associated Press, bound for greatness as a sports columnist with three Detroit newspapers, and headed for a place in the Baseball Hall of Fame. Joe had one special talent that surprised everyone. They knew he wrote long columns with extreme accuracy and perception. But they didn't know, until someone saw him and word got around, that he typed them with great speed, using only his two index fingers. Nobody on the team chided Joe about it, though; they all knew that the man who uses public ink has the final word. Anyway, they also liked Rosie Falls; she had a knack for drawing in friends. Joe and Rosie fit right in at Lake Morton.

Sam and Kitty Greene joined in on all the fun as if they belonged to the ballclub. Sam wrote a sports column for the Detroit News that made his readers feel as if they saw the game, whether they were there or not. Everybody liked Sam. He never showed a superior attitude like some members of the print media. He was a genuine, truly nice guy who respected a player's personal life. Of course, Sam made it clear that there was no such thing as "off the record" if someone talked about the job, the team, or anything else about baseball. Sam was the consummate newspaper reporter. He only had one thing noticeably unusual about him: Sam never drove a car; Kitty was his chauffeur. The two of them made a delightful pair.

Susan Lund and most of the other Tigers' kids attended Lake Morton Elementary School for about three weeks. The teachers were okay; the school was not. Susan, like her playmates at Lake Morton, normally attended school in accredited city school districts like Detroit, where school buildings were well maintained. Detroit classrooms were clean; floors were scrubbed; restrooms sparkled, and playgrounds had the latest equipment.

Lake Morton Elementary had none of that. Though the building itself seemed sound, corridors wore a perpetual scuff on their floors, furniture was old and shaky, and the girls' restrooms had soiled curtains in front of the stalls, rather than doors. And the playground was a fenced-in dirt lot holding a few rusted swings and teeter-totters. The bad news was that Lake Morton Elementary was much less than what the kids were used to back home. The good news was that the kids appreciated their schools back home and were anxious to return there.

When training camp ended, the Lunds and all the other Tigers who made the team roster said goodbye to Lakeland. The team boarded the northbound train; wives and children piled into cars. Their 1953 Lake Morton spring family vacation was over.

The Tigers began their 1953 season by trying to forget their 1952 season—that was the year the team compiled the worst winning percentage in Tigers' history. The only 1952 player who provided a beacon of glory had been pitcher Virgil "Fire" Trucks, an eleven-year Tigers' veteran. Trucks was a master of speed and control who had dominated every game he pitched that year—but he played with little support from teammates' bats. In fact, as his ERA went down, game losses went up. Virgil Trucks even pitched two no-hitters in 1952. The first one, on May 15 in Briggs Stadium against the Washington Senators, was a no-hit pitchers' duel for 8½ innings. The Tigers finally won the game, 1–0, when Vic Wertz hit a home run in the bottom of the ninth inning. Only about 2,000 fans witnessed Virgil's no-hitter that day. The rest of Detroit watched retired General Douglas MacArthur hold court in a triumphant parade down Woodward Avenue. The parade ended with a walk across the bridge to Belle Isle, named the Douglas MacArthur Bridge ten years before. Those who watched the parade missed one of the best head-to-head pitching contests in the major leagues that season. Those who attended the game missed a great moment in Detroit's history.

Virgil almost had another no-hitter against the Senators that year. In fact, it was a "might-have-been" perfect game. On July 22, again in Briggs Stadium, one of the greatest lead-off batters in baseball, Eddie Yost, started the game for Washington by hammering a solid single. Trucks thereupon retired the next twenty-six consecutive batters. The Tigers squeaked by with a 1–0 win.

Virgil's second no hitter of the season was hurled August 25, against the Yankees in New York. Again, the Tigers' offense produced just one run for the win. But it was only the fifth time in Yankees' history that they were no-hit. For Virgil, it was the sixth no-hitter of his professional career; he pitched his first four in the minors. Thus, only one player hung a shining star for the Tigers in 1952: Virgil Trucks. Virgil would have made immortal history by being the only pitcher to throw three no-hitters in a season, except for that leadoff single by Eddie Yost. Anyway, Virgil was deservedly named the team's MVP. He was on top of his career. The Tigers front office must have been at least grateful for their one bright light of the season—but they didn't show it. During the off-season, the Tigers traded Virgil Trucks to the St. Louis Browns. There, he would have his greatest season as a major league pitcher.

By the end of the 1952 season, the Tigers had 50 wins and 104 losses, which landed them in last place in the American League. They struggled at the plate for the entire six months. No batter who played in more than 19 games hit close to .300. Only three who played in 8 to19 games reached that magic mark: Harvey Kuenn, Russ Sullivan, and Don Lund. The front office tried to handle the frustration by switching managers in mid-season. Red Rolfe was replaced by Fred Hutchinson. The team still lost games.

Fate must have been grinning when she dealt the hand that scheduled the Detroit Tigers to meet the St. Louis Browns in the first game of the 1953 season. Then she must have started laughing when it turned out that Virgil Trucks would pitch that game for the Browns. Don watched it all from the visitors' dugout. It was April 14 in Sportsman's Park, the home opener for the Browns. It was also Virgil's first game as an ex-Tiger, and "Fire" Trucks was simply awesome. His fastball smoked; his curve left them swinging; his pace kept the batters off-balance. At game's end Virgil Trucks, last year's MVP, had shut out his former team 10–0. Someone in the Tigers' front office raced for the toilet.

Although the Tigers lost their own Opening Day game to the Cleveland Indians on April 16, the rest of their 1953 season turned out better than the year before. The team finished in sixth place, ahead of the Philadelphia Athletics and St. Louis Browns.

For Don Lund, however, 1953 was his most exceptional year as a player, and his only complete season in a starting role with a major league team. 1953 was his personal Year of the Tiger.

Don had first broken into the starting lineup when center fielder Jim Delsing injured his leg. Delsing would be out for only a few days, but that was enough time for Don to break in and stay there. When Delsing returned to center field, Don was moved to right field, where he played well enough to start there for the rest of the season. He wasn't the superstar; he wasn't the team standout. But he did have some heroic moments.

On Friday June 4, the Tigers entertained Philadelphia in Detroit, with a doubleheader for games 3 and 4 of a three-day series. Entertained is the right word. The first game had ended in a tie; the next two games saw the Athletics pound Detroit for two losses. However, Don brought the crowd to its feet during the second game on June 4. In his first time at bat he swung at a belt-high curve ball and hammered a towering drive into deep right center field. Ed McGhee, Philadelphia's center fielder, ran for the ball with everything he had and leaped in desperation, only to watch it miss his glove and roll to the flagpole. Meanwhile, Don was chugging around the bases as fast as his spikes could churn. The Athletics' right fielder, Dave Philley, chased down the rolling ball near the wall and heaved it toward home plate, ignoring the cutoff man.

Don was pounding for home. The play was close. Catcher Joe Astroth was forced to move out in front of the plate to grab Philley's one-hop throw. He made a ferocious lunge back toward the sliding Don Lund. He missed the tag. Don scored an inside-the-park home run, made more dramatic by his cloud of dust under the umpire's outstretched hands. The fans, eager for some excitement after the first game's nine-run loss, screamed as if Detroit had just won the pennant.

Don, of course, felt an adrenalin high—until he reached the dugout.

"Hey, Lundo," someone called. "You came around third like you had a truck on your back."

Everybody laughed, including Don, back to earth before the dust had settled.

After the game, which the Athletics won 9–6, Don was approached by Philadelphia's second baseman, his old friend

Cass Michaels. Cass was in his tenth year in the big leagues, playing for the Athletics after eight years with the White Sox, the Senators, and the Browns. He and Don had remained friends ever since their first meeting at Northeastern Field in Detroit, when Don worked for the Recreation Department and Cass was preparing to join the White Sox. Cass called to him as he trotted toward the Tigers' dugout. Don turned and shook Michaels' hand.

"Nice homer, Don," grinned Cass. "You sure were lucky."

Don matched his old friend's grin. "What do you mean, 'lucky'?"

Cass pointed out to right field. "Well, you know I was the cutoff man; if Philley threw it to me instead of Astroth, I would have thrown you out." They both laughed.

Don retorted, "I'm sure you're right. Of course, if I hit it farther, you don't have to worry about it, and my uniform stays clean."

They shook hands, and Cass trotted back to the visitors' dugout while Don went through the tunnel, still laughing. The laugh faded quickly when he entered the clubhouse.

Manager Fred Hutchinson was fuming in his small office. He hated losing. He took losses badly, to the point of destroying things. Almost everyone had heard about the times during his playing days as a Tigers' pitcher when he'd be taken out of a game and proceed down the tunnel under the stands, breaking every overhead light bulb in his path. Few knew, though, that Hutchinson was well aware of his anger problem and sometimes tried to overcome it.

In 1950, Fred had roomed with second baseman Jerry Priddy on road trips. One night before a game Hutchinson was scheduled to pitch, he told Priddy, "If I look like I'm starting to get mad, Jerry, come over to the mound and talk to me. Slow me down.

"Sure, Hutch," said Priddy, "I'll do just that."

The next day Hutchinson walked two batters in a row. He looked like he was about to blow. Priddy took the out-of-play throw from Tigers' catcher Aaron Robinson and walked over to the mound. Hutchinson stared at him. "Hutch," Priddy said calmly, "you need to slow down a little."

Hutchinson's eyes narrowed. "Give me the ball, Jerry."

Priddy persisted. "Hutch, you told me that ..."

Hutchinson's eyes became slits. "Jerry, give me the goddam ball!"

After Hutchinson became the Tigers' manager, he tried to control his temper after a losing game. He wasn't always successful. One time, after a 4–14 drubbing at the hands of the Washington Senators, Hutchinson walked from the dugout to the clubhouse. He didn't say a word to anyone, even as he showered and changed. He walked out the clubhouse door. He walked past his car. He kept walking until he reached home several hours later, fourteen miles to his place on Detroit's East Side, stopping on occasion to let off steam.

The event that finally cured Fred Hutchinson from showing his temper happened on May 19, 1953, when the St. Louis Browns beat the Tigers three games straight in Briggs Stadium. The third game was extremely brutal. The Tigers lost by twelve runs. Hutchinson grumbled all the way through the tunnel and up the stairs leading into the clubhouse. Hal Newhouser was right behind him, followed by Don Lund. The clubhouse doorway held wooden half-doors on spring hinges. The left door swung freely; the right door was held firmly in place by a piece of wood, about the size of a clothespin, that acted as a wedge. Hutchinson slammed through the right door with a vengeance. The wedge snapped free and rocketed backward, finding its target about a half-inch from Newhouser's left eye. Newhouser yelled.

Hutchinson saw the blood; his anger vanished immediately. "Oh no! Oh no!" Hutchinson cried. "Hal, are you all right? I'm sorry! I didn't mean to hurt you!"

Tension reigned until the trainer pronounced Newhouser fit. The pitcher's eye was fine. After that, Fred Hutchinson never displayed his temper to the players.

On this day, however, June 4, he was sitting in his office and brooding over the team's loss to Philadelphia. Don Lund walked into the clubhouse, wiping a smile off his face.

Hutchinson looked at his right fielder. His features softened. "Nice hustle, Don," he offered. "Next time we should have three runners ahead of you." The negative fog lifted throughout the room.

Don grinned and thanked his manager. The clubhouse bounced right back to normalcy. Fred Hutchinson, to everyone's delight, had changed.

On Wednesday June 23, the Tigers were visiting Philadelphia in the middle of a two-week road trip. Don felt comfortable about his playing on this tour. They had just finished a four-game split with the Yankees, and he had been an important part of the two victories. Monday they had beaten New York, 10–3. Today they faced the Athletics in Shibe Park. The whole team believed they were on a roll; Philadelphia would merely be their next victim. After breakfast that morning, they piled onto the bus, anxious to reach the park and get on with practice, but the bus didn't move. The team fidgeted. "Hey, let's get going," someone yelled. Others wondered about the delay.

Don sat in the back next to his roommate Hal Newhouser. They both shared the same curiosity, since it was highly unusual for a team bus to sit around full of players. Then someone noticed the front door of the hotel opening as two men walked outside. The older one was Ed Katalinas, a well-known Tigers' scout. The other one, a tall, thin kid who looked like he belonged in high school, was a complete stranger to those on the bus. The two men shook hands. Don noticed the kid's shy smile. The kid trotted to the bus and stepped up through the open door. The bus fell silent as he slowly made his way to the back, head down and his face a blank mask.

Don had never seen anything more intimidating than this stranger having to walk the length of a bus past silent men, all of whom were staring at him. Of course, the kid had no way of knowing that many of the players were annoyed by the delay, since they had to sit on the bus and wait for him. The silent treatment wasn't personal, but the kid didn't know that. Don immediately made up his mind to get to know him, to show him that his fellow players were basically nice guys. He would try to become the kid's friend. Later on, after they became friends, Don would recall the kid's silent introduction to his fellow players on that bus. Many years later he would remember that kid's first step as he jumped up from the curb into that bus.

Don would visualize that moment as the kid's first step into Tigers' lore and baseball's Hall of Fame. That tall, thin and modest young man would grow into superstardom. He would be respected universally as one of most decent men ever to play the game of baseball. Albert William Kaline, the Tigers' 1953 rookie from Baltimore, stepped on that bus and walked modestly toward an endearing legend.

Nearly a month later, on Tuesday July 21, Don produced one of the early milestones in Al Kaline's illustrious career. The Tigers were hosting the Washington Senators in Briggs Stadium. After nine innings, the score was tied at 6. In the top of the tenth, Washington scored a run off Detroit's relief pitcher, Dave Madison. The Tigers went into the bottom of the tenth one run behind, 6–7, and promptly hit fly balls that were caught for the first two outs. Then Washington's relief pitcher, Sonny Dixon, walked Pat Mullin. Don took his crouch in the on-deck circle and watched Walt Dropo take a ball and a strike, and then hit Dixon's next pitch over second base. The 6-foot-5-inch Dropo lumbered his 225-pound frame toward first base and stopped there, as Mullin held at second. Don strode toward the batter's box. He watched Dropo trot off first base toward the Tigers' dugout, while at the same time a Tigers' uniform number 25 sped past his right side. Wearing that uniform was the rookie Al Kaline. Hutch was sending him in to run for Walt Dropo.

Don stepped to the plate as Mullin and Kaline took short leads and crouched. Dixon's first pitch was high for a ball. The next one, a low and outside curve, never made it to the catcher. Don swung hard and felt the sweet crunch all the way up to his elbows. The ball rocketed toward left-center field. Mullin and Kaline were already running at the swing. So were Washington's left and center fielders, who glanced up as the ball ignored them and smashed into the wall just inches below the rail. Center fielder Jim Busby grabbed the bounce and heaved it toward the cutoff man, shortstop Pete Runnels. Mullin scored as the throw was in the air. Kaline, chasing Mullin's number 6 like a lion after prey, scored right behind him. Don reached second base as Runnels caught the ball and turned, too late. Kaline had scored the winning run; the first of his professional career. Don trotted back to the Tigers dugout to the screams of overjoyed fans. His teammates mobbed him. He was a ten-minute hero once more.

One of Don's best buddies on the 1953 team was pitcher Steve Gromek. Steve joined the Tigers on June 15 from a trade with the Cleveland Indians. The friendship was immediate. In fact, Betty Lund and Jeanette Gromek became pals. Susan and the Gromek kids would often romp in the deserted lower deck stands after a home game. Both families had strong roots in Detroit, which naturally brought them together.

It was sweet for Don when he was able to make a big contribution to one of Steve's wins that year. It was even sweeter for Steve, because the win was his first appearance against his former team of thirteen years, the Cleveland Indians. The game took place in Briggs Stadium on Thursday July 2. Mike Garcia was the Indian's pitcher. The game was tied at two going into the bottom of the ninth inning. Garcia fanned the first Detroit batter, and then allowed two men on base with a walk and a single. Don strode to the plate and faced Garcia with one out and Tigers at second and third.

One swing was all it took. Don hit Garcia's first pitch between third baseman Al Rosen and shortstop George Strickland, a long line drive that landed in deep left center field and bounced toward the wall. Cleveland's left fielder Dale Mitchell and center fielder Larry Doby converged on the ball. Mitchell scooped it up and fired it to cutoff man Strickland. Not in time. Two runners scored; Don was standing on first base. Strickland had no play; the game was over. The Tigers beat the Indians, 4–2. As Don trotted across the infield toward the Tigers dugout, a hyped-up Steve Gromek ran out to meet him.

"Yahoo!" Gromek grabbed Don in a bear hug. "I'm gonna buy this man a beer," Steve shouted. "I'm gonna buy him a beer!"

And he did, right there in the Tigers' clubhouse. Don thought of Virgil Trucks taking on his former team and beating them. And now Steve Gromek had done the same. He sipped his beer. Nothing tasted sweeter.

Don felt right at home with the 1953 Tigers, more than he had with any big league team. One of the main reasons was the fact that so many of his fellow players were home-grown Detroiters. They knew each other from local high school leagues and the sandlots. Pitcher Ted Gray was from Highland Park, which made him a "Detroiter." Highland Park, like its counterpart Hamtramck, was totally enclosed by the City of Detroit. Highland Park and Hamtramck high schools competed within the Detroit leagues. Only legal boundaries separated them. But for young athletes playing on the sandlots, all felt part of the same large community.

Steve Gromek, from Hamtramck, could also be called a Detroiter. Then there were pitchers Ray Herbert and Art Houteman, both from Detroit Catholic Central. Hal Newhouser pitched for Detroit Wilbur Wright. Catcher Joe Ginsberg played at Detroit Cooley. And infielder Reno Bertoia, although raised just across the Detroit River in Windsor, Ontario, played in the Detroit sandlots and was treated as a local boy. All these Tigers players, therefore, had known each other since they were kids. Their comfort level with each other, fostered by common memories, was almost unique among the big league teams. There were no barriers among them; they would all be special friends throughout their lives. There were all "Detroiters."

There were other Tigers on the team that year who were close friends with Don. One of these was Ralph Branca. Branca was famous (or infamous, depending on who was telling the story) for coming in as a relief pitcher for the Dodgers in the ninth inning of a play-off game against the New York Giants two years earlier. He threw "the shot heard around the world" to Bobby Thompson, who homered to win the 1951 pennant for the Giants. Amid rumors of "sign stealing" by the Giants and the resulting grumbles by Dodger fans and the Brooklyn newspapers, Ralph Branca took the high road and accepted everything good-naturedly. Don admired him for that. Moreover, it was another home run that drew Don close to Branca. He hit it against him in 1947, when he was with Montreal, driving in teammate Jackie Robinson in an exhibition game at Ebbets Field.

Don turned a Branca fastball into a towering blast that disappeared into the upper left field seats. Brooklyn's outfielders merely watched as it sailed over their heads. The next day the Dodgers called him up, along with Jackie Robinson and Spider Jorgenson. Maybe that home run did it; maybe not. Regardless, he liked to tease Ralph by thanking him for handing him his big league contract. Ralph would answer with some remark, like "Where's my commission?" The two hit it off very well as Dodgers teammates. Now, seven years later, they were together again on the Tigers' roster. Very nice.

Don and Ned Garver had at least one common career factor prior to the Detroit Tigers: they both played for the St. Louis Browns in 1948. Don had been sold by the Dodgers and played the outfield for the Browns, sharing uniform number 12 with fellow outfielder Ken Wood and infielder Jerry McCarthy. That wasn't unusual for the Browns of that year; several players shared numbers. Ned Garver joined the 1948 Browns as a rookie relief pitcher, and then went on two years later to set a record that has never been broken. Ned became the only pitcher in the history of major league baseball to win at least 20 games for a team that lost at least 100 in the same season. The 1951 Browns finished in the American League cellar, losing 102 games, nearly twice as much as they won. Jim Delsing played in the outfield for that team, as did Bob Nieman. And so it was that four 1953 Detroit Tigers—Delsing, Nieman, Garver, and Lund—shared the dubious honor of being losing-team St. Louis Browns alumni.

Their reminisces turned out to be frequent leisure-time highlights on road trips throughout the season. Left-handed pitcher Billy Hoeft became Don's friend mainly through Don's roommate and left-handed legend Hal Newhouser. Hal would frequently take other pitchers, particularly left-handers, under his wing as a much-appreciated mentor. Billy was one of these. A native of Oshkosh, Hoeft placed himself in Wisconsin's high school sports lore in 1950, by striking out all twenty-seven batters in nine innings on the mound for Oshkosh High School. The Tigers signed him before the ink on his diploma dried. Billy, Hal, and Don would sometimes hang around together on road trips. The talk would be mostly about hitting, hitters, and pitching techniques. Don learned a lot by keeping quiet and listening. Two ears were better than one mouth, any day.

To Don, the 1953 Detroit Tigers was a team composed of very special guys. Men like Ray Boone and Walt Dropo, who could hit Satchel Paige as if Paige were throwing batting practice. Few could handle Paige that easily. Most batters would see his whirling motion of arms, legs, head, and hands as something they'd prefer to stand behind, rather than face straight on. But not Boone and Dropo. They were among the few. Then there was Bill Wight, another left-handed pitcher who had the fastest and most deceptive first-base pickoff throw Don ever saw. One time

Manager Hutchinson had Wight deliberately walk a batter to fill the bases. Wight did, and then picked him off. Wight followed by striking out the next batter, to retire the side. In the clubhouse, Don walked over to Bill and congratulated him. Wight grinned and winked. "All in a day's work," he said.

One of the more hilarious things of that season happened away from Briggs Stadium. Hal and Polly Newhouser owned a farm in Franklin, Michigan. Franklin was a small village in Oakland County, about thirty miles northwest of downtown Detroit. Apple trees flourished in the surrounding countryside. So did corn, wheat, soybeans, cows, pigs, and horses. The Newhousers had horses. Their daughters, Charlene and Sherry, loved to ride. One day the Newhousers invited Don, Betty, and Susan to join them for an off-game day at their farm. The farmhouse was a white clapboard structure, well maintained by Polly, which featured a large, furnished, screened-in porch. The porch was where the Newhousers spent much of their time during nice weather. It was also where they liked to entertain guests. After dinner, everyone relaxed on the porch. The adults were talking about horses; the kids were reading comic books. Without preamble, Hal abruptly got up and walked outside, heading toward one of the barns, and saying he'd be right back.

Five minutes later he returned, leading a large, brown horse with a rope tied to its halter. Hal said the horse was his favorite. The children squealed with delight as Hal led his horse to the front of the porch. Then he led it up the steps and through the door, right onto the porch. Polly screamed. Don and Betty leaped from their chairs and backed up to the wall. Hal grinned like a first-grader holding forth with show-and-tell. The horse shook its head. Then it shook its tail. Then it did what most horses do when they're surrounded by yelling strangers. It voided, dumped, and whinnied. Polly screamed again. The kids laughed like they were watching a circus. Don and Betty stood with their mouths open. Hal yanked on the rope, hauled his horse back down the steps, and stomped back to the barn with the animal in tow.

Don followed and helped his friend put the horse back in its stall. When they returned to the porch, everyone else had fled inside the house. For the next hour the Detroit Tigers' starting right fielder and his future Hall of Fame buddy picked up, washed down, and scrubbed that nicely furnished porch. There was no multitude of fans to cheer them on. No peanuts, no popcorn, no Cracker Jacks. Just an hour of silent labor, followed by a lifetime of cracking-up laughter over the memory of Hal Newhouser and his favorite horse.

Being a Detroit Tigers' player in 1953 was a combination of hard work on the field and just plain fun in free times. Manager Fred Hutchinson's serious nature infected the entire squad during games. Hutch tried many strategies, including player platooning against right- or left-hand pitchers, or changing starting pitcher rotations, or using relief pitching to change a game's pace, or anything he could think of to affect a win. But the team still lost 94 games while winning 60.

Don played in most of the games as a starting regular outfielder. Hutch moved him around all three outfield positions, mostly to let rookie Al Kaline and veteran Pat Mullin join him and get some playing time. Don was the only regular outfielder to play all three positions consistently. He started in left field 37 times, center field 29 times, and right field 69 times. And yet, despite his being switched around, Don finished the season with a .980 fielding percentage, highest among the regular outfielders except for Jim Delsing's .992 in center field. One day the Tigers' play-by-play sports announcer Van Patrick commented about Don.

Patrick was in his first year with the Tigers, but he'd been around the Detroit media scene for many years. He remembered Don as a three-sport athlete in high school and college. Noting this on the air, Patrick drew an analogy between Don's three-sport background and his three-outfield platooning. He referred to the "multi-sport, multi-talented" Don Lund from Detroit. He invited his listeners to guess which position Don would play in the next Tigers' game. Only Hutch knew, Patrick said, and he wasn't telling anybody!

The "Iron Man" of the 1953 Tigers was shortstop Harvey Kuenn. Harvey played in every game that year and made 308 put-outs, which precisely equaled the numbers in his year-end batting average: .308. Kuenn was the Tigers' only American League representative to the All-Star Game on July 14, held at Crosley Field in Cincinnati. He got in the game only once, as a pinch-hitter for pitcher Allie Reynolds in the sixth inning. But Harvey made history, causing one of the great defensive plays in popular lore of the midseason game. He hit a screaming line drive to his opposite field, down the right field line. National League right fielder Enos Slaughter, figuring Kuenn for a pull-hitter and playing him toward right center field, raced toward the ball, dove, tumbled, stretched, and grabbed it just before it would have landed. Kuenn was robbed of a base hit; Slaughter gained an edge in his next contract appeal. The National League won the game, 5–1.

Then there was just plain fun. Steve Gromek owned a bowling alley, and many of Steve's fellow players would bring their families to try out Detroit's favorite indoor sport. Don, Betty, and Susan would join the Boones and other Tigers families for recreation after games or on off days at home. Sometimes Steve would arrange a party for all the players and their families. For these occasions, he closed his place to the general public. "Gromek's Alley" was a favorite spot for a good Tigers' team time.

As Steve Gromek provided indoor fun, a dedicated Tigers fan named Bill Murray gave the Tigers outdoor Michigan at its summer best. Bill owned a bar in Mount Clemens, Michigan, a small town about forty miles due north of Detroit. Mount Clemens had a world-famous reputation for its sulfur-laden mineral baths, which drew thousands of health-minded tourists each year. With seven bathhouses, the whole town smelled like rotten eggs through the first half of the twentieth century, but the townspeople were proud of their town and grateful for the mineral bath prosperity. In fact, Mount Clemens High School teams were known as the "Battling Bathers."

By 1953, though, the mineral wells had been capped, the bathhouses were razed, and Mount Clemens changed over to a typical pleasant Michigan town on the Clinton River. Little remained of the mineral baths but memory—except for the high school. The "Battling Bathers" continued to compete with great dedication. And Bill Murray's bar was also part of the town's tradition, with one exception: it was the only bar in town that featured wall-to-wall Tigers memorabilia. Bill opened his heart to the Detroit Tigers. And for the Tigers' players, he opened his home.

Murray lived in a large, wood-framed house right on the Clinton River. His home had multiple bedrooms, ample living spaces, a large kitchen, and a private bar that rivaled his place of business. He also had a 26-foot, open-bow, Chris-Craft speed-boat that dominated anything else that dared to wet a keel for miles around.

Murray wanted to entertain the Tigers and their families. He needed to let them know that. He needed a player contact. He finally found one through mutual friends and hooked up with one player who jumped at the invitation: infielder Jerry Priddy. Priddy happily took on the task of organizing Tigers family vis-its to Bill Murray's home. He arranged for these to be two-day affairs, on Sundays following a double-header, continuing into all-day on Monday. Jerry was the coordinator, along with his wife Evelyn.

The Lunds were eager participants, along with the Dropos, the Boones, the Garvers, and many others. They'd swim off Bill's dock; they'd play Bill's outdoor games; they'd raid Bill's bar; they'd take Bill's boat out to Lake St. Clair, and stop at Peche Island, a small, deserted clump of dirt and bushes surrounded by shallow water in the middle of the lake. They even stayed overnight in Murray's house. And Bill loved every minute of it. So did Jerry Priddy.

On Sunday, August 30, Priddy was at home getting ready to leave for Briggs Stadium to play the doubleheader against Phila-delphia. Evelyn's sister was visiting them for the week. As Jerry was leaving, Evelyn informed him that he'd better come home after the last game. They weren't going to Murray's, because Evelyn thought the parties would be too rowdy for her sister. A shocked Priddy drove to the stadium, practiced in pregame drills, managed to get in the second game for a couple of innings, and then trooped into the clubhouse without saying a word. That was unusual for him, especially since the Tigers had obliterated Philadelphia in both games, 10–1 and 9–1, but word had spread and the players knew what was bothering Jerry Priddy. They didn't interfere as he showered, changed, and walked out the door. They felt sorry for him. Priddy pouted all the way home. Then he just sat in his living room contemplating the tips of his shoes.

Meanwhile, players were arriving at Bill Murray's house on the lake, ready for the two-day blow-off that was about to start. Someone suggested they call Jerry Priddy, just to see if Evelyn might change her mind. Don made the call. Evelyn changed her mind. Jerry broke the land speed record between Detroit and Mount Clemens, smiling all the way. If a cop had been around, Detroit's veteran infielder, enjoying the final season of his remarkable thirteen-year career in the major leagues, might have been signing autographs for his fellow inmates at the Detroit City Jail.

Bill Murry's parties continued through the 1953 season

37

Still a Tiger

Monday morning, seven o'clock. Still dark outside, and cold on this December day. The only light in his apartment was in the kitchen, where he silently sat and nursed a cup of coffee. His family was asleep; their day wouldn't start for another hour. He, of course, was fully dressed and ready to go. He waited patiently for the phone call he knew would come at any minute. No problem. He'd been doing this same routine for years: early rise, light breakfast, wait for the ringing phone, answer it with your name, and wait for the matter-of-fact response. The drill never altered. The only thing that changed was his daily destination. So he waited, speculating where they might send him.

He grabbed the phone on the first ring and answered as prescribed: "Don Lund speaking."

The impassive woman's voice responded: "Eight o'clock; Stillwagon Elementary; physical education."

Don gave the expected response, "Thank you," and hung up. Stillwagon, he thought. Susan's school, right here in the neighborhood. An easy walk, even on a winter morning. He threw on his overcoat and headed out, not wanting to wake Betty or his seven-year-old daughter. Susan was in for a surprise.

Don watched closely as Susan strolled into the school gym with the rest of her third-grade class. When she saw her father standing in the middle of the floor and wearing slacks, a T-shirt, and a whistle hanging by a cord around his neck, she was totally astonished. Her eyes became bulging blue circles and her mouth opened into an o-ringed cave. "Daddy!" she squealed, as she broke ranks and ran to him. Don squatted and took his little girl into his arms, grinning like he'd just hit a grand slam. The third-grade teacher smiled; the rest of Susan's class took everything in and squirmed with delight. For the next hour, Don Lund taught the best gym class of his life.

The 1954 Tigers' spring training in Lakeland was almost unique for Don. For the first time in his major league career, he came into training camp having been a big-league starter all last season. This spring, he roamed the playing grass of Henley Field with the confidence of a regular player. His abilities had been well tested the previous year on the turf of Detroit's Briggs Stadium; all he had to do now was show everybody he hadn't lost a thing. So that's what he set out to do, and that's precisely what he did. He hit around .290; his fielding average exceeded .990, almost perfect. He even stole a couple of bases. He felt solid; he felt good; he was in the lineup.

Best of all, he was back with his team buddies. One of them was equipment manager John Hand. Don knew the Hand family from his old neighborhood. Isabel Hand, pretty and popular, was in his class at Southeastern High and the youngest of three kids. Her two older brothers, Bill and John, would ultimately be connected with the Tigers. Bill Hand took a job at the U.S. Rubber plant on Jefferson Avenue, and then joined the Briggs Stadium volunteer corps to work the huge center field scoreboard. Bill's job called for him to change the inning-by-inning numbers during a game. The standing joke behind the scenes: "There go the numbers, Hand over hand!" The third brother, John Hand, actually worked for the team. He started as a clubhouse attendant and then moved up to equipment manager.

John's friendship with Don had started during boyhood days in the old Detroit neighborhood. It was naturally renewed in 1949, when Don first joined the Tigers. And then, with Don as a regular in 1953, the two men had again become friends. So Don wasn't at all surprised to see John come running up to him one morning during 1954 spring training. John was fairly bursting with something he couldn't wait to reveal.

"Hey, Don," John said. "You'll never guess what Pat Mullin did!"

Don had no idea. Outfielder Pat Mullin was a close friend, but Don hadn't seen him much at Henley Field this spring. Mullin retired as a player at the end of last season, ending an exclusive fourteen-year career with the Tigers, interrupted by four years in the military during WWII. Throughout the years, Mullin had been an integral part of Detroit's lineup. His bat could be counted on in tight spots. He ran fast enough to score from second base on a long single, and his fielding was superb, topped in 1950 when his average finished at a perfect 1.000. Pat's last game, shared with fellow outfielders Don Lund, Jim Delsing, and Bob Nieman, was played on Sunday, September 27, 1953, in Cleveland Stadium against the Indians. The Tigers won, 7–3. Pat Mullin retired as a winner.

Now, in 1954 spring training, Pat worked for the Tigers as a scout and as a teaching coach for the organization's minor league teams. Those teams trained nearby at a converted military base dubbed "Tigertown." The facilities contained converted barracks, storage buildings, three baseball fields, and dining facilities. Pat's job consisted of working with young ballplayers, helping them develop their batting skills and fielding techniques. He was a natural teacher, well-liked and much respected. Moreover, Pat Mullin had the kind of personality that attracted people to him. He was a great storyteller who could relate to anyone, young or old. Don Lund was proud to call him a friend. Now what was John Hand so excited about?

"Pat Mullin just gave his number six to Al Kaline," said John. "He walked right into my area and told me to assign his number. I checked with Kaline. It's a done deal!"

Don was impressed. Pat had worn the number six for the past seven years, ever since he came back to the Tigers after the war in 1947. For seven years before that, Tigers' number six had also been worn by only one player, infielder Pinky Higgins, so number six was a consistent number for the Tigers. And now Pat Mullin was passing it on to Al Kaline. Don remembered his own game-winning double that allowed Kaline to score his first major league run. Al chased Pat Mullin's number six all the way around the bases that day. Now he would wear that same number and probably make it famous, Don thought. Just like Stan Musial was doing as he wore number six for the St. Louis Cardinals.

Don thanked John just as he heard the crack of a fungo bat. Both men looked up and followed the ball into deep right center field. They watched Kaline chase it down with long strides, make the catch, take one step, and then make a dead-on throw back to the infield. Magic in motion. John Hand looked at Don. Don smiled at his friend and said only four words before he walked away: "Bet on number six."

Don was a regular in the spring training lineup, starting in right field. His only disappointment during that time came through a missed game against Philadelphia in Clearwater. The Phillies' star pitcher, Robin Roberts, was scheduled to start. Don wanted to face him, and not just for the thrill of going up against one of the best pitchers in the game. He also had a mutual connection with Robin Roberts through Michigan coach Ray Fisher. Don, of course, played for Ray in Ann Arbor. Roberts met Ray differently.

Robin went to Michigan State College (later Michigan State University) on a basketball scholarship, but he also reigned supreme on MSC's baseball pitcher's mound. During the summer months he joined the Northern Baseball League, an amateur association of college player teams in Vermont, which was run by Ray Fisher. Ray immediately saw Roberts' potential and coached him, personally passing on techniques to improve the young pitcher's control and movements. Ray knew he was helping the young man to return to school and face his own Wolverines, but that didn't matter. Ray helped him; he was that kind of a man.

Don knew that Robin Roberts credited Ray as one of his mentors, as did he, so he was really looking forward to the game in Clearwater. It didn't happen. Rain, the inevitable spoiler, cancelled the contest. Don never had the chance to face Robin Roberts, the future Hall of Famer who shared with him the same mentor.

The 1954 Detroit Tigers were by all accounts an average team. Only Harvey Kuenn finished the season batting over .300. Ray Boone led the team in home runs with 20. Steve Gromek was the pitching ace, winning 18 games and finishing with the pitchers' lowest earned run average of 2.74. Manager Fred Hutchinson was determined to give his promising outfielder Al Kaline as much seasoning as possible, so he played him in 138 games. This was a smart move. Kaline needed to play, and his bonus arrangement made it impossible for him to be seasoned in the minor leagues. The move also affected Don, who was moved to utility status, playing when his right-hand bat was needed or starting as a replacement in left, center, or right fields.

A most embarrassing moment for Don came that season, after a game in Briggs Stadium against the Chicago White Sox. Tigers' first baseman Walt Dropo had blooped a floater to left field in one of the later innings. Chicago's left fielder Sam Mele, playing deep, tried to field the ball with a running stretch, only to see it tick his shoe tops and bounce away. Dropo stopped at first base. Everyone looked out toward the center field scoreboard. Tigers fans gasped as the "E" sign went up, signifying an error for Mele. Tigers players on the bench, believing that their first baseman had been robbed of a hit, reacted by booing and waving towels at the official scorekeepers in the press box. To no avail. Mele was charged with an error.

After the game, one of the scorekeepers, a reporter for the *Detroit News* named Watson Spoelstra, entered the Tigers clubhouse. Don knew him fairly well, since Spoelstra covered Michigan football and Don worked with Bob Ufer on Wolverines radio broadcasts. He and Spoelstra had shared conversations over the years in the Michigan Stadium press box. So as Spoelstra approached his locker, Don felt comfortable with a casual comment: "You know, Watson, I thought Walter deserved a base hit on that ball."

Spoelstra looked at him with hard eyes and responded with venom: "Get in the fucking game and get a hit before you pop off!"

That did it. Don grabbed him by the shirt collar and reared back with his right hand as the clubhouse went completely silent. Spoelstra's eyes bulged with fear. Then Don realized what he was doing, took a deep breath, and released the reporter. Spoelstra beat a fast retreat from the clubhouse. Completely chagrined, Don walked over to Hutchinson's cubbyhole office as the clubhouse returned to normal. "I'm sorry, Hutch," he said. "I guess I just lost it."

The manager looked at him and started laughing so hard he nearly fell off his chair. He continued to laugh as he waved Don away. So much for team apologies. The next day Don played in the game and got a hit, forcing Sam Mele all the way to the wall. After the game, Tigers' pitcher Paul Foytack sought him in the clubhouse.

Foytack was one of the most upbeat players on the team, always looking for ways to brighten things up, even during a losing season. "Hey, Lund," he said. "What was it that Spoelstra said to you about getting in the game and getting a hit before you pop off? Well, now you can go find him and pop off!"

Another embarrassing moment came on July 20 during the second game of a doubleheader against the Philadelphia Athletics in Connie Mack Stadium. Don became the first, and maybe the only, Detroit Tigers player to have his nose broken while sitting on the bench. It happened when A's pitcher Moe Burtschy, replacing starter Arnie Portocarrero, took his turn at the plate. Since Burtschy wore number 33, Don's number from his Michigan days, Don watched with interest from the bench as Burtschy strode up and took his stance. Then he turned his attention to infielder Fred Hatfield, who was sitting next to him and asking him a question. Don's face was turned away from the action. The first pitch to Burtschy, a right-handed hitter, was low and outside. Burtschy should have let it go. He didn't. The ball sliced off the end of his bat and shot toward the Tigers' dugout and Don's head. Hatfield saw it coming. "Look out!" Hatfield yelled, as he reached forward to block the ball. Don reacted by turning his head. The ball deflected off the meaty part of Hatfield's right hand and smashed into Don's nose. Someone grabbed a towel to soak up the blood as Don moaned in pain.

Quickly, Hatfield and Lund ran up the tunnel, through the visitor's clubhouse, and into a waiting taxi, with Don holding the towel to his face and Hatfield assuring the driver they wouldn't drop blood in his cab. When they entered the emergency room, Don looked around at the grisly sights of people in trauma. He saw broken arms, bloody faces, and just plain despair as persons of all ages waited for treatment.

"Let's get out of here," he told Hatfield. "All these people are worse off than me. The trainer can fix me up."

Hatfield was firm. "We're staying here and that's that."

Two hours later they were treated by an emergency room doctor. Fortunately for Hatfield, his throwing hand was only slightly bruised. He could play right away. Don, on the other hand, would be laid up a few days due to facial swelling. The doctor snapped his deviated septum back in place, cleaned up the blood, and worked on the broken nose while Don stared up at the white ceiling. After that, both men taxied to their Philadelphia hotel, where they learned the Tigers had won both games that day. At least, Don thought, that was some consolation.

A few days later, the Tigers were still on the road, this time against the Washington Senators in Griffith Stadium. Don wasn't

playing. His nose was still tender and swollen. Moreover, he was
breathing out of his mouth almost exclusively. He thought he
might have to see a doctor once he returned to Detroit, to find
out when his nasal passages would get back to normal. That
thought changed the next day, July 24.

Don was showering after a 2–1 loss to the Senators. As he
washed his face, he felt something hanging out of his left nostril.
He gently pulled on it. Out came a wad of cotton and gauze. He
reached up to his right nostril and pulled out another wad. There
was no blood, and he could finally breathe through his nose.
The doctor in Philadelphia hadn't told him about the packing,
let alone when to remove it. Later, in the clubhouse, he told the
story to Fred Hatfield.

"The Doc must have been an Athletics fan," said Hatfield.
"Maybe he didn't like the fact that we cleaned their clocks!"

The next day Don took batting practice and got in the game, a
3–11 drubbing from Washington, which completed three straight
losses to the Senators and ended the road trip. Nevertheless, Don
felt good about playing as the Tigers returned to Detroit. He was
again in the game, getting some hits, and scoring some runs. He
had no way of knowing how his career would turn abruptly in
just a few days.

It's called a "waiver." It's a secret known only to higher ups
in the chain of command of a major league baseball team. It's
the process by which a team notifies one or more other teams
that a player is offered up for sale or trade. Notification is made
by either written wire or by telephone, usually among general
managers. A player almost never knows he is "waivered." He
finds out only after a deal is made and he is forced to move on
to another team.

The waiver rules provide protection for teams in each league,
however. For instance, if an American League team puts one of its
players on waiver, it must first give the other teams in the American League a chance to react. Only after all the other American
League teams show no interest is the waiving team free to turn
to the National League. The same is true for waiving National
League teams. But there aren't very many other waiving restric-
tions, so it's common for a team to have several players on their
major and minor league rosters out on waivers during the baseball season. Sometimes even the stars and superstars are put on

waivers, just so a team can test the waters. If a bid is made and the waiving team changes its mind, it can always withdraw the waiver without penalty. Or it can make the deal, depending on the financial conditions. In the final analysis, waiving is all about making money for the team. The welfare of the player is seldom considered, unless there are special personal circumstances. Such was the case on July 29, 1954, which brought outfielder Hoot Evers from the National League New York Giants to the American League Detroit Tigers, in exchange for Don Lund.

Evers, in the twilight of his career after fourteen years in the big leagues, had been on waivers by the Giants for at least a month. In truth, the Giants didn't need him. They were the hottest team in the National League, led by a spectacular outfielder named Willy Mays. The Giants were on their way to winning the pennant and the World Series. Evers was expendable.

On the other hand, Don Lund was a strong factor in the Detroit lineup, even though he hadn't played in every game. The Tigers were far from being in contention, though, and manager Fred Hutchinson could easily change his outfielders around without fear of losing much in the American League standings. Besides, Hutch wanted to give Al Kaline lots of playing time. Even without the opportunity to get some seasoning in minor league ball, Kaline was showing great improvement, especially with his bat. Hutch wisely played him frequently. Don, along with several other players on this average-performing Tigers' squad, had been on waivers for at least six weeks. Here's the scenario:

It's the last week in July 1954. The phone rings in the office of Tigers' general manager Muddy Ruel. He's been expecting the Giants' general manager, Chub Feeney, to get back to him on his offer. Ruel takes the call. Feeney greets him back, and wastes no time in getting right down to the deal.

Feeney asks Ruel to tell him again why the Tigers want Hoot Evers. Muddy explains that his manager, Fred Hutchinson, has found out about Evers being on waivers, and that no team has expressed an interest. Hutchinson and Evers are tight friends, going back to the 1941 Tigers' team they both played on. Their families vacation together; they both have homes in the same neighborhood in Florida. Hutch doesn't want to see Evers' career stumble around. He wants his buddy on the Tigers' roster, even if Hoot doesn't play a game this year.

Feeney asks Ruel who he's willing to give up for Evers. Ruel tells Feeney he can have any one of the Tigers' players on waivers. Feeney tells Ruel that the Giants don't need any waivered Tigers players. Ruel understands. After all, the Giants are on top of the National League. Ruel asks Feeney if there's any other way the Tigers can acquire Hoot Evers. Feeney tells him yes, but to get Evers, Ruel still has to give up one of his other players in order to maintain the twenty-five-player limit. So Feeney tells Ruel he's been talking with Rosy Ryan, general manager of their Triple-A farm club the Minneapolis Millers, as well the Millers' team manager Bill Rigney. He says both of them want Don Lund. To them, Lund was a local favorite who played well for the St. Paul Saints and could hit the ball out of sight at Nicollet Park. But they can't get Lund directly from the Tigers. He'd have to be picked up by the Giants and sent right down to Minneapolis. Feeney tells Ruel he's willing to do that. Ruel accepts the deal. He wants Hutch to be happy.

So on July 29, 1954, Hoot Evers joins the Detroit Tigers. He would play in thirty games and hit .183. That same day Don Lund heads for Minneapolis, Minnesota. He would play for them the rest of the season, hit nearly .300, and blast the most unusual home run of his career. With two outs and nobody on in the last half of the ninth inning against the Kansas City Blues, Don stood at the plate with the score tied 3–3. The first pitch, low and outside, should have been ignored. Don reached out for it. The ball struck the end of his bat and sailed high toward the right field fence. As he ran toward first base, he figured he had just hit the final out of the game. But the ball kept sailing higher, arching above the right field wall, where it finally landed out of the park on Nicollet Avenue. The crowd went wild. The Millers won the game.

Don's "bad ball" swing had made him a ten-minute hero. Publicly, he gave all the credit to Nicollet Park and its 279-foot right field wall. He told a reporter that Briggs Stadium in Detroit, where he played before joining the Millers, had a right field wall of 325 feet. His hit would have merely been a long fly ball in that stadium. Personally, he laughed as he and Betty, who was there, recalled the home run. He was now part of the "Home Run in Nicollet" Club; a gag group of players throughout America's ballparks who had hit one in the street at Nicollet without much

Minneapolis Millers outfielder Don Lund is about to be tagged
out at home by Johnny Bucha of the St. Paul Saints, 1954.
This was Don's last season as a ballplayer. The rivalry between
these two Triple-A teams was intense. Lund and Bucha, good
friends, played for the Tigers and the Dodgers in their careers,
though not at the same time. (*Minneapolis Millers' Archives*)

effort. The saying "Home Run in Nicollet" gave bragging rights
to lots of guys. Don was delighted to be one of them.

His best experience with the Millers was getting to know
the best third baseman he'd ever seen, Ray Dandridge. Ray
was over forty years old. He'd been a superstar in the Negro
Leagues. Some said that Ray taught Willie Mays a lot about the
game, when both played for the Millers in 1951. Nearly all who
knew him, including Don, thought that Ray should be playing
for the Giants right now, despite his age. But the Giants, more
specifically their general manager Chub Feeney, claimed that
Dandridge was too old. Don believed Ray could play for the
Giants even if he were in his fifties; he was that good. Anyway,

he and Ray Dandridge quickly became friends, and Don played out the month of August with Minneapolis.

He, Betty, and Susan lived like royalty in a beautiful water-front house on Lake Minnetonka, thanks to a Millers' superfan named Doherty, who owned the house and ran one of the more popular bars near Nicollet Park. Doherty customarily rented his lakefront home to Millers' players for practically nothing. The Lunds happened to arrive, looking for a place to stay, just after another player had been traded and moved out of Doherty's house. The arrangement was perfect for Don and Betty. Whatever consternation they felt about Don's being abruptly sent to the minor leagues faded quickly when they moved into that lakefront home. Doherty gave them exactly what they needed.

At the end of the season, Don finished on a high note. In his final time at bat, with two runners on base, he faced Sam "Toothpick" Jones for the third time that day. Sam was a hard-throwing right-hander from the old Negro Leagues, who had been sent down to the Triple-A minors by the Cleveland Indi-ans. Sam's nickname came from the ever-present toothpick he clenched between his teeth when he pitched.

Toothpick seemed to have Don's number so far that day; he struck him out in his first time at bat, and forced him to hit a ground ball to third base for an easy out in his second try. As Don stepped in for the third time, Toothpick almost cracked a smile on his normally stone face. His first pitch, a fastball, came in low and inside. Don swung and connected, hitting a line-drive single that drove in the game-winning run. Toothpick walked slowly off the mound. Don walked toward him. They shook hands. This time Toothpick broke out a smile. Sportsmanship prevailed.

After the game, Don left Nicollet Stadium a contented man. He had played well, the fans liked him, and his family had just finished a month's "vacation" on one of the most beautiful lakes in the country. As he walked away, happy in his thoughts, Don Lund did not imagine he had played his last ballgame. The record would show that in his nine years as a professional, he had played in 281 major league games. In 753 times at bat he had 181 hits, including 15 home runs, 8 triples, and 36 doubles. His lifetime batting average would be .245. If game statistics could be found for the Triple-A teams he played for, they might show a better overall performance. But that's mere speculation. The fact is that Don Lund had unknowingly played his last game, going out a winner in Nicollet Stadium at the end of the season. He had every reason to believe his career in baseball would continue. He had no idea that it was about to change in a different, and much more rewarding, direction.

38
No Chance to Retire

Detroit John J. Pershing High School's gymnasium echoed with basketballs bouncing off the mirror-finish of its hardwood floor. Outside, a January morning's cold air pressed a thin layer of frost tight against the gym's huge windows. Inside, steam-heated air fought to bring the room's temperature up to nearly 65 degrees—about right for the thirty tenth-grade boys being drilled by substitute teacher Don Lund. Don had them organized into groups of six in front of the baskets around the gym. They were practicing lay-ups and one-handed shots, following Don's demonstrations of proper procedure. Don was moving among the groups, making comments and corrections as needed. The boys were dressed in typical gym class duds brought from home, including high-top gym shoes. Don wore his standard phys ed teaching garb: long khaki pants, white T-shirt, gym shoes, and the ever-present whistle around from his neck. He was content. He was doing what he loved to do: teaching sports fundamentals to young men. All the high school kids, no matter where he taught, called him "Coach." He liked it. As far as he was concerned, all phys ed teachers deserved the term.

Don was demonstrating proper lay-up technique when he looked up and noticed Pershing High's principal waving to him from the corner of the gym. He excused himself and walked over to the principal, who said, "Don, the Detroit Tigers called. They want you to contact John McHale."

Don was surprised. "John McHale? He heads up their minor league operations. What's he calling about?"

"No idea," said the principal, "but you can use my office phone when you're free."

Don thanked the principal and told him he'd be there after his class was finished. When he arrived and placed the call, he was put through right away to John McHale's office. McHale's assistant told him her boss would like to speak with him in person, as early as tomorrow morning. They settled on a time, and Don said he'd be there. On his way out of the office, he asked the school secretary to notify the teacher scheduling people that he wouldn't be available tomorrow. He had to attend a meeting.

That evening Don told Betty about the call from the Tigers. He was perplexed: "I still can't figure out why John McHale wants to see me," he told her. "Maybe the Tigers want me back. Maybe Hoot Evers is going to retire, and they'd like me to replace him."

Betty wasn't buying it. "That's not the way they'd do it, Honey," she said. "You know how they work. They buy and sell and trade players all the time and the players never know anything about it until the deal is done. Remember when the only way you found out you were traded was when you read it in the newspaper? I'm thinking it has to be something else." She went on, "Since McHale is in charge of the minor league teams, it can't have anything to do with the Tigers themselves."

Don thought about that. "Then maybe I did something last year that's getting me in trouble, but I can't think of what that might be. Or maybe they believe I might sue somebody over my broken nose." They both laughed at that idea, and then agreed to just wait and see what McHale wanted. Betty was skeptical; Don was optimistic. After all, he thought, John McHale is a friend. Besides, not too long ago John had brought an even better friend of Don's to work with him in Detroit, Jim Campbell. Jim had recently taken over the financial reins for the Tigers' minor league operations, after serving with distinction as general manager of the Buffalo Bisons. Campbell and McHale worked well together.

Don remembered his call to Campbell a couple of week's back, when he congratulated his old friend from Mud Hen days and welcomed him to Detroit. He didn't say it at the time, but he was convinced Campbell was a rapidly rising star in the Tigers' organization. Jim was also loyal to the core. The team's new owners would be crazy not to see that for themselves. And so, he reasoned, the Tigers must want him back in right field. McHale probably volunteered to tell him about it in person. Campbell would also be there tomorrow, he was sure. Don could hardly wait to see them both.

The next morning Don strode into the Tigers' front offices to the smiles and wholehearted greetings of everyone he saw. He heard one of the secretaries call out: "Mr. Campbell, Mr. Lund is here!"

Soon his old friend appeared and offered his hand, which Don took eagerly. "Hi, Don, now it's my turn to welcome you here. C'mon, John's waiting for you." The two of them proceeded to McHale's office. McHale met them warmly. After a few pleasantries, Campbell excused himself and Don settled into a chair across from John McHale.

McHale looked every bit the successful man he was. His tall, trim build was neatly covered by a gray suit, with wide lapels on the jacket and a knife-edged crease in the pants. His white shirt was fronted by a red tie. Don thought of Ohio State's colors; right now, McHale was a walking Buckeye ad. John's brown hair was neatly trimmed over his oval face. With his piercing brown eyes, thin smile, and forthright bearing, John McHale could have sat there and passed for the chairman of General Motors—except for his hands. They weren't the soft, manicured hands of a pampered executive. They were the strong hands of a ballplayer.

A standout athlete from Detroit Catholic Central High School, McHale went on to play football and baseball at Notre Dame. After graduation, he followed his dream of playing pro ball and signed with the Tigers. He played minor league ball for several years, most notably at first base. Then he had the good fortune of meeting a beautiful and vivacious member of the Briggs family, Patricia Cameron. They fell in love, married, and John McHale was welcomed into the world of big league baseball management. His role in the Tigers' front office could be whatever he wanted, automatically. But John quickly made it clear he wouldn't work in any job he didn't earn by his own merit. So he worked hard, and he moved up. Now he was the director of Minor League Operations, or Farm Director.

Spike Briggs, the owner's son and John's marital cousin, was Tigers' general manager and McHale's boss. Spike delegated everything, and John McHale was his delegatee. So John was, for all practical purposes, the default general manager of the franchise. No wonder he needed the talents of Jim Campbell.

McHale got right down to business. "Don, the Tigers need you back here in Detroit. I think so, Spike thinks so, and Jim

Campbell thinks so, too. The question is, can we get you to think the same way?"

Don smiled. This was going well. "I think that would be great, John. Have you talked with Minneapolis about buying my contract?"

John sat up and blinked. "Minneapolis? I'm not talking about you coming back here as a player," McHale exclaimed. "We don't need your muscles; we need your brain!"

Don gulped. "I'm not sure I understand."

McHale took a moment to compose himself. "Well, then, Don, let me clear things up. We need someone to run our Tigers Tryout Camps. We've been searching since last fall, and Campbell keeps bringing up your name. I agree. That's why I asked you to come in this morning."

Don suddenly understood. The tryout camps were held each summer in Detroit. Their purpose was to bring promising high school baseball players, all of whom had expressed an interest in becoming professionals, together in one location. The kids would come from the sandlots, mostly around Detroit. They'd be nominated by their high school coaches; they could be sent by "booster" type Tigers' fans, or recommended by Tigers' scouts, or even "walk on" by themselves. In turn, the Tigers could get a close look at youngsters who showed promise in competition with their peers.

Tryout camps weren't new to the Tigers, but for some reason they just weren't as popular as they were in past years. Maybe this was because the Tigers had been a struggling team for several years. Or maybe the tryouts weren't promoted as much as they used to be. Maybe both of these reasons were true. Nevertheless, he'd heard some negative talk about them from various high school coaches.

"Why me?" Don asked. "I mean, I'm still playing ball. Isn't this something that could wait until I retire?"

McHale sat back and stared at the big, muscular man seated in front of him. He knew that Lund was at the top of the Tigers' list for this job; everybody wanted him. And the number-two pick was a long way down. Lund was also the kind of guy who could smell bullshit a mile away. Plus, he still wanted to play ball, even in Triple-A Minneapolis. McHale decided he'd better level up and lay his cards right out.

"Don, let me be honest with you. From our point of view, you're a natural for running the tryout camps. You like kids, you work well with young players; hell, you've been a teacher in the off-season for ten years. And you're smart. You're an observer. Campbell told me about your bench comments when you're watching a pitcher's movements. You're what they call a dug-out player; always watching the game like a hawk and making remarks, even when you're not in the lineup. You can't shut it off. Most guys aren't like that. Some of them just sit there and brood until they can jump up and grab a bat. But not you; you're mentally in the game." McHale pointed his finger for emphasis. "That's why you're sitting here now."

Don just sat there, saying nothing. John was putting on a hard sell. But what he said about his being a game-calling chatterbox in the dugout was true. Plus, he really did like working with kids. So he put on his best smile and waited.

McHale went on, "Jim Campbell told me you've got as good a baseball mind as he's seen, and we were just talking in general. He didn't know I'd be looking to fill this job. And Gehringer said the same thing. Charley's the first one who talked to Spike about you. So you see, I'm not the only one looking your way."

Don was starting to get impressed. Jim Campbell and Charlie Gehringer. Hmmm.

McHale continued, "Now, as I see it, Don, you've got a couple of choices here; maybe more, but at least a couple." McHale looked upward as he gathered his thoughts. "First, you could return to Minneapolis this year, and I've checked with them; they want you back. You might have a good year, you might not. And what are your chances of being called up to the Giants? They won the pennant last year. They've got a whole slew of outfielders, including Don Mueller and Willie Mays. Mays won the batting title, and Mueller was right behind him. Do the numbers."

Don didn't have to do the numbers. Though he felt in peak condition, he was also thirty-one years old. Besides, the New York Giants were managed by Leo Durocher. Durocher wasn't favorably inclined toward him, as evidenced by his snide remark about college players. When he played for Durocher, the man never said anything positive to him. So Don had no illusions about being called up to play for the Giants. He continued to listen as McHale went on.

"Now please don't think I'm putting you down, Don. You may or may not play again for a major league team. We both know a lot of guys who finish out their careers in the minors. Some even stay around for years, never giving up even after they're booted all the way down to Class A ball. When they finally retire they're too old to find a regular job. That wouldn't be true in your case, because you're a trained teacher. You could teach school after you retire." McHale paused. "Oh, and by the way, I checked your career stats. For what it's worth, you've got enough years playing in the big leagues to qualify for the pension fund. You can retire any time and get your pension."

Don hadn't thought about that. He remembered Commissioner "Happy" Chandler, who had started the player's pension fund in 1947. He built it with proceeds from broadcast rights to the World Series. He was well known for his generosity to the players. The owners fired him in 1951. Don started to speak, but decided to keep quiet as McHale went on.

"I said you had a couple of choices. The other one, Don, is to take this job and come back to the Tigers. I'm offering you a full-time job. You'll work with high school kids and help us identify future players. More than that, you'll also help out with our minor league players in spring at Tigertown. You'd be working with guys, friends of yours, like Pat Mullin and Stubby Overmire."

Don was impressed with McHale's Tigertown scenario. He and Pat Mullin were indeed close friends. Pat had been doing some scouting for the Tigers. This year, though, he was being sent down to manage the Little Rock Travelers, a Tigers Double-A farm team in the Southern Association. Stubby Overmire was also Don's friend and a great guy. He pitched for the Tigers over seven seasons and then went on to pitch two seasons for the St. Louis Browns, followed by one with the Yankees. He earned two World Series championship rings during his career, first with the Tigers in 1945, then with the Yankees in 1951. Stubby retired in 1952. Now he was managing minor league farm teams for the Tigers. He most recently skippered the Little Rock Travelers to a winning season.

Now, Pat Mullin was replacing him there and Don wondered why. He had heard that Stubby was well-liked and respected, and since McHale indicated he was still around, he had to ask. "Stubby's still managing, isn't he?"

McHale smiled, "Oh, yes. We're sending him out to Terre Haute this year. They need a shot in the arm. Overmire's our shooter."

Don understood McHale's logic. The Terre Haute Huts (some called them the Tigers) were a struggling Class B team in the Three-I League. Stubby Overmire, with his ability to deal with young players, would do nicely there. His easy sense of humor would also bring him favor with the townsfolk of Terre Haute. Good move on McHale's part, he thought.

The prospect of joining Mullin and Overmire at Tigertown this spring was attractive, but Don needed to know more about the job. He had some additional questions, including how much administrative freedom he would have. McHale assured him that the tryout camps would be his to design, change, or develop in any way he saw fit, as long as they got results. The meeting ended with Don saying he had a lot to think about. He also wanted to talk things over with Betty. McHale agreed, but wanted his answer soon. Don said he'd get back to him the next day. After saying goodbye to Jim Campbell and some of the staff, he walked briskly out the door.

Back home over lunch, Don and Betty talked about his meeting with John McHale. They looked at the pros and cons of each choice Don could make, including his immediate retirement as a professional player to become a full-time teacher and coach in the Detroit schools. This option had been offered to him over the years by various high school principals, as recently as two weeks ago. He could coach football, basketball, baseball, or all three sports if he wanted. It depended on the school he chose. He had also been approached by schools in other districts around the metropolitan area. No doubt he'd have a nice career in high school teaching.

But Don had to admit that his heart was in pro baseball. More than that, he wanted to be with a major league team. And even more than that, he wanted to be with the Detroit Tigers. Sure, he could play out his years with Minneapolis. Betty disagreed with McHale's prediction that Don might not play again in the big leagues, and Don sided with her. Just imagine, she told him, if the American and National Leagues suddenly expanded to include more teams and more cities. He'd be a cinch to play big league ball. Franchises were moving all the time, like the Boston Braves going to Milwaukee only a couple of years ago in 1953. In fact, she added, the new County Stadium in Milwaukee had been built mainly to attract a major league team. The Milwaukee Braves had fans to the rafters at every game.

"It's all about money," Betty noted. "When those power moguls in major league baseball realize how much they can make by adding more big city markets, they're going to add teams. Why, even Minneapolis might have a major league team someday."

"Okay, you're probably right," Don answered, "but it's not going to happen tomorrow. Right now, I think I could play on any team in either league. But if I'm still with Minneapolis at the end of this coming season, my chances of wearing a major league uniform again will be getting pretty slim."

"So you're saying that John McHale's option looks like the best one?"

"I'm thinking it is," he answered. "Sure, I'd like to continue to play. And Mr. Doherty told me we could live in his home on Lake Minnetonka again all next season. Who knows? I might get a hot hand and have a great year. But staying in Detroit with the Tigers has a lot of appeal. The job John is offering plays to my strengths and experience with high school kids. And I'd be back in the big leagues, only in a different capacity. I'd be an ex-player who retired near his prime, rather than one who played until he was no longer of value to a team, even a minor league team. And I'd be with the Tigers. The Tigers were always my team, from the time I was a kid and Dad took me to Navin field. And frankly, I know I can do that job blindfolded. What do you think?"

Betty looked at her man through a film of tears. Here was the most compassionate, the tenderest man she had even known; a man who could rock Susan to sleep in his powerful arms with the gentleness of a soft breeze. Yet, here also was a man who could blast a baseball a country mile, who could run down a waiting catcher and send him flying off the plate without a second thought. This man of hers was a decisive man, too; able to teach a bunch of wild kids how to behave, or captain a team in three sports, leading his players to the win. And now, he was asking her to share in one of the most important decisions of his life. Extremely touched, she hesitated only a moment.

"I think you should move on to better things with the Tigers," she said. "You've had a great run as a player, and I've had a great run being right there with you. Besides, you're being recruited. That hasn't happened since you met George Sisler back in Ann Arbor. It's a new start for all of us, Honey; you, me, and Susan. We'll all move on together!"

That was it for Don. He hugged Betty for a long time and smiled. What had he ever done to deserve a woman like her?

"I'll call John McHale right away this afternoon and take the job. Then I'll call Rosey Ryan in Minneapolis and tell him I've decided to retire."

Betty laughed as she fairly shouted, "Detroit Tigers, here we come!"

McHale was of course delighted with the decision and went on for several minutes extolling Don's qualifications for the job. When Don told him he was going to call the Minneapolis Millers about retiring, John told him not to bother. He had already discussed the possibility with their general manager, Ryan. Now he would just need to call Ryan back and tell him the deal was done. Don said that was okay.

The next day, however, Don decided to call Ryan himself to confirm his deal with the Tigers. After all, he thought, I owe it to the Millers to let them know personally. When he placed the call to Minneapolis, he was put through immediately to Rosey Ryan's secretary.

"Mr. Ryan's not in at the moment, Mr. Lund. But we've all heard about your retirement. Congratulations and good luck. I'll be sure to let him know you called."

Don hung up the kitchen phone and looked at Betty. "How about that? I can't even announce my own retirement to my own team. John McHale did it for me!"

Betty gave him a knowing smile. "You're like General Mac-Arthur," she offered. "In that speech he gave to Congress after President Truman fired him. Remember what he said? 'Old soldiers never die, they just fade away.' Sound familiar? The Millers are letting you fade away."

Don sighed. "Oh well, who would we announce it to, any-way? Except the folks. Hey, we'd better run over there and tell them about this right away."

Betty laughed, "Before McHale does?"

He laughed back. "Before anybody does. Let's go!" They raced out the door, still laughing.

Spring training in 1955 at Tigertown in Lakeland was a new experience for him. For the first time, Don didn't have to be concerned with making a team roster. As an experienced teacher, he easily fell into the routine of instructing fundamentals. He showed young players how to improve their skills at things like base running, proper fielding position, sliding into base, even bunting. When he held a bat in his hands, it was usually to hit fungos. When he had a glove on his left hand, it was either to help another player work out, or to chase fly balls for pure exer-cise. He was having fun. He was also getting to know some very interesting people. Like Ralph Snyder, for instance.

Ralph, for lack of an official title (no one really knew it), was the man in charge of Tigertown. In fact, Ralph was one of the principal founders and designers of Tigertown. By 1955, he had already spent much of his adult life with the Detroit Tigers' organization. His was the responsibility for keeping track of the paper trails in the farm system, a job only the most highly organized person could handle. Ralph made it look easy. That's why the Tigers tapped him to start up and run Tigertown. They never regretted it.

Ralph became Tigertown's commanding general. He made sure that everything required to perform the daily regimen of spring training was in place, working, and ready to go. And noth-ing escaped his demanding eyes; no job was too big; no detail was too small. He saw to it that equipment was ready, schedules were maintained, and needs were met. So it was no surprise that everyone involved considered Ralph Snyder to be the most important person in the entire Tigertown minor league camp.

Everyone, that is, except Ralph Snyder. His unassuming style, coupled with a nearly obsessive drive to do things the right way, made him one of the most likable men in Lakeland. Just being with Ralph was nice. He was pleasantly plump at two hundred pounds, which floated easily around his six-foot frame. His balding, gray-haired pate rode comfortably over his round face, which never seemed to lose a continual, toothy smile. He looked right at people as he talked to them, making them feel like they were the only ones in the world at the moment. This approach was natural for him. It drew people in and made them glad to be there. Ralph Snyder was the kind of man who could get people to do all kinds of logistical stuff without getting them riled up. A nice guy who got things done pleasantly was somewhat rare in pro baseball.

Ralph Snyder and Don Lund had first become acquainted in 1949, when Don was a Tigers' outfielder. They knew each other as casual friends over the next six years. Now, in 1955, their paths crossed directly as Tigertown got under way and Don started helping with everyday logistics. The two of them worked well together. They became better friends. Then they became buddies when Betty Lund and Ralph's wife Jeanette got to know each other. The four of them related easily. Love of baseball brought them together; love for the Tigers cemented them.

Tigertown for Don that year was almost like a reunion. He felt at first like a long-lost fraternity member coming back to his old school to see his brothers of years past—only this time the brothers wore baseball uniforms, even though they were no longer players. Another thing that sets this sport apart, he thought: managers, coaches, and instructors all wearing uniforms. He liked the tradition. Some things should never change, and this was certainly one of them.

One of the most prominent instructors was Joe Gordon, one of the great second basemen of the 1940s. Noted for his acrobatics at the keystone, Joe starred for the Yankees, then served in WWII, and then came back and starred for the Cleveland Indians. After retiring from the majors, Joe went to the Pacific Coast League as player/manager for the Sacramento Solons in 1951 and 1952. In 1953, he joined the Tigers' organization as a scout and a Tigertown instructor. When Don went down to Lakeland in 1955, one of the first guys to greet him on the Tigertown practice field was Joe Gordon. Their friendship was instant.

Another impressive instructor at Tigertown was Wayne Blackburn. Blackburn had spent his entire playing career as an infielder in the minors. What made him significant, though, was his skill at drawing a walk. As a player over a period of nineteen years, he drew 1,400 walks. Wayne had heard the expression "Good eye!" so much he listened to it in his sleep. So it was no surprise that he became one of the most sought-after batting instructors in camp. Ask Wayne what he taught the guys every day, and he'd say "patience." He also scouted for the Tigers. Ask him what he looked for in a batter and he'd give the same response.

Beyond the new friendships for Don that year was the renewing of old friendships. Foremost of these was Jim Campbell, whom Don now saw as the man who pushed John McHale to hire him. Jim was the principal founder/developer of the Tigertown complex. He put the whole thing together, including land development, staff, and finances. No one questioned his ability to manage the American greenback. Most agreed that Jim Campbell was on his way to becoming a baseball legend, doing it all without wearing a pro uniform. They were right, of course. But for now, in spring training of 1955, he was simply a well-known presence.

Jim Campbell was also one of Don Lund's best friends. Jim and Don had become pals many years ago, ever since Don's playing days with the Mud Hens. Their friendship was forged over many hours of baseball talk. Jim the Buckeye and Don the Wolverine; Jim the strategist in cost controls and belt tightening to increase profits; Don the believer in calculated spending; Jim the pragmatist; Don the dreamer. Both men were willing slaves to the game that ruled them. The game. It was everything to them. It's what fueled their friendship. That, plus a lot of fun together. Nothing during that entire spring training at Tigertown meant more to Don Lund than getting together again with Jim Campbell. For him, that was the way it would always be.

Other friends he met again included Pat Mullin and Stubby Overmire. Both men were friends of long standing. Both were outgoing. Both looked at the world with a grin and a gleam in their eyes. Neither had much patience for a dull moment. Pat was always cracking jokes and making people roar. Stubby was more subtle.

A good example of the Overmire mirth came one day after practice. Stubby and Don were making the long walk from the playing fields to the locker rooms. They were accompanied by Cy Williams, a scout from Buffalo, New York. Cy often took kidding about having the same name as the famous left-handed pull hitter for the Cubs and Phillies from 1917 to 1930. But this Cy Williams, the one walking with Stubby and Don, had never played in the majors, even though his reputation as a Tigers scout was notable.

However, Cy wasn't a Tigertown instructor. He sort of hung around. He was there, he said, to help any way he could. In other words, Cy Williams was on vacation. Anyway, the three of them were heading back to the showers. Stubby was carrying the portable phone they always used when they had to place or receive calls from the practice area. The phone needed to be plugged into a jack at one of the dugouts in order for it to operate. Someone on the staff would unplug it after practice and bring it back to the camp office. This day it was Stubby.

Without breaking stride, Stubby stuck the phone to his ear and mumbled something. Then he held it out to Williams, saying "It's for you, Cy."

Williams grabbed the phone. "Hello, Hello?" He looked back at Overmire. "There's nobody ..." Then he got it.

Don started laughing. So did Stubby.

Cy flipped the phone back, grinned at Stubby, and blurted: "You sonnama ..." Then he also laughed.

The story of Cy Williams and the portable phone was all over Tigertown the next day. Don and Stubby never said a word; they didn't have to. Cy blabbed it to everyone he saw.

Marv Owen and Bernie DeViveiros were two men who made tremendous impact on the entire Tigertown Program. Marv Owen was an integral part of the Tigers' fearsome infield of the 1930s. With Owen at third, Billy Rogel at shortstop, Charlie Gehringer at second, and Hank Greenberg at first, the combination became one of the most formidable infields of their time. They were essential to the Tigers' World Series win in 1935. Now, in 1955, at the age of 49, Marv Owen was again in Tigertown. He worked primarily with infielders on a device he invented in 1953, which he installed with everything else needed to open Tigertown. It was designed to build short-hop fielding skills. Marv called it the "trap wall."

Located on grass along the edge of the workout field, the trap wall was a solid, cement barrier measuring approximately twelve feet long and six feet high. The infielder would set himself several feet in front of it, crouching much like he would during a game when facing a batter. Then someone would bounce a ball off the wall, making the fielder charge in and trap it on the first hop. With practice, the thrower could put various types of spin on the ball, causing it to bounce unpredictably. The purpose was to make the ball move as if it were coming off a slashing bat. The fielder had to be decisive and quick in order to trap it in his glove. Players treated it like a game. Some made side bets and competed. Others became almost addicted to it, returning several times during the day to "beat the throw."

There were at least a couple of good reasons for the trap wall's popularity. First, bouncing the ball off the wall onto the grass gave it a realistic spin. Second, the small area needed by the trap wall made this particular fielding practice faster and more efficient than it used to be. In the past, short-hop practice consisted of someone throwing or batting a ball directly at the fielder. This process was time consuming. Plus, the percentages of a thrown or hit ball landing in front of a player sufficiently to allow for a one-hop trap were small, maybe one out of three or four times. But the trap wall eliminated this problem by giving the fielder a one-hop chance nearly every time.

The Tigertown trap wall was so simple, so effective, that it fit into the "Why didn't somebody think of this before?" category. Don, Marv, and other Tigertown instructors took turns throwing at the trap wall, trying to make the ball spin in every direction possible. And it worked like they'd hoped. Marv Owen's trap wall became one of the most popular practice features in Tigertown.

Naturally, word got around. Soon other teams in the Grapefruit League were having trap walls installed on their own workout fields. Someone said Marv should have patented his wall. Marv scoffed at the idea. All he wanted to do was make it more efficient for infielders to practice trapping the ground ball. The fact that it worked so well was enough for him.

Bernie DeViveiros was a Tigers' scout from Oakland, California. An infielder, Bernie played for two major league teams: the 1924 Chicago White Sox and the 1927 Detroit Tigers. The rest of his playing career was spent in the Triple-A minors, most notably with the Minneapolis Millers and the Spokane Indians, where he was player/manager. His claim to fame, however, was his ability to teach players how to slide properly. In fact, Bernie DeViveiros was known affectionately as "Doctor Slide."

Sliding into base to avoid the tag is as old as the game itself, and the techniques varied. Ty Cobb was known to slide head-first in a cloud of dust. He was also known to slide with spikes up and pointed at the defender, but there's some doubt whether that was entirely true. In any case, all base runners are prepared to slide. The problem is many of them don't know how to slide properly, or they change their mind just before they slide, thinking they can beat the throw standing up. That decision puts undue stress on the legs and sometimes can result in serious injury.

A sad example of this happened to Tigers' second baseman Jerry Priddy in 1951. Jerry was preparing to slide into home plate when the next Tigers' batter, standing behind the action, signaled him to come in standing up. Jerry pulled up out of his slide and tried to run in. His ankle twisted. The leg snapped. The crowd gasped as Jerry lay at the plate with a broken leg. His indecision cost him dearly.

Bernie often used the Jerry Priddy example in his sliding sessions at Tigertown. "When you decide to slide, don't change your mind," he would tell them. "And don't let anybody else change your mind." Bernie taught the "bent leg" slide, wherein the player puts one leg under the other, while the leg on top points toward the base. The technique protects the legs, while also allowing the runner to use his bottom leg to thrust him upward, ready to stand on the base or run to the next. Bernie taught his sliding procedure by telling the players to remove their spikes and slide with just the socks on, or perhaps wearing tennis shoes. This built confidence. Then he would graduate them to wearing spikes.

Don was so impressed with Doctor Slide that he joined one of his classes and did the drill. He vowed to himself that, if and when the time ever came for him to coach, he would teach this sliding skill to the players. He had no way of knowing, of course, that the time would come when he would actually do it as a coach.

Don savored every minute of spring training in 1955. From time to time, fans would come by and ask him for an autograph. As a matter of fact, Don signed more autographs that spring at

Tigertown than he ever did at Briggs Stadium. Don was always flattered and happy to oblige.

After practices and on days off, he and Betty enjoyed relaxing with their friends. The Boones, the Gromeks, the Garvers, and others would all join in on barbecues and picnics. Stories would be swapped, kids would romp together, marshmallows would be roasted, and laughter would reign supreme. The Lunds would always cherish fond memories of spring training in Lakeland, and the one in 1955, with friendships cemented forever, would remain extra special throughout their lives.

Back in Detroit, Don went right to work setting up the tryout camps. He attended high school games and roamed the sandlots scouting for talented athletes. He chatted with parents to find out what their sons might be thinking about a baseball career. Plus, he added a new dimension to promoting the camps: he actively recruited the ones who showed real promise, rather than waiting for them to answer newspaper ads. As a result, the 1955 Tigers tryout camps, held at sandlot fields all over Detroit, were filled with skilled young players as never before, the cream of high school youngsters who thrilled with the chance to show their stuff on a ball diamond.

The Tigers took notice. Players sometimes dropped in to meet the kids and sign autographs. Manager Bucky Harris showed up for a day. Don's old friend and manager from his years with the Mud Hens and Bisons, Jack Tighe, made several visits. Jack was now one of the team's coaches under Harris. He and Don went back a long way.

A big plus for Don personally that summer was getting to know Tigers' head scout Louie DeNunzio, who showed up nearly every day at the tryout camps. Louie was a master at spotting real talent in a player. He could pick out weaknesses and strengths like few others. He could determine a player's attitude after just a few minutes of casual conversation with him. He could observe whether a certain player was playing his best position or not. He could predict potential with reasoned logic, rather than gut feelings. In short, Louie DeNunzio epitomized the finest example of a professional baseball scout. And, best of all, he was willing to share what he knew with Don Lund. Don didn't know it at the time, but what he learned from Louie would prove invaluable to him in later years.

At the end of the 1955 season, the Tigers finished in fifth place. The shining spot belonged to Al Kaline, who hit .340 and became the youngest player ever to win a league batting title. The National League champion, seven months older than Kaline and hitting .328, was a Milwaukee Braves' outfielder named Henry Aaron. Another bright mark that season belonged to Don Lund and his tryout camps, though he would never admit it or accept any personal credit.

Thanks to the tryout camps and Don's presence around the sandlots, an overwhelming percentage of Detroit's graduating seniors who chose a baseball career instead of college were signed up to play in the Tigers' minor league farm system. This was quite an accomplishment, considering that the Detroit sandlots were among the best baseball breeding grounds in the country, and scouts from every big league franchise were frequent visitors. It didn't hurt Don that many of the kids knew him, not only through his reputation and his Detroit roots, but also because he taught many of them in their high school phys ed classes. It also helped that Don had a penchant for remembering names and school situations; he could talk to the youngsters on a personal level. Out-of-town scouts didn't have that advantage. For the Tigers, then, the season was average, but for batting champion Kaline and for talent scout Lund, the season was a screaming success.

Over the 1955–56 winter months, Don began a series of organized conditioning sessions for Tigers' players, with the encouragement of Tigers' manager Jack Tighe. He secured an indoor workout facility belonging to Detroit Edison, so that the team could work on physical conditioning away from the public eye. Any male member of the Tigers organization could join in, and the Tigers paid all costs. Most of the team players who lived in the Detroit area eagerly participated. Such a program had not been attempted before in Detroit; professional ballplayers had always been expected to keep in shape on their own.

Nevertheless, the regimen was so successful that Hal Middlesworth, a reporter for the *Detroit Free Press*, wrote a complimentary article about it, citing Don Lund as the innovator. But true to form, Don passed on sole credit to Detroit Edison, who "so generously donated their facility." The real test of Don's program, however, came when 1956 spring training started in Lakeland.

Sure enough, several Detroit-residing players, who normally showed up each spring with weight gain and a loss in muscle tone, avoided those first-week aches and pains. They arrived ready and able to suit up for the Grapefruit League games.

Don also tried something new with the 1956 tryout camps. He arranged to have an All-Star Contest between outstanding tryout camp players and a select group of similarly qualified young men from Buffalo, New York. He secured the help of Cy Williams, one of the scouts who covered the Bisons, to play the game in Offermann Stadium. The contest would be a double-header. Don, with help from Louie DeNunzio, selected a group of ten All Stars, who would travel with them to Buffalo for the games.

They all went by car in a caravan, made the trip in one day, and checked into one of Buffalo's finest downtown hotels. The Detroit delegation, including Lund and DeNunzio, was assigned rooms on the seventh floor. That's when the fun began. Immediately after registration, the whole group headed for the elevator. The boys piled in quickly, purposely leaving no room for their two coaches. As the elevator doors closed, the boys laughed and said things like "See ya later!" and "Try the stairs!" Don and Louie laughed with them.

The elevator then lurched up about seven feet and stopped dead, trapping the boys inside. The boys weren't to blame; their elevator had frozen between floors. But for about one frantic hour the Detroit All-Stars hung there, until people from the Otis Elevator Company were able to bring them down to freedom. For the rest of their stay, Don and Louie were the only ones in the group who rode the elevator. The rest of them lumbered up and down seven flights of stairs. There was one huge salvaging factor, though. The Detroit boys won both games by large margins. On the way back home, all agreed to tell families and friends that the trip was great, but it had its "ups and downs." They would all savor that inside joke and the wins in Buffalo.

Don's 1956 Tigers Tryout Camps were as popular as the year before, but the big news hit on July 12. It was announced that the Detroit Tigers and Briggs Stadium had been purchased from the Briggs family through a syndicate headed by Fred Knorr and John Fetzer. The record selling price was 5.5 million dollars. Few were shocked that the sale took place. The Tigers were not very exciting again this year, wallowing in fifth place with not much outlook. Many fans hollered for a change in managers. Others cried out for wholesale trading. Still others merely moaned about what they saw as overwhelming disinterest by the players. Nevertheless, popular thought held that a change at the franchise helm might be welcome, if the new owners were able to give the club a big shot in the arm.

Don stayed away from discussing the controversy publicly. He knew there was no simple solution to any team's problems, no matter the sport, no matter the ownership. Building a winner was a complicated process of hard work, team leadership, player motivation, talent merge, and sometimes just plain, old-fashioned luck. There was no way he was going to join any chorus of quick fix, band-aid-pressing voices. His experiences had taught him better. Let's wait and see what the new owners have in mind, he thought. So he went into the winter months with an open mind toward the future.

In January 1957, Don did something that was very special to him. He signed a Michigan mid-year graduate to a professional baseball contract. As a matter of fact, he signed his favorite Michigan baseball player of that year. He'd known the young man for a long time. He'd watched him play both basketball and baseball for his old high school, Detroit Southeastern. The kid was a 5-foot-7-inch bundle of explosive energy named Moby Benedict.

Don had never seen a high school or a college athlete so enthusiastic and so highly motivated as Moby. On Southeastern's basketball court, Moby could outjump guys nearly a foot taller. He could outhustle, outmaneuver, and outrebound the bigger players, making it look easy. And he wasn't a blowhard or a loudmouth. He just played hard. Don Lund's kind of guy.

Baseball turned out to be Moby Benedict's favorite sport. He played shortstop like a hawk on the hunt. He wasn't a power hitter, but he could place the ball around the field and usually beat out the throw at first. And in 1952, sixteen-year-old Moby Benedict's star was hung forever in the annals of Detroit area youth baseball. It happened during the American Legion All-Star game at Briggs Stadium. The stars from Detroit City posts were playing the stars from Detroit's Downriver area posts. All of the players were fifteen or sixteen years old.

Moby represented Detroit Briggs Post, and was chosen to be the leadoff batter. With his typical enthusiasm braced with surging adrenalin, Moby darted from the dugout to the plate. He ignored the catcher's barbs and stared at the pitcher. Moby was so hyped and ready for action that he couldn't resist the tempting first pitch. He swung hard, connected, and blasted a high, soaring missile toward the left field seats.

Moby wasn't used to hitting home runs, so when he smacked the ball, he threw down his bat and took off toward first base like Seabiscuit leaving the starting gate. Legs pumping, arms churning, Moby chewed up the bases so fast he was practically crossing the plate as the ball sailed over the fence. With that one mighty swing, Moby Benedict became the first American Legion ballplayer, and probably the first high schooler, to hit a home run in Briggs Stadium. He may have also set the record for the fastest homer ever run in that fabled ballpark. For the few fans scattered around the stadium that day, the joke went like this:

Q: "Did you see Moby Benedict's home run?"
A: "Nope. Cloud of dust was too thick!

That was Moby Benedict. Hustle all the way, no matter what. The person who eventually picked up his home run ball surely walked away with a valuable treasure, but he or she would never realize just how valuable that treasure would have been to a certain sixteen-year-old shortstop, who swung from the heels and ran like the wind.

After Southeastern High, Moby moved on to star at short-stop for the Wolverines under Ray Fisher, from 1954 to 1956. When he graduated in December 1956, he let it be known that he was interested in a pro baseball career. That got attention from several teams, including the Tigers. When Don heard about it, he grabbed a contract from the Tigers front office and raced to Ann Arbor.

Don and Moby met in January 1957, at the Men's Union on the University of Michigan campus. As Moby inked his signature, neither man realized that the occasion marked the start of a life-long friendship. Both would eventually grow together as buddies, coworkers, and honored Wolverines of Michigan lore.

39
Dialogue

"Let me finish this and I'll be right there. Go on in and make yourself at home."

He was finishing up sweeping the floor of his garage when I popped in unexpectedly, so I walked in his condo and settled on the couch in his living room. The October midmorning sun was struggling to push its way through a gray overcast left by a midnight rain. The weather broadcasters promised a pleasant day. Perfect for those inclined to clean their garages, or simply sit around being interviewed by an author.

I looked around the now-familiar walls and shelves, again marveling at his total lack of personal photographs. Don Lund was not one to display his own likeness. Instead, the eyes that beamed back from numerous picture frames belonged to friends and family members. Here was a man, indeed a celebrity, whose photograph had been taken thousands of times. Yet not one of them was placed for viewing in his home. His face was shown in one photo: a smiling pose of Don and Betty Lund, taken sometime in the 1980s. They looked great together.

Finally, the old coach joined me in the living room and sat in his favorite chair. We exchanged a few pleasantries, most of which consisted of him asking about me and my family. I was anxious to turn the conversation back around to him. It took only two words.

"Moby Benedict."
DL: "Moby? We already talked about him."

"Right. But we just covered the early years, when you signed him as a minor league player. We didn't touch on your connections with him later on, when you pulled him out of pro ball and

recruited him as your assistant at Michigan. You're still friends many years later."

DL: "Still friends? I'm closer to Moby than just about anybody I know. So let me tell you a little bit more about him. Moby Benedict is the most dedicated guy you'd ever want to meet. And that includes anything he does. He plays to win; he coaches to win; he'll make you try to win whether you want to or not. Yeah, Moby is baseball through and through. You know, after he was my assistant at Michigan, he replaced me as head coach and did fine. Later on, he went back to the pros and managed the Jamestown Expos in New York. They're a minor league affiliate of Montreal. Now he's retired. But they still love him in Ann Arbor. In 1994, he was inducted into the University of Michigan's Hall of Honor."

"Ten years after you were inducted."

DL: "Well, Moby's younger than I am."

"Let's go back to 1956. You just finished two years of representing the Tigers to high school players around Detroit. You built the tryout camps to be the best ever. You established yourself in minor league spring training at Tigertown ..."

DL: "Wait a minute. You're making me look like a one-man band. There were lots of good, solid people I worked with."

"I know, Coach. But all I'm saying is that, here you are, two years into a specialty job put together by General Manager Muddy Rule. Then the Tigers are sold to a financial syndicate. Heads were bound to roll. Weren't you a little concerned about your future?"

DL: "Sure I was. So was Betty. But I got lucky."

"Lucky?"

DL: "Yes. I got a call from Jack Tighe."

40
First-Base Coach

The first big change for Don Lund and his family in 1956 had nothing to do with baseball, yet it changed their lives like nothing had before. It came in the form of a miniature black poodle they named "Inky." They had been living in a rented upper flat on Chatsworth Street, in a working-class neighborhood on Detroit's far East Side. Several of Susan's friends had dogs. Susan also wanted a dog, so she brought the subject up one night around the dinner table. Don and Betty were skeptical at first, not only because they had no experience with dogs at home, but also because they were merely the tenants in someone else's house. Their landlady, Mrs. Humphries, was kindly and understanding, but she might balk when it came to having an animal living in her house.

Don and Betty finally agreed to let Susan have a dog, providing Mrs. Humphries went along with it. They charged Susan with the task of getting the landlady's approval. Their ten-year-old daughter excused herself from the table and ran downstairs to see Mrs. Humphries. Ten minutes later, Mrs. Humphries came upstairs with Susan in tow.

"Susan just asked me," said Mrs. Humphries in a somewhat stern manner, "if I would let her have a dog in the house. She said she doesn't have a brother and she doesn't have a sister. But she sure would be happy if she had a dog."

Don and Betty held their collective breaths and didn't respond.

"So I ask you," Mrs. Humphries laughed, "how can I refuse a request like that?"

The next day Inky joined the Lund household. And like most other family dogs, he happily took over their lives.

The second big change that year involved the Detroit Tigers. Fred Knorr and his group wasted no time in making changes to the Tigers organization, once they purchased it from the Briggs family. Knorr, a wealthy radio station owner, headed the group as president. John Fetzer, even more renowned as a broadcasting pioneer than Knorr, was second in command but without a title. The rest of the ownership group included mere investors. Walter O. "Spike" Briggs Jr. was made executive vice president as part of the sales agreement. Knorr's group had wrested complete control of the Tigers. They were free to make any changes they wished, and they started right after the 1956 season ended.

First to go was General Manager Muddy Ruel. Knorr replaced him with Spike Briggs, who obviously knew the organization, and who wanted more than a ceremonial executive VP's job. Next was team manager Bucky Harris. Spike liked Jack Tighe and promoted him from coaching to the playing helm. Spike also negotiated the largest single trade since 1952. On December 5, he sent pitchers Ned Garver, Gene Host, and Virgil Trucks, plus first baseman Wayne Belardi and $20,000 in cash to the Kansas City Athletics. In return, the Athletics traded pitchers Jack Crimian and Bill Harrington, plus infielder Jim Finigan and first baseman Eddie Robinson. Many Detroiters scoffed at this particular trade, especially since acquiring Crimian and Harrington while losing Garver and Trucks didn't seem to beef up Tigers pitching at all.

What it did, however, was feed rumors that the club was making changes for the sake of change itself. Fans were upset; the Tigers front office was nervous. Only a few selected staff were confident about their futures as the winter months progressed in 1956–57. They were those with the special skills or experience deemed necessary. They included administrative assistants and long-term secretaries, as well as other key support staff who were too knowledgeable to let go. They also included baseball professionals—former players who acted as scouts, coaches, and player training experts. All of these "essential" employees were told in the fall of 1956 that they would play an important role in the newly organized Detroit Tigers. One of them was Don Lund.

The call came in mid-October. The Lunds were enjoying Friday night dinner at home. They were following their typical ritual of evening meal reverie, which started with Betty describing her day's activities, followed by Don reviewing his day "subbing" at school, followed by ten-year-old Susan talking about her fifth-grade adventures. Dinner had started about five o'clock, a little earlier than usual. Don was scheduled to referee a local high school football game that night. Just as Susan had finished describing her assignment in English class, the phone rang. Betty answered it.

"It's for you, Don. It's Jack Tighe."

Don was surprised. I wonder what he wants, he thought, as he took the receiver. "What do you say, Jack?"

"Hi, Don," said his old friend. "There've been some changes here in the front office, and I thought I'd call you about 'em before the news hits the papers."

Don grinned and blurted into the phone, "We're all out of a job!" Betty's eyebrows jumped for the ceiling. Don winked at her.

"Not quite," Tighe answered, "but Harris is gone, and I'm the new Tigers manager."

"Congratulations, Jack," Don said, and he meant it. Jack Tighe had paid lots of dues over the years with the Tigers' minor league system. And he had served the major league team well as a coach under Bucky Harris. Jack was an obvious choice for the helm.

"Thanks," said Tighe, "but I'm not calling to tell you about myself. I'm calling about you. I want you to be my first base coach. We go back a long way, and you're the guy I'm looking for. Are you interested?"

Don came right to attention. Jack was offering him a coaching job! He didn't hesitate, "Sure I am. And Betty's right here; let me check with her." Don placed his hand over the receiver and whispered to her, "Jack's the new Tigers' manager. He wants me to be his first base coach." Betty grinned and nodded her head. That cinched it.

"Jack, you've got yourself a coach," he said. "What do you want me to do now?"

"Enjoy the winter," said Tighe. "I'll see you next spring in Lakeland."

One phone call. That's all it took for Don Lund's career in major league baseball to change back to being part of a big league team on the playing field. Once again, he would suit up for the season. Only this time, he'd be a coach rather than a player. He felt as if he'd prepared for this over many years of playing and

Basketball referee Don Lund shows the game ball to Nancy Laws, three, and her brother Gene, four, prior to a high school contest on January 11, 1957. Their father, a technical automotive instructor at Henry Ford Community College, wanted his kids to meet this "well-known referee." Don had recently started his job as first base coach for the Detroit Tigers. Refereeing high school and college games, as well as substitute teaching, helped support his family. (*The Detroit News*)

learning the game. He knew how to study pitchers to learn their strengths and weaknesses. He could predict certain batters well enough to position outfielders against them. He could teach the fine points of base running. And most importantly, he would be in an authoritative position. He knew players would likely follow his suggestions. He couldn't wait to get to Lakeland and Henley Field.

The winter months of early 1957 dragged slowly. Don went about his usual duties of substitute teaching and officiating high school basketball games. Occasionally, he'd drive from his home on Detroit's East Side to Ann Arbor, where he'd spend time with friends in and around the university. Ann Arbor seemed to have a special draw for him, especially since the campus was radically changed from the war years when he was a student-athlete. West Quadrangle, for instance, was no longer a "ship."

Students used its doors at all hours, day and night, without fear of curfew. And women students were prominent, particularly in the undergraduate ranks. It wouldn't be long before women would be an equal force with men in Michigan's graduate and professional schools. Don hoped this trend would also bring a surge in women's athletics on campus. He firmly believed that college sports should echo the makeup of the student body, including race, gender, and ethnic background. He also hoped that one day Susan would enroll at Michigan. Although he and Betty would never pressure her, they would both be exceedingly proud if she chose his alma mater.

When the time came for the three Lunds to travel to Lakeland, they piled into the family car and drove the 1,300 miles in two days. By now the Lakeland area was like a second home territory. They found a place to live and settled in. Betty tutored Susan in all her classes and prepared her for exams when she would return to Stillwagon School in April. Don assumed his coaching duties.

Spring training in 1957 was as much hard work for Don as it was fun. The first thing he had to learn was to hit fungos effectively. A fungo bat is much different from the typical game bat, in that it almost resembles a straight piece of solid round stick, rather than a round piece of wood that tapers from a thickness of three inches down to a little over one inch at the handle. A fungo bat is much lighter. It must be swung with less power to control the flight of the ball.

Sluggers have a hard time hitting fungos. Don was a slugger. So he turned to the one class of players who weren't sluggers—the pitchers. They could hit fungos, and one of them, Steve Gromek, could hit beautiful fungos all day. Steve agreed to teach his friend, and Don became skilled at fungo hitting. He especially liked hitting them to Al Kaline, because no matter where he placed the ball, no matter how high or how far he hit it, Kaline was always under it, making the catch look easy. Don actually felt challenged to make hard ones for Kaline to field and he tried. Then he tried harder. Kaline always got to it and pulled it in. Magic in motion.

A new pitching coach joined the Tigers that year. Willis Hudlin, a right-hander who pitched for Cleveland from 1926 to 1940, was famous for his side-arm sinker. He was also famous for yielding Babe Ruth's 500th home run on August 11, 1929, in Cleveland's League Park. Although he took some kidding about that, Willis always had a great comeback: he still beat the Yankees that day, 6–5.

One of the training duties Don took on that spring was pitching batting practice. He was still in excellent shape, and his throwing arm was nearly as strong as it was in his playing days. He had no trouble getting the ball in the strike zone over the plate, and he could vary the speed of his delivery. However, pitching batting practice wasn't easy. If one man did it first for the reserves, who each took three swings, and then the regulars, who took three or more swings, he could be on the mound for at least a half hour with no break. That could be especially tough in the baking Florida heat. Batting practice pitching became a lot easier when training camp ended, and the Tigers went up to cooler summer days in Detroit.

The 1957 Tigers ended their season in fourth place—an average finish for an average team. Management decided more changes were needed. So they traded players like kids traded comic books; fast and speculative. The biggest trade took place on November 20, when the Tigers gave up six players (and a player to be named later) to Kansas City. In return, they received six players from the Athletics.

One of these was Billy Martin, who had played second base for the Yankees from 1950 to 1956. Billy was known for his ability to come up with clutch plays, one of which saved game seven of the 1952 World Series. He was also known for his hard drinking and rowdiness off the field, so he was dealt to the Athletics by Yankees' general manager George Weiss. Weiss thought Martin was becoming a bad influence on two of his star players, Mickey Mantle and Whitey Ford. Yankees' manager Casey Stengel, whom Martin considered a father figure, did nothing to prevent the trade. Martin felt betrayed. His performance as an infielder declined. He lasted only one season with Kansas City. Now it was the Tigers' turn to see if they could bring Martin back to his glory days.

Despite all the changes in their roster, the 1958 Detroit Tigers fared no better than the previous season. In fact, they would finish in fifth place. Don Lund continued mostly as a batting-practice pitcher. He was actually good at it. His arm was strong, and he could place the ball well. The players liked his practice pace. He liked the challenge of giving them a good workout. He would pitch first to the reserves for three swings each, and then to the regulars who entered the batting cage in their normal batting rotation.

On one hot day before a game in May, Don had been throwing to the reserves for twenty minutes and working up a nice sweat. The bell rang to signal the start of batting practice for the regulars. First in the cage was leadoff batter Billy Martin.

Don knew that Martin liked to begin with easy pitches. He threw a medium-fast one, right over the middle of the plate—a pitch any hitter would happily crunch. He threw it well. Martin watched the ball go by him. Don thought Billy wasn't ready. So he waited for Martin to assume his stance. Then Don threw the same pitch again—right down the middle, belt high. Martin also watched the ball go past. Don became frustrated. It was hot, he'd been throwing for thirty minutes, and he thought there was no reason for Martin to ignore two perfectly thrown pitches.

So Don called out, "Hey, Billy, why don't you just swing?"

Martin answered, "Why don't you just throw the fucking ball and keep your mouth shut?"

That did it. Don wound up and threw at Martin's head. Billy hit the dirt, completely surprised. Then, without even a glance at the prone Martin, Don walked off the mound. He told one of the other coaches to take over for him. When he reached the dugout, Jack Tighe came over to him.

Don said, "I'm not going to fight that big mouth."

Tighe walked away without a word. Martin didn't pursue the incident with Don, and the two of them got along the rest of the season.

Also in 1958, Jack Tighe added a fourth coach, legendary Yankees right fielder Tommy Henrich. Together with Joe DiMaggio in center field and Charlie Keller in left field, Henrich had played in one of big league baseball's all-time greatest outfields. Mel Allen, the Yankees' famous sportscaster, dubbed Henrich "Old Reliable" for his ability to get a hit when it counted.

Henrich played his entire career with the Yankees. He retired as a player in 1950, and then went on to coach for the Yankees and the New York Giants from 1951 to 1957. By joining the Tigers' coaching staff in 1958, Tommy Henrich gave the team an extra measure of class, experience, and name recognition.

Tighe assigned Henrich to no other duties except coaching first base, replacing Don, which left Tommy free to mix with the players in practice and before games. In the dugout, between puffs of his cigar, Tommy enjoyed freely dispensing wit and wisdom to those around him. The players loved every minute of it. So did Don Lund and the rest of the staff. Tommy Henrich was a booster shot to the 1958 Tigers.

So Don Lund coached for the Tigers during two seasons, 1957 and 1958. In between he continued substitute teaching for the Detroit public schools, as well as officiating high school football and basketball games. He also worked with his friend Bob Ufer, doing color commentary for Bob's popular Michigan football radio broadcasts. This allowed him to be part of the fall football scene in Ann Arbor. He knew the Wolverine coaches; he knew the players; and he knew most of the people in the Athletic Department.

From time to time, Don would run across his former baseball coach and mentor, Ray Fisher. Ray was nearing seventy, the mandatory retirement age at the university. Don refused to think about that. To him, Ray Fisher and Michigan baseball were like Siamese twins: inseparable. He couldn't imagine Ray being replaced as head baseball coach.

In his two years of coaching for the Tigers, Don felt he was highly productive. He was, after all, a part of the team at all times in a useful role. Every time he put on the Tigers' uniform he was energized. Never mind that he no longer roamed in right field. Kaline bought and paid for that piece of turf with unmatched skills, a winning attitude, and never-ending hard work. He was better than good, plus a super guy to know. And never mind that Don no longer had the chance to stare down a pitcher while cocking his 32-ounce bat. Now he could help others with their skills at the plate. What really mattered to him, however, was the chance, every day, to be a part the action, to make suggestions that were followed, to matter in the grand scheme of Detroit

Tigers' baseball. Don Lund was indeed happy being a Detroit Tigers' coach.

Some of the players he worked with during those two years had quite an impact on him. One of these was Reno Bertoia. Reno grew up in Windsor, Ontario, just across the Canadian border from Detroit. During the summer months of his high school years, however, Reno would cross the border every day to play in the Detroit sandlots. Don first saw him there. He was impressed, not only with Reno's great talent in the infield, but also with his serious determination to win. Reno never let up; even if his team was rolling over its opponent. Reno played with intensity every minute he was in the game.

Off the field, however, Reno Bertoia was almost a different person. He seemed to change instantly from the hard-charging, determined ballplayer to this mild-mannered, calm, nice guy who would do anything for you. He was, in fact, one of those rare men who's easy to know, easy to get along with, and easy to like. Don took to Reno like a magnet, especially since he'd known him from Reno's sandlot days.

It had not taken the Tigers long before they enticed Reno Bertoia to sign a contract after only one year of playing freshman baseball at Michigan. When he joined the team, Don was delighted. The two became close friends. Don's only concern was that manager Jack Tighe picked on Reno for no apparent reason. To his credit, Reno took Tighe's barbs without comment or retort. He just played harder. Don admired that. To him, Reno Bertoia was one heck of a guy.

There were some Tigers' pitchers who stood out in Don's coaching experience. Paul Foytack was fast, had great control, and lots of energy on the mound, but Mickey Mantle had his number. The Mick could hit Foytack almost at will. Whenever Mantle strode to the plate with Paul on the mound, Don almost cringed. It was like a jinx. Foytack was a fine pitcher. Nobody understood why Mantle could hit him so easily. To his credit, Mickey never gloated or made a big deal out of it. He just hit the ball and ran. Don Lund and Billy Hitchcock were talking about the Foytack-Mantle phenomenon one day.

"Foytack's just building up Mantle's batting average," said Hitchcock.

"Yeah," Don answered. "If Paul doesn't watch out, he's gonna put that guy in the Hall of Fame!"

Then there was right-hander Frank Lary to provide the balance. They called Frank "The Yankee Killer." Those pin-striped New Yorkers, including Mickey Mantle, couldn't seem to beat Frank Lary. If Foytack had a jinx, Lary had a better one, and both involved the Yankees. *Free Press* columnist Joe Falls and Tigers' first base coach Don Lund were chatting one night before a game. The subject got around to "jinx" factors in baseball and, in particular, the two involving Foytack and Lary. Joe and Don had been friends for years.

"What do those two think about it?" asked Joe.

"Why, nothing at all," said Don. "Good thing pitchers aren't superstitious!"

They both rolled their eyes.

The Tigers' pitcher Don remembers best during those two years he coached is Jim Bunning. Bunning was the team's ace on the mound. Great form, great speed, great control, great attitude—all describe Jim Bunning. And one could add a whole lot more descriptives to the man, all beginning with the word *great*. Bunning's big moment came on July 20, 1958, in Fenway Park. Jim had a no-hitter going against Boston; the Tigers were ahead through eight innings, 3–0. Of course, nobody on the bench said a word to Bunning about his progress throughout the game. The "jinx" might rear its ugly head. In the bottom of the ninth, Jim managed to retire the first two batters.

The third batter, representing the final out for a Tigers' victory, walked briskly to the plate and assumed his left-handed-batter stance. He was confident; he was smiling; he was Ted Williams. On the second pitch, Williams hit a towering fly ball toward right-center field. Everyone in the Tigers' dugout gasped as the ball sailed high and far. Al Kaline beat the ball to the fence, took a leap forward, and buried the final out in his glove. The Tigers' bench erupted and mobbed their star pitcher. Don would always remember that special moment, when Jim Bunning took another step toward baseball immortality.

One of the most profound things during Don's two years of Tigers' coaching happened on Tuesday, June 10, 1958, in Boston. The Tigers were in the middle of a road series against the Red Sox. They had lost the first game, 9–4. There was no game today.

Don just happened to be in his room at the Kenmore Hotel when the phone rang. The caller was Tigers' general manager John McHale. John had been promoted to the job from his post as Farm Director after the resignation of Spike Briggs.

McHale got right to the point: "Don, we just let Jack Tighe go. We're replacing him with Bill Norman."

Don wasn't surprised to hear that Tighe had been fired. The team was not having a good year. They wouldn't be a pennant contender. Rumors had flown regarding Tighe's tenure as manager. Don, as well as others on the team, had only been waiting for the axe to fall. But why select Bill Norman? He decided not to ask.

McHale continued, "You have two options. You can stay on or you can leave. I personally would like you to stay. So would Bill Norman."

Don spoke right up, "I'll stay, John. I'll finish out the season."

McHale expressed his thanks and hung up.

Henry Willis Patrick "Bill" Norman had spent most of his career as an outfielder, coach, and manager in the minor leagues. He was virtually unknown to Detroit's world of baseball fans and sportswriters. So naturally, Detroit's Fourth Estate was quick to question the sanity of the Tigers' management. The writers said that a struggling major league team like Detroit should have the benefit of a manager with major league experience. Nevertheless, Bill Norman had been picked. It would turn out to be an unfortunate decision. The Tigers won about half their games under Norman from June 10 until the end of the 1958 season, ending up in fifth place.

Nevertheless, Don Lund finished out the 1958 Tigers' season after two years of coaching, still delighted to be a part of his favorite major league team. He went into his usual off-season routine of substitute teaching and officiating. He had every intention of rejoining the club in Lakeland, teaching in spring training, coaching again, and helping the 1959 Tigers improve over last season. Coaching for his major league dream team was exactly what he wanted to do. He couldn't imagine doing anything else.

All that would be instantly changed by another career-changing phone call to his home.

41
Going Back to Settle In

Sunday evening, August 3, 1958. A most relaxing twilight time. Don's home on Detroit's far East Side was quiet and peaceful. Betty was outside talking with a neighbor. Susan played quietly in her room. Don reclined on the living room sofa, eyes closed, a smile on his face. His mind roamed over the past three days at Tiger Stadium. The Tigers had just won four straight from the Baltimore Orioles, leaping from seventh to fourth place in the American League standings in less than seventy-two hours.

The streak began with a thriller Friday night. Herb Moford, a right-hander who wasn't even a regular Detroit starter, hurled the game of his major league career in a 3–1 win over the Orioles' ace Jack Harshman. The next day Jim Bunning edged out veteran Orioles' left-handed All-Star Billy O'Dell 8–7, in a game filled with relief pitchers and the solid crack of bats. In the doubleheader on Sunday, the Tigers won the first game, 3–2, behind the deadeye throwing of Paul Foytack. Then Billy Hoeft hurled enough smoke in the second game to allow the Orioles only one run as the Tigers triumphed, 4–1.

Don's memory brightened as his mind relived highlights of the series. Reno Bertoia, who had been the youngest player in the American League during his first two years with the Tigers, 1953–54, guarded third base as if he had bought and paid for it with his last dollar. Nothing got by him in all four games. Charlie Maxwell, "Mr. Sunday Hitter," made good on his nickname by hitting safely in both Sunday games. And Al Kaline proved without fanfare that he was the best right fielder in the game, time after time.

Don admired Kaline's professional, almost modest approach to the way he played. He never "cut the pie" or showboated like some outfielders do. He never displayed exceptional emotion, never appeared angry or upset. He just got under the ball, made the play look easy, and did his job better than anyone else who roamed right field. There was a rumor that some fans bought their tickets and came to the park just to watch Kaline work his magic. Don believed the rumor was true.

Nevertheless, superb Tigers' pitching had made the difference throughout the entire series. Hoeft, Foytack, Bunning, and even Moford showed off their talents, aided by some pretty nifty relief throwing. After the second win, Detroit's clubhouse showed more spirit than Don had seen in at least a month. Manager Bill Norman was happy; the players were happy; the press was bound to beatify the entire team. Fourth place! Onward and upward!

All this was cruising pleasantly through Don's mind as he relaxed in the stillness of his living room. He was content; life was good. Nothing could bother his daydreams, he thought; unless it's the ringing of that stupid telephone and Susan's frantic steps to answer it.

"Dad, it's for you. Mr. Fritz Crisler is calling from the University of Michigan!"

Don's eyes flew open as he jumped off the sofa. Fritz Crisler? Why would he be calling me? Don gathered his thoughts as he walked toward the phone in the kitchen. Herbert Orin "Fritz" Crisler was his former football coach at Michigan. He was also a mentor of Don's, mainly because Fritz always demanded such things from his players as total dedication, impeccable character traits, and an appreciation for Michigan traditions. Fritz seldom praised his athletes for possessing these; he expected it.

Don remembered the time when his buddy Bob Chappuis was a standout on Crisler's 1947 team, known as the "Marvelous Magicians." Bob, who was on his way to becoming an All-American, lay prone on a practice field in Pasadena, two days before the 1948 Rose Bowl. Chappuis was moaning in pain from a pulled muscle in his thigh. Crisler strode over to the small group standing over Chappuis and asked the Michigan trainer, Jim Hunt, what happened.

"Bob pulled a muscle," said Jim.

"Well," answered Crisler as he walked back to the sidelines, "I'm glad it didn't happen to somebody that could run."

Hearing that, Chappuis jumped up, grumbled something to himself, and ignored the pain through the rest of practice. Two days later, Bob Chappuis proceeded to run, pass, score, and set

Rose Bowl records that made him the game's MVP in a 49–0 Michigan romp over Southern California.

That was Crisler. Don't ask for a guy's best performance; just presume you're going to get it. That's one of the reasons why Don considered Fritz an example for his own approach to coaching. Although Don believed himself to be more affable and approachable than the austere Crisler, he nevertheless adopted those same coaching principles for himself. After all, Fritz was one of the most renowned college coaches of his day. He couldn't have picked a better person to emulate.

Don reached the phone and picked up the receiver. "Hello, Coach, this is Don."

Crisler's voice was friendly and upbeat as he greeted his former gridiron star. He asked about Don's family, remarked about the Tigers' weekend victories over the Orioles, then got right into the purpose of his call. "Don, you may or may not know that Ray Fisher retired in June," said Crisler. "He reached the mandatory age of seventy."

"Yes, I knew about that," answered Don. "It must have been tough for him to let go."

Crisler agreed, and then went on. "The reason I'm calling you, Don, is to talk to you about Ray's job. Do you think you might be able to come here to Ann Arbor so we can discuss it?"

Don was astonished. Michigan's head baseball coach? He'd never thought about that possibility. Better keep a cool head with Fritz, he thought; don't seem too excited. "Well, Coach, you sure called at a good time," he responded, "The Tigers are scheduled here in Detroit for another ten days, and tomorrow's an off day. Could we get together tomorrow?"

Crisler didn't hesitate. "Tomorrow's fine. If you can be here in my office at ten o'clock, I'll see you then."

"Tomorrow morning at ten," said Don. "Thanks, Coach, I'll look forward to it." They said their good-byes.

Betty walked into the kitchen with Susan at her heels. "What did Mr. Crisler want?" she asked.

Don detailed his conversation with Fritz. He told Betty about the job of head baseball coach at Michigan in great detail. When he finished, Betty agreed with him. The opportunity at Michigan was indeed attractive. She also pointed out that Ann Arbor was practically a second home to them; he seemed to be driving up there whenever he could, just to see old friends like Ray Fisher and some of his other buddies. Susan said she'd like to go to school in Ann Arbor. He had the green light from both of them, and he left early the next day for Ann Arbor, intending to see a couple of people before his appointment with Fritz.

Ray Fisher wasn't at all surprised when he opened his front door at eight o'clock the next morning to see Don Lund standing there. He knew Fritz was going to call Don about the job. He was also certain his former star player would see him before he saw Fritz. They sat in Ray's living room and, after the usual banter they both enjoyed, Don got right to the point.

"Coach, Fritz called me about the job. I can't believe you have to retire. I never thought about that. In my mind, I suppose, I thought you'd be coaching here forever."

Ray laughed. "Nothing's forever, Don. The calendar catches up. But I'll still be around here; Ann Arbor's my home. Besides, my life isn't what it used to be."

Don knew what he meant by that. The only child of Ray and Alice Fisher, daughter Janet, had been taken from them three years before by cancer. Ray had been extremely close to Janet; he brought her into his baseball life as if she were a son as well as a daughter. He taught her to throw, catch, and bat as good as any neighborhood boy. And Janet responded by being bright, energetic, competent, and enthusiastic about everything her father taught her. Janet adored him; Ray adored her back. Janet's marriage to John Leidy, an Ann Arbor retail merchant, had been happy and successful. Their two children, John and Ellen, were, according to Ray, the only two perfect kids ever created. So until 1955, when Janet died, Ray Fisher's life with his family and with Wolverine baseball had been most fulfilling. After that, Ray was never the same.

"Well, Coach, I'm glad you're staying here in town," said Don. "You're a fixture here; you have family and lots of friends. If you moved, you'd be sorely missed by everyone, including Betty and me."

"Thanks for that," Ray answered. "Now let's get to Fritz's call. Did he offer you the job?"

Don shook his head. "No, he didn't. But you know Fritz. He wouldn't do that over the phone. We're meeting at ten o'clock. My guess is he'll offer it to me then."

"I'm sure he will," answered Ray. "I should tell you that Fritz asked me to recommend my replacement. I gave him only one name. I'm glad he called you."

"Thanks for the recommendation," said Don. "I'd like the job; I'll probably take it."

"Good for you," said Ray, "but you also know Fritz. He hangs onto the dollar with a closed fist. So be careful of letting him get you too cheap."

Don thanked him for his advice and turned to go. Ray stopped him with one more comment. "By the way," he said, "Bob Ufer's been talking you up for the job all over town. He even asked me to recommend you to Fritz. I told him I already did."

"Thanks again, Coach," said Don, and he left Ray's house. He thought about Bob Ufer as he drove to his meeting with Crisler. Bob had tremendous clout with Michigan Athletics. Not only had he been a world-class runner for the Wolverines, but he also was one of the University's most vocally loyal fans. Plus, Bob knew his way around the Athletic Department. Several of the coaches carried life insurance policies through him. In addition, Bob's Michigan football broadcasts, which Don shared with him on fall Saturdays, made him a guest in almost every "Maize and Blue" home in this area. So with Ufer supporting him, he reasoned, he was a cinch to get the job.

Some fond memories hit him as he entered Michigan's Athletic Administration Building. Located at the junction of State Street and Hoover, the building anchored the northeast corner of Ferry Field. It was a straight-walled dark-brick solid two-storied rectangle, measuring about 300-by-500 feet, with unadorned windows and thick wood doors. No one would accuse it of challenging the stimulating architectural styles found throughout the rest of Michigan's campus. But this building housed more visibility, perhaps even more public power, than most of the others within the University complex, for it contained the heart and soul of the Michigan Wolverines.

Decisions were made inside the Athletic Administration Building's walls that led to well-known and observable results. People identified with the university by attending public performances by its students. The School of Music, for instance, enjoyed much of its excellent reputation through public concerts by student bands and orchestras. And William Revelli's Michigan

Marching Band, with its preponderance of non-music majors, brought together parents, alumni, and friends from virtually all university departments. However, nothing brought more attention to the university than the performances of its athletic teams, particularly the football team. Victories and defeats at Michigan Stadium stirred the passions of thousands connected even remotely to the university. And the genesis of it all took place within the plain, fortress-like structure at State Street and Hoover. Don Lund was no stranger there.

Don had first become acquainted with athletics administration as a student-athlete, when he was appointed to the Board in Control of Intercollegiate Athletics. This board, created by the university's regents as an advisory body to help maintain Athletic Department autonomy, consisted of faculty, alumni, and students, all appointed by the regents. When Don served on the board, there were five faculty members, three alumni, and two students. Fritz Crisler was the athletic director. He was also Don's head football coach. So Don approached his membership on the board with courage, conviction, and his sense of duty as a concerned student. In other words, he kept his mouth shut and listened.

Don learned a lot about the process around which Michigan athletics was driven. He also gained appreciation for the enthusiasm among those volunteers who served with him on the board. They were all highly successful people in their chosen fields. They also were Michigan loyalists to the core. They were bright, knowledgeable, astute, and in tune with the traditions of Michigan's Wolverines. They also admired Fritz Crisler. He was their leader; they were there to support him. Don appreciated being a part of that effort as a student. He also enjoyed getting to know some of the Athletic Department staff during his tenure there.

Now, the first person he saw as he entered the building was Dotty Wilkins at the switchboard. He liked Dotty. Everybody did. Her job called for immediate response to anyone calling in or out of the building. Consequently, Dotty knew more about what was going on in the Athletic Department than anybody else, including the director, but she was discrete. When it came to business, Dotty's mouth was Fort Knox itself. That's why she was so appreciated by everybody. That's why the office joke

"Don't tell Dotty!" was exactly that—a joke. Anything confidential was sealed tightly in her mind. As Don walked past her work station, Dotty was processing a call. She looked up and smiled at him as he waved.

He walked on, past the ticket office on the right and down the hall to Fritz Crisler's office. He was met by Norma Bentley, Fritz's secretary, who greeted him by name. Norma was a career professional. She took her responsibilities seriously and carried them out with supreme efficiency. She was Fritz's gatekeeper, who guarded her boss's calendar with determination, knowing how much Fritz liked the effort. Norma never suffered rudeness, or impatience, or abruptness on anyone's part. For those who showed courtesy and were well-mannered, Norma was always helpful, friendly, and accommodating. It was easy for Don to return her smile.

As Don walked into the athletic director's office, Fritz greeted him with a firm and formal handshake. Fritz wore a dark blue suit, white shirt, a narrow solid blue tie, and a squared white handkerchief in his breast pocket. His black shoes looked brand new. He was a ruggedly handsome man, with large ears, a prominent nose, and an oval face that bottomed out with a strong chin divided by a cleft, much like the actor Cary Grant. All this was dominated by a huge smile and a commanding voice. At just under six feet and 180 pounds, Fritz looked fit and trim, much younger than a man who would celebrate his sixtieth birthday in about five months. He carried the image of a man in charge of things.

Herbert O. Crisler was one of the few men in Don's life whom he practically revered. Fritz had been a nine-letter winner in college, playing football, basketball and baseball at the University of Chicago. His football coach in those years, the legendary Amos Alonzo Stagg, nicknamed him after the famous violinist Fritz Kreisler. As a coach, Crisler was one of the most successful of his time. He was also an innovator. He designed his own version of a "winged" helmet when he joined Michigan in 1938. That helmet became a famous Wolverines standard. Fritz also chaired the NCAA Rules Committee, one of the most powerful positions in college sports. And he preached the doctrine of fair play. Many times, Don remembered, Coach Crisler would tell his players, "There's nothing in the rules that says you can't block and tackle as hard as you can; but this is Michigan. We block clean and we tackle clean; that's it!"

Don admired Fritz Crisler more than any other coach he had ever known. Out of pure respect, he would always address him as "Coach," never by his first name.

Fritz sat down at his desk and pointed for Don to sit on one of the two chairs facing him. As he sat, Don quickly glanced around. The small office was simply modest. Nothing adorned the walls. None of the many awards Fritz had received over the years was displayed—no diploma, no certificates, no pictures of Fritz with any of the many celebrities he knew. Just like Ray Fisher's office, Don thought, unpretentious. He decided right then that he would follow this example in his own office. Fritz broke his reverie.

"So what's going on with you and the Tigers, Don? Do you like coaching?"

"I guess so, Coach," said Don. "I like the team; I like the players."

Fritz grinned. "Is it true that some of those fans in Detroit buy their tickets just so they can watch Al Kaline play your former position?"

Don grinned back and lied, "Nah!" They both laughed.

Then Fritz became serious. "I think you're ready for something better, Don. I think you're ready to manage a team."

Don knew exactly where this was going. "Maybe so," he said.

Fritz continued. "We'd like you to come here to coach our baseball team. You've been highly recommended by people I respect."

Don didn't respond. Fritz reached into a desk drawer and pulled out a few sheets of paper. "Our Board in Control has commissioned me to offer you this contract at a salary of ten thousand dollars a year. We'd like you to start as soon as the Tigers' season is over."

There it was, Don thought, the low-ball. A pay-cut offer. No way could he take that proposal. "Thanks, Coach, but no thanks," he stated firmly. "As much as I'd like the job, I don't think I could sign for that amount."

Fritz eyed him carefully and saw he wasn't bluffing. "Okay Don, I'll go back to the board and see if I can get more for you. You'll hear from me within a week."

Don smiled tightly as he stood to shake Fritz's proffered hand. "Thanks, Coach, I'll look forward to hearing from you."

As he left the building, Don smiled to himself. He knew Fritz didn't need his Board of Control to approve anything about his employment, but he also understood Fritz's strategy. It was the athletic director's way of making sure whatever happened didn't seem personal. In case of conflict or disagreement, Fritz could refer to the "higher authority" to resolve it. Don admired Fritz for that. He also hoped he hadn't blown the deal. He'd know within a week.

The next evening Don was relaxing on the couch in his living room after dinner. He was commiserating about the 6–1 pounding the Indians gave the Tigers that day. George Susce had taken the loss. Detroit was back in fifth place. Too many Tigers' players had been stranded on base today. We had our chances, he pondered. Maybe tomorrow …

His thoughts were interrupted as Betty walked in and sat in a chair opposite him.

"Honey," she said, "it sure would be nice if you took the Michigan coaching job. But I understand how it wouldn't be worth it at the money you were offered."

"You're right," Don answered, "but I think Fritz will raise the offer. If he comes up with another thousand, I'll probably take it. But there still might be a slight problem."

She stared at her husband, "A problem?"

"Well, it could be," he said. "I've been thinking about how I would approach that job, based on what I've learned in pro ball. I think the Michigan baseball program should have both a full-time head coach and a full-time assistant coach. I'm not sure I could sell that idea to Fritz."

Betty thought for a moment. "Why don't you try selling it to me first? That might help you organize your arguments, so that when you talk about this to Fritz, you'll be able to convince him."

Don liked that approach. "Okay, here goes. I intend to actively recruit my players. And most of them are going to come out of the Detroit area high schools and sandlots. In fact,

I probably know many of the ones coming up now. These kids are going to know me personally, and even more so if I can get them to play at Michigan."

Betty smiled, playing the role of Fritz Crisler. "So?"

"So the way things are," he went on, "freshmen can't compete. They go out for freshmen baseball, but they only drill in fundamentals and play inner-squad practice games way down in the corner of Ferry Field. But these are my personally selected players. I recruited them, but I don't get to work with them until their second year at Michigan."

"But those are the rules, and you're stuck with them," said Betty.

"I know," he answered, "but if I had a full-time assistant who could coach these freshmen, while at the same time working with me on the varsity program, there'd be some consistency and a smoother transition between the first and second years. It would be almost like I was coaching my freshmen players through my assistant."

Betty nodded. "How is it being handled now?"

"Right now," he told her, "the football assistant coaches work part-time in the other sports. For instance, freshmen baseball is coached by Matt Patinelli. Now, Matt's a good coach, one of the best. He could coach any sport on campus. But he's really part of the football program. He doesn't represent varsity baseball to the freshmen kids at all. I'd try to change that by bringing in my own full-time assistant. And I'm sure Matt Patinelli would understand."

"That's a pretty big change," said Betty, playing the 'devil's advocate,' "hiring a full-time person to do the same job that someone already on the paid staff is doing might be wasting money." As she said that, Betty saw her husband's eyes darken. Had she played Fritz's role too intently? She was relieved in an instant, however, as she watched them brighten again.

"But that's just it," Don answered forcefully. "My assistant wouldn't just be doing the same job someone else did. He'd also be helping me recruit kids during the summer months, so the freshman players would have been recruited essentially by both of us. Transition to the varsity would be easy and familiar to them."

Betty broke out in one of her familiar huge smiles, jumped up from her chair, and hugged him. "Okay, my handsome warrior," she chuckled, "You've sold me. Now all you have to do is sell Fritz Crisler."

About half an hour later the phone rang. Betty answered it. "It's Coach Crisler." She passed the receiver to him.

"Hello, Coach," said Don.

After they exchanged a few amenities, Fritz moved right to business. "Don, the board has authorized me to offer you twelve thousand dollars a year to become our head baseball coach. That's as high as we can go."

Don didn't hesitate. "That's fine, Coach. I'll take it."

"OK," said Fritz, "nice to have you aboard. You'll take over Ray's office, on the second floor."

Although he was pleased with the offer, Don was fresh from his role play with Betty. There wouldn't be a better time to ask Fritz for a full-time assistant than now, he thought, and he was prepared to make his case. He decided to seize the moment.

"Coach, there's one more thing."

"What's that?"

"I'd like to hire a full-time assistant coach."

"No problem," said Crisler, "maybe it's about time. Got anyone in mind?"

"Not yet," answered Don. He couldn't believe what he'd just heard.

"All right," Crisler responded, "let me know when you do. Just stay away from any of the assistants already working here."

After agreeing on a start date, the two said good-bye and Fritz hung up. But Michigan's new head baseball coach just stood there next to the phone, looking at the receiver. Betty came up to him and asked about the call from Fritz.

"I didn't have to sell him at all about an assistant coach," he said to her. "Fritz was so agreeable; he acted as if the whole thing was his idea."

Betty laughed. "Maybe you should have asked him for two assistants," she teased. "And a staff car, and an unlimited expense account."

"And my wife on the payroll, plus the moon and half the stars in the sky." He laughed, "Ann Arbor, here we come!"

The two men had agreed that Don would start his new job on Wednesday, October 1, three days after the Tigers ended their

1958 season in Cleveland. There was no way the team was a pennant contender. Don would finish his term as a Tigers coach on September 30. He would be moving on; his future would be filled with promise. He'd be going back to his college roots. He'd be coaching the Michigan Wolverines!

Before all that, however, Don first had to finish out his Detroit Tigers coaching job. He made that commitment to John McHale, and he intended to keep it. His best effort was needed during the next six weeks, until the end of the season. The Tigers were sinking in the American League standings. Don would have to give his all to help keep up his team's spirit. He would try his best to focus the players on winning their few remaining games.

So Don forgot about his next job and gave full attention to the Detroit Tigers. He seldom spoke about Michigan baseball to others on the team. He wore the Tigers' uniform; he spoke the Tigers' talk; he cheered the Tigers onward day after day. Only once did he step out of his major league roll to act on behalf of his future team in Ann Arbor.

It happened at Fenway Park in Boston, where Don had arrived a few hours early before a scheduled Tigers–Red Sox game. He noticed some unusual commotion around home plate during the Red Sox practice period. Nosing around, he learned that the Red Sox had invited a high school senior from Revere, Massachusetts, a catcher named Joe Merullo, to work out with them. As Don watched Merullo perform, he was impressed with the kid's lack of nervousness around the big leaguers. Merullo had a strong arm, good moves behind the plate, and a healthy swing. Don wanted to talk to him about playing at Michigan, but would he violate any NCAA rules by doing so?

Don thought carefully about that. The last thing he needed was to do something stupid before he even started his new job. But that's just it, he realized. He hadn't started yet; hadn't signed the contract. And one thing he'd learned over his nine years in pro ball: nothing's official until you sign your name to it.

He waited patiently until Joe Merullo finished his workout and was standing alone behind the batting cage. Don approached him and began to talk. Joe was receptive. Several minutes later Don walked away, feeling that Joe Merullo would be interested in attending Michigan, especially if he received a scholarship. Merullo would do well at Michigan, Don believed. Joe seemed smart enough to make it through the demanding curriculum, tough enough to stick it out through his degree, and talented enough to be a key asset to the baseball team.

Of course, Don had no way of knowing just how accurate his thoughts about Joe Merullo would turn out to be. Joe would indeed enroll at the University of Michigan, becoming Coach Don Lund's first recruit. And he would go on to exceed every expectation his coach would have of him, on and off the baseball field.

On Wednesday morning, September 3, Don and Betty were relaxing at home in Detroit. Don was happy to be home after a grueling road trip. Twenty-one games in twenty-one days; ten wins and eleven losses. The Tigers remained stuck in the middle of the American League standings, with just over three weeks left on the schedule. They were becoming predictable as middle-of-the-pack performers. Don felt like his personal "balloon" of team optimism was constantly being attacked by a swarm of needles. So he had to keep blowing it up every day and showing it off to all those around him. That was the core of his job, he reckoned; that's what he owed the team.

Still, he felt good this morning. The Tigers were beginning a home stand of nearly three weeks. He looked forward to the familiar sights and sounds of Briggs Stadium and those wonderful, enthusiastic Detroit fans. In all his travels around ballparks in the major and minor leagues, Don had never found more dedicated fans than the ones who filled the stands in Briggs Stadium. Other parks would cascade with boos and catcalls from fair-weather fans, or the home crowd didn't show up in big numbers if the team was on a losing streak. Not so in Detroit. Detroit fans came to the park and cheered. Catcalls were reserved for the visiting team, or the umpire whose call didn't favor the Tigers. On nights and weekends, some fans could be seen among the packed crowd, peering out from behind a post because they had paid for and occupied one of the stadium's "blind" seats. It didn't seem to affect their attendance much if the Tigers were struggling. Of course, it would be standing room only in a pennant race.

Yes, Don thought, there weren't better baseball fans anywhere than at Briggs Stadium. And some would go to great lengths to be there for a game. He remembered standing next to the dugout before the opening game on April 18. A *Detroit News* photographer was standing near him, taking pictures of the crowd. Suddenly, as the photographer swung his camera down to shoot a group of men in the front two rows of prime seats next to the dugout, someone shouted "whoa!" from the second row. Don turned and saw one of the men practically hugging the stadium floor in front of his seat, trying to avoid having his picture taken by a newspaper photographer. When the photographer walked away, the man sat back up in his seat.

Don grinned at him and said, "Your boss thinks you're home sick, doesn't he?"

"Yeah," said the man, "and my wife thinks I'm working!"

As he remembered this, Don laughed to himself. Detroit fans were a special breed. They were another reason why he was feeling good and looking forward to this long Tigers' home stand.

The telephone interrupted his reverie, and Don answered it on the second ring. It was his old friend Moby Benedict. "How's it going, Moby? Are you here in Michigan?"

"Actually," said Moby, "Pat and I are in Walker, Minnesota, just finishing up a vacation. We'll be back in Ann Arbor in a few days, but I wanted to call you now, when I know you're home."

"What's up?" Don could hear some excitement in Moby's voice.

Characteristically, Moby got right to the point. "When I was back in Ann Arbor I found out you were going to be Michigan's new baseball coach. That started me thinking about my own career. I've given pro ball a good try for the last two years. In the meantime, I've also been substitute teaching in the off-season, like you did all those years. Maybe it's time for me to retire as a player and look into something else."

Don had closely followed Moby's two-year career in the Tigers' minor league farm system. In 1957, Moby played for Idaho Falls. The next year he was sent to Lancaster, Pennsylvania, where he played most of the 1958 season. In August, the Tigers had moved him from Lancaster to Montgomery, Alabama, where Moby finished in September. Moby had spent the last two seasons, plus each year in spring training in Lakeland, away from the love of his life, Patricia. Perhaps that fact alone had cooled his fire for playing the professional game.

Head Coach Don Lund (*left*) and Assistant Coach Moby Benedict get
ready for their rookie season in March 1959. Three years later, they
would bring both national and world championships to the University
of Michigan. (*Bentley Historical Library, The University of Michigan*)

Don responded, "What did you have in mind, Moby?"

Moby went on, "Well, I thought I might go back to Michigan
for my master's. I could then get a full-time job as a high school
coach. Maybe also you could use a graduate assistant while I'm
there going to school. Pat has already looked into transferring
to Ann Arbor to teach there. What do you think about me being
your graduate assistant?"

Don was struck by his good fortune. Here was Moby Benedict, a three-letter winner and captain of the 1956 Michigan
squad, a Big Ten standout during all three years he played, and
the very definition of the word *hustle*, asking him for a graduate
assistant's job. He was about to blow Moby's mind.

"How would you like to be my full-time assistant coach?"

There was a moment of silence on the other end of the line.
Then Moby came back, "Are you kidding?"

"Nope," said Don. "Fritz gave me the OK a while back. You're my obvious first choice. I just wasn't sure you were ready to retire as a player. I'd really like to have you with me. What do you think?"

Moby fairly shouted into the phone. Maybe he wanted Pat to overhear. "I think you just hired an assistant coach!"

They agreed on a salary and worked out a mid-October starting date. And just like that, over a long-distance phone line, Milbrey (Moby) Benedict became the first full-time assistant baseball coach in the entire ninety-two-year history of the game at the University of Michigan.

The 1958 Detroit Tigers season ended without fanfare. Don cleaned out his coach's locker at Briggs Stadium with bittersweet emotions. He was a man who knew he belonged in spirit to two organizations, each having his loyalty and devotion.

First, he was a born-and-bred Detroit Tigers' fanatic. They were "his" team, from his earliest memories of boyhood. Second, he was a "Man of Michigan." If you cut him open, someone once told him, his insides would glow maize and blue. Now, as Don cleared out his locker and walked out of the Tigers' clubhouse, he knew a part of him was staying behind. Like the guy who loved his new watch, but kept the old one fondly tucked in his dresser drawer, Don Lund was placing his Detroit Tigers in the folds of his memory and setting out for his newfound quest in Ann Arbor. He drove from Briggs Stadium to the administrative offices of the Detroit Public Schools. There, he placed himself on the inactive substitute teaching list. No use quitting completely, he thought; you just never know when you might need the job again.

Don thought his first day at work in Ann Arbor would be routine. In fact, he worked out the schedule as he drove that morning from his East Side Detroit home. First thing, he thought, was to find the shortest way from his Detroit home to his office. Until he found a house in Ann Arbor and moved his family there, he'd be driving his '57 Pontiac nearly a hundred miles a day, round trip. That could become expensive. Gasoline was selling at 28.9 cents a gallon, up from the 26.9 cents a week ago. Last night he was lucky enough to benefit from a "price war" between a Standard Oil station and a Shell station on Jefferson Avenue. He had filled up at the Shell for 24.9, but that was pure luck.

Mostly he'd been paying full price at the pump. Find the shortest route, he figured, even if it took a little more time.

He'd left the house just before 7 AM, intending to get to his new office around eight o'clock, so he could be one of the first ones there. He'd be assigned Ray Fisher's old office on the second floor; no problem. The rest of his day would be spent just getting acquainted with the normal things that made the Athletic Department run smoothly. It was football season. The team had squeaked by Southern California last Saturday in Michigan Stadium, 20–19. Everybody would be pretty happy about that. This coming Saturday's game against Michigan State in East Lansing was a toss-up. Evenly matched teams. Big rivalry. No bet on the outcome. He thought about his coming day.

First thing he'd do when he settled in, he decided, would be to walk around, see who's there, say hello. No way would he wait for them to come to him; that wasn't his style. Just take it easy, get settled, learn procedures. First day should be an easy one. That's what he thought as he drove into Ann Arbor. It didn't take long for him to change his mind.

Don pulled into the parking lot behind the Athletic Department around 8:15, thinking he had made good time from Detroit. He was pleased to find several spots available. He knew that parking around the rest of the campus was very limited; some faculty had to walk long distances to their offices and classrooms. But parking was no problem for the athletics staff. Nice perk, he thought.

Don was not prepared to walk into the office before 8:30 in the morning and see it bustling like the New York Stock Exchange at crunch time. But that's what he saw. People were at their desks, or walking deliberately around, or meeting in small groups. Three or four typewriters fought for the rights to control the sound throughout the entire first-floor space. Was this business as usual? At this early in the morning? He walked in practically unnoticed, except for a friendly wave from Don Weir in the ticket office. Fritz must be on the warpath, he concluded, nobody works like this without somebody pulling their clocks. Anyway, he'd better go back and say hello to the boss. He got three steps down the corridor when Les Etter, the sports information director, pounced out of his office on the left with a handshake extended.

"Don Lund," said Les. "Welcome back to the fold, Coach!"

Les pumped Don's hand and pulled him into his office. Don said hello to Jean Etter, Les's wife, who worked with her husband. For the next half hour, Les and Jean interviewed him for a press release about Michigan's new head baseball coach. Don was impressed with how much the Etters already knew about his background. When it was over, Don told Les he was going across the hall to greet Fritz. Les told him Fritz wasn't in this morning; he was meeting with President Hatcher and a couple of the regents. Don might want to just step in and say hello to Norma Bentley, anyway.

On his way out to do just that, Don chided Les Etter, "Fritz isn't here and everybody's working so hard so early ... Does that mean when the cat's away the mice don't play?"

"Are you kidding?" Les laughed. "Fritz just slows us all down!"

As Don climbed the stairs to the second floor, he noticed less movement and noise. It figured. People up there were usually self-confined in their offices rather than moving around. But he was excited; a lot of the coaches on the second floor were longtime friends. He could hardly wait to see them again.

First to greet him as he stepped on the second floor were Betty Ann Bacon and Lillian Duford, secretaries for the head coaches and their assistants. The two of them handled secretarial work for all sports at Michigan except football. Football needed its own secretary, and that would be Dorothy Johnson, Lillian Duford's sister.

Betty Ann introduced herself to Don as his secretary. "Let me show you to your office," she said, and she led him to a familiar corner room with windows overlooking Hoover Street.

He and hundreds of other Michigan ballplayers over the past thirty-eight years had spent countless hours of time in this office where Coach Ray Fisher presided. He looked around the room. There were now two desks: the one Ray had used (which he would take), and another one for Moby when he came on board. There were also four extra wooden chairs in the room for office visitors. He thought of the history of the room. Now it was assigned to him. He appreciated Betty Ann for her kindness. She could have called it "Ray's office, or "the baseball office";

she didn't. She called it "your office." Betty Ann had won him over immediately.

For the first few minutes, Don sat at his desk and went over the Athletic Department staff list, figuring out who occupied various offices in the Administration Building, and who were placed elsewhere. He already knew the first-floor dwellers, including Fritz Crisler, Les and Jean Etter, Don Weir, and Associate Athletic Director Bert Katzenmeyer, who also was the golf coach.

As he looked over the second-floor list, some familiar names stood out. One end of the floor held the football staff: Head Coach Bennie Oosterbaan, plus assistant coaches Don Dufek, Bump Elliott, Jack Blott, Cliff Keen, Matt Patanelli, Bob Hollway, and Wally Weber. Quite a list, he thought.

Benny Oosterbaan was arguably the best athlete ever to play at Michigan. Don Dufek had played fullback with power, courage, and determination, which led to Michigan's MVP and All Big Ten honors in 1950. Plus, Dufek was everyone's role model for great attitude; players followed his directions without question. Bump Elliott was, according to Fritz Crisler, "One of the greatest halfbacks I ever saw." Don knew he was even more than that. Bump earned three letters in three sports at Purdue while in the Marines, then came to Michigan and became the league's MVP. As a coach, one of his strengths was being able to explain complicated strategy in the simplest of terms. No one ever had to ask Bump to describe a play twice.

Jack Blott had been an All American center and place kicker for Michigan in the early 1920s, plus a star baseball catcher. Now Jack was one of the best line coaches in the NCAA. Matt Patanelli was a motivator for every player on the team. He played end for the Wolverines and was the only Michigan player drafted by the NFL in 1936.

Bob Hollway was born to coach. A local Ann Arbor native, Bob grew up never wanting to play anywhere else but Michigan. It didn't hurt Bob that his dad, Lou Hollway, was a legendary high school football coach for Ann Arbor High School. In fact, the new Ann Arbor Pioneer High football field had been named after Lou a few years earlier in 1956. His son Bob's cradle toys probably included a football.

Don looked at two other names on the list of assistant football coaches, Cliff Keen and Wally Weber. Cliff Keen was Michigan's head wrestling coach. More than that, Cliff was considered one of the most outstanding college wrestling coaches in America. And Cliff did more than coach college wrestling. He designed the helmet worn by wrestlers in schools throughout the country. He created the circular ring, which revolutionized the sport itself. He promoted better equipment, not only for wrestling, but for other sports as well. He coached the 1948 U.S. Olympic wrestling team and served on the U.S. Olympic Board. As a college wrestler at Oklahoma A&M University, Cliff was undefeated in all heavyweight divisions and became a national champion. He also starred as a lineman on the football team and ran track as a sprinter. Cliff Keen was an amazing man.

Wally Weber was also more than an assistant varsity football coach. As a Wolverine, Wally played on the same team in the mid 1920s with the most famous forward pass combination in school history, Bennie Friedman and Benny Oosterbaan. Wally coached freshman football for many years. Freshmen couldn't compete with other schools, but Michigan's freshmen were mostly recruited high school standouts. Coaching their practices without giving them any more status than fodder for the varsity team required a delicate but forceful touch. Wally had that, and more. He was a dynamic speaker, much in demand by alumni groups and service clubs. Wally often carried game movies wherever he went, always making sure that the films merely served as support material, never superseding what he personally had to say. Wally Weber might be the best-liked person on the entire staff, thought Don. He wouldn't be surprised if they phased him out of coaching altogether, just so he could devote full time to being the Wolverines' ambassador-at-large. Wally Weber would probably like that.

Don continued to scan the list, mentally placing the location of his fellow coaches on the second floor. Head basketball coach Bill Perigo shared offices with assistants Dave Strack, Jim Skala, and Tom Jorgensen. Tennis coach Bill Murphy, hockey coach Al Renfrew, and wrestling coach Cliff Keen had offices not too far away from Don's. Track coach Don Canham and his assistant Elmer Swanson completed the list.

He looked again at Al Renfrew's name. Renfrew had been Michigan's standout hockey player in the late 1940s. He was an All-American left-winger who scored with abandon and captained the team in his senior year. In his last season, he scored two goals in seven seconds against Michigan Technological University. That must have shocked them. When he graduated, Michigan Tech promptly hired Al Renfrew as their coach. Now, in his second year of coaching Wolverine hockey, Al was putting his own recruits on skates and leading a Big 10 contender. Don couldn't wait to meet him.

Two other coaches, both of whom were famous in their own sports, had offices in the Intramural Building. They were swimming coach Gus Stager and gymnastics coach Newt Loken. Gus had been a championship swimming and diving coach at Dearborn Fordson High School, where he captured three successive state championships before coming to Ann Arbor. Now Gus was quickly gaining national respect with back-to-back NCAA national championships, 1957–58. Most fans believed that only a coach like Gus Stager could have replaced the one and only Matt Mann at Michigan.

Newt Loken was in a class by himself. A college All American and NCAA All Events National Champion at Minnesota, Newt went on to serve with distinction in the U.S. Navy during WWII, teaching physical conditioning to naval aviators. While there, he co-authored the Navy's book on gymnastics and tumbling. He also introduced the trampoline for conditioning while stationed as an athletic welfare officer aboard the aircraft carrier U.S.S. *Prince William*. He was just getting started. After the war he went to Michigan and earned his master's degree. Then he convinced the university to re-establish its intercollegiate gymnastics program, which had been dropped during the Great Depression.

Insisting that Newt be the head gymnastics coach, the university reestablished the program. Then Newt reinvented it. Now, ten years later, Michigan's gymnastics teams under Newt Loken were a recognized NCAA force. And Newt himself was the unlimited personal energy that drove them. He was also a celebrity. For instance, people loved his annual appearance in Detroit's Thanksgiving Day Parade. Newt would ride the entire parade on a float, bouncing with amazing coordination and doing tricks, while the adults and children along Woodward Avenue screamed at his antics. Yet, with all of his accomplishments, Newt Loken was just a regular guy. Nobody at the university had more friends and fans than their head gymnastics coach.

Don scanned the list of his fellow coaches one more time. He could hardly believe where he was. For the first time in his career, Don Lund had merged into a peer group of national legends. Kind of like scoring the game-winning home run without having to hit the ball. Looking over the list of Michigan coaches had suddenly humbled him. He had driven to work full of pride and confidence, the one anointed to replace the great Ray Fisher. Now, he saw how shallow his thinking had been. He was on the bottom rung of his own ladder, which stretched up to infinity. Most of the guys on this list were well up their own ladders, and some were at the top of theirs after many years. At the age of thirty-five, Don Lund felt once again like an entering freshman at the University of Michigan. He had a long way to go to prove his worth, in a school that was used to producing winners.

Over the next few weeks, Don threw himself into his new job with three goals in mind: One, he needed to get to know the players as soon as possible; two, he had to find a permanent place to live in Ann Arbor; and three, he should develop Moby to help him build the team from the time they entered as freshmen.

In addition to these targets, Don knew he had to learn to work within the political system of the Athletic Department. The university, like nearly all very large organizations, was a conglomerate of political systems. Each was supervised by a department head, or a dean, or a director, or a university officer. Many of them had little to do with setting up the political system under them. In fact, the real authority for putting out the daily grind rested with those who fell under the generic title of "staff."

No matter what the individual titles were, they were "staff." They did the everyday work, and they did it well. At Michigan, they were the "Go" in "Go, Blue!" Trying to fight their rules, procedures, or personal work habits (i.e., the political system) would be a one-way ride to career disaster. The last thing he needed was to twist the ego of a staff member by trying to get something done his own way. His secretary, Betty Ann Bacon, would be a big help, he concluded. That turned out to be the best decision Don Lund made all year.

He needed to find a place to live in Ann Arbor. He and Betty had always rented, wherever they went. Now they wanted to buy a house. Susan was twelve and into junior high school; she needed roots and the chance to establish long-term friends. So

Betty was riding to Ann Arbor with her husband every morning and then taking the car to search for a home. As the weeks went on, "house hunting" became Betty's job.

At first Don wondered how long it would take him to "break the ice" and join in the camaraderie shared by his fellow coaches. He got his answer the first time he went to the lunchroom in the basement; there was no ice at all. Right away they accepted him into their ranks. After handshakes all around, Don was pleasantly surprised and totally comfortable. Where he might have expected the more renowned coaches to be somewhat aloof and self-absorbed; where he might also expect the more experienced coaches to simply see a "newbee" and treat him with detachment, there was none of that. Personally, Don had been a little concerned about possibly having a negative image thrust at him. He thought he might be seen as a guy who was trying to grab the limelight of a fabled Michigan coach, a legend who was forced to quit only because of his age. But that turned out not to matter at all among these coaches. When he met them all together over lunch, his welcome was warm and genuine.

The lunchroom also gave Don a lot of exposure to the personalities of his fellow coaches. Naturally, the talk was mostly about sports, and it ran the whole spectrum of sports, from high school through the pros. At first Don took some good-natured kidding about the Tigers' 1958 season. For instance, someone would ask the group what the Tigers would have done if Don had managed them this past year. Probably the same, someone else would say, except they'd be wearing maize and blue uniforms. Everyone would laugh, including the new baseball coach.

Sports stories were rampant in the lunchroom, and some of the coaches were really good at telling them. Al Renfrew who could break up the whole group, and even Fritz Crisler, who "had a million of 'em." Lunchtime usually lasted about an hour, but when Fritz showed up, the clock was thrown away and the stories began.

A typical Fritz Crisler story would feature one of the guys on the staff, told in a positive way, like this one about Elmer Swanson, Don Canham's assistant track coach:

Swanson had a foghorn voice; you could hear it anywhere, even from the middle row of Michigan Stadium in a packed crowd. And he loved to pick on opposing head coaches. He showed no mercy, either. One time at a baseball game here, we were playing Ohio State. Their head coach was Marty Karow. Swanson was on Karow from the first pitch, like an ant on a lump of sugar. "Hey, Karow, why don'tcha let your kids call the pitches? They'd do better'n you!" You know, stuff like that. Well, Karow managed to get himself thrown out of the game. He walked back to the locker room in Yost. But Swanson wasn't through. He decided to turn Karow into a phantom. "Hey, Ump! Karow's still here. He's in the stands behind their dugout." The umpire would look at the stands, then scan the Michigan rooting section to see who was yelling. Of course Swanson had moved. A few minutes later: "Hey Ump! He's back in the park! He's standing behind that pole, throwing signals!" The umpire would glance at the posts holding up the stands, then try to locate where the yelling came from. Our fans loved it! Nobody would think of ratting on Swanson. And when the game ended, we'd beaten their pants off!

Fritz liked to play the card game of hearts; he was also good at it. Hearts is a trick-taking game, the object of which is to win by having the lowest score at the end of a hand. Players try to avoid taking tricks that contain hearts or the queen of spades, all of which add up to high points. Fritz, the "King" of Michigan athletics, won a lot of games by somehow avoiding the high-point queen. A few good-natured barbs about the king not wanting a queen were heard at times around the lunchroom, but not when the boss was around. Stupidity seldom showed up during lunch in the Athletic Department basement.

Two or three times a year, Fritz commandeered the lunchroom for staff meetings. The King summoning his court. Prompt attendance was mandatory. Fritz didn't pass out an agenda. He was the agenda. Nearly always, the theme of these meetings centered on NCAA rules and rule changes for college sports. And nearly always, Fritz would repeat his own rule: "If you cheat, you're fired!"

Don wondered why Fritz would continually bring that up to coaches who would never even think of cheating. Then someone reminded him that Fritz chaired the NCAA Rules Committee. His job was to investigate rules violations allegedly being committed by major college coaches. Some of these coaches were ultimately found guilty, and Fritz was charged with bringing them down. That wasn't fun for him; as a matter of fact, he hated it. There was no way Fritz Crisler was going to allow the cheating question to arrive one day at his own doorstep. And there was no way any of his coaches were going to allow even the hint of cheating to appear among the athletes, their parents, or any "boosters" associated with them. So Crisler's words "If you cheat, you're fired!" were actually meant for everyone associated with sports at the University of Michigan. No exceptions.

Fritz Crisler was not the type of boss one could simply access at any time. He wasn't the desk-bound type. Nor was his schedule consistent and predictable. If someone wanted to meet with Fritz, the unwritten rule was to set up an appointment through his secretary, Norma Bentley—like the sheep setting up its own shearing time. But the Athletic Department coaches were anything but sheep. No one ever accused them of being typical subordinating types. Their jobs demanded them to be aggressive, dominant men, despite their outward "nice guy" demeanors. In fact, they were trained to approach the process of getting results through direct action, even though they were polite and professional in doing so. When a problem occurred, they charged forth to solve it; they didn't avoid it or go around it. So when a coach wanted to talk to Fritz, he'd call him directly on the phone, even at home if necessary. He'd walk right in Fritz's office looking for him, whether or not the boss was there. Sometimes they'd merely leave a note for him. Sometimes that turned out to be funny.

At the start of one of his staff meetings, Fritz announced, "Someone's been sending me notes telling me he wanted to see me, but not signing them." Fritz looked around the table. "Anybody here know anything about that?"

Nobody said a word. As Fritz moved on to other business, Al Renfrew glanced at Newt Loken and grinned. Don Lund looked at Al, then at Newt. Newt's face remained as blank as the ones on Mount Rushmore. Only the redness on the back of his neck gave him away. Finally, as Fritz droned on, Newt grinned back at his two friends, knowing he was the victim of a "gotcha." For a long time, the story of "Newt's notes," which never got back to Fritz, was a department favorite.

Don decided the best way for him to get to know his players right away was to have a fall practice. The baseball team
had never before practiced in the fall, but that didn't mean it
couldn't be done. Ann Arbor weather in October usually wasn't
too severe to work outside. Besides, the players were all on campus and tended to hang out together. They'd be easy to bring
in. And those who weren't on the football team were keeping in
shape by playing intramural sports or just working out on their
own. So he contacted the players who weren't out for football
and called for the first-ever baseball team fall practice. To his
delight, the players were eager. He set up their first meeting for
Monday, October 15, at Yost Field House. Then they'd go on
to practice four days a week, Monday through Thursday, for
four weeks. After that it would become too cold to continue the
outdoor schedule.

Don first chose the varsity baseball stadium for practice,
rather than the freshman diamond way out at the south end
of Ferry Field. The varsity stadium was conveniently close to
the locker room. Plus, Don liked the idea of practicing where
the team played its home games. But he overlooked one item,
and that turned out to be a big mistake. He didn't remember
that the varsity stadium's left field foul line was wide open. It
had no stands or other barriers to block a foul ball from going
astray. And less than 150 feet beyond it was the football team's
practice field.

Don saw the potential problem as soon as his team walked
onto the field. He could have moved everybody out right away
to the far-distant freshman area. Instead, he cautioned them to
hit only to right field, not realizing that doing so would direct
everyone's attention to the wide-open left field line. Sure enough,
the inevitable happened as soon as a right-handed batter took his
stance at the plate. He swung at the first pitch, an inside fastball
that caught the bat's handle, and launched a towering foul ball
over the left field foul line, straight toward the practicing football
squad. It landed without hitting anybody, and rolled right to
where Coach Bump Elliott was drilling his starting backfield.

Bump picked up the ball, threw it back, and yelled something
that was lost in the wind. And like burglars caught by a screaming
alarm, the entire baseball team and their new coach scrambled
to action. They grabbed their gear and scampered like a herd

of zebra from a pursuing lion, toward the freshman diamond, which was tucked into a corner of Ferry Field. They raced the entire 250 yards. Nobody yelled; nobody spoke, nobody even breathed hard. They dashed past the football team as if the guys with pads and winged helmets weren't even there. They loped the entire distance with Moby Benedict setting the pace in front.

When the players reached their destination, they all formed in a tight circle around their head coach. Don tried to look deadly serious. Large and in-charge. "Hey, guys," he began, but that's as far as he got. He started to grin; the players grinned with him. Then he laughed; the players howled. They had launched themselves into the archives of Wolverines lore: stampeding out of a practice session because of a foul ball!

Recruiting players is never far from a coach's mind, no matter what the sport is. It's a simple assumption: recruit the best players and you'll have the best team. It works if the coach is good enough to forge the recruited stars into a cohesive, competitive unit. It doesn't work if the coach is merely a good recruiter. The stars perform for their own glories and don't meld together. Like the house builder who finds the best materials, and then builds a structure that leaks when it rains.

Don Lund was well aware of this when he accepted the job from Fritz Crisler. He knew he could coach the team. He also knew who the better player prospects were in Detroit's high schools. What he didn't know was how successful he'd be at recruiting them. His competition would be fierce. Michigan State's John Kobs had a network of supporters, alumni, and friends around the Detroit area. Notre Dame's Jake Kline had just lost his standout player to the Boston Red Sox, a promising outfielder named Carl Yastrzemski. Jake would be after Carl's replacement like a race dog after the rabbit. And Notre Dame had plenty of alumni in the Detroit area. Don would be up against strong odds.

He had two things going for him. One was the academic worth of the University of Michigan. A degree from Michigan opened doors to great careers. The other was the NCAA rule on recruiting athletes. All coaches had to follow the same limitations and guidelines about direct contact with student-athletes. He would have just as much access to these kids as John Kobs, Jake Kline, and all the other coaches; no more, no less.

It would take him up to the middle of October before Don could concentrate on recruiting his team. Joe Merullo was almost an accidental discovery in Boston. Most of the other kids he wanted were in school through the middle of June; he'd have to wait until he could see them on the sandlots next summer. But there was one very special young man Don wanted to attract, ever since he got the Michigan job. The kid starred in football and baseball at Detroit Denby High School. He was also an honor student. Plus, he had torn up the sandlots as an outfielder on the Modern Hard Chrome Team. Don had known this young athlete for nearly ten years, more than half the kid's life. He was someone special. His name was Ed Hood.

Don first met little Eddie Hood when the boy was a third grader at Detroit's Hosmer Elementary School. Don was substitute teaching during his off-season winter hiatus from pro ball. Eddie showed up in Don's recreation class. At the end of class, Eddie came up to him as the rest of the boys were leaving.

"I know who you are, Mr. Lund. You're a baseball player. Can I have your autograph?" The kid produced a slip of paper.

"Sure," Don said, and signed his name.

"Gee, thanks Mr. Lund!" Eddie grabbed the paper, turned, and ran to catch up to his class. Don never forgot that incident. All through his substitute teaching years, lots of boys had approached him in school, produced a ball or a piece of paper, and walked away with his signature. But they were older kids, mostly in the fifth grade and up. That's why the memory of little Eddie Hood from Hosmer School stayed. He was the youngest kid to ever ask him for his autograph.

The next time he saw Ed Hood was during the two years Don ran the Tigers' high school summer camps, 1955–56. Both years Ed was selected as a league All-Star to play in the game at Briggs Stadium. Both years Ed was a dominant player. The Tigers' scouts thought he was worth watching. Don thought so too, but he also knew that Ed was an academic standout at Denby. He wouldn't be the type to play pro ball without first going to college, probably all the way to a degree.

Now it was the fall of 1958, and Don was starting his Michigan coaching career. He made up his mind to try to recruit Ed Hood. He learned three things about Ed right away. First, Ed was a second-semester senior at Denby, due to graduate in

December. Second, Ed was also being recruited by Bump Elliott for Michigan football. Third, Denby's highly successful football coach, Ed Rutherford, cheered for Michigan State. Rutherford was probably trying to steer Ed toward the Spartans in a big way. Knowing all this, Don was determined to bring Ed Hood to Michigan. And it wasn't just because the Denby standout would enhance his team; that was a given. Don was selfish enough as a coach to badly want Ed's considerable skills, but Don was also convinced that Michigan was the best place for Ed.

Ed Hood's grades were good enough for admission on his own merit. Also, many of Denby's graduates went on to Michigan. Ed would have lots of friends in Ann Arbor. Don knew Ed Hood. He knew that this young man's character was forged as he rose up from childhood in Detroit's East Side housing projects, to the top of his senior class in one of the highest-rated schools in the state of Michigan. There are those who get ahead by having doors opened for them. And there are also those who rise up by opening their own doors. Michigan, Don firmly believed, was for students who opened their own doors. Michigan was for Ed Hood.

Don arranged to meet Ed during the young man's official fall visit to Ann Arbor on November 1, which happened to include good seats for the Wolverines' home football game against Iowa. They sat together and enjoyed themselves, even though Michigan lost, 14–37. Ed volunteered that his choice for a college was between Michigan State and Michigan. Three weeks later Don heard that Ed was coming on his own to the Michigan football "Bust," which annually honors the graduating seniors on the team. It was held at the Book Cadillac Hotel in downtown Detroit. Again, Don arranged for them to sit together, and again they had a good time.

While reminiscing, Ed told Don he had gone to Briggs Stadium in 1953 and watched Don play in right field for the Tigers. Don was about to quip about Ed picking up some pointers while watching him, until Ed followed immediately with a comment about also watching Al Kaline play a couple of years later. Don smiled and kept quiet. After the seniors finished their individual speeches, Wally Weber announced the results of a raffle that was held, using numbers from the ticket stubs. One of the prizes was an autographed team football. They called Ed Hood's name.

When Ed returned to the table, carrying his prize aloft like the Olympic Torch, he sat down with a huge smile on his face.

"Guess what, Coach?" he exclaimed as he looked at the ball. "Tomorrow I'm going to call Coach Elliott and tell him I'm coming to Michigan!"

That said it all for Don Lund. Ed Hood became his second recruit. "Way to go Ed," he said as they shook hands. "You made the right choice."

It was a choice Ed Hood would never regret.

By the end of November, Betty Lund had enough of house hunting. Running around with a realtor like mice after the elusive cheese revealed nothing she liked, so she asked her husband to take over. Don knew better than to say anything else but yes. If one of his players complained about going to classes or something like that, he'd be all over him like bees on a hive. But Betty could mold him like he was soft clay. She could turn him into a hot roll smothered in butter. With her, he forgot that the English language had a two-letter word beginning with "N" and ending with "O." He agreed with a smile.

The next day Don started his hunt for a house with a firm resolve. He was the man of the house, after all. He was tough-minded. He decided right away that he would create the most meaningful, the most deliberate, the most sophisticated, and the soundest plan he could think of. He could do it, by golly. He'd attack the problem straight on; he'd go for it like he was charging with a football at the Michigan State line. He would be fearless. He would fill himself with a single-minded purpose. He knew exactly what he had to do. So he went right over to Ray Fisher's place to ask his mentor if he might possibly know someone who could help him find a house.

"Sure, I know someone," said Ray. "How about me?"

Don couldn't believe his luck. It turned out that Ray had just finished helping a friend move into town. Thus he knew the market; he knew where houses were selling; he even knew some of the local builders who were putting up new houses around town. They chatted for more than an hour. Don told Ray about Betty's unsuccessful waltz around town with a realtor. They both agreed that Don should use another strategy. No use trudging down a worn-out path. They finally agreed that Don's best move would be to contact a builder who might have something available. Ray suggested a man named George Airey. He'd heard that Airey had some activity going, but he'd never talked to him, because his friend had found a house before Ray had a chance to contact any of the local builders. Don left Ray's house, amazed that his quest for a house had been so easy. He set out immediately to contact the builder George Airey. It took him just one phone call.

"I'm here in Ann Arbor working for the university, and I'm looking to buy a house for my family," said Don. "Ray Fisher gave me your name and said you might have something available."

Airey's first response surprised Don. At once he started talking about Michigan baseball like a diehard fan. Mentioning Ray's name had apparently pushed Airey's button, because he was quoting stats and records that only a serious follower would care about. Plus, he knew about Don being the new coach. Airey spoke at great length, even citing Don's three-sport achievements at the university as if he had memorized the record. This guy, thought Don, was either an immensely dedicated fan or a smart salesman who was blowing smoke at him. He decided on the former.

Don decided to test this by changing the subject to his immediate need for a house—and that brought the second surprise. Almost instantly, Airey switched from being a Michigan devotee to a serious home builder. His telephone voice calmed. He spoke slower and more deliberately. He asked pointed questions about what Don was looking for. Finally, Airey told him about a house he had recently built on Barrington Place in Ann Arbor. He described it as a three-bedroom, ranch-style brick home, with a two-car garage and a large family room with a fireplace. Don liked what he heard, figured he could afford Airey's price, and told the builder he was interested. He also said he wanted to bring Betty to see it with him, and she could be there the next day. They agreed to meet the following morning.

That afternoon, Don drove by the house to check it out before going home to Betty and Susan in Detroit. George Airey's new house at 1565 Barrington Place was a ranch house in a quiet residential subdivision of ranch houses. Most of the homes looked new. Only a few front yards had grass, probably planted this past summer. Barrington Place was a short street in an area of short streets, located off Stadium Boulevard, about two miles west of Michigan Stadium and the university's athletic complex.

He could walk to work in about ten minutes. Regarding Betty, Don felt confident she would be impressed with this house. He also believed she wouldn't be upset over how quickly he found it without her. After all, he used networking resources that weren't available to her. He was right on both counts.

Betty loved three things about the house right away. First, the kitchen was large enough for her to move around comfortably, but small enough for her to easily reach all appliances. It overlooked a large back yard through a window that dominated the back wall, making it easy to see kids playing. Also, there was an outside kitchen door that opened into the garage, making it convenient to bring in groceries, even in bad weather. Second, the one-story ranch design meant no more hauling things up and down flights of stairs. And third, the living/family room had a fieldstone fireplace along the wall opposite the kitchen. She liked that.

Don was impressed by the full basement, which measured about 30-by-60 feet. When finished with a tile floor, paneling, and a standing bar, he could entertain large groups of friends.

Within an hour they closed the deal with George Airey and made plans to move to Ann Arbor in December. The city where so much of their lives had been shaped, where Don Lund had established himself as one of the premier college athletes of the mid-twentieth century, would now be their own hometown.

It didn't take long for the Lunds to start fixing up their new house. Betty divided the decorating chores. She would take charge of selecting colors and fabrics for the kitchen, the master bedroom, the large den, and the long hallway. Susan would furnish her own bedroom. That left Don with the garage and the big basement with its cement walls and concrete floor. No problem, he thought. The garage is fine; let it be. As for the basement, I'll just paint the floor light gray and the walls white. Then I'll pick up some used folding chairs and a couple of card tables to use for a bar. We'll be having parties in no time at all. I'll ask Moby where I can buy some paint.

"You're gonna do what?" Moby Benedict looked aghast as he stared at Don. The two of them were enjoying morning coffee at their desks in the baseball office. "Paint all four of the walls white? Your basement will look like an explosion in a dairy!"

Don laughed. "You have a better idea?"

"Sure," said Moby. "You could turn that space into a real party room, with a tile floor, paneling on the walls, a built-in bar, and so on. Then you can entertain in style."

Don thought about it for a moment. "That's a great idea, Moby. But I can't afford a contractor. I also don't have a clue about doing it myself. That's why I thought I'd just use paint."

"Well, maybe you could find somebody to give you a hand," Moby suggested. "Someone who'd be willing to help you do the work. And maybe bring in others who knew how to do things like lay tile."

Don looked hard at his assistant. "How about you?"

Moby grinned, "I thought you'd never ask."

So Moby arranged for others to help him turn Don's bare basement into a first-class entertainment room. Among his choices were assistant basketball coach Jim Skala and assistant football coach Jocko Nelson. Both men knew their way around hammers and saws.

Skala could have made a good career from just building things, but basketball was his first love. He was a good coach and an even better recruiter. In a few years Skala would find himself as the top assistant to head basketball coach Dave Strack. He would recruit some headline players for Michigan, including Oliver Darden and Cazzie Russell. Even though Strack, the decision-maker, would have the player-signing credit, it was Jim Skala who would make the contacts and close the deals. But now, in the winter of 1959, Jim Skala couldn't predict his future successes. He was simply a good guy and a good coach, who lent his abundant carpentry skills to Don Lund's basement project.

Jocko Nelson was known far and wide as a great recruiter. He was like the pied piper of Michigan football. Give him the name of a prospect and the next thing you saw was that same kid wearing a winged helmet. Of course, Moby Benedict was also a pretty good recruiter. Somebody told him that Jocko Nelson liked to build things. The next thing Don saw was Jocko, standing in his unfinished basement, covered in sawdust.

When the job was completed at the end of January, Don and Betty had a basement to be proud of. The entire floor was covered with brown speckled tile. The recreation room was separated from the furnace and laundry area by a floor-to-ceiling studded wall with an archway set in the middle of it.

Walnut paneling adorned all four walls. A built-in corner bar had been put together by Moby and Jocko. It was made of clear pine and stained to match the walls. The two of them built it without drawings or plans, which led them to question each other constantly. Don would sometimes referee their arguments. The end result was a Moby/Jocko bar, built so strong that the Lunds could hide in it to escape a tornado if the house fell down around them.

The room's most distinctive feature, however, was the hand-rail that framed the stairway leading up to the main floor. Jim Skala made it from baseball bats and balls, set together under a top rail, and shellacked to shine for the ages. The handrail was the first thing noticed by visitors who descended the stairs. It gave a powerful first impression, and it provided opening lines for countless conversations. This, of course, was exactly what the Lunds intended when they saw it built.

A few months later, when warm spring air started to wake up winter's dormant vegetation, another unusual incident occurred at 1565 Barrington Place. Don came home one Friday evening to find three huge piles of grass sod heaped in his driveway. His first thought was that Betty had ordered the delivery, since both front and back yards looked like an advertisement for topsoil. Don knew that turf would soon be required, not just for looks, but also for Susan and her friends at play. But he soon dismissed the idea of Betty ordering the sod; she would have told him first. He found Betty preparing dinner in the kitchen.

"What's with the sod in our driveway?"

"Oh, Honey," answered his wife, "this afternoon some workers from the university came by with a truckload of sod. They said they were replacing the turf in Michigan Stadium, and someone told them we might be able to use the old grass for our yard. So I thanked them and told them to leave it."

Don laughed, "You mean you didn't tell them to lay it? You just let them dump it on the driveway?"

Betty played along. "That's right. You'll just have to park the car at the curb for the rest of the year. Maybe next winter we can build a neighborhood ski slope!"

He grabbed her in a bear hug and swung her around. "Wow!" he yelled. "Free grass and it's from Michigan Stadium!"

She: "Hallowed ground!"

He: "Tradition-filled!"

She: "Stained with the blood of generations!"

He: "Big Ten blood!"

She: "Theirs, not ours!"

He: "Wisconsin red! Indiana crimson! Ohio State scarlet!"

She: "Michigan State green! Green?

He: "Whatever ..."

They both nearly collapsed in laughter.

The next morning all three Lunds spent the whole day laying their Michigan Stadium sod, occasionally helped by one or two neighbors. Later, they relaxed and admired their work. They were happy and honored that their new lawn came from such a special place. They would never find out who decided to deliver the sod, even though they asked around for several days afterward. Whoever it was gave the house at 1565 Barrington Place a special distinction: one of the only residential homes in the Ann Arbor area to have both front and back lawns covered with Michigan Stadium grass. That story would be told thousands of times as years went on, becoming one of the favorite neighborhood yarns of its day.

Yost Field House was the busiest building on campus during the school year. The library probably hosted more students per square yard, but its mission was to provide a quiet, sedentary place for academic preparation. Yost, on the other hand, was like a colony of ants with amplified sound, a three-ring circus without the animals and pretty girls. Three teams used the building for practice every day in the winter months. Two of them, the basketball and the track squads, also played their home games and meets in Yost. The baseball team held off-season practices there. So on most winter weekdays, a visitor to Yost could walk in and smell the fragrance of athletic energy coming from all distant corners of this steam-heated, closed-air cavern.

The continuous "thump, thump, thump" on the basketball floor would be interrupted at various times by a shrill whistle held in the teeth of a determined coach. Above on the track, pounding feet would follow the unmistakable "Bang!" of a starting gun, in a continuous loop of runners racing to beat the judgment of an ever-vigilant clock. And way over on the far end of this enormous open room, the constant "twark" of a round bat hitting a round baseball defined the action in the batting cages. And every few seconds, the distinctive "plock" of a catcher's mitt receiving a hard-thrown horsehide sphere broke into the other noises around it.

Yost in winter assaulted all three senses at the same time—sight, sound, and smell. The athletes in training, though, had an advantage over the visitor. They could also feel the bounce of the track and the boards of the court, and they could touch the basketballs, the baseballs, and the other items of their sports. At times they could taste their own sweat as it dripped down their faces. Yost Field House. All five senses at once, crammed into the conscious brain. To those who dwelled there, it was heaven.

Before each home basketball game, Yost became a study in organized chaos. Fans would line up outside, patiently waiting for the doors to open about an hour before the opening tipoff. Nobody had a reserved-seat ticket. All spectators would sit on temporary bleachers, which were arranged around the court from the floor up to the edge of the balcony, a distance of about twenty feet up at the back. Once the doors opened, the fans were supposed to walk in, hand their general admission tickets to an usher, and then, with genteel and orderly decorum, move on to occupy a seat anywhere in the bleachers.

Yeah, right.

What actually happened was that the fans ignored any line formation protocol. They formed in a huge crowd outside the classic oak doors of Yost Field House. They started assembling about three hours before game time. They stood quietly in the cold, bundled up in coats and scarves, each one shifting weight from one foot to the other to ward off chills. Male students who considered themselves macho enough to go without a hat would smoke cigarettes and perform the "red ear dance" with their buddies.

At last the doors would open, and the 500-plus crowd of people would surge slowly forward, like a herd of cattle to the warm barn, patiently flowing inside through a bottleneck where they handed over their tickets to the ushers. Once they were past the ticket takers, everyone stampeded for the bleachers. Some fans would walk fast, some would jog; some would break into a run for their favorite seats. There was little shouting or shoving. What counted were speed, direction, and determination. The phrase "Excuse me" mostly meant "Get out of my way," so people simply ignored it. Within ten minutes, all the good bleacher seats were taken. Within a half-hour, there was standing room only. By game time, Yost Field House was crammed with die-hard Michigan fans. The herd awaited its nourishment.

The basketball season was over by the end of February. Yost was then changed to allow for more convenient baseball training. The bleachers came down and were stored. The wood floor and its spring support system were lifted, revealing hard-packed dirt. Moby set up an infield and worked the players through their defensive fundamentals. Don installed a sand pit in the corner so the players could practice their slides. Ray Fisher came in as a volunteer to work with the pitchers, continuing what he started back in November.

Moby's mother, Rose Benedict, was the heroine of batting practice that winter. She designed and made a canvas cover that slipped over a track hurdle. When placed in front of the practice thrower, the canvas blocked grounders and other low hit balls from causing injury below the navel. Of course, she probably had a special incentive for inventing such an important safeguard. Her son, Moby, was the main batting practice pitcher.

And so, for at least two weeks into March, or until the weather outside turned mild enough for outdoor training, Yost Field House was a baseball practice building. The only other sound on weekdays was the pounding feet of the track team, as it raced on the lanes above, and the "Bang!" of that diabolical starting gun.

In the first week of April, Don and Moby took the team to the Seminole Spring Tournament in Tallahassee, Florida. They won only the first game against Duke, 6–2. They dropped all their remaining six games before returning to Ann Arbor. Then they lost their home opener against the University of Detroit, 9–3. The team would go on to compile a conference total of five wins against seven losses, placing them in the middle of the final standings. However, there were a lot of good players on this team, despite the win-loss record. Every starter had his moment of greatness: a mind-boggling catch that would end an inning, a blazing third strike that retired the side, or a base hit that drove in the winning run. Two players, Dave Brown and Bill Roman, were exceptional all season.

Dave Brown, a junior from Battle Creek, Michigan, had enough blast as a right-handed hitter to knock all 108 waxed red cotton double stitches, the leather cover, and three miles of twine off the ball. His average for the spring tournament was .395; for the season it was .333. In the spring tourney at Tallahassee, Dave smashed a screamer just over the pitcher's head, which landed safely in center field for a single. If the ball had been a few inches lower, it would have probably hit the pitcher in the head. Don looked across the dugout at Moby. Moby looked back with relief on his face. Then they both looked at the pitcher, whose face was the color of milk as he picked himself up from the dirt.

Finally, Don and Moby looked at Dave Brown as he stood comfortably on first base. Dave's face was a mask of indifference as he watched the pitcher get up. Moby walked over to Don.

"Brown is either one hell of an actor or his veins are filled with ice," said Moby.

Don looked back with a wry grin at his assistant. "Probably a little of both."

Later in the season the Wolverines were playing the Michigan State Spartans at home. The game turned out to be a hitting contest, with the Spartans smashing out a 17–12 win. Dave Brown caused a stir in one of the early innings when he slammed one over the shortstop's head. Or rather, it should have gone over the shortstop's head. Richard Golden, playing shortstop for the Spartans, jumped straight up like he was nine feet tall and caught it for the out. Then Golden picked the ball out of his glove and threw it to the first baseman. He took off his glove, looked carefully at his hand, and then called timeout. There were some anxious moments as the team doctor examined Golden's hand, but it wasn't injured. Golden stayed in the game, and Dave Brown stood in the dugout watching the entire scene, his face a mask of indifference. After the Wolverines won their next game against Michigan State, Don quipped to the squad that he was going to have Brown's bat registered as a lethal weapon. Dave's mask of indifference suddenly became the grin of the century.

Bill Roman was a left-handed hitting junior from Detroit's St. Cyril High School. Bill showed major league potential at first base constantly, turning in a .987 fielding average, while playing in every game. He also batted .331 for the season. Don was convinced that Bill could make it in the big leagues. Naturally, he preferred that Bill's team would be the Detroit Tigers.

The worst defeat in Don Lund's rookie year came at the hands of Notre Dame. They were playing at South Bend, Indiana, on April 30, 1959. Moby had remained in Ann Arbor to work with the freshman team. Michigan couldn't put anything together that day, and the Notre Dame bats connected like they were a homing device for the ball. Final score: Fighting Irish 21, Wolverines 0. Notre Dame's head coach Jake Kline was sympathetic but realistic. Between innings, he said the same thing Don would have if the situation had been reversed.

"Sorry, Don, but you know I can't tell them not to hit."

Don nodded and smiled through his teeth. "Let's just get the game over with."

And they finally did. Afterward, Don held a team meeting on the bus. He tried to console the players as best he could. Don told them stories of his own miseries as a player, including his going zero for ten in a 21-inning game as lead-off batter for the Mobile Bears. It appeared to help. When the bus arrived in South Bend, Don told the team to find some place to eat, and he waited as they sauntered off. Then he did something he had never done before. He went to the nearest bar and had a drink. A double whiskey. Straight up. Almost choked on it.

Betty would certainly understand. Don Lund had just become the only rookie head baseball coach in the history of NCAA Division 1-A to be shut out by more than twenty runs.

The next day, Michigan faced Indiana at Bloomington. The Hoosiers had a quality team, led by head coach Earnie Andres. In his customary pregame briefing, Don once again stressed the importance of putting games already played in the history file. "Today's the only game that counts," he told them. "I'd put your talent right next to anybody else and compare it with pride. Now go out there and play to win. Let 'em know we're Michigan!" The team took the field like a pack of hungry wolves. In a hard battle, the Wolverines pulled in the win, 7–5. After the game, Andres walked over to the Michigan dugout: "We just couldn't put your guys away today," he told Don, "and we had our chances out there. After yesterday at Notre Dame, I figured your team might be a little down." Don put his hand out to the Indiana coach and they shook. "Nice game, Earnie," he smiled. "See you around." Then he walked over to his celebrating team.

Michigan's 1959 baseball season ended on May 26 with a game against Eastern Michigan College at Ypsilanti, practically next door on the Michigan map. The Wolverines won it, 7–4. Don Lund's rookie coaching year was finally over. His team had given a good showing by finishing in the middle of the league, he reflected, even if some of their losses were brutal. They were good kids; they never gave up. He was proud of them all, and some of them would be back next year. Now it was time to head down the recruiting trail on Detroit's sandlots. He'd take Moby with him. He knew he could find and build a winning team at his alma mater. And he was determined to make that happen.

42
Recruiting the Champs

"How would you like to come over to my house next week and talk to my kids about baseball?"

It was Friday morning, June 19, 1959. The speaker was Phil Frakes, volunteer coach of a Detroit Sandlot League Class D team, sponsored by Lundquist Insurance. Like every other sandlot coach, Phil was fanatic about baseball and also totally committed to making the sport an ideal venue for teaching boys the many values of healthy competition. Unlike the other coaches, however, Phil had only limited experience in personally playing the game. He had a physical deformity called kyphosis, or an abnormal upward curvature of his spine, which prevented him from swinging the bat properly. But Phil Frakes easily overcame his physical handicap with an encyclopedic knowledge of the game and how it's played. He also had a good-humored approach to the kids, never sarcastic, always helpful. Like the other volunteer sandlot coaches, Phil Frakes also had a "real job." He worked for the sponsor. He was one of the top salesmen for Lundquist Insurance.

When Don Lund and Moby Benedict started visiting the Detroit sandlots, their first approach was to get to know the various coaches. They couldn't arbitrarily talk to the kids. NCAA recruiting rules were clear on that, but they could talk to the coaches. They decided that Don would approach the Class D coaches, who were working with high school boys, while Moby would concentrate on the American Legion teams for younger players. They both agreed to narrow their contacts to the coaches of the more successful teams, which probably had the better players.

Right away Don decided to focus on what could be the best Class D team this year: Lundquist Insurance, coached by Phil Frakes. He knew many of the players on the Lundquist team; he had seen most of them in his gym classes over the years. Floating nomadically around as a substitute teacher has its peculiar advantages. You get to meet a lot of kids.

It didn't take long before Don became friends with Phil Frakes. They talked frequently as Don visited the Northwestern Field diamonds and observed the Lundquist Insurance players. Then, on June 19, Phil asked him to go over to his house and talk to his players about baseball.

"I'd very much like to do that," said Don, "but I have to be careful about the NCAA rules. I can't compromise myself by trying to directly recruit the players as a group."

"Don't worry about that," answered Phil. "Just talk about baseball in general; about your experiences as a pro. Things will go just fine."

And they did. Don met the players at Phil's home. He spoke about his experiences on major and minor league teams. They asked him to talk about famous players he knew; they asked him what it was like to play in both major leagues. They wanted to know "inside stuff" about the Tigers. They also asked him about playing for Michigan. In his answer, he stressed that he wasn't there as a recruiter, so he wouldn't talk about playing for him at Michigan. He talked instead about the many traditions that were held sacred throughout all university athletics. He answered all their questions as thoroughly as he could. Then he thanked them and said good-bye.

Phil walked him out. "Thanks, Don," he said, "It's nice of you to do this, and it's also nice to see Michigan recruiting on the sandlots this year."

Don knew what Phil meant. He and Moby were almost a novelty as Michigan recruiters around the sandlots. Ray Fisher didn't recruit like this. To some extent, Ray followed the Oosterbann recruiting theory, which held quite simply that Michigan was its own magnet for players. Benny was known for saying things like, "After all, this is Michigan. The best athletes want to play right here." On the other hand, Ray just wasn't around Detroit during the summer months. For years, he coached in New England's Northern League. With Don and Moby haunting the Detroit sandlots, Michigan became a newly visible program to the kids and coaches from the area. It was good for the young players; it was bad for the other college recruiters. Don Lund and Moby Benedict were a compelling presence.

As he left Phil Frakes' house, Don hoped he'd be able to recruit some of those Lundquist players. He had his eyes on several of them. So did other college coaches, of course, like John Knobs of Michigan State and Jake Kline of Notre Dame. And then there was Charlie Maher from Western Michigan. Charlie did most of his recruiting in the western part of Michigan, but he also paid attention to Detroit. And Maher attracted attention because he was riding the crest of a winner's wave. His squads were the champs of the Mid-American Conference.

Therefore, Charlie was Don and Moby's chief recruiting rival. And Charlie also liked the Lundquist Insurance squad, for the same reason everybody else did. Simply put, the Lundquist players were better than their peers. It would turn out that Phil Frakes would take his 1959 team all the way through the sandlot tournaments, to the finals in Johnstown, Pennsylvania. Tournament rules allowed Frakes to take along a couple of extra players from other Detroit sandlot teams. Phil chose wisely. One of them was a kid named Willie Horton who could knock the cover off a ball. Without much of a struggle, Lundquist Insurance under Coach Phil Frakes won the 1959 National Sandlot Class D championship.

Don and Moby structured their recruiting to focus strictly on the Detroit sandlots. They knew who they wanted; they knew how to go after them within the constraints of NCAA rules. They also knew how to leverage the university and the desirability of a Michigan diploma. It didn't hurt that both of them were bona fide, degreed alumni who could speak from experience.

By midsummer, three of Lundquist's players were committed to the Wolverines. Outfielder Denny Spalla from Detroit Catholic Central was powerful at the plate. Second baseman Jim Steckley from Detroit Mackenzie would switch to the outfield at Michigan and be a clutch player who could produce when it counted. Lefty pitcher Fritz Fisher from Adrian High School would use his fastball artistry at Michigan to tame the best batters during the toughest games.

Two more Lundquist players, right at the top of Don's recruiting list, showed very high interest in Michigan but wouldn't commit. Shortstop Dick Honig, an all-around game breaker and Jim Steckley's keystone partner from Detroit Mackenzie, had tremendous baseball instincts. He was also a standout high school basketball player and a football star. Catcher Bill Freehan, from Bishop Barry High in St. Petersburg, Florida, was a top-of-the-line athlete, one of the most sought-after prep players in the country in football, baseball, and basketball. Bill nonetheless chose baseball as his preferred sport. He grew up in Royal Oak, Michigan, and had lots of family ties and friends there. So it was natural for him to come up to Michigan each summer to play in the Detroit sandlots, where he starred. Pro scouts built Freehan files; college coaches saw him in their dreams.

Both boys had narrowed their choices down to two colleges: Michigan in Ann Arbor and Western Michigan University in Kalamazoo. Don Lund and Charlie Maher. Michigan had sports tradition and national records, especially in football. It also had Lund, a superstar in their young minds. Their parents liked Lund. On the other hand, Western Michigan was a baseball power in the Mid-American Conference and had a winning coach in Charlie Maher. The big leagues watched Western closely, and the boys knew it.

By the beginning of August, both Freehan and Honig had decided to accept the scholarship offer from Western Michigan. Their main reason was Western's national baseball reputation. They imagined playing under the watchful eyes of big league scouts. They had just won a national sandlot championship; they could win a college one at Western. Surprisingly, they hadn't told Coach Lund of their decision. Nor had Coach Maher asked them to sign a letter of intent. These two issues would turn out to be fortuitous.

Late in August, Bill Freehan and Dick Honig were driving to Kalamazoo. They were on their way to freshman orientation at Western Michigan. With them was Patricia Wagner, another entering freshman and the daughter of close friends of the Honig family. As the trio drove west from Detroit to Kalamazoo on I-94, they passed by Ann Arbor and began reminiscing. The boys recalled their visits to Michigan's campus with coaches Lund and Benedict. Lund, they agreed, was pretty "low key" for a guy who was a living sports legend. He hadn't tried to "sell" them on the university. Over dinner, he simply said, "Here's what we have, here's what we offer; we'd like you to come here." Coach Benedict also pretty much said the same thing. It was almost as if these two coaches were so confident in what their programs could offer they didn't have to brag about them. They just laid it out and let the recruits make up their own minds.

That approach was a far cry from what they'd been through with other coaches. Except, they agreed, for Coach Charlie Maher at Western Michigan. He seemed like a pretty straight shooter. Besides, Western was the reigning MAC League champion. They'd won that title in seven of the last nine years. The boys had based their decision mainly on that record.

As they drove toward Kalamazoo, neither boy knew that Charlie Maher and Don Lund had a history together, and it wasn't very pleasant. Back in 1955, when Don was scouting for the Detroit Tigers, he went to a Western Michigan game at Hyames Field in Kalamazoo. He was interested in talking to a WMU outfielder named Bill Lajoie, a hot major league prospect. During the game, an opposing player hit into a sure double play, a slow grounder to Western Michigan's shortstop—except the first-base runner didn't slide into second, and the shortstop held onto the ball instead of possibly hitting the runner with his throw. The umpire ruled the runner safe. Maher protested in vain. After the game, Don walked up to Maher on the field, intending to ask his permission to talk to Bill Lajoie. He greeted the WMU coach. Maher shook Don's hand half-heartedly.

"What did you think of that incident at second base?" asked Maher.

Don replied with his usual candor. "Well, to be honest, I think your shortstop should have thrown the ball."

Maher glared at him and fairly screamed in his face, "You fucking big leaguers think you know it all, don't you?"

Don grabbed Maher by the neck in his left hand and lifted him up until the WMU coach was standing on his toes. Don raised his right fist, prepared to do some damage. Then he relaxed, let go of Maher's neck, and stepped away.

"Get out of here," shouted Maher. "There's no way I'm gonna let you talk to Lajoie. Get the hell out of here!"

Back in his room, Don called general manager John McHale at the Tigers' offices and explained the incident. McHale was sympathetic, nearly suggesting that Don should have decked the Western coach. Even so, Don immediately called Charlie Maher and apologized for his part in the incident. Charlie accepted his apology over the phone, but didn't offer any regrets for what he'd said. Later on, Don learned that Charlie was continuing to degrade him to others, but there was nothing he could do about that. He let it go and kept quiet about it.

Now, four years later, Lund was Michigan's coach. And when Michigan played against Western Michigan, Don and Charlie were merely civil to each other. The 1955 incident was never brought up, but it was clear there was no forgetting or forgiving. Don Lund and Charlie Maher would always be less than personal friends.

Neither Bill Freehan nor Dick Honig would hear about the incident between Lund and Maher, but as the two boys continued their drive toward Kalamazoo, they started to have second thoughts about their decision to play for Western Michigan. First, they began to seriously compare the two programs: both Michigan and Western Michigan had strong baseball traditions. Both schools had played in the national championship game. Michigan, under Coach Ray Fisher, beat Texas to win the 1953 title, 7–5. Western Michigan lost the 1955 final game to Wake Forest, 7–6, under Coach Maher. The boys agreed they would do well playing for either school.

Next, they considered the academic programs they'd face. Honig, an honor student, believed he'd do well at either school. He was right. Freehan thought that a person got as much out of education as he or she was willing to put into it. He was also right. To their young minds, the two schools were an academic toss-up.

Finally, they settled on a comparison between the two coaches, Maher and Lund. Maher was a tested, experienced, winning coach. Lund was brand new to college coaching but had coached in the big leagues. Maher was a powerful college coach who made all his decisions without much counsel. Lund sought out others' opinions, especially those of Moby Benedict and Ray Fisher. Maher was a power broker; Lund a power consulter, at least as these boys saw it. But one fact about Coach Lund finally settled their thinking: Lund was a three-sport letter winner. So were Bill Freehan and Dick Honig. As they saw it, Coach Lund was "one of them." By the time they reached Kalamazoo, their decision was made. They were going to play baseball for Don Lund.

They sought out Coach Maher right away and told him they had changed their minds. Maher wasn't happy, but he didn't

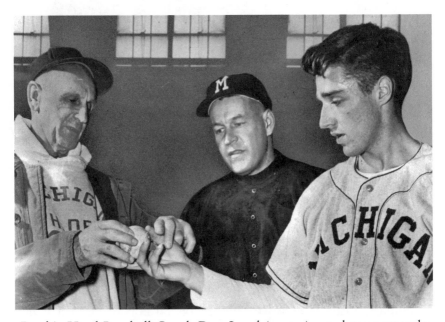

Rookie Head Baseball Coach Don Lund (*center*) watches as recently
retired Ray Fisher demonstrates proper grip to Wolverines'
pitcher Bob Stabrylla on January 23, 1959. Ray stayed on to help
Don by teaching the pitchers as an unpaid volunteer. He was
Don's mentor and confidant from 1942 until he passed away
in 1982 at the age of ninety-five. (*The Detroit News*)

give them a hard time. After all, neither had signed to accept
their scholarships. And so, like excited first graders setting out
for their first day of school, they hopped back in their car and
returned to Ann Arbor. Bill Freehan and Dick Honig, fresh from
the Detroit sandlots and Lundquist Insurance, would play for
the Michigan Wolverines. An astonished Don Lund felt like he
had won the Irish Sweepstakes.

That summer of 1959 saw Don and Moby as the dominant
recruiters around Detroit's sandlots. People from the coaches, to
the players, to the groundskeepers, to the parents, and even to the
everyday fans either knew them personally or knew about them.
Both of them had cut their baseball teeth on these very fields.
College coaches and pro scouts had watched them both play there
as standouts from Detroit Southeastern ten years apart. And Don
Lund had played in the big leagues. He played for the Tigers.
Lund was, to those who hung around Detroit's Northwestern

Field and the area's other sandlot parks, a local celebrity. People wanted to meet him, to talk with him, to seek his advice or his opinion. And sometimes, just to get his autograph.

Don was almost never alone on the sandlots. His naturally pleasant demeanor drew people to him, and his ability to remember names, faces, and personal facts about others kept them coming around. For the most part, Don was comfortable being the center of attention wherever he was on the sandlots. There were, however, a few drawbacks to his notability. They chiefly involved players whose skills were less than Don was looking for and who wanted a Michigan scholarship, or their parents who couldn't understand why Don wasn't looking hard enough at their talented youngster. Through it all, Don tried to let them down diplomatically. For the most part, he succeeded.

By the end of summer, Don and Moby had successfully recruited every player they wanted. In addition to the Lundquist Insurance recruits, these players represented the best high school baseball talent in and around Detroit. Right-handed fastballer Jim Bobel from University of Detroit High School, though only a junior, would be eligible to compete for the Wolverines in 1962. Second baseman Joe Jones from Southeastern High School—a Jungaleer grad—would be playing for two other Jungaleer grads. Outfielder Jim Newman from Lutheran East High School was one of the fastest kids on the sandlots. He would round out a formidable outfield for the Wolverines, along with Ed Hood and Denny Spalla. Right-handed pitcher Mike Joyce from Royal Oak Dondero was a clutch competitor and a gamer. Lots of college coaches were looking at Mike with a scholarship tender in one hand and a pen in the other. But fortunately for Don, Mike really wanted to go to Michigan. He would play a key role in the Wolverines' quest for a title.

By September 1959, all of Don and Moby's recruits from Detroit's sandlots were ensconced in freshman classes at Michigan. Ed Hood was fulfilling his scholarship requirement by playing non-competitive freshman football, which was fine with him, mainly because the new freshman coach was Don Dufek. Ed remembered listening on the radio to the 1951 Rose Bowl game, when Dufek starred and was named MVP. Ed was only ten years old at the time, but he never forgot that game or Dufek's stardom. As a result, Ed Hood would gladly have played for

Coach Dufek anytime, anywhere, even non-competitive freshman football. Soon after practice began, Ed and the other freshman footballers were joined by an extremely talented walk-on. It happened without fanfare.

Two weeks into the school year, Bill Freehan stopped by Don's office. "Hey, Coach," asked Bill, "how would you feel if I went out for football?"

Don smiled. "Remember what I told you this summer, Bill? Here at Michigan we won't restrict you from playing any other sport. You're free to go out for football."

So Bill went to Coach Dufek and was accepted on the freshman squad. His experience as a standout high school player, plus his stellar athletic ability, brought attention right away to his performance as an offensive end in the freshman scrimmages. The following spring, Don and athletic director Fritz Crisler were sitting together in the Michigan Stadium stands. They were watching the final varsity spring practice game.

Abruptly, Fritz pointed at Bill Freehan and said to Don, "Is that the kid you recruited for your team?"

"Yes," Don answered, "his name's Bill Freehan."

Fritz nodded and said, "I can't keep my eyes off him."

Neither could anybody else. Bill would go on to play football one year for the Wolverines, dominant in his position at offensive end. At the conclusion of the season, the coaches would honor Bill with the Meyer Morton Award, designated for the most improved player during spring football.

Don started his second season as head baseball coach in 1960 by moving the spring trip to Arizona. In addition to Moby, he took along a man named Morrie Moorawnick, a good friend and one of the best scorekeepers Don had ever met. His talent wasn't limited to one sport. Morrie was also the official scorekeeper for the Detroit Pistons basketball team. Morrie was so good he could keep score in three games at once without making a mistake. Thus, to a college recruiter roaming the sandlots, or a college coach attending a tournament, Morrie was priceless. On the Arizona trip, Don put Morrie in the same room with Moby Benedict, which led to one of the funniest incidents of the year.

Late one night, Morrie returned to the room he and Moby shared. Moby was already in his bed. Not wanting to disturb Moby, Morrie undressed in the dark and groped his way toward his own bed. Or so he thought. He pulled down the covers and jumped into bed, right beside his roommate. Moby practically defied gravity by executing a full-body, vertical jump about a foot in the air.

"Hey, Morrie, what are you doing?" shouted Moby, by now fully awake.

Morrie's feet hit the floor before Moby finished his question. He leaped toward his own bed, hoping to hit the mattress as he came down. Fortunately, he did. Moby started laughing. So did Morrie. It was quite some time before both men fell asleep. Later on this incident, known as the Moby/Morrie story, would become one of the most famous tales in the annals of Maize and Blue lore.

The team did well on the Arizona trip, winning eight and losing three, with eight of the returning regulars hitting at least .300 for the tournament. Everyone on the team, including the coaches, returned to Ann Arbor with high hopes for the season, but reality didn't match their visions.

The problem wasn't hitting. Michigan outscored their conference and non-conference opponents by eighty runs overall (242–162), but they just couldn't put enough wins together. Their non-conference record was eleven wins, six losses, and an eight-run tie with Western Michigan. Western also won the other game they played, 8–6. In addition, Notre Dame beat them 8–4. Rain prevented the rematch. These losses were tough to take, especially since four games on the schedule were rained out. Michigan split its conference games, posting seven wins and seven losses. Minnesota was the walk-away powerhouse of the season, easily winning the conference championship.

The problem wasn't fielding, either. Michigan placed third in league final fielding percentage, close behind Wisconsin and Michigan State. Joe Merullo had some problems at third base, but that's understandable. Joe had never played that position in competitive ball. He was a catcher. But Michigan's 1960 squad already had a catcher in senior Dick Syring. Syring, from Bay City, was a returning letterman with a strong bat. Coach Lund needed him in the lineup. He also needed the strong bat of Joe Merullo. And so, following what Jack Tighe did to him in Buffalo by pulling him from his natural outfield position and putting him at third base, Don Lund did the same to Merullo. Joe, at least, worked third base well enough for him to get by. Don, on the other hand, had booted everything that came his way, until an exasperated Jack Tighe moved him back to the Bison's outfield. Joe Merullo would play third base for the entire year.

At the end of the season, no one could ultimately figure out why the 1960 Wolverines baseball team didn't place higher in the league. They had some mega-talent players. Senior Bill Roman, from Detroit St. Cyril, was unquestionably the best first baseman among the Big 10 teams. He was also a first-class young man. He would sign with the Detroit Tigers when he graduated, only to lose out on their major league roster to another first baseman named Norm Cash. Then they attempted to trade him to the New York Mets. Bill wasn't about to let that happen, so he left pro ball for a lucrative career as an engineer. Bill Roman thus became a brilliant example of the benefits for those great athletes who get their college degree as a backup, in case their dreams of a pro career don't turn out the way they expect.

Other super talents on that team included Wilbert Franklin, who led the team with a final batting average of .347; Dave Brown, who often hit the clutch drive to keep the game alive; John Halstead, among the top eight leading hitters in the conference, and Ed Hood, who started every game as a sophomore and became a fixture who could get on base.

So what was the problem? It had to be the pitching. Michigan struggled on the mound all year, allowing teams that were behind in the early innings to catch up and finally pull ahead. As the team arrived home after the Arizona spring trip, hopes were high for a winning season. Pitching was a big part of those hopes. In the end, however, pitching was also the biggest part of their losses.

As the season progressed, the Lunds enjoyed themselves as an Ann Arbor family at 1565 Barrington Place. March, April, and May of 1960 showed the typical climate changes of the area: mud, created by warming temperatures and melting snow, gave way to all-day rains, which in turn brought blossoms, buds, and berries. The outdoor world transformed itself from gray skies and gloomy days to bright sunshine, emerald grass, and rainbows of flowers. At fourteen, Susan was a happy ninth grader at Slauson Junior High. Betty was making friends in the neighborhood and around the university. Don was busy with his team. Inky tried in vain to catch squirrels, rabbits, or birds who dared to invade his backyard domain. There were lots of memorable events at their home that spring, only one of which was a little scary.

The scary episode took place around the middle of April. Betty was home alone with Inky. She was standing at the kitchen sink when there was a knock at the side door. That could only happen if the garage door were left open. Inky began to bark, but Betty quieted him down and answered the knock.

Sure enough, the garage door was open. A man was standing at the side door. He was in his thirties, about 5-foot-10-inches and 180 pounds. He had dark hair and dark eyes. He wore a light blue uniform-type jacket, gray trousers, and a matching uniform cap with a black brim. He said he was from the gas company and needed to check the meter. Betty pointed him to the basement stairs and waited in the kitchen while the man went down to the basement. After about ten minutes, the man came back up. He stood at the side door and started to engage Betty in conversation about the neighbors. Betty became uncomfortable, and Inky must have sensed it; he began to growl at the man. The man looked at Inky. Then he looked at Betty. Then he said good-bye and left. Betty closed the garage door.

She was curious, so she called the gas company and asked if they had a meter reader in the neighborhood. They said no. Then she called Don and asked him if he had left the garage door open. He said no. She told him what happened. Don came right home. He drove around. There was no sign of the intruder. Betty had been very lucky, thanks to Inky. She remembered the man asking her to show him where the meter was located, and her telling him he couldn't miss it in the back room below. She shuddered at the thought of what might have happened had she gone with him down the stairs. But Inky, their friendly, gentle black poodle, had saved the day. He would always be the Lund family's four-legged "hero."

The Lunds frequently threw parties in their finished base-ment. Coaches and their families would get together for rousing games of ping-pong and sometimes cards. Only one guest took the ping-pong games too seriously and was not invited back. Those who frequently attended came there to unwind with people they knew and trusted. They lived in the world of highly visible athletic competition, with its abundant pressures and recognitions. Many of them were national figures, or at least local celebrities. Their public behavior was necessarily guarded. That's why parties with close friends, like those the Lunds threw, were highly valued by the well-known and carefully selected attendees. The alcohol flowed freely but not dangerously, the jokes were continuous but not too raucous. Nobody got drunk, nobody got mad. Everybody simply relaxed and had fun. Plus, they came back for more.

Don liked his lawn at 1565 Barrington Place, and that makes sense, because every blade of grass in it came from Michigan Stadium. He had played on that grass, wearing maize and blue number 33 and running around, over, and through people as hard as he could. So did many of his friends, including Bob Chappuis, Elroy Hirsch, and Bump Elliott. To him, that lawn was a treasure trove of memories. He tried to find out who made the decision to dump that storied grass on his driveway back when they had barely moved in, but people either didn't know, or they wouldn't tell him.

Even Fritz Crisler had no idea. But Fritz had a thought: maybe it was someone who wanted to be sure that Don would be motivated to cut his lawn and maintain his outdoor property. "Like Betty?" Fritz grinned.

Don grinned back, "You're kidding."

Without another word, Fritz kept grinning and walked away.

And so Don Lund's second year as Michigan's head baseball coach ended with great satisfaction for him. His team had consisted of fine young men, talented and full of spirit. They never gave up. He firmly believed that the final standings didn't reflect the true worth of his squad. He was proud of all of them, without reservation. As for 1961, his premier Detroit sandlot recruits had finished their freshman year and would compete for the Wolverines next year. With returning players, this would be a team he and Moby had personally found and recruited. Some of them, like the Lundquist Insurance players, knew what it was like to win a championship. So did Don and Moby. All it would take would be practice, hard work, and better luck than he dared to hope for. He could hardly wait to start.

43
Dialogue

"I'll tell you ... If I'd have caught that guy I'd still be serving prison time!"

Don was recalling the perilous 1960 incident, wherein Betty escaped trouble from an intruder in the house. Thanks to fierce growling by Inky, the family dog, the man fled. Don had driven around the neighborhood, trying to find the man, but wasn't successful.

"Well, I'm glad you didn't, Coach," I said, "I wouldn't like to interview you through steel bars." He laughed.

We were seated in his living room in front of the fireplace. Gas-fed yellow flames danced over the logs, daring us to stare at their constant, captivating routine. Outside, a few inches of snow had paid an overnight visit, making the entire condo complex look like a polar bear's fondest dream. The only marks disturbing this immaculate early-morning scene were tire tracks on the road. There were only two; they left the road at Don's driveway and were now resting underneath my car. To me, it was a beautiful Ann Arbor midwinter's day. To him, it was the middle of basketball and hockey seasons. Guess it just depends on one's perspective.

"You know, Inky was quite a dog," he mused. "Nobody ever trained him, but he acted like he was trained professionally. For instance, Inky would walk the lot line. We didn't have fences in the yards, but Inky wouldn't stray. It's like he knew where the boundary was."

"Pretty amazing," I added. "Lots of dogs need to be tied in their yards or fenced in."

"Well, Inky was a pretty amazing dog."

I changed the subject back to 1960. "After the 1960 season, what were some of the things you and Moby did to focus on the following year?"

The old coach thought for a minute, then said, "Well, the first thing, of course, was to go in every day to the sandlots. My players were there; at least those who lived in the Detroit area. As for Moby, he couldn't go in with me, even though he wanted to. Money was tight with him; he worked extra jobs that summer. But I drove to Detroit every day but Friday. They didn't play on Fridays."

"You'd watch your players. Would you coach them a little?"
DL: "Oh, no," he answered quickly. "That wasn't why I was there. I could talk to them, though. Since they were already at Michigan, I wasn't violating any NCAA rules by talking to them."

"What about recruiting?"
DL: "That was my year of being Mr. Lucky. I got three outstanding kids that summer. One of them I went after in a big way. The other two sort of came my way. That's what I mean by lucky."

"Tell me about them."
DL: "The one I went after was a pitcher, a right-hander who batted left named Jim Bobel." He pronounced the last name to rhyme with *hotel*. "Jim was from University of Detroit High School. He knew how to pitch, and that impressed me. He was playing in the sandlots for Modern Hard Chrome. He was friends with Joe Jones and Ed Hood. That was a plus."

"What about the other two?"
DL: "The first one was an infielder named Dave Campbell. Dave was from Sexton High in Lansing. The connection there is his dad, Bob Campbell. Bob played football and baseball for Michigan in the 1930s. Then he went on to become a successful high school coach. His son Dave practically grew up hearing maize and blue stories. They must have sunk in, even though he grew up near Michigan State, because Dave chose Michigan. His dad, naturally, wanted him to come here. As a matter of fact, it was Bob who introduced me to his son. I took one look at Dave in action and made my mind up right away. We brought him to Ann Arbor.

"The second one was Harvey Chapman, from Farmington High School near Detroit. By the time I met him on the sandlots, Harvey had already committed to Michigan as a football player. His dad, Ted Chapman, played here in football, hockey, and baseball. As a matter of fact, Ted's the one who introduced me to his son. Harvey played infield. He wanted to play baseball for us. It was as simple as that. Let me tell you, though, Harvey Chapman was one of the brightest kids I ever met. One time, as we were getting ready for a road trip, I gave Harvey his final exam in economics."

"You personally tested him?"
DL: "Well, I talked to his economics professor and explained that the team would be away during Harvey's final exam. I asked him if Harvey could take the test in advance. The professor was real nice about it. He trusted me to give Harvey the exam and monitor him as he took it. Harvey took the test in my office. I watched him. His pencil never stopped moving the whole time. Afterword, I took Harvey's exam back to the professor. Then we went on the road trip."

"Did Harvey pass his final?"
DL: "Did he pass? When we got back, the professor called me and said Harvey's test was number one in the whole class! I'll tell you, he was one smart kid."

"So you recruited three players who would be eligible for your 1962 team."
DL: "Well, there was a fourth. But I didn't meet him that summer. He came to me the following spring, when he was already a freshman here. He first approached Moby during the freshman baseball workouts. Then Moby had me talk to him."

"What happened?"
DL: "Well, his name was Ron Tate. Ron was from Akron, Ohio. He'd never played in the Detroit sandlots, so I really didn't know anything about him. Ron was recruited by a lot of colleges, by the way."

"And you never heard of him?" At this point, I saw the twinkle in his eye.

DL: "Nope," he grinned, "because Ron Tate was recruited in football!" He also played baseball in high school, but it was football they all wanted him for. Bump Elliott was the one who signed him, so he came here to play football. As it turned out, Ron preferred playing baseball."

"Where have I heard that before, as I sit here with the only guy who turned down the Chicago Bears' first round draft to sign with the Dodgers? Ron Tate was singing your song!"

DL: The old coach laughed, "You're probably right. Plus, Ron told me he was also going to switch his academic program from engineering to education. So I told him I would move his scholarship from football to baseball, providing I could square things with Bump, and also providing he got his academic program in order. Bump said okay, Ron changed his academics, and I moved his scholarship. Things worked out fine for everybody."

"Ron Tate must have looked pretty good to you, or you wouldn't be telling me all this."

DL: "Ron was a good player and a fine young man. And he just walked into the program. As I said, call me Mr. Lucky."

"Did any players on your team work that summer, besides playing baseball?"

DL: "Oh, sure. Some of them had good jobs, too. Dick Honig and a few of the others did quite well. You remember that 1960 was an election year? Well, these guys made fifteen dollars an hour setting up voting booths all over Detroit. That's a lot of money, even now."

"That brings up the subject of players working during the school year to make ends meet. You personally worked at Edwards Brothers, even though you played three major sports. Then, during the summer, you held all kinds of different jobs in your neighborhood. What about your players?"

DL: "A lot of them held part-time jobs. That's the only way they could make ends meet. I'll give you a couple of examples: Dick Honig worked at the railroad station as a baggage handler. He made a small wage, plus tips. One day some guy gave Dick a five-dollar tip; we all heard about that one.

"Joe Jones worked at a popular restaurant on State Street called The Parrot. Joe worked the cash register, which says a lot for his character. Most owners of cash-type businesses want themselves or a trusted relative at the register. Joe liked that job; he also liked the owner, a man named Charles Reinhart."

"You mean Charles Reinhart, the Ann Arbor realtor?"
DL: "That's right. After he sold The Parrot, Chuck Reinhart went into the real estate business. As you know, he became the leading realtor in town. Plus, Chuck did many good things for the community. Anyway, when he owned that restaurant Chuck employed lots of Michigan students, not only athletes. He was a good guy that way."

"Let's go back to what you did that summer of 1960. What else do you remember?"
DL: "Well, that's about it as far as my coaching job. We pretty much hung out in Ann Arbor. Betty planted flowers all around the yard. And we'd have visitors: my mom and dad; my sister Virginia and her husband Bill Lyle. We also drove into Detroit to visit them. We entertained friends quite a bit. I guess you could say we had a good time all summer."

"So now we head into the school year, 1960–61. What were some of your highlights?"
DL: "Let's just say I had only one highlight. I counted the days until I could meet my eligible players on the baseball field."

He was sitting up straight now. I could tell he'd been waiting for the chance to talk about his next two years as head baseball coach for the Wolverines. They were memorable years; they were extra-special years for everyone involved in that program.

44
Victors Valiant

"C'mon, Eddie, way to go! Let 'er rip!"

As Don yelled this from the dugout, Ed Hood, batting for the Wolverines in the first half of the eighth inning, listened real hard. He heard his coach's words like a tiger catching sound in the wind. He set himself for the pitch.

Michigan was playing the first game of a doubleheader against the University of Illinois in Urbana-Champaign. The 1961 baseball season was nearly finished. The Wolverines needed one more win to clinch the Big Ten title. Only the Fighting Illini stood in their way, and Michigan had to win one of these two games. So Coach Don Lund decided to gamble with his pitching schedule.

The team had two top-ranked starting pitchers, right-hander Mike Joyce and southpaw Fritz Fisher. Both had enjoyed peak-performance games this year. Mike had pitched on Fridays, Fritz on Saturdays. This rotation, first Mike and then Fritz, had paid off in victories, right down to the conference championship they were playing now. But now Don had reversed things. Fritz was pitching this game; Mike was slated to pitch the second one. Their reasoning was simple: Mike Joyce was considered the stronger of the two pitchers, even though the margin was pretty close. The Fighting Illini were tough. If Michigan lost the first game, they would need their strongest pitcher in the second. Besides, Mike had closed out the final two innings of yesterday's win against Purdue. Holding him back to pitch game two would give him additional rest. So it made good sense to make the rotation switch.

Illinois sent its best pitcher against Fritz Fisher in game one. That was smart strategy, since a win for them would put tremendous pressure on Michigan to go for broke in the second game, and possibly make enough mistakes to lose the championship. But Fisher wasn't about to let that happen. The left-hander seemed to get stronger as the game went on, and by the end of the seventh inning of a pitcher's duel, both teams were tied at one run. Then, at the beginning of the eighth inning, when Michigan's first batter had taken a pitch for one strike, Don noticed something that made his mind jump to attention. The Illinois catcher was giving away the signs! Don watched with a stone face as the catcher hung two fingers below his thighs. A curve ball. Sure enough, the curve came in and missed the outside corner. Right then, Don knew just what to do.

All season long, Don had been able to catch telltale signs from various pitchers or catchers. Sometimes a pitcher would hold the ball with his fingers pointing down before he started his motion—a sure fastball sign—or he'd betray a curve by holding the ball with his fingers turned in toward his leg. And sometimes a catcher would give away the pitch by either opening his legs far enough to expose his hands or by dropping his fingers below his thighs. Most of the time these "telltales" weren't noticed; they were too subtle to attract attention from most people. But not Don Lund.

Don had been picking up pitching signs since he was a kid watching the older guys play ball in his neighborhood. A flip of the glove, an extra-high leg kick; a facial expression, or anything nonverbal that changed the pitcher's regular throwing motion were all signs of a particular pitch about to be thrown. Don trained himself to watch for them so well over the years that not even a raised eyebrow escaped his notice.

It was natural, then, for Don to observe pitch telltales. This year he'd been doing it to Michigan's opponents since the first game of the season. He even developed a special code he'd shout from the dugout to let his batters know what pitch was about to be thrown. For a fastball it was "Let 'er rip!" For a curve ball he called "Wait for it!" And now, in the final innings of Michigan's most important game, the Illinois catcher was giving telltales. Michigan runners hugged second and third base. There were two outs. Right-handed batter Ed Hood stood at the plate with the count at two balls and one strike. Don watched the catcher hold down one finger. Fastball about to be delivered. He yelled to the batter, "C'mon, Eddie, way to go! Let 'er rip!"

Ed set himself for the fastball he knew was on the way. It came in toward the outside corner, just above his belt. He felt the sweet connection through his hands, then he charged across the plate and down the first-base line. He saw his line drive landing in deep left-center field, so he ran on to second base as the ball was thrown to the plate. As both Michigan runners scored, they were mobbed by their teammates to the tune of a collective groan from the Illinois fans. The Wolverines moved ahead, 3–1. Ed Hood stood nonchalantly on second base, outwardly showing no emotion except for a slight grin. Inside, he was the happiest and most excited college ballplayer in America.

The score held at 3–1 until the end, as Fritz Fisher shut down the Fighting Illini and the Illinois pitcher held back the Wolverines. Michigan was now the undisputed 1961 Big Ten Champion.

Naturally, that win made the second game of the Illinois doubleheader anticlimactic. Michigan's star right-hander, Mike Joyce, was therefore faced with pitching a game that meant nothing except a notation in the record books. As a result, Michigan turned off its spark against an Illinois team set on avenging their first game defeat. The Wolverines lost, 4–1, with a solo home run by Bill Freehan being the only Michigan score. Nevertheless, they had won the day. They ruled the Big Ten. They were "Victors Valiant"* indeed.

The Big Ten champs hosted the regional tournament in Ann Arbor. They lost out to Western Michigan in the final game, 4–3. Western Michigan went on to the national championship tournament in Omaha, Nebraska, which was ultimately won by the University of Southern California.

Two special awards were presented to cap out Michigan's 1961 season. First, Bill Freehan was named an NCAA All American. He was nominated by Indiana University coach Ernie Andres, who sat on the selection committee. After presenting Bill as a candidate, Ernie punctuated his speech: "If Freehan doesn't make it, I'll resign from this committee." That wasn't needed, though. Ernie Andres, one of the most respected college baseball coaches in America, was merely underscoring the committee's unanimous decision. Plus, they all knew that Ernie had first-hand

---

* From the chorus of the Michigan fight song, "The Victors" by Louis Elbel, 1898.

Bill Freehan knowledge: Bill was the unstoppable phenomenon in Michigan's rout of Indiana that year, 24–5.

The second award was given to Don by *Coach and Athlete Magazine*, the leading publication in America for high school and college coaches. The periodical named Don Lund "Midwest Baseball Coach of the Year." The editors sent him a suitable plaque; other coaches sent congratulatory letters.

A few days after the season, Don and Moby were settled into their office chairs, enjoying morning coffee.

"So Mike Joyce is talking with the White Sox," Moby remarked.

"Yes, and they're not the only ones after him," said Don. "I hate to see him go after only one year here. I think he could use some more seasoning. Mike's a good kid, however, with talent for the big leagues. If the White Sox sign him, their gain will be our loss. But I haven't heard anything about it. If we're lucky, we'll have him back next year."

Moby shot him a glance. "Speaking of losing players after only one year, what about Freehan? We knew we wouldn't be able to hang onto him."

"Bill's a special situation, Moby. Also a special guy, as you know. And you're right, he was being bombarded with offers. When his father, Ash, came to me and told me about the pressure Bill was under, I had to agree it was in Bill's best interest to turn pro."

Moby nodded, "What did the Tigers finally come up with?"

Don grinned as he counted off Freehan's offer particulars: "Over a hundred thousand dollars for signing, all of his tuition to finish his Michigan degree, the biggest Oldsmobile that General Motors makes, plus a few other things."

Moby's eyes widened. "A hundred and eighteen thousand? That's a fortune!"

"And he won't touch any of it," answered Don, "until he gets his degree. His dad made him promise that."

Moby sipped his coffee. "It's amazing how Bill had such an impact on us and on the Big Ten in only one year. Just think of his final .585 conference batting average. That record will never be broken."

"Probably not," Don agreed. "The nearest guy to him was Bart Kaufman from Indiana at .452. That's 133 percentage points, which compares to a horse winning the Kentucky Derby by 500 yards. It'll take some doing for another Big Ten player to break Bill's record."

"There's only one thing you ever had to teach Bill," Moby said.

Don knew exactly what Moby was thinking. He taught Bill to keep his emotions away from the public. Bill was such a fierce competitor. He hated it when he struck out, which was seldom, made a bad throw, which was rare, or hit for an out, which was less frequent than most other batters. Nevertheless, his emotions flared when his performance fell short of what he expected. Unfortunately for him, he showed his displeasure in front of the crowd. Fortunately for him, Don noticed it immediately, as early as the spring trip to Arizona. Michigan played their first game against the University of Wyoming. The Wolverines won, 4–1, but Freehan drew catcalls each time he openly displayed his frustration. After the game, Don took Bill aside and told him how bad he looked when he released his temper in front of the fans.

"Wait until you get inside the dugout," Don said, "then let it out if you need to. If you don't, the fans will ride you without mercy."

Bill took his coach's comments to heart. For the rest of the season, nobody in the stands ever saw Bill Freehan get mad. As a matter of fact, no one saw much of his temper at all, for by the time he reached the dugout, whatever had bothered him was mostly forgotten during the walk. Bill became a model of decorum on the field, never again deliberately causing fans to pick on him.

Don laughed at Moby's comment about there being only one thing he had to teach Freehan. "That," he answered, "and also maybe how to tag the runner charging in from third base without killing him." They both laughed.

Moby went on, "What's your favorite Bill Freehan story?"

"Probably the same one as yours," said Don.

They both exclaimed, "Michigan State!"

"I still can't believe how you talked John Kobs into playing that twenty-one game triple header," said Moby.

Don remembered it well. Their first scheduled game in Ann Arbor had been rained out, so when Michigan went to East Lansing for their normally scheduled doubleheader, Don asked MSU coach John Kobs if he'd consider playing three games in order to make up for the rainout. Kobs hesitated at first, but perhaps considering his home-field advantage, he agreed. Twenty-one innings later, Kobs regretted the decision. Michigan swept the Spartans, 5–1, 6–4, and 4–3. Bill Freehan not only caught the entire three games, he was a big-hit factor all day. Bill's effort was nothing less than superhuman.

Don responded, "That was something, all right. After the game, one of our fans came up to me and asked, 'How come you had Freehan catch all three games?'"

"What'd you say?" asked Moby.

Don's grinned. "I said, 'You want to win, don't you?'"

Moby laughed so hard the typewriters stopped in the secretaries' area. Everybody wondered what was so funny. Moby repeated Don's story in his own inimitable way. He broke everyone up, including Don. Moby was on a roll, so he continued.

"And to think it all started with spring practice in Arizona," he drawled. "I heard the whole team went to the dogs."

"Went to the dogs?" asked a staffer. "What's that about?"

Don knew that Moby was referring to the evening when a bunch of players followed Joe Murello to the greyhound track in Tucson. It was innocent fun, and they all had a good time, but Don didn't want to bring the subject up to the staff.

"Oh, that's just an expression," he answered, "not much else."

After things settled back down, the two coaches resumed their reverie. Moby broke the silence.

"Isn't it something that both of us were asked to coach a team this summer in South Dakota?"

Don allowed that it was. Their Big Ten Championship had drawn attention from officials who coordinated the various NCAA approved summer leagues for college baseball players. Don and Moby were contacted by a man named Gordon Stout, who represented the Basin League in South Dakota. The league consisted of teams in six towns in South Dakota: Pierre, Huron, Winner, Sturgis, Mitchell, and Rapid City. Pierre was the state capital and the other towns were the county seats. The teams played each other in a schedule that gave the players daily games, minus travel days between cities.

Players and coaches would travel between cities in cars loaned by townspeople or local car dealers. Two factors, therefore, closely paralleled the experiences of minor league baseball: daily games and team travel. The South Dakota Basin League, therefore, attracted top-level NCAA players and coaches from all over the country. In addition, major league franchises sponsored Basin League teams. They were eager to do this. Their scouts were able to see the best level of college players competing under minor-league conditions. It was a near-perfect college recruiting setup for the pros.

Stout asked Don to coach the team in Huron, known as the "Jims"; he wanted Moby to coach Winner's team, called the "Pheasants." Both squads were sponsored by the Philadelphia Phillies.

"How long did it take us to think about Gordon Stout's offer before we accepted it?" asked Moby.

Don caught his friend's eye. "Oh, about two, maybe three seconds!"

The next week Don, Betty, and Susan crammed a month's worth of luggage and an excited Inky into the family Pontiac and set out for Huron, South Dakota. It took them three days, after a brief stop in Minneapolis to see old friends, along with detours to sightsee along the way.

The family arrived in hot, dry, dusty Huron with all four windows rolled down to combat the car's lack of air conditioning. Don stopped for gas at the edge of town. He needed directions to their rental house. They also needed to refresh, and Inky had to take care of business. When Don stepped from the car, he gazed back at the road they'd travelled. It looked like a black ribbon someone had lowered carefully among the rocks and sand, stretching way out to a fine line that met the horizon. The rest of the landscape was barren. All he could see was miles, and miles, and miles of nothing but miles, and miles, and miles.

Huron, South Dakota, is found on the eastern side of the state, 123 miles northwest of Sioux Falls, off route 37. Its population in 1961 was around 10,000, scattered here and there around 8.3 square miles, nearly all of it dry land. The people were friendly, politically conservative, hard working, and clean-living. Of the numerous small rural-town advantages found there, three stood out as sources of local pride. First, the only woman U.S. senator ever elected by the state of South Dakota, Gladys Pyle, was born in Huron on October 4, 1890. Second, Huron is permanent home to the South Dakota State Fair. Third, Huron is a ring-necked pheasant paradise.

This third source of pride may be the biggest. The Chinese ring-necked pheasant is South Dakota's state bird. It's the only state-designated bird that serves dramatically at the heart of its state's economy. Each year, thousands of hunters trek into South Dakota to test their skills against it. They spend millions in pursuit of the sport. They don't care that the birds they hunt are raised for that purpose on local ranches and farms. Huron honors its state bird in a big way. Visible from almost anywhere in town is a gigantic statue titled "The World's Largest Ring-necked Pheasant."

The three Lunds had little knowledge of the proud history of Huron, South Dakota, as they meandered through town looking for the address of the house they had rented. They knew they would recognize it when they saw it, thanks to the glowing description given by the landlord. They soon found the street and began searching for the address.

"It's got to be close by," said Betty, "probably near that lot with the three-foot-high weeds."

"Could be close," agreed Don. "Now that you mention that lot with the tall weeds, it's funny how a nice, well-kept neighborhood like this would allow a property to grow wild like that."

Betty pointed toward the lot. "Look, dear, there's a house on it. I wonder if people actually live there."

Don was counting the address numbers. He stopped counting when they pulled up in front of the weeds. Only the roof of the house could be seen from the car. He let out a huge sigh as Betty and Susan turned toward him, wide-eyed and aghast.

"Oh, no!"

"Oh, yes," he answered with a frown. "People live here, all right, and it's us!"

The man who rented this property to them had lied about its pristine condition. But the Lunds were stuck with it; they had nowhere else to go. The three of them bravely moved in.

It took Don a week of cutting the near-jungle of weeds by hand with a scythe. Then another two days of cutting with a lawnmower. Huron town workers hauled away the cuttings. As for the house itself, lots of elbow grease from the three of them finally made it clean and livable. The Lunds had created a comfortable home, no thanks to the landlord. Meanwhile, Don had a baseball team to coach.

Before he left Ann Arbor, Don had asked four of his players to join him in South Dakota. Three of them, pitchers Fritz Fisher and Mike Joyce along with second baseman Joe Jones, were part of his Big Ten champions. The fourth one was a brand new Michigan transfer student named Dave Roebuck, but Roebuck wasn't new to Don. Dave was a right-handed pitcher from Bryan, Ohio, who first came to Don's attention during spring baseball in 1959.

Dr. Neil Levinson, a physician in Bryan who spent his undergraduate years at Michigan, called Don about this remarkable pitcher from Bryan High School. His name was David Roebuck. He was, according to the doctor, setting statewide high school records and winning every game he pitched. In 1959, Dave Roebuck set a single-season record of eleven wins for Bryan High School, which still stands. Acting on Dr. Levinson's words, Don called the Roebuck home and set up a meeting with Dave and his father, Victor. Then he proceeded to use his well-established Wolverines' network to find out as much as he could about young Dave Roebuck.

Lund learned three things that made him glad he'd set up the meeting: First, and most important, the young man had a superb character. He came from a good home that subscribed to high moral values. Those who knew him said Dave was a first-class kid. That was good. The same could be said about the rest of his players. Second, Dave Roebuck was at the top of his senior class academically, and Bryan High School was fully accredited. That was also good. Dave would make it in Ann Arbor. Third, Dave was a premier all-around athlete. In his four years at Bryan, he earned sixteen letters in football, basketball, baseball, and track. It was said, however, that he liked baseball as his college sport of choice. That was outstanding. Dave was singing Don's melody. His Michigan baseball scholarship was waiting for the signature.

The three of them had met at a restaurant in Adrian, Michigan, a small town about halfway between Bryan and Ann Arbor. Dave's father Victor, a minister, was a pleasant man with a clear, deep voice and a smile that lit up the room. To Don's dismay, though, Victor seemed skeptical about his son attending a large public school like Michigan. He favored Wheaton College in Illinois, where his daughters had gone. Wheaton, a small Christian college located about twenty-five miles west of Chicago, was known for its strong liberal arts curriculum. Plus, Wheaton had a successful baseball program coached by Lee Pfund, who also happened to be Don's friend.

Pfund had been a pitcher who signed with the Dodgers in 1945, the same year as Don. The two had remained friends over the years. When Dave mentioned Coach Pfund, Don explained how he knew the Wheaton coach from his early Dodgers days. He also said that if Dave would play anywhere else but Michigan, playing under Lee Pfund would be a good thing for him. Nevertheless, Don did his best to present his Michigan program to both father and son. When the meeting ended, Don sensed that Dave Roebuck was interested in coming to Ann Arbor, but his father preferred him to attend Wheaton. He believed Victor would prevail. He was right. In September, 1959, Dave enrolled as a freshman at Wheaton College.

One year later, near the end of his second season, Don took a call from Dave Roebuck. Dave wanted to transfer to Michigan, providing his scholarship would be available. He knew he'd have to wait one year to regain his NCAA eligibility and play in 1962, but that was OK with him. Don told him he could count on the scholarship, but he also asked Dave why he wanted to transfer. He'd heard the right-hander was having a good year.* Dave's answer was simple. Lee Pfund had been in a car accident at the start of the season and hadn't coached the team all year. Dave's main reason for playing at Wheaton was gone. He therefore wanted to play for Don Lund.

And so, at the end of Michigan's successful quest to rule the 1961 baseball Big Ten, Dave Roebuck became eligible to play for the 1962 Wolverines. Don asked him to come along in summer

---

* Dave Roebuck's season 1.41 ERA, set in 1960, stood as a Wheaton College record for twenty-seven years.

ball, so Dave Roebuck, Fritz Fisher, Mike Joyce, and Joe Jones left Ann Arbor for Huron, South Dakota. They would all play for Coach Don Lund and the Huron Jims of the Basin League.

The Huron team had its problems at the start of the season, winning only one and losing nine in the first ten games. Despite strong efforts by Don's Michigan men, plus some heads-up contributions by players from Notre Dame, Rutgers, and the University of Oregon, the squad just couldn't pull out a win.

Then Dave Roebuck came up with a sore right elbow. Don sent him back to Ann Arbor to work with Michigan's trainer Gus Crouch, with fervent hopes that Roebuck's arm would come around by next spring. Gus was the most thorough trainer Don had ever seen. Roebuck's right arm was in good hands.

With the departure of Roebuck, combined with the staggering win-loss record, Don took a hard look at his team. There was no question he needed stronger players, particularly in the infield. He first approached Jim Gallagher, the farm director of the sponsoring Philadelphia Phillies. He asked Gallagher if there were any Phillies' prospects he could bring out to South Dakota to play for his team. Gallagher said no. Don then asked if he could bring some of his own players out from Ann Arbor at the Phillies' expense. Gallagher said yes.

Don's first call went to Dick Honig. His plan was to shore up Huron's keystone with Honig at shortstop and his Michigan teammate Joe Jones at second base. The two of them could break the Jims out of its doldrums, he felt, like the proverbial dynamite blast that opens the mine. But Honig was committed to playing in a Canadian league. He couldn't join the Jims.

Then Don contacted his outfielder Jim Steckley. The team could use Steckley's power at the plate. Jim said yes.

Two more Michigan men agreed to join their coach: outfielder Denny Spalla and pitcher Jim Bobel. Don was sure these three would provoke the Jims into winning some games, and they did. The team galvanized and soared when Steckley, Spalla, and Bobel linked up. The Huron Jims went on to win twenty-one of their remaining thirty-two games. They finished the season just under the .500 mark, not bad for a squad that started out losing nine of their first ten games.

The Lunds arrived back in Ann Arbor just before the 1961–62 school year began. Susan at fifteen was entering her junior year at Ann Arbor High School. She was one of the youngest in her class, but she merged easily. Her knack for making large numbers of friends with little effort helped a lot. And Betty, ever the doting mom, referred to her gregarious daughter as "fifteen going on twenty-five." Susan could hardly wait to start classes.

As the university began fall classes, Don checked the enrollment lists to make sure his players were able to get the classes they needed. This procedure was part of his routine to help them with their academics. This time, however, he noticed a glaring omission. He couldn't find Mike Joyce on any of the class lists. He checked with his university network, and then with his usual "grapevine" contacts. Mike had not enrolled. He had signed with the Chicago White Sox.

Like other years, the 1961 autumn in Ann Arbor meant maize and blue football, with its traditions dating back eighty-two seasons. Football has always been the major revenue-producing sport at the University of Michigan. Football money kept the athletic department financially independent from the rest of campus. So everyone on Fritz Crisler's staff pitched in, and that included all the coaches and assistants.

Don followed his usual practice of many years and joined Bob Ufer in his radio booth. He did the spotting for Bob and gave expert commentaries when asked. Moby Benedict took charge of the game films, from preparation before games through the filming, to the distribution afterward. Moby always made sure that Wally Weber, the department's "ambassador" to the public, was the first to get a copy of the finished film. Weber used these films in his presentations to alumni groups and service clubs. He needed the latest information available. Moby guaranteed he got it.

Over the winter months Don, Moby, and Ray Fisher held informal practices with the players in Yost Field House. Yost held the basketball games each year. It also served as the winter practice stage for track and baseball. Pick any daytime from October through March, and you'd pick a time when Yost would be packed with men in organized chaos. Each group had its designated workout area. The basketball players had the most space, of course, since the court and bleachers took up two-thirds of the huge cavern. And to make sure the basketball team practiced undisturbed, someone had set up a ten-foot canvas wall around the court.

Only the basketball regulars thought the wall was a good idea. The rest of the Yost crowd looked upon it as an affront to the other loyal Michigan teams. One day, in a laughable gesture, hockey coach Al Renfrew demonstrated the preponderant feeling toward the wall. He mounted a ladder outside the wall and peered in. Those on the court looked up and saw Renfrew's face grinning at them. After that, there were no "off limits" areas to the athletes and others who trained in Yost Arena. Al Renfrew had made everyone's point.

During these Yost practices, Don would teach sliding and base running, Moby held forth with batting techniques, and Ray worked with the pitchers. Things got easier when basketball season ended. The court floor was removed and the bleachers were rolled back. Everyone had more room and the noise decreased.

Springtime at the Lund's Barrington Place home always brought out Betty's flowers, the Michigan Stadium green lawn, and parties. All of their friends had an open invitation to drop by at anytime, and many of them did just that, especially on weekends. One day head basketball coach Dave Strack, Don's longtime buddy, stopped by with his entire family in their huge station wagon. Dave had just completed his first Wolverine season after a one-year stint as head coach at the University of Idaho. He was back in Ann Arbor and on his way to what would become a remarkable career.

With Dave on this visit were his wife Ruth Ann and their five children: Sally, David, Ruthie, Amy, and Julie. Julie Strack and Susan Lund attended Ann Arbor High School together and were close friends. After a cordial visit, the Stracks hopped in their car and took off. Don and Betty relaxed in the family room. A half-hour later the doorbell rang. Dave was back, asking for the whereabouts of his daughter Julie. Betty immediately looked in Susan's room. There was Julie, reading quietly with Susan. The Stracks had left for home without her! Dave's concern changed to relief, then to laughter. He knew Don had him and would never let him forget it. The 1962 "phantom daughter" story was as solidly planted as Betty's flowers.

As April drew near, Don could hardly wait for baseball season. He knew he had a very special squad of young men. He wanted like anything to mold them into a winning unit, and he was more than ready. After all, he personally had recruited most of them, so he knew their strengths and weaknesses. With this team, he told somebody, the sky's the limit. The person replied that he might not be right about that. Last year the Soviets put a guy in space. He decided to never again use that phrase to describe potential. After all, potential never won a ballgame. Hard work and smart preparation did. He was anxious to get started.

45

National Champions!

"Guys, just remember this: Good defense and good pitching will win you a lot of games."

Don looked at his assembled team, trying to catch the eyes of every player as he said these words. He knew their individual strengths and weaknesses. In fact, he knew them so well he could accurately predict how each one would react to different game situations. After all, he had watched most of them play since they were kids in high school. He saw them as winners, either in their schools or on the sandlots. Those who had played for Lundquist Insurance had helped that team win a national championship three times. The others had won several times in their respective leagues. They were winners, all right, and they had won with good defense and good pitching.

The team would miss Freehan's bat this year. None of these players would lead the Big Ten in hitting. But they were scrappy; they were motivated. No pitcher they'd face would intimidate them.

So let's just see what happens, he thought, as he followed them out to the practice field. Once there, Don placed himself next to the batting cage and watched everybody go through the drills under Moby's enthusiastic orders. He let his thoughts meander randomly through the squad, focusing on each of his young players.

He watched as Ed Hood gathered in a fly ball and returned it to the infield in a single motion. One of three seniors on the team, Ed had been elected team captain. His natural leadership style, combined with an upbeat attitude, went a long way with his fellow players. Plus, Ed was completely unselfish. As badly as he wanted to be a part of all the action on the field, he respected the talents of his fellow players, and knew he might not play in every game. That was okay with him. He put the team first. He was their unanimous choice for captain.

Don took in his group of pitchers as they worked under the watchful care of Ray Fisher. John Kerr was the most improved man on the pitching rotation. A walk-on as a freshman, John was a left-hander from Royal Oak High School. He had good control and a natural gift for changing speed on the ball with the same motion. John didn't throw hard; he just got it over the plate. During the past two seasons, though, John gave up a lot of hits. Many of them were long drives; some of them were home runs. Most of them were solid hits, and Ray Fisher had decided to do something about it.

Ray taught John Kerr to throw a screwball, by turning his hand opposite the way he would throw a curve. Instead of turning the bottom of his left hand to the right for the curve, John learned to turn the top of it to the right for the screwball. His curve broke to the right; his screwball broke to the left. And fortunately for John, his control stayed sharp. Coming into this 1962 season, John Kerr was now a pitcher with a formidable repertoire. And since he didn't throw hard, he had lots of staying power. He wouldn't wear out. Plus, he had one other thing going for him: John Kerr was a good hitter.

Fritz Fisher, another left-hander, was nearly the opposite of John Kerr. Fritz threw a blazing fastball. Where Kerr's pitch might bounce off a pane of glass, Fisher's would break the entire window and put a hole through the wall inside. But Fritz had some control problems. He walked more than his share of batters. Nevertheless, he also had more than his share of strikeouts. In a word, Fritz Fisher on the mound was intense, which was exactly opposite his persona off the field. In everyday life, Fritz showed an easy-to-like, carefree spirit that made him lots of friends. Meet him on campus and he was your buddy. But face him at the plate with a bat in your hands and he'd blow you away.

Right-hander Jim Bobel was a smart pitcher. He didn't throw hard; he just threw strikes. Jim also had extreme concentration. His eyes seemed to bore right through the batter like a steel drill, taking away whatever edge of confidence the guy thought he brought to the plate. When the ball worked for him, Jim Bobel was all smoke and mirrors. The batter didn't have a chance.

Dave Roebuck, the other right-handed starter, was a strong, disciplined, natural athlete. He also threw one of the sharpest curveballs Don had seen in a college player. And this year, working with Ray Fisher, Dave had learned when to throw it. Off the mound, Dave was one of the hardest-working academic students on the team. On the mound, he gave everything he had into every pitch. Added to that, he could hit with confidence. For sure, no coach could ever want more from one of his players than that which Don received from Dave Roebuck. The kid from Bryan, Ohio, had come of age.

Don noted his relief pitchers. Franz Neubrecht, a right-handed senior from Berkley High School, could throw hard. He also had control problems, but Franz took his pitching seriously, even though his motions were more "mechanical" than intuitive. Don would definitely use him against lesser opponents this year, to give his starters some rest. He had no doubts about Franz in the relief role. The other relievers were junior John Lengemann, a right-hander from Royal Oak, and sophomore Bob Dunston, a southpaw from Flint Southwestern.

Don turned his attention toward his two catchers as they warmed up the pitching staff. He smiled as he watched senior Joe Merullo. With Freehan gone, Joe would finally get away from playing third base, a position relegated to him because of his bat, to behind the plate where he belonged. His teammates saw him as a street-wise, free spirit from New England, who could back up his talk with a rifle arm. Joe Merullo was Don's catcher number one.

Catcher number two was junior Ron Lauterbach, from Chaminade High School in Dayton, Ohio. Ron was also a substitute tackle on the football team, seemingly destined to play a secondary role in both of his sports. He knew that, unless something happened to Merullo, he wasn't too likely to see game action. But that didn't seem to bother him. He was one of the most entertaining guys on the squad, never letting anything bother him personally, and always cracking jokes. But none of that meant a thing to Don or Moby. What mattered most to them were Ron's quick mind and his dead-on perception about things around him. Early on, Don had picked Ron to be his third-base coach. In his own way, Ron Lauterbach would prove indispensible to the team.

Don next studied his infielders who were drilling their defensive plays. He counted the seconds as shortstop Dick Honig grabbed a grounder on one hop, flipped it to second baseman Joe Jones, who stepped on the bag and tossed a perfect throw to first baseman Dave Campbell. Under four seconds—a sure double play in game action. Pick the adjectives, Don thought— peppy, lively, dynamic—they all fit, and then some. Maybe "explosive" was more appropriate for the way these infielders, including third baseman Harvey Chapman, responded to a one-hop ground ball. One of them set the charge; another ignited the fuse; and the third one (Bam!) put it away. Two outs in less than four seconds. These guys were as good as or better than any other college infield he could name.

Don's eyes went around from one to another. Honig led them in sheer energy. Jones was a high-speed vacuum cleaner. Jones was also ideal for lead-off hitter; he had a knack for finding ways to get on base. Campbell could run like that cartoon devil from Tasmania. He also had upper-deck blasting power. Harvey Chapman defined the term *heads-up*. Few runners could beat out a grounder hit to him, because his quick charge would turn it into a one-hopper, and his throw to first base, from most any angle of balance, would pop Dave Campbell's glove like a cannonball. Harvey could also run the bases like a guy who owned them. He was a pitcher's bad dream.

Don walked down the line toward third base. Along the way, he picked up a bag of balls and a fungo bat. He also asked one of the student assistants to grab a glove and help him retrieve the balls. The outfielders had been playing catch in center field. Now they turned toward him as he stood outside the foul line and set up to hit fungos. As he began to launch the balls, he sorted his thoughts about each one of his outfielders.

Jim Steckley was a coach's blessing. An infielder from the time he was a grade-schooler in Detroit, he wasn't used to roaming the broad grass around the fences. Don had switched him to the outfield last summer in South Dakota. He counted heavily on Steckley's natural athletic talent, as well as his sense of the game itself, to make the transition a smooth one. The gamble paid off. Jim had no trouble getting under the ball and making the catch. He certainly was fast enough. He also satisfied Don's initial concern about him having only an "infield arm." Steckley could throw the ball from the boonies with runner-holding power. He also took to the position change without complaint. As a matter of fact, Jim Steckley never said a bad word about anything or anybody. That's one main reason he was a team favorite.

Don held up for a moment and watched Jim Newman make an effortless catch and a return throw with poise that could only describe a superbly gifted athlete. Newman was that special all-around player, who could play any position on the field with style. He would therefore be the Wolverines' utility man this year. Don grinned to himself as he recalled Moby's comment when he talked to his assistant coach about Newman's versatility. He told Moby he believed Jim Newman could fill in for anybody on the team.

"Maybe even me," Moby had said with a huge smile.

"Well, maybe," Don answered. He paused for effect as Moby's smile faded. "... but I'd never consider letting Jim Newman build a bar in my basement!"

Moby had laughed like crazy as he threw his cap at his boss.

Yanked out of his reverie by the need to keep hitting fungos to his outfielders, Don swung too quickly and drove a line shot far deeper than he had intended. His center fielder, Denny Spalla, sprinted toward the ball, reached up, and caught it over his left shoulder on the run. Then, in almost the same motion, he pivoted on his right foot and made a one-hop left-handed throw back to the student assistant helping Don. Picture perfect, thought Don. Denny just doesn't make mistakes. He's a steady, no-fooling, reliable outfielder, good for the team, good for Michigan.

Don's next fungo sailed high and started its descent toward Ron Tate, who signaled for the catch and made an easy one-handed grab. Ron was not only a good fielder, thought Don, he was also a long-ball threat every time he stood at the plate. What's more, nothing seemed to rattle him. Ron's easy-going demeanor made him well liked by his teammates. But what would matter most to them, Don knew, would be his ability to come through with his bat when it counted. Ron Tate would make some noise this year.

Don's last fungo was hauled in by Dick Post. Dick was from Essexville, Michigan, a transfer from Bay City Junior College. He wore glasses and tended to squint while at the plate, giving pitchers a false impression that something was wrong with his eyes. That was their mistake. Dick would take full advantage of the misconception, sometimes drilling it right back through the mound. Don knew that Dick Post would be a valuable utility player, one who would be an asset to the team throughout the year.

The season began with a spring trip to Arizona, the third year in a row for the Wolverines. Don liked the dry Arizona climate over the humid, and sometimes rainy, Florida weather. On the other hand, he didn't particularly like the reception they annually received when they arrived in Tucson at the University of Arizona.

Arizona's coach, Frank Sancet, wouldn't let the Michigan team practice on the Arizona Stadium infield. They had to work out in center field. Moreover, Don and his players had to sleep underneath the stands on mattresses laid out on the cement floor. The players actually liked this less-than-dignified cement-floor camping. It reminded them of the loft they all shared each fall on the third floor of their Ann Arbor dorm, before classes began and before they were each assigned to rooms.

Don, however, didn't like this "roughing it" arrangement at all. The team's almost cavalier spirit over being housed like cattle in a barn bothered him. He wanted his players on edge, not comfortable. Besides, he felt cheated by not being allowed to practice on the diamond where they would soon compete against the nationally ranked Arizona Wildcats. But he wouldn't complain. After all, the Wolverines had been invited to Tucson and were guests of the Wildcats. The smart thing was to go along with whatever their hosts arranged. He decided to keep quiet.

Michigan lost all three games in Arizona Stadium. Don made no excuses, although he could have complained about lots of things, including the general disrespect he felt was given to his team. Besides, he didn't want to use his temper to destroy any ambience of the visit. The players were thoroughly enjoying Tucson, especially at night, and especially with the help of catcher Joe Merullo.

For the second year, Joe spirited his fellow players out from their stadium sleeping cavern to Greyhound Park for some dog racing fun. "This team is goin' to the dogs," someone would shout, and off they'd go with Joe in the lead. Dog racing was big in Tuscon, especially during the winter months. Tourist dollars from the northern United States and Canada kept the turnstiles spinning every night. So naturally, some of the best racing kennels in the country brought their dogs to the Tuscon track. Racing competition on the track was fierce. Betting in the stands was wild. Some people won; most people lost. Then there were others, like certain guys from that university in Ann Arbor, who had a "sure thing" like Joe Merullo. Because Joe had his own "sure thing": his dad, back home in Revere, Massachusetts.

Joe's dad was a likable, hard-working man who loved the sport of dog racing. He studied the dogs and their records. He knew which dogs ran extremely well or extremely poorly under any kind of distances and track conditions. He didn't wager much, but when he did he usually won. He was, therefore, the perfect source for his son and Joe's fellow Wolverines at the dog track in Tuscon. Joe never promised anything. He'd merely phone his father before a race and get a recommendation, and then he'd pass it on to his teammates. Call it fate at its best, or call it just plain good luck, but by the end of the last race, all of Joe's teammates who'd bet that night according to his dad's recommendations left with more money than they brought. Joe was the prince those nights; his dad was the far-away king.

And so, with marvelous memories of good times for the players and with a sigh of relief from their head coach, the Michigan Wolverines said goodbye to Tucson. Their next stop was Tempe, and seven games against the Sun Devils of Arizona State University.

The welcome Don and his Michigan men received at Arizona State was the exact opposite from the one they got in Tucson. It was like someone suddenly switched on the light. Sun Devils coach Bobby Winkles was one of the nicest guys Don had met in his NCAA coaching travels. Winkles couldn't do enough for his Ann Arbor visitors. He placed them in a first-class Tempe Hotel. He made sure they had plenty of good food. And he not only let them practice on the ASU game diamond, he made sure the entire field was kept maintained to the highest standards.

Bobby would say, "Whatever you want done, just let me know." And he kept his word. Don and Bobby got along famously. The two would frequently head out for a beer after a game was over and just sit around swapping stories. It didn't take long for them to find lots of things they both had in common, and one of the more interesting of these was George Kell, the renowned Detroit Tigers third baseman of the 1950s.

Currently, Kell was broadcasting play-by-play for the Tigers on one of Detroit's TV stations. And he was good enough to keep his audience interested. He'd do more than merely describe what people could see for themselves on the screen. He'd put in anecdotes about players, teams, umpires, the crowd, and other happenings, all gleaned from his own experiences as a big leaguer. Many fans considered a TV broadcast of any baseball game to be quite boring. The black-and-white picture showed mostly the view from above and behind home plate, only expanding to a broader scope when the camera followed the ball around the field. Thus the viewer could only stare at the limited scene. Even the crowd noise was subdued and distant. The announcer, then, had to make things interesting. And George Kell, with sheer force of his experience and credibility, was one of the most interesting baseball commentators in the business.

Don Lund and Bobby Winkles found their mutual connection to Kell because the Arizona State coach was from Arkansas. As a matter of fact, Bobby went to school in Swifton and George Kell was born and raised in Swifton. Bobby said Kell was his teacher in the seventh, eighth, and ninth grades. That made sense to Don. Many professional ballplayers taught school in the off-season, including him. George Kell would be no exception, especially in Swifton, where he was a hometown hero. Bobby couldn't say enough good things about his former teacher, whom he considered his mentor. When Don told him that he and George were road roommates when they both played for the Tigers, Bobby appreciated the connection. And so, the remarkable George Kell, a mutual friend, became the link for Don Lund and Bobby Winkles becoming lifelong friends.

* * *

At the start of the season, Don made a lineup change. He put Harvey Chapman at third base, moved Joe Merullo to the catcher's slot, named Dave Campbell the first baseman, and Dick Honig became the shortstop. Moby agreed with the change, stating that this would ensure the best possible defense. He couldn't have been more right.

Out of the 24 regular season games, the Wolverines won 19, scoring a total of 166 runs while allowing their opponents only 85. Moreover, in 12 of their wins, Michigan's opponents only scored 2 runs or less. Few other teams in the NCAA would have such a strong a defensive record that year. Only three teams beat them in1962. They lost their Big Ten opener to Illinois in a remarkable pitching contest, 0–1. The University of Detroit and Wisconsin were the other two teams, each winning both of their scheduled games.

It was the second loss to Wisconsin that cost Michigan the Big Ten Championship. The Wolverines needed to win one game of the doubleheader in Madison in order to move ahead of Illinois and retain the title they had won last year, but the Badgers were tough and won the first game, 6–3. The second game, however, was a battle down to the last inning, with both teams tied at five runs. In the last half of the ninth inning, Wisconsin's left fielder, Pat Richter, strode to the plate. Don watched him. Richter was a dangerous hitter; a three-sport athlete who fairly rippled with power. He looked relaxed and confident. Don saw trouble. He decided to change pitchers and brought in Fritz Fisher to wrap it up, not realizing he should instruct Fisher to jam Richter or otherwise not give him anything good to hit. But he didn't say anything to Fritz, and Fritz proceeded to throw with his usual intensity. Richter swung at a blazing fastball and hit the longest home run Don had ever seen in college ball. Good-bye Big Ten title; hello second place to Illinois.

Back in Ann Arbor, Don made another mistake that might have cost his Wolverines any chance for a play-off berth. He took their next game, a non-conference match against Wayne State in Detroit, too lightly. He assumed there was no way they should lose to Wayne State; the Tartars weren't having that good a season. Besides, he thought, they just don't have the talent we have. Even Moby, whose fierce and competitive passion was renowned, seemed unenthusiastic about the game.

Consequently, Don didn't prepare the team as thoroughly as he usually did. He didn't extol the possibilities of defeat against a tough opponent, because he didn't think the Tartars were tough. So away they went to Detroit, everyone from the head coach to the seldom-used utility player thinking they were merely on a mopping-up mission, much like Custer sauntering off to the Little

Big Horn. They didn't change that thinking until the middle of the fourth inning, when they woke up to find themselves behind four runs and being rapidly shut down. Good-bye play-offs; hello to losing.

Don changed pitchers and began to shout encouragement to his players. Moby started acting like their lives were on the line, which was true from the strict sense of the rest of the season. The players responded like a racehorse in the stretch when its jockey applies the whip. The final score was Michigan 10, Wayne State 7. Only one other school had scored that many runs against Don's team that season. The Michigan State Spartans had forced the Wolverines to beat them, 16–13, in the first game of a three-game series. In the next two games combined, the Spartans only scored one run as the Wolverines had blown them away.

The season ended with three games against Western Michigan, all of which Michigan won with ease. Don learned two valuable lessons from the Wayne State game: never under-prepare for a game, no matter who you're playing, and always try to schedule the last game against a Big Ten team. There's not much to be gained, he believed, by non-conference competition after the Big Ten season is finished.

Their second-place conference finish earned Don's Wolverines an invitation to the NCAA District IV Tournament. It would be held at Western Michigan University's historic Hyames Field. Hyames was considered to be one of the best college baseball venues in the country. One measure of its claim to renown was that Hyames Field hosted the first College World Series in 1947, between the University of California and Yale, which California won. The game itself was significant, being the first of its kind. More than that, however, was the fact that each team had a player who was destined for fame. The winning pitcher for Cal was Jackie Jensen, who would go on to win many major league awards, including American League MVP. The first baseman for Yale was a WWII hero named George H.W. Bush, who would become the forty-first president of the United States. Hyames Field deserved its historic fame.

There were four schools represented in the District IV double-elimination tourney: Michigan, Big Ten champs Illinois, University of Detroit, and Western Michigan. Both U of D and Illinois had beaten the Wolverines during the regular season.

Western was playing on its home field. Don prepared his team to climb the mountain.

The mountain became an even steeper cliff when Western beat the Wolverines in the first game, 6–5. Michigan had to win the rest of its games to stay in the tournament. Their second game against U of D, which they won 12–6, was payback for losing two games to them in the season. So was their third game against the Fighting Illini. Michigan sent them packing, 5–1, aided by the superb pitching of southpaw John Kerr. That left the final tournament game, to be played between the Wolverines and the Western Michigan Broncos. The game would begin after a twenty-minute rest period.

What followed was one of the most remarkable achievements in the history of Michigan baseball.

Left-hander John Kerr had shown that his game was on, as he allowed Illinois only one run. While watching that game, Don recalled how John had come up with a slight change in his motion in midseason, which allowed him to throw while not wasting unnecessary movement and energy. Don remembered watching him hurl one of the Michigan State victories; John hardly broke a sweat. Today, as he watched John mow down the Illinois lineup, Don had marveled at his southpaw's stamina.

As soon as he ran off the field, John Kerr approached Don with a big smile on his face. The two shook hands.

"Nice going, John," said his coach. "You looked good."

Kerr's face turned serious. "Coach, I feel strong. I'd like to pitch the Western game. If you'll let me, I will."

Don was stunned. Sure, John looked sturdy out there and he seemed eager and confident. He was also the kind of kid who'd always acted sensibly around the team. John Kerr was solid. He wouldn't push himself if he thought it would hurt the team.

"Are you sure about this, John?"

"Yes, Coach, I am."

That was good enough for Don. "OK. As long as you finish hard, you can pitch."

John Kerr did pitch hard through nine innings, allowing the Broncos only 5 hits. The score was tied at two.

Before the start of the tenth, Moby grinned as he asked Don, "You thinking of replacing John?"

Don didn't look at Moby as he watched his team take the field and answered, "Not a chance."

John Kerr retired Western in the first half of the tenth inning. Then he came to bat with one out and a teammate on base. Eager to win the game, he slapped the first pitch for a long fly ball. His teammate scored the winning run. John Kerr's sacrifice fly had won the tournament. That, plus nineteen innings of outstanding pitching in one day, made him legendary. John Kerr became Superman in maize and blue!

When Don got back to his room, there was a telegram waiting for him from Fritz Crisler:

Don, congratulations to you and your team. Stop Buy John Kerr the biggest steak in town. Stop Slap some oil on his arm and send him in there tomorrow stop

Fritz.

The "tomorrow" Fritz referred was the game for the regional championship, once again to be played at Hyames Field between the Wolverines and Western Michigan. Again, it turned out to be a ten-inning game, with a tie score of 6 after nine. And again it was the pitcher, this time Jim Bobel, who brought home the winning run. Jim Newman's single allowed Bobel to scramble in for the score. The Michigan Wolverines were regional champions. They would soon be on their way to the College World Series in Omaha, Nebraska.

The day after he returned from Kalamazoo, Don spent much of his time in the office talking with reporters from Ann Arbor, Detroit, Toledo, and other places. He also took congratulatory calls from friends and fellow coaches who wished the team well in Omaha. He chatted with Fritz and his fellow Michigan coaches who were in town and dropped by. He met with some of his players. He completed some necessary paperwork. Finally, at the end of the day, he and Moby relaxed at their desks and reminisced about certain highlights of the season.

"Remember the second game against Minnesota," asked Moby, "when we edged 'em out 3–2?"

"Sure do," Don answered. "They were tough that game. Wayne Slusher turned in one of the best relief jobs of the season."

"Couldn't have done it without him, that's for sure," said Moby. "And what about Richter's home run? That cost us the conference championship."

Don laughed. "Man, that ball is still going. Illinois should retire his Wisconsin number. Richter handed them the prize. He's a superb athlete and a nine-letter man in football and basketball, as well as baseball. He's also a two-time All American in football. He'll go high in the NFL draft. I heard he'll probably turn pro after he graduates."

Don didn't know at the time, but his prediction would prove accurate. Pat Richter was a first-round draft pick and went on to star for eight years with the Washington Redskins. A bronze statue of him stands outside Camp Randall Football Stadium in Madison, Wisconsin, honoring him for his many contributions to the university as an athlete and as one of their greatest athletic administrators.

Moby continued, "I was kind of pleasantly surprised when we got chosen for the district tournament."

"I was, too," said Don. "When we lost that last game, I thought we were out of it, but when they picked us, I couldn't wait to tell Fritz. He wasn't surprised at all. He told me to go there and show 'em who we are."

"And we did," Moby grinned, "we did indeed!"

Don considered a moment. "Remember our game against Wayne State? We barely won it. But what grabs me most about that game is Joe Jones making that double play by himself."

Moby recalled it. "Yeah; man on first, the batter hits a grounder to Jones, who tags the runner and throws to first to get the batter out and wrap up the inning. Nice play."

"That's right," said Don, "but I was watching Dick Honig wait at second base for the force-out. I expected Joe to toss it to Dick, who would tag the base and throw it to first and get the batter out. Typical double play. Instead, Joe tags the runner in the base path, flips it to first for the putout, then keeps running straight for the dugout. Me, I keep watching Honig. Suddenly I see Dick leaving second base and trotting in toward me in the dugout, followed by the rest of the team. I ask myself what's happening. I look in the dugout and there sits Joe, calm and collected. He looks at me with a straight face, as if he's saying 'Wasn't I supposed to do that?' I had all I could do to keep from busting a gut. Joe had me fooled."

Moby laughed. "I had no trouble seeing exactly what happened. You must be losin' it."

"And you're sitting there with a straight face," Don retorted.

Moby laughed. "OK, OK. But I guess if we picked a certain series of games this year that stand out in our minds, it would have to be the games against ..."

"Western Michigan!" Don interrupted.

Moby followed. "That left field fence and the hill behind it. Remember Jim Steckley getting his foot caught in the fence? Prevented him from a sure catch. Lousy home run instead."

Don agreed, and Moby continued.

"And what about Dave Campbell's home run over that left field fence? The ball rolls back down the hill and stops just inside the fence. Their left fielder reaches under, picks it up, and throws it in to third base."

Don completed the scenario, "The umpires call a ground rule triple."

"You charged out like a wild bull," said Moby. "Didn't get us anywhere, though. The umps were hired by Western, but I suppose it's not fair to use that as an excuse. Thank the Lord we ended up winning the game."

Don turned serious. "Speaking of umpires at Western Michigan, what about that time Mo missed the call on one of Fritz Fisher's pitches, then refused to admit his mistake?" Don was referring to Mo Kunka, a Detroit police officer who moonlighted as an NCAA umpire. In this particular game between Michigan and Western Michigan, Mo was behind the plate when the WMU batter swung at a Fisher fastball and missed it. Mo called a ball instead of a strike.

"Mo," Don yelled from the dugout, "he swung at it!"

Mo trotted over to the first base umpire for confirmation. That umpire nods to Mo, then yells back to Don, "He didn't swing!" Mo ambled triumphantly back to the plate as Don fumed silently.

"Yeah, I remember that," said Moby. "I also remember we got that batter out on a fly ball."

"Right," Don answered, "but later on in the game there was a close call at first, and we got the ruling. Afterward, I said to that ump: 'You were real decisive on that close call at first, but you didn't have the guts to admit Mo's mistake on that obvious strike.' And you know what he said to me? He said: 'Mo told me to tell you he didn't swing.' I just walked away."

Moby shook his head.

It wasn't long before the conference announced its 1962 All Big Ten Baseball Squad. Michigan was represented by eight players, twice as many as Ohio State and conference champion Illinois, and more than twice those of any other member school. On the first team were center fielder Dennis Spalla and pitcher Dave Roebuck. The second team included second baseman Joe Jones and right fielder Ron Tate. The third team was dominated by Wolverines Dave Campbell at first base, Dick Honig at shortstop, Harvey Chapman at third base, and John Kerr at a pitching slot.

Michigan was also the only team represented by its entire infield. Perhaps Don and Moby were surprised at their invitation to the district tournament. But one look at the All Big Ten Squad reveals no surprise at all. Those extending the invitation knew exactly what they were doing.

The winners from all eight NCAA regions traveled to the 1962 College World Series. They were Michigan, Florida State, Holy Cross, Ithaca College, Missouri, Northern Colorado, Santa Clara, and Texas. They would pilgrimage to Johnny Rosenblatt Stadium in Omaha, Nebraska. "The Blatt," as it was popularly termed, is the largest non-major league baseball stadium in the country, and it's owned and operated by the city of Omaha. Since 1950, the stadium has hosted the College World Series, and there were strong signs it would continue to do so. The NCAA favored a permanent location for the tournament, plus the city was committed to funds for keeping its stadium in first-class shape. "The Blatt" would continue its tradition.

The five-day, double-elimination tournament was slated for June 11–16. All participating teams arrived in Omaha around June 6. They were sequestered in various hotels/motels around town.

The Wolverines, like the other teams, worked out on a high school practice field. The only glitch to this came on the first day of batting practice, with a combination of sweet pitches allowing nearly everyone to blast the ball over the fence, and only a small number of balls supplied by the high school. Soon the entire team was combing the outlying fields to find the lost balls. Welcome to Omaha, thought Don.

Don attended the draw meeting, to determine the first day's games, along with the rest of the coaches. Michigan drew the University of Texas, which was making its sixth appearance in the national tournament. After the drawing, Don was standing with a couple of the other coaches when Bibb Falk, the storied

Texas coach, walked up. Bibb was highly respected as a former major leaguer with the Chicago White Sox and the Cleveland Indians. But more than that, Bibb Falk starred for Texas in football and baseball, and then came back to the university as head baseball coach once he retired from the big leagues. Over his years as coach, Bibb coached numerous Southeastern Conference championships, plus back-to-back national championships in 1949–50. His nickname, earned as a big league player, was "Jockey," for his propensity to ride opponents with abandon. Don was about to find this out personally.

Bibb approached Don's group and shook hands around. He looked at Don, narrowed his eyes, and adopted the look of a fisherman about to fillet his latest catch.

"I guess we got each other in the draw."

"I guess we did," answered Don with a slight grin.

"Then I also guess," said Bibb as he changed his expression to match Don's grin, "that we'll just have to kick yore ass!"

Don continued to watch as Bibb slowly ambled away toward another group. He and the other two coaches shared a laugh over Bibb's remark. Only Don's laugh was a little more on the nervous side.

Michigan beat Texas in the first round, 3–1. After the game, Don shook hands with Bibb Folk, who said "nice game," and winked.

The Wolverines won the next two rounds, 11–4 against Holy Cross and 10–7 versus Florida State. After three rounds, Michigan was the only undefeated team.

Four teams comprised the fourth round. Santa Clara eliminated Florida State, 11–6. Texas shut out Michigan, 7–0. After the last out, Don again shook hands with Bibb Falk, who merely said "nice game" and winked.

Opponents for the semifinal game were chosen among the three remaining teams by draw. Michigan drew the bye, and Don seemed to be the only one breathing a sigh of relief. Moby and the players weren't happy to sit by and watch; they were on the hunt and didn't like the hiatus.

It took ten innings for Santa Clara to finally dispatch Texas, 4–3. That set up the final game between Santa Clara and Michigan, to be played the next day. Don's players could hardly relax, they were so eager. Don tried as best he could to settle them down, get them relaxed, and off for a good night's rest. He and Moby would spend lots of time going over their notes for tomorrow's contest. Neither one would clock many hours of solid sleep.

The championship game on June 16 was as hard-fought a battle as any throughout the history of the national tournament. Both teams were tied at 3 through fourteen innings. In the later innings, Don noticed that Fritz Fisher seemed to be getting tired. So he substituted Jim Bobel, and that decision proved right. Bobel would become the game-winning hitter as well as the winning pitcher.

In the top of the fifteenth inning, the Wolverines began to tag Santa Clara's ace reliever Bob Garibaldi. They scored one run to move ahead 4–3. Then, with two outs and a man on third, Jim Bobel crunched a long drive between the center and right fielders for a triple, scoring the runner and putting the Wolverines ahead 5–3.

Bobel came back in the bottom of the inning with his usual tight control, but a determined Santa Clara batting order was able to score a run, making it 5–4. On a remarkable defensive play, Jim Newman, who some thought was the most intense man in the dugout, noticed that a Santa Clara runner failed to touch first base on his way around the bag. Newman fairly screamed from the bench, and the umpires agreed. The runner was out, making the next batter approach the plate with two outs. He hit Bobel's second pitch, a long fly ball to left field, which was caught by Jim Steckley. The Michigan Wolverines were National Champions!

Pandemonium broke out among the Michigan players on the field and the Michigan fans in the seats. Jim Steckley ran the ball in from left field and promptly found Don in the crowd. "Here's the ball, Coach," said Steckley. "I know you'll want it, and if I don't give it to you now, I'll probably lose it." He gave the ball to his coach, ran over to celebrate among his teammates, and threw his glove in the air as high as he could. Jim Steckley never found that glove.

Len Honig, Dick Honig's father, was so excited by the win that he leaped out of his seat and jumped down onto the field to congratulate his son. In doing so, he slipped and went down on his back. His subsequent injury turned out to be minor, and fortunately it was the only upsetting incident during the entire celebration.

In winning the biggest prize, Don's team became famous in the annals of Michigan athletics. They were known as opportunists who made the breaks that won games. The press referred to them as the "Comeback Kids' and "The Miracle Team." They were rightly honored, because they were only the second Michigan baseball team, after Ray Fisher's 1953 squad, to become the national champions.

Head coach Don Lund, in a ceremony held at the Biltmore Hotel in Los Angeles, was named the NCAA Coach of the Year. When interviewed by reporters, he was asked what he attributed to his team's success.

He answered very simply, "Good defense and good pitching; that's what did it."

1962 Coach of the Year. On January 6, 1963, Don accepts the award from Glen Daniel, baseball coach at the University of Wyoming and President of the American Association of College Baseball Coaches. The ceremony took place at the association's annual banquet in Los Angeles. (*AP Images*)

46
Hawaii

"Hone-e-y, I'm ho-ome!" Don walked in his house from the side door off the garage, doing his best impression of Ricky Ricardo, Lucy's husband on the hit TV series of the 1950s *I Love Lucy*. He was returning from Los Angeles after receiving the NCAA Coach of the Year award. Since Betty was standing in the kitchen a mere ten feet from him, he was looking at her as he sang out.

Betty laughed and ran to him for a big hug. "So how's my famous coach husband?"

"I don't know about the famous coach part, but your husband is pretty tired," answered Don. "That plane trip was grueling." He had flown on a United Airlines DC-8 from Los Angeles to Detroit. The trip had taken twelve hours, with two brief stops along the way. Don could still hear the loud drone of the four propeller-driven engines. He had hoped to fly in one of those new big jets that can travel coast-to-coast in about six hours. But so far, they weren't flying in or out of Detroit. Besides, travel to the West Coast was expensive. Round trip was somewhere around eighty dollars. That's why he had to go out there by himself. While Fritz was generous when travel involved entire teams, he was quite frugal when it came to individual trips, especially across the country, even to get an award. Betty stayed home.

Susan bounced in as Betty turned to finish preparing dinner and greeted her father with her normal enthusiasm. Then, after typical family conversation that brought everyone up to date, the three Lunds sat down to dinner.

"Mom," said Susan, "tell Dad about your meeting the priest after Mass last Sunday." Betty and Susan, both Catholic, attended church at the St. Mary Student Parish chapel on the university campus. Don, a Protestant, sometimes went to church with them.

"Oh, yes," Betty smiled, "Father was greeting everyone coming out of Mass, and when Susan and I walked up, Father shook our hands and said to me, 'I haven't seen the big guy around here lately.'"

"Uh-oh," said Don, "and how did you answer that one?"

"I just said, 'That's interesting, Father; we haven't seen you in the stands during our games, either.'"

All three laughed. Don made up his mind to go with them to church next Sunday.

Betty asked, "How did the team celebrate our win in Omaha?"

Don told them about the pandemonium on the field, how other players and coaches who were there, as well as NCAA officials, plus the fans, came onto the field to join them. He mentioned the fact that Santa Clara coach Paddy Cattrell was especially gracious in defeat. This was his school's first appearance in the national tournament.

He also told them about going back to the hotel, where he and Moby had a bite to eat while the players went up to their rooms. "Later on," he related, "we were all up in the rooms and spilling out into the hall, celebrating, making a lot of noise. I was in the hall, and I turned around just in time to see this little old lady open her room door and stick her head out. I walked over and said to her 'Sorry, ma'am, I hope we aren't keeping you up. My team just won the national championship and we're just having a good time.' She smiled at me, this little old lady with gray hair, and she said, 'Enjoy yourself, enjoy yourself' and closed her door. I couldn't believe that little old lady. I felt pretty good about her."

"The whole town of Ann Arbor felt good about the team, Dad," said Susan. "Yost Field House was really jumping!" She was talking about the reception and celebration held at Yost, which was sponsored by the Athletic Department. Hundreds of people were on hand to cheer the national champions, including the movers and shakers of both the university and the city of Ann Arbor.

"That's right, Honey," said Don, "and now there's been a new development. Before I came home from the airport, I stopped at my office and talked to Fritz."

"And?" asked Betty.

"And Fritz is going to Hawaii."

"That's nice."

"And I'm going with him."

"What?" Betty was sitting up straight now, looking at her husband's blank face. "What's going on?"

Don grinned. Time to stop playing the game. "As a matter of fact, Honey, the whole team's going to Hawaii. Fritz told me he got a call from Rod Dedeaux, the coach at Southern Cal. His team won the National Championship last year. Anyway, Dedeaux tells Fritz he's put together an exhibition series between us and Hosei University of Japan. Hosei won the Japanese College Championship. Dedeaux is calling it the 'International World Series of College Baseball.' We'll also be playing some military teams in Honolulu, so I think the U.S. military is footing the bill for our trip."

"Do we get to go on this trip with you?" Betty was asking about her and Susan.

"No, I'm afraid not," answered Don. "I asked Fritz about bringing you. He said no families were going with us, unless they went on their own and paid their own way."

Betty and Susan frowned at this, but didn't say anything. They both knew Crisler's rules about including families in team travel. It wouldn't do any good to complain.

Before they left for Honolulu, Don learned that Moby wouldn't be going. His wife, Pat, was due to deliver their first child any day. Moby would be missed.

Also, Fritz told him he was arranging to buy gifts for the Japanese team. "It's their tradition," he had said. "They'll be giving us gifts, so we'll need to reciprocate." Don decided to let Fritz determine what kind of gifts Michigan would give the Japanese. He just wanted to concentrate on the trip and the upcoming games.

Don and Fritz were joined by a mutual friend, Bill Snyder, to accompany the players and staff assistants to Hawaii. Among other things he did for the university as a volunteer, Bill was in charge of the sideline chains during football games. He also was a familiar figure at most of the other sports contests on campus. Everybody liked Bill Snyder. Don was pleased that Fritz had brought him along.

The team received a cordial welcome when they landed at Honolulu Airport, complete with a garland of flowers, called a "lei," placed around their necks by young and beautiful Hawaiian women who met them at the plane. Don, Fritz, and Bill accepted their leis with dignity and a smiling "Thank you." The players, being young, aggressive, and filled with testosterone-driven energy, did their best to maintain decorum as the beautiful women placed the leis over their heads. They succeeded. Don was proud of them.

After retrieving their luggage and gear, all were whisked away by Navy personnel to the naval base at Pearl Harbor, where they were billeted in dorms. Then the tours started.

Foremost on everyone's agenda was a visit to the brand-new U.S.S. *Arizona* memorial, which had been dedicated only three weeks before, on May 30. Don marveled at the difference in everyone between the boat ride out to the memorial, when there was a lot of talk, laughter, and joke telling, and the ride back, when there was almost complete silence. He couldn't remember having a more solemn and patriotic feeling, as he had stood over the sunken *Arizona* and the watery graves of more than 1,100 sailors. They had lost their lives on the same day he listened to their story in the Michigan Union on December 7, 1941.

His feelings about Japan had begun to boil at the memorial, until he saw a group of Japanese tourists, some of them crying silently, standing with quiet reverence. He cursed himself for even thinking about hating any class of people, and he hoped his team would feel the same way. After all, he told himself, they were only babies during the war. They would have no personal memories of it.

The series with Hosei University was to be a five-game tournament. The team that won three games would be the winner and "International College Champion." They would play at the public stadium in Honolulu.

At first, Don's players weren't impressed by the Japanese team when they met them on the field. They were nice enough, all smiles in fact, during the gift exchange. But overall they were smaller and thinner in stature compared to the Americans. It wasn't until their pitchers started warming up that the Michigan team began to see how they could win Japan's championship. The Japanese pitchers were full of extra motions and moves unfamiliar to the Wolverines. One of them stretched like a rubber band. Another seemed to wind up like a samurai warrior about to cleave in somebody's head. Don hoped his batters wouldn't be dumbfounded by all that motion on the mound.

Before the start of the tournament, Don and the coach from Hosei went over the rules. To his delight, Don learned that he would be allowed to personally coach at third base. He couldn't wait to get out there and be part of the action.

Michigan won the first game, 3–0, behind the turned-on throwing of Fritz Fisher. Hosei came back in the second game with their best pitcher, a guy whose contortions made it seem like he was throwing from center field. The Japanese won game two, 6–1. Then Michigan edged out Hosei in game three, 4–3. In game four, the score was just the opposite: Hosei 4, Michigan 3. With both teams even at two games apiece, game five would decide the winner.

Don called his players together before they took the field for the final game. They needed encouragement. They had faced a different style of pitching, which had been effective; they had seen numerous reporters from Japan swarming all over the Hosei team, while few American press people were around. The tournament appeared to be far more interesting in Japan. Don could sense his players were a little down. He spoke slowly and deliberately.

"Guys, let me tell you something. A lot of people might think this is just a match between the University of Michigan and Hosei University. The winner will have bragging rights around campus for a while, and that's it. But you and I know it's more than that; it's more than our university against their university. It's the United States of America versus Japan. Pure and simple. We've seen the memorials. We're living on that base with dedicated men who'd gladly give their lives for our country. Well, today we're called upon to represent America, to fight and win this game. Now get out there and make us proud!"

The team charged out with a roar.

The final game was a pitcher's duel. Hosei brought back their second-game pitcher, who was as tough as before, and held the Wolverines to one run through eight innings. Michigan returned Fritz Fisher. Fritz promptly walked the first four batters, as his infield griped and grumbled behind him. But the run Fritz walked in would turn out to be Hosei's only score in the game, and the fact that Don allowed Fritz to stay in and pitch was a vote of confidence that transferred to the infielders and the rest of the team. They all settled down as Fritz threw brilliantly and allowed only two hits from the Japanese. Going into the ninth inning, the score was tied at one. They all felt the pressure. United States versus Japan.

Batting in the top of the ninth, Harvey Chapman hit a triple. With Don behind him in the coaching box, Harvey took a slight lead and watched the pitcher, who didn't seem to be paying attention to him. Harvey studied the elaborate windup. If Coach Lund would let him, Harvey wanted to try for home. The pitcher threw a strike. Harvey walked back to third base and looked at his coach. Lund nodded slightly; he'd also noticed that windup. The pitcher began his motion. Harvey streaked for home like a fox with hounds on its tail. With wide open eyes and a startled look, the pitcher reared back and hurled the ball with all his strength ...

Right into the screen behind the plate, about twelve feet high. Harvey Chapman scored what proved to be the winning run, as Fritz Fisher retired Hosei's final batters. Final score: Michigan 2, Hosei University 1. The Michigan Wolverines were, according to promoters of the tournament, the College International World Champions!

The Associated Press carried the story, and the Detroit, Ann Arbor, and other local papers picked it up and ran it big. European papers covered it, as did certain ones in Asia, especially Japan. As a result, Don Lund's 1962 baseball team became the first in University of Michigan history to receive world coverage for a game.

All wasn't over for the Wolverines in Hawaii, however. They still had to play several military teams on the playing field at Pearl Harbor. After, all, the Navy was their host and paying the tab. There was no question these games would be played. And Don found another reason to be glad the war was over.

During WWII, the military's baseball teams were made up of professionals who had been drafted into the service. Their duty included playing ball, representing their various outfits. Those teams were formidable. However, after the war these players were discharged and sent back home to the big leagues and the minors. That left the military teams with soldiers and sailors whose first job was to defend the country. They were good athletes, but baseball wasn't their calling.

So the Michigan Wolverines beat all comers. Don was almost embarrassed, but he didn't let it show. There even came a time when one of his players came up to him and asked if they should

HONOLULU, HAWAII   JUNE 1962

The NCAA National Baseball Champion Wolverines arrive in
Hawaii to take on the Japanese national champions. The contest
was described as the "World Series of College Baseball." Michigan
went on to win and was hailed by the international press as World
Champions. Pictured (*left to right down the stairs*) are Jim Bobel,
Dave Campbell, Wayne Schlusser, Fritz Fisher, Harvey Chapman, Joe
Murello, and Ron Tate. Standing (*left to right*) are Head Coach Don
Lund, Dave Roebuck, Jim Steckley, Team Captain Ed Hood, John
Kerr, Dennis Spalla, Dick Honig, Dick Post, and Ron Lauderback.
Assistant Coach Moby Benedict couldn't make the trip because
of his child's imminent birth. (*Lund Family Collection*)

let a team win a game, just to save a little face. Don told him
that everybody should play hard to win.

One light moment came when a fan who must have had several beers kept heckling the Michigan players. Taunts like "Hey
you college hot dogs!" and "Go back home to your classes!"
were starting to grate on Don. Finally he turned toward the
stands, cupped his left ear, and yelled back, "I can't hear you!"
The guy yelled louder. Don yelled back, "I can't hear you!" This

continued a few more times, until the guy's buddies caught the joke and pulled him down, laughing.

Don laughed with them. No more heckling from that guy.

One other thing happened after one of the night games on the base, which Don perhaps treated more lightly than he might have. When he had finished hanging up uniforms with the equipment manager, he went over to the base bowling alley, which was the central spot for entertainment. He had a burger and a beer. Then he went to the admiral's quarters, where he, Fritz Crisler, and Bill Snyder were staying, and went to bed. Later on he was roused from sleep by Fritz and Bill, who had been out having a good time.

"Hey, Don," they said, "wake up. C'mon, have a drink.

So Don got up and joined them in a drink.

During the conversation Fritz asked, "Say, Don, have you ever thought about being an athletic director?"

Don answered, "Not really. I'm still thinking about coaching and stuff like that."

The conversation went on to other things, and then they all turned in for the night.

The next morning Bill Snyder sought him out. "Don, you didn't run with the ball when Fritz handed it to you."

Don looked at him. "What do you mean, Bill?"

Bill went on to say that Fritz just didn't bring up things like an athletic director's job without having an agenda behind it. He might have blown an opportunity. Don thanked Bill and let the matter pass.

The flight home was one-of-a-kind in a very special way. The Michigan people were in one of three military Lockheed Super Constellations that were flying in formation east out of Honolulu. It was July 9, 1962. None of the passengers flying with Don were aware that, about 800 miles to the north, a Pacific atoll called Johnston Island was about to become the site of an atomic blast from a bomb called "Starfish." Johnston Island had been used by the U.S. military for atomic bomb testing for about ten years. Today, "Starfish" would release a 1.4 megaton explosion into the atmosphere above Johnston Island. It would be seen for a thousand miles.

Don was sitting back, resting his eyes, when someone shouted "Look, out there in the sky!" Everyone scampered to the left portholes and saw an orange glow in the sky. It seemed to grow bigger and lighter in color, turning to yellow as it climbed higher. In a minute, it was gone. They all returned to their seats. Soon, a flight officer entered the cabin and announced that they had witnessed an atomic bomb test. He said they weren't in any trouble. He also said that, because the blast disturbed radio waves, they didn't have communication to or from the plane. He told them not to worry. In a little while, he said, all would be back to normal. When it was, everyone breathed a little easier.

Back home, the team was given another victory celebration. This time, there was an additional honor awaiting them. On June 28, while Don and his squad were in Honolulu, the Michigan Senate passed a resolution to honor them. The resolution, proposed by State Senator Stanley G. Thayer of Ann Arbor, was adopted without debate:

A resolution of Congratulations to the University of Michigan's 1962 National Championship Baseball Team

Whereas, In a thrilling 15-innings that lasted past midnight at Omaha, Nebraska, June 16, 1962, The University of Michigan Wolverines Baseball Team won the 1962 NCAA baseball championship by defeating Santa Clara 5 to 4; and

Whereas, On June 25, the University of Michigan Baseball Team won the fifth and deciding game for the Intercollegiate International World Series against Hosei University, National Champions of Japan, in a thrilling series in Honolulu; and

Whereas, Throughout the 1962 season, which was the longest season in Michigan baseball history—a season during which 31 victories were won in 44 starts—the Michigan team demonstrated the true spirit of which champions are made. They overcame obstacles of having to rebuild a 1961 team, which had won the Big Ten title but lost the NCAA title, after which two of the 1961 team's best sophomore players yielded to professional offers; and

Whereas, Labeled the "Comeback Kids," the 1962 Wolverines Baseball Team became a "one for all and all

for each other" team under the talented leadership of the
University of Michigan coach, Don Lund, and, as such,
brought the second national baseball trophy to Michigan
since 1953; now therefore be it

Resolved by the Senate, That the members of the
Michigan Senate hereby extend their sincere congratula-
tions to the University of Michigan's 1962 Baseball Team
on winning the 1962 NCAA baseball championship; and
be it further

Resolved, That copies of this resolution be transmit-
ted to the University of Michigan, to Coach Don Lund,
and to members of the 1962 Michigan Baseball Team—
champions all.

Later on, the Senate changed the title to include the Intercollegiate International World Series. Don considered this resolution to be the highlight of the statewide recognition he felt his players deserved.

47
Dialogue

"What a dump!"

He grinned at me. "Are you talking about this place here or the snow outside?

I grinned back. "The snow, of course." I was looking out the window at the snow dump.

We were sitting in the old coach's living room on a January midmorning, after an overnight blizzard had buried the landscape beneath about two feet of snow. The plows had worked on the roads and driveways during the night, but the relentless cascade had nearly filled them in again. Early this morning, the plows had returned to fight the battle. Now the paved areas were passable. Only a few flakes were falling; the rest had returned to hide in the unbroken gray sky.

I turned back to the room. The gas-fired logs flamed yellow in the fireplace. Two table lamps gave light to offset the gray and white gloom outside the window panes. Don was staring at the fire. I grabbed his attention with my first question.

"Hey, Coach, do you ever see any of the guys who played on that 1962 team?"

DL: "Sure do. There's a reunion every year, usually during the summer. It's held at various places, sometimes at one of the players' homes. They also try to include the '61 team as well.

"How well do you know those guys? I mean, do you know what each of them did after they left Michigan?"

DL: "I think so, but let's get one thing straight. Those players on that '62 team just didn't leave Michigan; they all graduated. They got their degrees."

"All of them?"

DL: "Yes. And I'm quite proud of that fact. Bill Freehan also came back and got his degree. The '62 team made him an honorary member."

"Do you know how your players spent their careers?"
DL: "Pretty much, I think. All of them led very successful, productive lives. Some became quite famous in their careers. That sets them apart from a lot of other teams. Why do I have the feeling you're about to run through a list?"

"Because I am. Is that OK?"
DL: "What do I get if I pass your test?"

"You'll go to the head of the class."
DL: "Fire away, teacher," he laughed.

"OK. Let's start with the captain, Ed Hood."
DL: "That's easy, because I see him all the time. He lives right here in Ann Arbor. Ed stayed at Michigan and went to law school. Then he practiced law in Detroit and Ann Arbor, becoming one of the most successful attorneys in the state. Over the years, Ed's represented some of the guys he played ball with, handling their business dealings."

"How about Joe Jones?"
DL: "Joe spent his entire career in pro baseball. After his playing years, he managed in the minor leagues for the White Sox. Then he was hired by the Kansas City Royals to manage in their minor league system. Joe took his teams to several league championships in both organizations. He also ran the minor league instructional program for the Royals."

"Dick Honig?"
DL: "Dick went into the sports officiating business. He formed a company called 'Honig's Whistle Stop,' which sells officiating clothes and equipment worldwide. He was also a Big Ten football referee for many years, rated number one in the conference."

"Ron Tate?"
DL: "Ron played pro ball in the Tigers' organization. Then he worked several years with Johnson and Johnson on the west coast. But he really hit his stride as a broker in the real estate business in San Antonio, Texas. He owns several offices and employs well over a hundred people."

"Jim Steckley?"
DL: "Jim helps doctors keep their money."

"Really?"
DL: "Yes, really. You'd never think it, but many doctors aren't good at working the business end of their practices. Jim takes care of that for them. He also helps doctors buy and sell practices."

"Joe Murello?"
DL: "Joe got his degree in education here and went back home to the Boston area, where he became a teacher and a coach. He later went into school administration."

"How about a hard one? Dave Campbell?"
DL: "A hard one, yeah, right. Everybody knows Dave. Eight years as an infielder in the big leagues, then a great career as a sports broadcaster. Now he does color commentary for ESPN. You'll even hear Dave's voice if you buy one of those video baseball games. I hear him on ESPN all the time."

"Harvey Chapman?"
DL: He's another one who's been successful in commercial real estate. He's an owner and broker in California.

"Denny Spalla?"
DL: "Another success story in commercial real estate. Denny lives in Minnesota and works as director of real estate for a group that builds and manages shopping centers, office parks, warehouses, and so on.

"It's interesting that some of your former players made their mark in commercial real estate."
DL: "Interesting, yes, but not surprising. Think about what it takes to make it in real estate. You have to be aggressive, you have to be smart, and you have to be organized. But most of all you have to be disciplined."

"I suppose you could say that about the rest of the guys on the team, no matter what they ended up doing."
DL: "Absolutely. But this team was exceptionally filled with those attributes, to the man. Not all teams are like that."

"How about Fritz Fisher?"
DL: "Fritz played a season or so in the Tigers' farm system after he graduated. He probably would have played in the majors, but two things happened to him at that time. First, a large bank in Toledo, Ohio, was after him to join their executive training program. Second, the Tigers were preparing to trade him to another organization. Fritz decided to go with the bank. He spent the rest of his career as a bank executive, survived at least two bank mergers and came out on top. That's something."

"Jim Bobel?"
DL: Jim stayed here and got an MBA, then went on to work for several small companies as a financial manager, among other things. Finally he bought an engineering firm, which he built up and eventually sold to a publicly traded company. Took his money and retired.

"Dave Roebuck?"
DL: "Dave stayed in Ann Arbor and went to medical school. He became a radiologist and spent his entire practice back in his hometown of Bryan, Ohio."

"John Kerr?"
DL: "John made it big in the automotive world, and then some. Eventually he became president of Volkswagen of North America."

"Dick Post?"
DL: "Dick became a world-known specialist in information systems, working all over the globe as an IT troubleshooter. He lives in France. He speaks French, German, and Russian."

"Ron Lauterbach?"
DL: "Ron established himself as a successful real estate broker, like some of his teammates. Also, like some of them, he went back to his hometown. In Ron's case it was Dayton, Ohio."

"And Jim Newman?"
DL: "Jim taught and coached in high school. Then he went into administration. Tragically, he passed away while still in his prime. His death shook up all of us: me, Moby, and the players."

"I'm sure it did. Tell me, Coach, how come you know so much about these guys?"
DL: "Actually, it's no big deal. I talk to some of them regularly. I go to the reunions. All of us are sort of like an extended family. By the way, you missed one on your list."

"I missed one? I thought I covered everybody. Who did I leave out?"
DL: "Bruce Kropschot, our student manager. He also went to Hawaii with us."

"And what does Bruce do?"
DL: "Oh, not much. He just buys and sells companies!"

I sat back in my chair, stuck in amazement as this magnitude of life accomplishments for the entire 1962 Michigan baseball team. National Champions? World Champions? Champions in life? This was certainly a stand-out group of men. What was even more amazing is that they'd stayed close. They kept in touch, and Don Lund was still a focus in their lives. I continued.

"So you get back to Ann Arbor in July," I said. "The 1962 baseball season starts becoming a treasured memory. It stands to reason you'd want to get over to the Detroit sandlots right away and start recruiting. Is that what you did?"

He gazed out the window at the frozen landscape. He spoke softly. "No, I didn't go out recruiting. That became Moby's job."

"Why was that?" I asked, not realizing the abrupt change the conversation was about to take.

He turned and looked at me with the hazel eyes glowing. "Because I got a phone call from Jim Campbell that changed everything."

48

Running the Farm

Betty had just finished washing the supper dishes when the phone rang. She dried her hands on the dish towel and let it ring for a second time before she picked it up. "Hello?"

"Hi, Betty," a familiar voice said. "This is Jim Campbell. How are you?" Jim Campbell from the Tigers, she thought. Now there's a friendly voice from the past.

After a few pleasantries, Jim asked to speak with Don. Betty called her husband to the phone. Don quickly grabbed the receiver and proceeded to get reacquainted with his old friend, who congratulated him and his team on their accomplishments. Finally, Jim mentioned the reason he called.

"I wonder if we could get together soon. Any chance you might be able to drive up here to my office in the next couple of days?"

"Sure," agreed Don, "what have you got in mind?"

"I'd like you to see what's going on here. Thought I'd have our new general manager to show you around."

Don responded immediately. "Congratulations, Jim. I'd heard you might get the job, but I didn't know it happened. I'm delighted. No one's more qualified than you. I'm real happy for you."

"Thanks, pal," said Campbell. "I hope Rick Ferrell and Mr. Fetzer share your confidence in me. Anyway, can you get over here, maybe tomorrow? We can start with lunch."

Don didn't hesitate. "Sure, Jim. Tomorrow's fine. I'll be in your office at noon." He hung up the phone and told Betty about his conversation. Betty confirmed her husband's suspicion that Jim had a job with the Tigers in mind for him. They both began to speculate. They narrowed it down to two possibilities—team manager or director of minor league personnel, more popularly known among baseball people as "Farm Director."

"I'd give anything to manage the Tigers," mused Don. "But Bob Scheffing's been doing a pretty good job, even if the team finished in fourth place this year."

"Well, you never know," Betty answered. "After all, you've proven yourself as a manager. Also, Jim Campbell and you go way back."

"That's true," he agreed, "but the more logical conclusion would be the farm director job. That's what Jim was doing before he was promoted to general manager. That job's open, unless of course Jim has already hired somebody."

Betty sighed. "I guess we'll just have to wait and see. But there's something else, Honey."

"What's that?"

"If you went with the Tigers, I wouldn't be too happy about us moving back to Detroit. We have so many friends here in Ann Arbor; so does Susan at Pioneer High. We just couldn't …"

Don interrupted. "Don't worry, Honey. Ann Arbor isn't far from Detroit. It's an easy commute. Besides, we're just talking here. Anyway, I'm not anxious to leave the University; right now, I'm riding high. Let's see what Jim has in mind. Maybe I'll just get the grand tour tomorrow and that'll be it."

The next day with his old friend Jim Campbell proved to be more than merely a grand tour of the Tigers' front office. Jim wanted Don Lund to be his successor as Director of Minor League Personnel, or Farm Director. Don would be in charge of the entire farm system of Class Triple-A, Double-A, A and Rookie teams. Managers, coaches, players, and support people would be under his supervision. His office would be right next to Campbell's, and it was almost as large. It was a big job with big responsibility. And after all, it was with his favorite major league franchise. He'd be back with the Detroit Tigers. He would, in fact, run their minor league teams.

He took the job.

And with that, he became unique in all of American baseball. No man had ever served the same major league team as a player, a scout, a coach, and as part of front-office top management. Don Lund had become a special part of pro baseball lore.

Fritz Crisler took the news of Don's leaving with regret, but with understanding. Although he knew where Don stood when it came to the University of Michigan, he also knew how much

Tigers Farm Director Don Lund throws out the first ball at a
Mud Hens' night game, 1966. Playing for the Toledo club produced
some of Don's fondest memories. (*Toledo Mud Hens' Archives*)

he loved the Tigers. "I had plans for you right here, Don," noted
Fritz. "I felt you were ready for phasing into an assistant athletic
director's position, along with being baseball coach. Sort of
groom you to be an athletic director some day. Unfortunately, I
didn't tell you that."

"I had no idea you were thinking along those lines, Coach," said Don. "If I had, it probably would have made a difference in my decision." He meant it.

After securing Crisler's promise to make Moby Benedict the head baseball coach, Don said good-bye, promised to stay in touch, and headed for Detroit and his new job. He had mixed feelings. Although directing the Tigers' farm system excited him, he couldn't help being sad about leaving the university. He was one of those "blood runs maize and blue" Wolverines, loyal to the core. Anyway, he thought, he'd still be available to help Bob Ufer with football radio broadcasts. Those kept him in the loop. He started feeling better about the whole thing as he drove north to the Motor City.

* * *

As he settled in with the Tigers, Don wouldn't have made it the first couple of weeks without the help and guidance of Ralph Snyder. Although he officially reported to Don, Ralph was more of a partner on the job. Ralph knew the farm system so well, he could tell a person anything about it without having to check notes, reports, or the big organization board in Don's office. He knew where the players were, how they were doing, whether they were ready to be reassigned, and anything else about them that was important to the franchise. Ralph knew all this because he'd spent almost his entire career with the Tigers' farm system. He played for a short time, then moved into administration of the farm teams. He was bright, well liked, highly respected, and knowledgeable, perfectly suited for Don's job.

Don wondered why Campbell hired him as farm director instead of promoting Ralph. It wasn't long before he found out.

Ralph Snyder had another thing going for him. He was one of the best facilities guys in baseball. He could manage all the ins and outs and the ups and downs of a baseball park, and keep people mostly happy at the same time. Every year for several years, Ralph was the one who opened Tigertown. He was so good at making it fit for use, that everyone there unwittingly paid him the highest compliment: they took his work for granted. But one man who seemingly didn't take Ralph Snyder's work for granted was the one man who mattered: Jim Campbell. And Campbell wanted Ralph to run his ballpark in Detroit.

Don soon learned that Ralph Snyder was to become superintendent of Tiger Stadium. For a few weeks he would help Don learn the minor league farm system. After that, Don would be left with only Ralph's occasional counsel. For those first few weeks, then, Don Lund the farm director turned himself into Don Lund the sponge. He soaked up Ralph's knowledge of the Tigers' minor league teams, managers, players, and prospective players like someone trying to get a degree in farm system trivia. Soon he felt he was up to speed and ready to make things happen.

Jim Campbell didn't hire Don to be a "maintenance" guy. Jim wanted a leader with enough savvy and stamina to make the farm system a fertile ground for developing new players properly. Don set out to do just that, to hire the best young players he could attract, put them with the appropriate teams, and move them around when they're ready. Get the managers and scouts to provide continual feedback, not just win-loss data, but also feedback on every player they work with. Get out in the field and visit the teams. Give them as much support as possible.

It worked. For the next six years, Don ran the Tigers' farm club system with one goal in mind: make the farm system turn out the kind of talent that leads to championships for the Tigers. If it's done right, the Tigers should be able to count more on its own player development program than on trades. Trades worked out well some of the time, but too often turned out to be costly mistakes. Players from the farm system were tracked, continually evaluated, moved around to enhance their skills, and talked about by scouts, coaches, managers, and, of course, the farm director. It took the whole of six years, but by 1968 Don had achieved his goal.

When he had started the job in 1962, the Tigers had ended their season placing fourth in the American League. Among the eight regulars on that team who took the field most games, only Al Kaline had never played in the minor leagues. Of the remaining seven, only two, second baseman Jake Wood and third baseman Steve Boros, were products of Detroit's farm system.

Don set out to change that ratio, to see if the farm system could contribute more to the success of the team. Here's what happened.

The 1963 Tigers finished in fifth place again with only two of the seven daily regulars, not counting Al Kaline, coming from the Tigers' farm system. They were second baseman Jake Wood and shortstop Dick McAuliffe.

In 1964, four of the seven daily regulars were Tigers' farm promotions. They were catcher Bill Freehan, third baseman Don Wert, shortstop Dick McAuliffe, and left fielder Gates Brown. The team moved up to fourth place and also improved dramatically over the 1963 season. They won 85 games and played .525 ball. The previous year they had won 79 and played .488. Things were looking up.

Five of the seven daily regulars not counting Kaline were Tigers' farm system graduates in 1965. In addition to Freehan, Wert, and McAuliffe, outfielders Jim Northrup and Willie Horton took the field most games. Although they again finished in fourth place, they continued to improve. They posted 89 wins and played .549 ball.

The 1966 Tigers moved up to third place with virtually the same daily regulars as last year. Another home-grown farm system player, outfielder Mickey Stanley, was a big factor in many of the wins. Mickey, in his third season with the Tigers, had improved steadily since his debut with the team in 1964. He would continue to be a big contributor. Pitching was a huge factor that year, and it came chiefly from three starters: Denny McLain, Earl Wilson, and Mickey Lolich. Of these, only Lolich had come up directly through the farm system. The team needed a fourth in order to move ahead next year. It would arrive in farm system graduate Joe Sparma.

All the daily regulars of the 1967 Detroit Tigers had come up through their farm system, except first baseman Norm Cash. With the addition of Sparma, two of the four starting pitchers were farm grown. They were a winning team. Tigers' lore was on everybody's lips; newspapers were generous with space for Tigers tales. Until Sunday July 23.

Don was watching the second game of an afternoon double header between the Tigers and the Yankees from the third deck of the press box in Tiger Stadium. That's as high as any spectator can go. Birds fly lower when they're migrating. Look down at home plate and the entire playing field looks about as big as a card table. Look up over the outfield roof and the rooftops of city dwellings spread out from the stadium like an aerial photograph. Late in the game, Don was gazing out toward the cityscape below when he noticed that smoke was steadily rising about a mile away. He saw that the smoke was spreading. Then he heard a chorus of sirens. Something was wrong.

The Detroit Riots of 1967, starting on July 23 and continuing for five days, was one of the most violent urban uprisings of the twentieth century. The entire city was virtually shut down. The Tigers, nearly immune to the trouble, went on the road and didn't return for another home game until August 8. When they came back, they were still a winning team, and they continued to prove it through the rest of the season.

They nearly won the pennant, finishing in second place by just one game. Detroit had no complaints against its baseball team. Even though they didn't win the pennant, the Tigers provided a welcome break from the traumas of Detroit's social unrest. As the riots had opened a wound, the Tigers at least had provided a small bandage of relief. But it would take more than a second-place finish to raise cheers in Detroit. It would take something big and positive. And the Detroit Tigers would turn out to be the ones who would provide it.

The 1968 Tigers blew away the season's competition, winning the American League pennant by twelve games. That was the highest margin since 1947, the year the Yankees won the pennant by 12 over the Tigers. There's another similarity between the 1947 Yankees and the 1968 Tigers: both teams took seven games to win their World Series, besting the National League champs 4–3.

World Series' celebrations in Detroit brought pride back to town. The Motor City was once more alive with cheers and beers. "Bless you, boys!" became a common phrase, and congratulations poured in from all over the world. To be a Detroiter was to be a Tigers fan; it was that simple.

Don and Betty Lund had their own way of celebrating the World Championship. They built a new house. It was a four-bedroom, colonial style, two-story house with a huge back yard. Located at 2222 Delaware, only a few blocks away from their former home, it was a mansion compared to where they had been living.

Don was included among those on the Tigers' staff who received one of the 1968 World Series Championship rings. He was proud of the team, proud of the organization, and proud of the exceptional players who made it happen. More important to him personally, though, was the fact that this World Championship team fielded mostly players from the farm system he supervised. He had exercised a direct influence in their careers for the past six years. To some extent, their success represented a personal triumph, though he never would have expressed that publicly. But there were two players on this team who gave Don an even greater lift.

The first was Bill Freehan. Bill had become the dominant catcher in the American League. He was strong, quick, smart and decisive, among other things. He also had both feet on the ground. He never bragged, didn't put on airs, and treated everyone as friends. Bill had become the epitome of a great major league ballplayer. Don also considered him family.

The second was utility infielder Dave Campbell. Dave was on Don's 1962 NCAA National Champion team, and now he played for the Major League Champs. Don had recruited him to Michigan, coached him, and later on watched him play in a Tigers' uniform. Dave Campbell, he believed, would one day achieve national recognition, either in baseball or elsewhere. He had the guts and he had the brains.

* * *

For the next couple of years Don continued to manage the Tigers' farm system. He forged ties and friendships with managers, scouts, players, and staff that would never be broken. He continued to look for ways to improve the farm system, as he had from the start.

Early in his tenure, Don had formed an "Instructional League" team in Dunedin, Florida. The team was devoted exclusively to winter practice for promising rookies and Class A players. The main goal was to help these players move more quickly through the farm system, by providing coached fundamentals and game experience during about six weeks of the winter months. Other major league franchises also formed these instructional teams. The games were played in minor league parks throughout Florida. The whole program proved to be a big success. Don considered it one of his milestones.

He also refused to do something else, which turned out to be a good decision. He wouldn't emulate the Chicago Cubs. The Cubs' farm director had started a program of arbitrarily switching minor league managers around. The idea was to give the managers broader experience running a wider variety of levels. The managers rebelled. Chicago eventually stopped admitting they had even tried it.

One evening, after the 1969 Tigers season was over, Don and Betty were in their new home, remembering some of the events that had faced him as farm director over the past six years. One of these had to do with a plan that emerged from one of the league general managers' meetings. If the teams got together periodically to share scouting reports, they reckoned, the increased information on players would be a good thing for each team. A nice idea, perhaps, but one that was doomed. There was no way a scout was going to share his hard-earned intelligence on player prospects. The farm directors knew this, but none of them, including Don, was willing to take on a general manager with an argument that scouts were entitled to keep secrets. The plan was tried. It failed almost immediately.

"How has it been for you, working for Jim Campbell?" Betty asked. "He's pretty much a workaholic and you aren't."

Don answered quickly, "But he doesn't expect me to be, Honey. Jim has no one to go home to and I have. He'd be the first one to send me home if he thought I was neglecting you. Jim likes you a lot."

She laughed. "Even though I sometimes go into his office after games and turn around that Ohio State picture he has hanging on the wall?"

"He gets a kick out of it, but he'd never let you know."

Betty remembered something else. "What about when he called you 'Santa Claus'?" She was talking about the time, just before spring training one year, when Don sent an internal office memo to Campbell about spring training compensation. All spring training athletes were required to live at Tigertown. Their pay didn't start until the season began, so they received nothing but room-and-board from the Tigers, except two dollars a week for laundry expenses. In his memo, Don proposed that each player, regardless of his status in the farm system, be given an additional dollar a day for personal expenses. Two hours after he had sent the memo, Jim's voice came over his intercom.

"Hey, Santa Claus, get in here."

Don laughed as he recalled the story. "I didn't win that one, but I did win quite a few with Jim. As a matter of fact, I think I won the other day."

"Oh?"

"Well, you know those daily reports I send to Jim, the ones he sends on to Mr. Fetzer? I mentioned in one of them that we have a catcher in our system who shows promise."

"That's unusual?"

"Well, no," he answered, "but this guy has been around a while, and he's fine as a minor league catcher, but he probably won't be a major league player. On the other hand, I think he'd be an excellent manager. That's what I recommended to Jim the other day. We talked about it, and I think it might happen."

"Who's the catcher you're talking about?" Betty asked.

"His name is Jim Leyland."

Their conversation turned toward reminiscing about highlights in Don's career with the Tigers. The World Championship was obviously one of them. His 1953 year as a regular player was another. There were lots of strong memories of Tigertown, especially over the last several years with Don in a principal role. There were Jim Campbell stories, too numerous to count, that reflected how close the two of them had become. Now they were like brothers.

Betty suddenly asked, "What's your biggest Tigers memory? I'll bet it has something to do with the 1968 pennant race or the World Series."

"Not really."

"What then?"

"It happened during my last year as a coach. We were playing the Yankees at the end of the season. I wasn't coaching at first base that day. Tommy Henrich was taking my place ..."

Betty suddenly remembered. "Mickey Mantle's home run!"

"Bingo!"

It happened on Wednesday afternoon, September 17, 1958, in Briggs Stadium. Don was in the scouting office during the game, one of the rare occasions when he wasn't coaching on the field. The scouting office was behind the right field stands, but there were no windows to the field. Instead, the windows overlooked Trumbull Avenue. It was a warm day, so the windows were open. There was hardly any traffic on Trumbull during the game. Don was pouring through the files, listening to the familiar play-by-play from radio sportscaster Van Patrick. Mantle was the batter. Don heard the crack of the bat as Patrick shouted, "There's a lo-o-ong high drive to right field … it's going over the roof!"

Don leaped to the window in time to see the ball hit the front of the cab company building across Trumbull, about ten feet up. It bounced into the street and rolled to the curb. A cab coming down the street squealed to a halt and the driver got out. He ran to the ball, picked it up, ran back to his cab and sped off, taking that historic ball into eternity.

Detroit cab drivers are notorious baseball fans. They all listen to the games. There was no question that the driver knew what he had. Don was dumbfounded. He never thought of getting the cab's license plate, but that wouldn't matter. The ball was gone forever. But he'd never forget that moment when he saw Mickey Mantle's home run hit the building across the street. Thousands of fans saw the ball fly out of the stadium. But Don, and possibly that cab driver, actually saw it land.

"I can see why that's your biggest memory with the Tigers," said Betty. "Want to hear what mine is?"

"Sure."

"You'll remember this well. It was back in 1965, sometime during the middle of the season. I was home here, listening to Ernie Harwell broadcast the game at Tiger Stadium. Ernie called a high foul ball heading toward the upper right field stands. Then he said the ball was caught by the only fan sitting in that area, the ball went right to him. He didn't even have to stand up to catch it. I thought that was pretty amazing. Then you came home later and told me the fan who caught that ball was you. That just blew me away!"

Don laughed. "That was me, all right. I took a break from my office to watch the game in the stands. I was sitting just inside foul territory about halfway up. It was one of those afternoon games when attendance was light. There was nobody around me. Then this fly ball was hit in my direction, and it kept coming toward me. When it came down practically in my lap, I just caught it in both hands. Pretty amazing."

"I've told that story to friends lots of times," said Betty. "Gets a reaction every time. We've had good years with the Tigers, and you've loved every minute of them. But there is one downside."

Don was surprised. "What's that?"

"Remember how you said when you took this job that the commute to Detroit would be easy? What do you think now?"

She had him. The commute was anything but easy. Betty needed the car most days, so he drove to Tiger Stadium only when the team had a night game. The rest of the time, she would drive him to Ann Arbor's Michigan Central Depot so he could catch the 6:30 AM train to Detroit. An hour later he would arrive at Detroit's cavernous Michigan Central Depot and then walk the few blocks to the stadium and his office.

Sometimes Don would take the bus, which was cheaper than the train, from the Ann Arbor Greyhound Terminal directly to his office at Michigan and Trumbull. But he didn't like that option, since the bus trip took lots of stops along the way and lasted more than two hours. The regular bus riders called it a "milk route."

A third alternative was to hitch a ride with someone else who lived in Ann Arbor and worked in Detroit. This was fine during the off-season months, when Don worked regular nine-to-five hours, which matched the hours of most companies, but during the season, with his long daily schedule, there was no way a driver would wait for him. Nevertheless, Don finally found a friend, Garner Wilson, who could drive him back and forth in the off-season. Garner was a manufacturer's representative whose office was in downtown Detroit. He was a pleasant guy and a Tigers' fan. Don enjoyed riding with Garner. He was also grateful to him.

"Yes," Don told his wife, "this commute gets tiring at times. Maybe we should think about moving back to Detroit sometime."

"No way. We just moved, remember?"

"Oh, well," he answered, "it was just a thought."

* * *

As early as 1967, Don had brushed close to being given a leadership position at the university. Shortly after Fritz Crisler announced his retirement, Don received a phone call from Wilbur Pierpont, vice-president for business. Pierpont chaired a search committee to find a new athletic director. Someone had nominated Don, and Pierpont wanted to know if he might be interested. Don said he was, and he traveled to Ann Arbor for an interview with the search committee.

Early the next year Don again heard from Wilbur Pierpont. Pierpont told him the candidate list had been reduced to two: track coach Don Canham and himself. He agreed to a second interview, and then he told Jim Campbell about his candidacy. He assured Campbell that he wouldn't take any time out from his job with the Tigers to interview for the position. He had never campaigned for election, and that included way back when he was elected president of his high school senior class. Campbell was extremely supportive.

Don was at Tigertown during 1968 spring training when he got a call from Betty. She had just read in the *Ann Arbor News* that Don Canham had been appointed Michigan's new athletic director. Don promptly called Canham at home and sincerely congratulated him. He could tell that the new AD was pleased. Then he went on with his own career, as the Tigers sprinted toward the World Championship.

Two years later, during 1970 spring training at Tigertown, Don received a phone call from Don Canham. They exchanged a few pleasantries and reminisced a little. And then Canham told him that Dave Strack, assistant athletic director, was being promoted to associate director, replacing Bump Elliott. Bump had taken the athletic director's job at the University of Iowa. Canham wanted Don to return to Ann Arbor to replace Dave Strack as Assistant Athletic Director. Don told Canham he needed a day to decide. He used that day to confer with those who needed to know.

Betty was overjoyed at the prospect of her husband returning to work in Ann Arbor. His long commute, which often involved Betty driving him back and forth to the train or bus station, would be gone. Plus, she'd be back again with the coaches' wives and all her other friends at the university.

Jim Campbell showed his friendship by wholeheartedly endorsing his farm director's potential with a huge grin. "If you

A smiling Don Lund becomes Michigan's Associate Athletic
Director in 1970. He still has that full head of hair.
(*Bentley Historical Library, The University of Michigan*)

work real hard, Don, and if your successors work real hard
over the next hundred years, you might come close to bringing
Michigan athletics up to the level of Ohio State."

So that was that. He would part with the Tigers on excellent
terms. He would also be going back to the university that held
his heart. He took the job the next day.

49
Dialogue

An early spring rain was dissolving the snow and giving the roads a thin coat of liquefied mud. I hardly noticed it in the warm refuge of his living room. The two of us were completely immersed in tales about people who place their fortunes on a five-ounce, leather-covered sphere held together by 108 double stitches. He was in a storytelling mood.

"One of the funniest guys I ever played with was Bob Swift."

"He was a catcher when you played your last three years with the Tigers?"
DL: "Yes, and he also managed the Tigers for a while when I was farm director. You might remember Bob as the Tigers catcher in 1951, when the St. Louis Browns sent that midget to the plate."

"Eddie Gaedel?"
DL: "That's him. His head wasn't much bigger than the ball. Anyway, Bob Cain walked him while Bob Swift stayed on his knees. By the way, here's a trivia question: When Gaedel got on first base a pinch runner came in for him. Who was that runner?"

"That's easy. It was Jim Delsing."
DL: "And exactly twelve years later, Jim Delsing played center field for another major league team. What team did he play for, and who were the other two regular outfielders?"

"Uh ..."
DL: "I'll give you a hint: 1953 Tigers."

"The two other outfielders were you and Bob Nieman! You didn't give me much time."
He laughed.

"You said Bob Swift was a funny guy."
DL: "He could break you up, especially at parties. One time he came up to Betty and me looking like he could tear somebody's head off. He said 'You know what really burns my ass?' We took him serious and said 'What?' He changed his face completely to a grin, put his hand, palm down, next to his hip, and said 'A flame about this high!'"

I'm laughing.
DL: "And then one time when Bob was managing the Tigers in 1965, he came up to us at a party and said to Betty, 'You know what a one-eyed sex fiend looks like?' Betty said, 'What?' And Bob put his left hand over his left eye. We both laughed. A couple of days later Betty and I were sitting next to the dugout during a game, when Bob strolls back from his third base coaching box between innings. He looked at Betty, grinned, and put his left hand over his left eye. Betty laughed so hard I thought she'd fall off her chair!"

I laugh. The old coach is on a roll.
DL: "Dick Wakefield was another funny guy."

"You knew him well."
DL: "Oh, yeah. Anyway, Dick was playing left field for Oakland, in the Pacific Coast League. It was a night game. The other team had runners on first and second with two outs. Then the batter hits one just over Dick's head for a home run, but Dick knows the lights aren't that strong in the outfield, so he jumps up, stretches, and comes down like he caught the ball. The runners stop. Dick starts trotting in toward the dugout, and everyone is moving off the field. The shortstop came over and said 'Throw me the ball, Dick.' Dick said, 'I ain't got the ball.' The shortstop said 'You ain't got the ball?' Boom! Oakland loses the game. Afterward, Dick expected his manager, Chuck Dressen, to climb all over him. Instead, Chuck asked him, 'Why didn't you take an extra ball and put it in your pocket?' Dressen also had a sense of humor."

"I bet you have lots of Dick Wakefield stories."
DL: "Sure; and I'll tell you one more. Dick was with the Tigers in left field. Hal Newhauser was pitching. Beautiful day. Not a

cloud up there. The batter hits an easy fly ball and Dick catches it, then drops it. Batter on first. Newhauser fumes. After the inning, Newhauser is waiting in front of the dugout for Dick to trot in, Hal is looking like a bomb about to explode. Dick doesn't give Newhauser a chance to say anything. He flashes his usual grin full of teeth, and says 'Harold, just as I was about to catch that ball, a drop of rain hit me in the eye!' Newhauser looked up at the clear sky, tried not to smile, and stepped into the dugout."

"That's funny."
DL: "Lots of funny things happen in a game. Reminds me of Frenchy Bordagaray. I was a rookie with the Dodgers during his last year with them as a player. He was quite a guy. One day Frenchy was at the plate when the pitcher threw a curve over for a strike. Frenchy steps back and says to the catcher, "Man, that's the best curve ball I've seen all season. What a pitch.' Then he puts a bewildered look on his face and steps back into the box. The catcher signals for the same pitch. The pitcher throws it. Frenchy smacks it to center field for a double, then stands on second with a blank face, looking like the luckiest guy in the world. The catcher glared at him!"

He continued.
"I also remember a good one with Tony Lupien. Tony was our first baseman when I played with Toledo in 1949. He was a Harvard grad."

"Is he the same one who coached baseball at Dartmouth?"
DL: "One and the same. Tony Lupien coached there for over twenty years. He's a legend. But let me tell you this story. Tony's at bat. George Corona is at first base. Tony signals for the hit and run."

"That's when the guy on first base should run on the next pitch, regardless of what it is, and the batter will try to hit it. You're trying to fool the catcher."
DL: "That's right. Hopefully, the batter hits it fair and the runner, who's already moving, can pick up extra bases. The least you want is a stolen base."

"So Tony Lupien signals the hit and run."
DL: "And the pitch comes in high; Tony swings and misses. George Corona doesn't move and Tony looks at him. Tony signals for the hit and run again. The pitch comes in; Tony swings and misses. George stands on first like his feet are part of the bag. So Tony steps out of the box, looks at Corona, and yells, 'Hey George! On the next pitch, I want you to run!'"

I'm still laughing. "You've seen some funny things."
DL: "There's one about Jim Campbell and me during spring training in 1969. The two of us were playing golf in Lakeland, at a course near a place called the Carpenter's Home. Jim was struggling, and things were getting tense. I wanted to lighten things up. I saw my chance when I was standing just off the green, as Jim put his fifth shot on from about 100 yards away. The ball rolled to about six feet from the cup. Without him seeing me, I replaced Jim's ball with one of those trick balls that rolls every way but straight. Jim rolled his putt. The ball moved like a snake, ending up about four feet from the hole. Jim stares at the ball, looks up at me, and says 'Did Lolich give you this?' That took away all the tension and we had a great time the rest of the round."

"Lolich?"
DL: "Yes. Jim knew my favorite Mickey Lolich story."

"You mean the one where you ask him if he can move the ball like a snake, and he does?"
DL: That's the one."

"That's a great story."
DL: "Mickey's a great guy."

"We've talked a lot about your seven years as the Tiger's farm director. Is there anything you'd like to add?"
DL: "Just that I got to know a lot of outstanding managers in the organization who made life easy for me and a lot of other people."

"Such as?"
DL: "Well, I'll name a few of them, not in any particular order. Frank Carswell made things happen wherever he went. Al Federoff, Al Lakeman, and Gail Henley were superb with their players. Any manager could learn a lot from them. Bob Mavis, Frank Skaff, and Wayne Blackburn were outstanding scouts for us, and they also served as "emergency" managers. They could step right in and take over a team when the regular manager was sick or something like that. Wayne also ran my Instructional League. I honestly don't know what I would have done without those guys."

"Pretty impressive."
DL: And I can't stop here without mentioning Joe Gordon. He taught at Tigertown, but he also had a lot of influence on me through the years. Joe has now been voted into the Hall of Fame, thirty years after he died. I practically jumped up and cheered when I heard about it."

"Those men must have meant a great deal to you."
DL: "I'll never forget any of them."

"So there you were in 1970, after seven years with Tigers management, coming back home to Ann Arbor and the university."
DL: "As a matter of fact, I could hardly wait."

50

Long Labor of Love

Thwack!

The ball slammed off the tee with a force that only powerful coordination and the latest forged-steel driver could provide. It started low and straight, continued to climb for about 200 yards, then reached its peak and fell in a graceful ark in the middle of the fairway. It passed the first tee shot by twenty yards, and rolled to a stop within 150-yards of the green. Don watched it all the way. It was clearly the best tee shot of the round.

Only he didn't hit it. His ball was the one laying twenty yards behind the ball he just watched.

"Nice shot, John," said Don, as head basketball coach Johnny Orr picked up his tee. "You think we might be able to find it?"

It was mid-April of 1975. Don Lund was now associate athletic director under Don Canham. He and Johnny Orr were playing golf at one of the more renowned courses in Palm Springs, California, in a tournament sponsored by a local Michigan Alumni Club. The other men in their foursome were two of the most prominent and wealthy alums in the Los Angeles area. That's why they were paired with two renowned Michigan coaches, rather than just one.

But the main foursome had teed off first in the morning, and was about six holes ahead. In it were four high-powered Michigan alumni, one of them famous. Secret Service agents stuck to them like paint on canvas. Because the famous one was the thirty-eighth president of the United States, Gerald Ford.

Don had set it up that way. In fact, he had set up the entire tournament.

Michigan coaches were paired with successful alumni in a subtle effort to use the camaraderie of the golf course to raise money for the Athletic Department. Head football coach Bo Schembechler was in the foursome ahead of him. Head hockey coach Dan Farrell was in the foursome behind. Other coaches were scattered around the course. Some of them, including

Schembechler, Orr, and President Ford (if he stayed around), would speak at the awards banquet that night. They wouldn't come right out and ask for money, but the implication would be there, and the money would come in through follow-up calls and other personal contact under Don's direction. Nobody was fooled; the alums wanted to support their university. They just needed the right stimulus. The golf tournament worked just fine.

From his first day on the job in 1970, Canham had stressed that Don's mission was to raise funds for the Athletic Department. He was to be the fundraising catalyst for major donors, as part of Canham's overall quest to make the Athletic Department financially strong. The other part of raising funds, appealing to the general public as well as students, staff, and alumni, would be handled by Don Canham himself. It would involve merchandising the Michigan logo, marketing the winning traditions of revenue-producing sports, and promoting the enjoyment of attending football games. To this end, he said, he had hired the three most important people he could find: Bo Schembechler, Johnny Orr, and Don Lund.

One of the first things Don did when he arrived on board in 1970 was to attend a campus meeting of the University's development directors. Several schools and colleges, including Engineering, Medicine, Literature, Science and the Arts (LS&A), Business, Law, and a few others all employed full-time fund raisers. When Don met with them, he found he had walked into a turf war. They all wanted to protect their own graduates from contact with anyone from the university but themselves. When Don said that no one graduated from Michigan with a degree in athletics and he had no direct prospect list, his words were ignored. They all claimed proprietary rights to their own major donors. Any contact from Don would have to go through them.

Don decided to ignore them and do his own thing. Canham approved.

The university already had a major donor group, called the Presidents Club, that was formed in 1961. Named to honor the university's presidents, it was in fact not formed by the university. A group of highly influential and well-connected men and women decided that their alma mater needed an organized means of attracting big-money donors. The university agreed, and the Presidents Club soon grew from a handful of individuals to hundreds of people willing to put up $10,000.00 to join an elite group of Michigan supporters.

For their contributions, members of the Presidents Club received a ceramic and wood plaque, plus an annual invitation to meet on a fall home football weekend. On Friday they would mingle with fellow donors from around the country, attend lectures given by prominent faculty on vital topics of interest, and participate in a special dinner that featured an address by the university president. On Saturday they would attend the football game dressed in maize and blue, all the while cheering, chanting, and singing "The Victors." Presidents Club weekends, as they were called, brought the moneyed people back to campus in grand style. They were successful beyond even the founders' expectations.

Don reckoned that the Athletic Department could also benefit from such an organization. They had in place the "M" Club, but regular membership in it was open only to letter winners. There was no other special group in athletics, especially for major donors. However, his research into the Presidents Club revealed a high interest in Michigan athletics among the members. Many of them were season ticket holders for both football and basketball games. Some Presidents Club members also belonged to the "M" Club. And even one of the founding members, Paul Goebel, was an All American who played for Yost and was now a regent of the university. He was betting that many Presidents Club members could be enticed to join a similar group in athletics. And he knew just how to entice them. He'd offer them special privileges.

Don formed the University of Michigan Victors Club in 1970. It was patterned on the model of the Presidents Club. Membership cost $10,000.00, which could be paid through installments. Matching gifts and corporate memberships were encouraged. A plaque, nearly matching the one for the Presidents Club, was given to each new member. The big difference was that the Athletic Department held full control over the Victors Club. Unlike the Presidents Club, there were no volunteer officers or board members. The department itself had its own volunteers on its Board of Control. That was enough for Canham.

As he put the Victors Club together, Don heaped on the benefits. Members would have the chance to improve their season ticket seats. They'd be granted special parking locations for football and basketball games. Membership cards would gain them free admission to non-revenue sports events. In addition, there would be an annual meeting for Victors Club members, where they would hear from various coaches about the teams. So as not to conflict with Presidents Club meetings, the Victors Club would meet in the spring, near the end of spring football practice. Members would then be invited to see the final spring practice game, free of charge.

And the one agreement from the university that was most important to Don, one that he was able to get with a single phone call, was that the purchase of a Victors Club membership was also good for Presidents Club membership. For $10,000.00 to Michigan athletics, one could join both clubs at the same time. He was glad nobody asked him if it would also work the other way; if joining the Presidents Club would be an automatic entry to the Victors Club. He would have said no.

The Victors Club would become the prime fund-raising arm of the Athletic Department. Don would do everything he could to make that happen. But he had to broaden his member prospect base. He had to go beyond the former athletes and Presidents Club members. He had to find other major donors. He had to find someone with the key to broader horizons. And he did. He arranged a meeting with Bob Forman.

Bob Forman was more than the director of Michigan's Alumni Relations. He was a phenomenon. Under his direction, alumni groups sprang up all around the country, eager to collectively watch the televised football games, sharing in the feast of an emerging football juggernaut under Coach Bo Schembechler. Forman's staff would also arrange for well-known university people to travel to alumni meetings, to talk about whatever exciting things were happening "back home" in Ann Arbor. To belong in an alumni club under Bob Forman was to practically have your alma mater parked at your doorstep.

In addition, Forman was credited with taking the university out of the campus classroom and into the world, by establishing one of the most comprehensive alumni travel programs of any major university. Michigan alumni could travel anywhere with their maize-and-blue cohorts. That included seminars in other cities, bowl games, and world-wide destinations. Forman actively led the whole thing with charisma, personal drive, and an ability to hold an audience spellbound with his words. Bob Forman was a larger-than-life Michigan celebrity. Don Lund needed him if he wanted to build the Victors Club exponentially.

Lund decided to approach Bob with the concept of alumni golf tournaments. They would be sponsored by a local club, and put together by Don's office. The subtle purpose would be to raise funds for athletics and promote Victors Club memberships. Bob and his staff would preside; Don and his coaches would play in the tournament and say a few words at the banquet. The tournaments could be held all year long; East and Midwest in spring and summer, and West and South in fall and winter. The plan, he thought was workable.

So did Bob Forman.

For the rest of his tenure as associate athletic director, Don Lund and Bob Forman presided over alumni-sponsored golf tournaments throughout the country. The two could have been brothers; both of them blond, blue-eyed, physically fit, popular, cast in maize and blue, and close as brothers they were.

In 1977, Don decided to start a "Hall of Honor" to recognize former athletes and others who have made a difference in their own lives and in the overall reputation of the University of Michigan. He obtained the support of Canham and the coaches, and then received overwhelming enthusiasm from the "M" Club, who agreed to preside over selection of nominees. The first group was inducted in 1978. They were:

Gerald Ford—Football
Bill Freehan—Baseball
Tom Harmon—Football
Cazzie Russell—Basketball
Bob Ufer—Track
Bennie Oosterbaan—Football, Basketball, Baseball, and
    Coaching

Don Lund himself was inducted in to the Hall of Honor in 1984, for football, basketball, baseball, and coaching. In 1987, he was inducted into the Michigan Sports Hall of Fame.

Don spent the last twenty years of his career as Associate Director of Athletics at his beloved university. In that time his Victors Club brought in thousands of friends and millions of dollars to Michigan's sports programs. The Victors Club remains his legacy.

Sometimes his job was a struggle. He regularly fought for funding the emergence of women's sports at a higher level than the department was willing to budget. It wasn't easy.

There were also sad times along the way, as there will be in any life. His father, Andrew, died from a heart attack on March 1, 1976. Three years later, on September 16, 1979, Marguerite, his mother, succumbed after a long struggle with dementia. They are buried in a cemetery along Detroit's Woodward Avenue.

On the afternoon of February 9, 1992, sixty-eight-year-old Don Lund was celebrated on his retirement from the university. Called "Lundo's Retirement Roast," the event was held in the Track and Tennis Building, a facility large enough to hold the hundreds of friends and admirers who were there. Bob Forman was Master of Ceremonies. Speakers were Jim Brandstatter, a former Michigan football player and local media sports celebrity; Bill Freehan, at the time Michigan's head baseball coach; Athletic Director Jack Weidenbach; Al Renfrew, Michigan hockey great and coach; Moby Benedict; Jim Campbell, chairman of the Detroit Tigers; and Bo Schembechler, retired from Michigan and now president of the Detroit Tigers.

During his speech, Jim Campbell brought out Don's recommendation to him that Jim Leyland be moved into a manager's job. Jim was now managing the Pittsburgh Pirates in the National League. Someone called Don "Swami." All told, the words spoken by his friends were hilarious. Those unspoken were tender and touching. They all bore witness to the winding down of a long labor of love. Don Lund was saying good-bye.

On the drive home after the retirement party, Don and Betty reminisced about a lot of things. They speculated over the future.

"What are you going to do now, dear, with all the time you'll have on your hands?" she asked.

He thought for a minute. "Well, the first thing is to get going on the move to our new condo." He had said the right thing.

She smiled and agreed, "Right."

He went on. "By then it will be spring and the Tigers will be training in Lakeland; Jim will be there, Bo will be there ..."

"Don't even think about it."

He winked at her. There was silence for a moment. "But then there's another possibility; something I'd sort of like to do."

"What's that?" She was skeptical.

"Why don't we drive out to Ames, Iowa, and spend a few days there? I hear they've got a university nearby. They call it Iowa State, or something like that. They might even have a basketball team."

Betty brightened. "And a champion coach named Johnny Orr!"

"I thought we might visit them sometime in April when the weather turns nice."

"I'll call them as soon as we're home!"

"That's good," said the retiree, "and who knows? Maybe John and I can find an excuse to get in a couple of rounds of golf!"

Don and his biographer attend a musical performance at the University of Michigan in October 2007. Notice his 1968 World Series ring, presented when the Detroit Tigers beat the St. Louis Cardinals in seven games to win the championship. At the time, Don was farm director for the Tigers. (*Photo by Dick Gaskill, Livonia, Michigan*)

51
Afterglow

"Beep-beep!"

The coach waves from his doorway in response to my horn as I drive away. His broad smile is bright. His eyes follow me as I steer around the bend in the road and drive slowly away from his condo. We're close friends now, though I still call him "Coach" rather than Don.

Betty was able to share his retirement for only six years and eleven days. Cancer took her away on February 20, 1998. She is buried at Forest Hill Cemetery in Ann Arbor, the historical resting place for University of Michigan presidents and prominent citizens whose names are found on city street signs. Someday Don will rest next to her. They were married for fifty-three years.

On Sunday, May 11, 1999, the University of Michigan retired Don's baseball jersey, number 33. The ceremony was held in Ray Fisher Stadium, just prior to a game against Indiana. Don stood on the mound, in front of a half-circle of the Michigan players. Outfielder Jay Dines, wearing number eight, stood there smiling among his teammates. He had been wearing number 33. He gladly gave it up for posterity. Jim Schneider from University Media Relations was at the microphone upstairs, reciting Don's contributions with eloquence and style. Don followed with brief remarks of thanks. All this was raptly watched from the stands by many friends of the honoree, plus a proud and happy Susan. She and her family would never forget this touching tribute to her father.

Over time, many of his old friends have passed away, but some still remain close. Al Renfrew, Bob Chapuis, and a few others are regular cronies who see him all the time. He regularly sees former members of his 1962 championship team, like Ed Hood and Dick Honig. The team has an annual reunion that Don attends.

He doesn't lack for things to do or places to go.

Don also sees his family regularly. Susan and her husband, Bruce Allison, are with him nearly every evening for dinner, either at his place or theirs. His two grandchildren, Don Allison and Elizabeth Martin, are not far away. Don attends law school at Northwestern. Elizabeth is employed in the area, as is her husband, Alex Martin. Alex played baseball at Michigan. His conversations with his wife's grandfather are stimulating to say the least.

On May 18, 2008, his eighty-fifth birthday, about seventy close friends gathered at a local country club to celebrate with him. Bob Forman was the Master of Ceremonies. Speakers included Moby Benedict and Ed Hood. Even Pete Elliott came all the way from Illinois. It was a love affair.

As I leave his neighborhood and head back through Ann Arbor on my voyage home, I look through the windshield at the sky on this bright spring afternoon. There are no creatures in the clouds this time, as there were when I first arrived months ago. Only a big blue ocean of air.

I drive on past emerging flowers beds and budding fruit trees eager to paint their landscape of glamour. And in the distance, I can see the highest point on the University of Michigan's campus—the Burton Tower and its world-renowned carillon, standing like a sentinel on its own special hilltop. Ann Arbor, Michigan, and its university. Or maybe it's the University of Michigan and its town. Either way, both have made an indelible mark on the life of Don Lund. And now they've made an indelible mark on me. I ask myself: Am I a better person because I know this man? I think back on his life and the stories he's told me. And then I look around as I motor along.

Driving through Ann Arbor, Michigan, feels good this afternoon. Very good. Very good, indeed.

Acknowledgments

Many people contributed to this book. They range from information science professionals to friends of Don Lund, plus relatives, former colleagues, former major and minor league ballplayers, and men who played under him at the University of Michigan. Some of them work in research libraries, such as the Baseball Hall of Fame in Cooperstown, New York, and the Bentley Historical Library in Ann Arbor, Michigan. Others adroitly staff library archives in Detroit, St Louis, Minneapolis, Saint Paul, Lakeland, Florida, and Toledo, Ohio. I'm profoundly grateful to all of them.

But most of all, my path to writing the manuscript was smoothed by the verifiable memory of the subject himself. Don's accurate recall of people, places, and events in his life goes beyond normal. He not only remembers friends he knew from his childhood, he can also spell their names and, if they're still living, tell you where they are. And that goes for everyone he's known throughout his life.

Finally, a big thank you to those who made their scrapbooks available. It's amazing how pointedly the past can be chronicled by those who have a vested interest in preserving special memories.

Bless you all.
J.R.I.

James Robert Irwin has been in the computer business from the early days of data processing up through the latest in information technology. His company operates throughout the United States.

His writings include contributions to standard library reference books and articles for magazines and trade journals.

He and his wife, Millie, reside in Florida. Reach him at jrimail@comcast.net.